TRUTH OR DEATH

TRUTH OR DEATH

THE QUEST FOR IMMORTALITY
IN THE
WESTERN NARRATIVE TRADITION

Thierry Hentsch

Translated by Fred A. Reed

Talonbooks
2004

Talonbooks
P.O. Box 2076, Vancouver, British Columbia, Canada V6B 3S3
www.talonbooks.com

Typeset in Times and New Baskerville and printed and bound in Canada by
AGMV Marquis.
Printed on 100% post-consumer recycled paper.

First Printing: September 2004

Raconter et mourir. L'Occident et ses grands récits was published in the original
French by Les Éditions Bréal (France) in 2002.

National Library of Canada Cataloguing in Publication

Library and Archives Canada Cataloguing in Publication

Hentsch, Thierry, 1944-
        Truth or death : the quest for immotality in the western narrative tradition
/ Thierry Hentsch ; translated by Fred A. Reed.

Translation of: Raconter et mourir.
Includes bibliographical references and index.
ISBN 0-88922-509-5

        1. Truth in literature. 2. Death in literature. 3. Narration (Rhetoric) 4.
Literature, Comparative--Themes, motives.
I. Reed, Fred A., 1939- II. Title.

PN3383.N35H4613 2004   809'.923   C2004-903255-0

The publisher gratefully acknowledges the financial support of the Canada Council
for the Arts; the Government of Canada through the Book Publishing Industry
Development Program; and the Province of British Columbia through the British
Columbia Arts Council for our publishing activities.

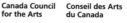

TRANSLATOR'S NOTE

I wish to thank Thierry Hentsch and Betrand Pirel for their unflagging and enthusiastic support. Grateful acknowledgements as well to Dina Cindric, who tracked down many of the references that enrich this book, and to Davinia Yip, of Talonbooks, whose devoted attention to detail helped give it its final shape. Ultimately, though, responsibility for its inevitable errors is mine alone.

CONTENTS

A Word to the Reader

This is a book of narration—and of reflection. Its form, a series of essays that explore how the West has fashioned its self-image, is drawn from a close reading of several of the *grands récits*, the great stories that lie at the heart of our cultural tradition.

An introduction places these essays within a common perspective. Though it is intended to give shape to my argument, this perspective is not meant to be either conclusive or exclusive. Each chapter is structured so that it can be read separately from the others. Even the introduction itself is not indispensable, nor need the chapters themselves be read in order. I offer them to the reader in a sequence which, taken together with the introduction, constitutes one way—but not the only way—in which the book as a whole can be read.

My principal—and ultimate—ambition is to encourage readers to plunge back into the original texts themselves. If I have assigned order to certain ideas, it is because any attentive reading is necessarily a kind of rewriting. As such, my interpretations strive to capture something of the narrative breath of the texts that have inspired them.

INTRODUCTION

I

The Story of the West

DEATH IS man's great obsesssion. It reveals all that has gone before; it is the ultimate moment of truth, the final reckoning whose ineluctable advent illuminates our lives. Life, death, and truth are inextricably joined in a linkage that consciousness can only fail to recognize at the risk of diminishing itself. It is precisely the threat to consciousness—the uniquely "Western" consciousness we share—that this book addresses.

How could the West's self-awareness possibly be threatened by diminished consciousness? Or, to rephrase the question in more fundamental terms, how does the West view itself? What are the truths that sustain it?

Such are the questions upon which this book proposes to throw light through a close reading of several of the great texts that have given shape to our collective imagination, and which we consider as central to our tradition. These texts stand in our memory as way stations along a narrative journey that I call, quite simply, "the Story of the West." But the Story of the West is *not* the history of Western civilization, even though the two are closely related. In the narrative chain we hold dear, and to which we owe to a significant degree our view of the world, it consists of that which we should read—and which we generally do not. As we might have guessed by now, the Story of the West does not exist. It can only be *read*. And the only way it can be read is through its texts.

Why through its texts and not through its history? Might they tell us something that history does not? No, for they are part and parcel of the history they have helped create. My preference for the texts themselves is a practical one: they are *readable*. I know that reading texts is a perilous enterprise. But so is reading history, to an even greater degree. And though their interweaving has fashioned only a portion of our history, the texts are at least, for all the mediation of time, immediately accessible, almost palpable.

Time has caused them to undergo a process of selection, has worked and reworked them, in the manner of those venerable masterpieces whose varnish has grown darker over time, whose colors have become burnished through the course of centuries. The selection process, though at times fickle, is generally coherent: a text that is strong enough to endure and to transmit itself has broken free from the circumstances of its birth. If it had no meaning other than that which it once derived from its immersion in the environment in which it was written, we would have before us a lifeless text that would be at best historical, like a notarized document or a letter of credit. By definition, the collective imagination can only travel through time along with those writings which have never ceased to be read and re-read, copied and re-copied because of the inexhaustible richness of meaning that transforms each reading into a new experience, not to say a new writing.

So it is that the *Epic of Gilgamesh* speaks to us today because it evokes not only Sumerian or Babylonian antiquity, but also the human condition. Even though the version we have recently been able to reconstitute is incomplete, even though the deciphering of cuneiform script and its translation into modern languages cannot bridge the abyss that separates us from its inception, the bare fact that it is read today not simply as an archeological remnant but as a story that can touch us, bring us sadness or pleasure, is in itself enough to make of the epic a living treasure and well justifies the risk of a *reading*. It is of little concern to the non-specialist whether, today, such a reading is "accurate," faithful to some original meaning to which we can hardly pretend to enjoy unimpeded access. No, what matters is that the text, after a long eclipse, is once more being read.

Any text, even if it has been preserved whole, comes down to us in mutilated form: removed from its context; orphaned, as Socrates so elegantly puts in Plato's *Phaedo*, and deprived of the voice and the support of its father. During his own lifetime the text's progenitor must, whether he likes it or not, bid farewell to his creation. It is a commonplace that, once delivered over to the public, a book no longer belongs to its author and follows a path independent of him. For all its visible and invisible lacunae, a text stands before us (in the condition in which it has come down to us) like something which, without being either whole or even necessarily complete, is nonetheless final and circumscribed. Quite unlike a series of events or a cluster of occurences, whose concluding act can always be relocated or called into question, and where delimitations themselves form a part of a set of problems to be resolved, a text is limited while open to infinite interpretation—perfectly closed with respect to its writing, perfectly open with respect to its reading. This is not to say that all readings are of equal value—setting aside those that the text simply cannot support. A reading is valid insofar as it illuminates the text from within, gives it life and relief. A text draws its richness from the successive strata laid bare by the passage of time. The "great" texts, the texts that endure, are those whose meaning is never exhausted.

Rare are the texts that endure, but they are still too numerous to be read with identical attention. I therefore had to set myself limits, to make choices. This book ends at the threshold of the classical age, at a time when a significant break took place, one that fully justifies considering it as a chronological end point. This first volume will be followed by a second, which will examine the great stories bequeathed to us by Western fiction from the mid-seventeenth to the twentieth centuries. My choice of texts is, rigorously speaking, unjustifiable. Only use, and of course the interest that reading them may spark, can justify it. Most turn upon the lives of heroes whose names are familiar to a broad audience in the West. This knowledge is limited to a handful of exploits, to a scattering of powerful character traits. Of Ulysses we know that he wishes to return to his homeland, of Oedipus that he has killed his father and wedded his mother, of Don Quixote that he jousts with windmills, but very few, aside from the intellectuals and the specialists, read Homer, Sophocles, or Cervantes. We have a vague idea of the richness of their works, we know that they do not owe their survival to chance, and we know that their enduring popularity must have something to do with their power, their quality. But for all that, their interpretation remains the preserve of the erudite.

Yet the stories they tell touch us to our depths. Each of them, in its own way, seeks answers from humanity in its most fundamental aspect: in its relationship with reality and with death. Where, for us mortals, lies the truth of our being in the world? In this life, in another, or nowhere? Where if not, as a simpler form of diverse and shifting truth, in that most human of necessities: to tell one's story, to create meaning by telling the story? To what extent does our vision of the world depend on these accumulated, preciously neglected narrative treasures? This precisely is what our age, which tells stories no less assiduously than any other, is hard put to resolve and to learn; precisely what I set out to investigate in my effort to understand the stories we tell, and those that we repress, about ourselves today.

Beginning with the desire better to understand ourselves, this book attempts to throw light on several key moments in the spiritual and intellectual journey through which our civilization claims to recognize itself. There is nothing new about the enterprise; the journey has been undertaken thousands of times. Each of us has followed in its footsteps, to greater or lesser degrees of distraction, from our desks in the classroom, around the family dinner table, in the theatre, at the movies, in the tumultuous silence of our own reading. We are possessed by a world as imaginary as it is familiar, to which under normal circumstances we pay little heed. We take it for granted that the West exists as a succession of largely fictitious, plausibly heroic or revolutionary works and events which from antiquity down to the present create meaning, of which we consider ourselves the heirs, and which without a second thought we subsume as part of the general thrust of history.

That history moves in a particular direction and that we, as Westerners, see ourselves as the bearers of time's arrow must be among the most powerful and the least investigated features of our conception of the world. But a persistent doubt has, for more than a century, been shaking our certainties down to their philosophical foundations: the structure of metaphysics has collapsed and nothing enduring has been reconstructed upon its ruins. While technoscience and capitalism surge gloriously forward along the well-marked highroad of history, relativism has made spiritual inroads, and deconstruction haunts art and literature. We have let go of all certainty in the maelstrom that carries us, almost in spite of ourselves, toward a fate that we are not at all certain we desire and which we have all but abandoned the effort to understand. The desire for understanding is clearly not dead, but it increasingly finds shelter in technoscience, which seems to be hurtling headlong toward the unforeseeable.

A sense of the unknown, along with the excitement it generates, may be enough to compensate us for our lost certainties. But the need to believe is so powerfully rooted in the human heart that it continues to seek justification in formulae, in discoveries, in the laboratory. The subject of our beliefs has changed, but we still live in a state of expectation, though not of some extraordinary event: we hope neither for a Second Coming nor for political revolution. We live out our lives in the apprehensive expectation of where the technological accumulation over which finance speculates day and night may be leading us. We no longer see the present as the outcome of the past but as a springboard to the future. The arrow of time has not been broken, but events around us take place as though we no longer cared about its point of release, as though that point of release had all along been a matter of course, as though we knew whence we have come.

If this knowledge were really all that it appears, I would not hesitate to describe my enterprise as an anachronism. Indeed, in strictly etymological terms, it is: the idea being to retrace our steps through time, upstream from memory, to rediscover a hidden part of what makes us who we are. For it is perhaps there, where we believe we best understand our roots, that the forgetfulness woven by habit and sloth has drawn its most impenetrable veil; it is there, where we fancied we knew ourselves so well, that we see with the least clarity. The task then becomes one of recognition: to identify in the literature the cardinal points around which our collective self-image has been articulated, and to renew our acquaintance with them. It is not like happening upon old mementoes in a dusty attic, but like discovering new, unknown, or neglected properties in the objects that have never ceased to be before our eyes. The troubling novelty, not about the works themselves but about what they encompass, is that they may well reveal as foreign what had heretofore seemed familiar.

The foreign and the familiar are nowhere so closely wedded as in death. Nothing is at the same time so near, and yet so far from us. Death is the proverbial shadow about which we never think. It surges into our consciousness only at extraordinary moments, in the gleam of ecstasy, of grief, of danger, of sickness, only to be quickly repressed. Whether it be openly spoken or passed over in silence, death, life's inseparable companion, winds its way through every story. The manner in which it is related, evoked or eluded makes it the principal characteristic of the "great stories." The "greatness" of a story derives from its capacity to leave a lasting imprint on the collective imagination, and that imprint in turn owes its depth to the underlying tensions that the text sets up between truth and death. Finally, death provides the horizon against which the reading of the great narrative texts seems richest and most promising.

This is particularly true in the West, the first civilization to define itself in terms of a cardinal point. The West, in a kind of genial intuition—by identifying with the setting sun—set death as its horizon. But it is unaware that it has done so. Instead, it has identified itself with the "discovery" of the New World, with the cycle of the sun and with its eternal return. Like the solar orb itself, the West, civilization of change and of revolution, holds out the prospect of perpetual renaissance. The continuous return of the identical removes the seal of death, and our unconscious designation remains without echo. Our civilization wishes to know nothing of its fall. Yet the idea of its fall secretly preoccupies us beyond all else. For all its occultation, we are totally possessed by the horizon of death.

Death, the umbilicus of life, the banality and mystery of our condition, lays at the feet of analysis a prey that is at once apparent and evanescent. That stories should inscribe themselves in the memory of generations as an attempt to survive should come as no surprise. The desire to endure, by definition, runs through all civilizations like a red thread, or at least, through all those civilizations whose footsteps we have been able to follow. The enterprise of speaking to one another, of telling stories, of leaving tracks, milestones, and landmarks is shared by all civilizations. But that of the West is unique in its exorbitant pretension to transform, more than half consciously, its own self-awareness and its own footsteps into the highroad toward universal truth. In the Western vision of history, this highroad is not simply evidence of a particular experience, or of a specific human moment; no, it blazes a trail, which, though incomplete, fully intends to determine the future of the world.

For a civilization that, today more than ever before, cannot but call into question the truths it has helped ground, beginning with the idea of truth which was to touch off the upsurge of modern science, this is a paradoxical affirmation indeed. But the paradox is immediately, and reassuringly, explained away: does not the critical faculty of the Western spirit bear yet more eloquent witness to the universal character of the civilization that exercises it? Is it not the most revealing of all the signs—to our eyes—that the general truth of our Western experience is capable of leading to the destruction of the ideational foundation upon which our civilization's power is based? Not only has this power not been lessened; it has grown. The critical capacity of our thought and the technical achievements that have flowed from it almost without interruption for the past two centuries are the finest proof that we Westerners are at one with truth. It is because metaphysical truth has ceased to prevail that scientific truths, which once rested upon it, have been able to develop their full practical force. Today the sciences stand alone; their self-sufficiency points better than anything else to the rightness and the necessity of the path that has led to their flowering. Such is the polyphonic song of the apprehensive sirens of our destiny.

So, while alongside constructive scepticism rings a hymn of victory, beneath this hymn lingers a nagging sense of disquiet that the accomplishments of technoscience have powerfully contributed to repress. Undeniably marvelous, these accomplishments reveal first and foremost the matter that they have shaped. Paradoxically, they also screen from view that which, today, could be described as a reading of the question of truth. By its very success, science appears to shelter its engineers and its users—all of us—from the very critique that has become its emblem of truth. The implicit truth of our era can only be that no solid truth exists outside science, that it is useless to seek elsewhere, that finally no domain lies outside the purview of scientific investigation, and that art, literature, and poetry have no other objective than to express states of mind and residual idiosyncrasies (whether collective or individual). Bluntly put, the idea that we are situated within truth deceitfully resists all relativism, especially when relativism is the idea's most faithful witness. The question of truth seems to have been disposed of once and for all; in fact, its disposal ranks high among our received ideas.

But this "philosophy" leaves us mute in the face of death, the death to which our civilization, as long as it could still be described as Christian, had a response. The response was a powerful one. It postulated death, the passage into the hereafter, as the moment of truth when the meaning of our lives would be illuminated. Whether we like it or not, we belong to a civilization that linked truth inextricably with death. The manner in which Christendom has forged—and continues to forge—this linkage is deeply unfortunate. But its rejection as belief cannot bring us relief from the misfortune it has brought about. For all the decline of religion, we are far more Christian than we imagine. Death and truth remain secretly interconnected, and their invisible link pervades our collective concerns to this day. It is only by virtue of a rather superficial maneuver carried out by modern reason that death and truth appear to have parted company; or that the link that might still bind them has been relegated to the private sphere. It is as though, on this matter, our civilization no longer had anything to say, and was correct in choosing silence.

I wish to call into question precisely this self-imposed silence, this reasoning. For they conceal broad areas of darkness, particularly in the sensitive area of our relations with the Other. The civilization that expels death from its field of inquiry clearly has no interest in that which incommodes it. Like death, the Other stands at risk of becoming an object of unutterable fear and exclusion. So it is that beneath the encounter between truth and death lies the double question of identity, and of how we relate to the world.

The conviction that lies at the core of this book is that the great texts of our tradition are the bearers of a superior kind of knowledge, of a better use of life, than those that satisfy our civilization today. Does this sense of satisfaction arise from the fact that we may well—and for how long now?—

have ceased to read? Or is it because we may no longer see in the great texts of our narrative tradition anything more than interesting, all-but-outdated myths? Have they, for us, ceased to be "true"? It is here that the function of the story comes into play, in all its ambiguous relationship with truth.

II

Of Truth and Stories

STORIES TURN THEIR BACK on *the* truth. The truth of a story lies in its capacity to create meaning. It thus stands as our supreme connection with the world because it is the freest, the least censored among them. Its freedom places it at a distance from the designs of religion, philosophy, and science, each of which attempts in its own way to impose itself as the discourse of truth. Nothing, of course, can stop such a discourse from assuming the narrative form. Stories of truth also exist. Moreover, any story can be read as an expression of truth, but at the risk of losing its plurality of meaning. For meaning is never entirely protected from the imperative of truth. Nor does it definitively succumb to this imperative; its latent subversive capacity remains. Truth's campaign against narrative freedom has, happily, always been defeated before it begins.

Fable, Philosophy, and Science

Philosophy has little patience with stories. It distrusts them, and is constructed in large measure in opposition to them when it does not seek to subordinate them outright, most often without any great success. If we were to take seriously Plato's remonstrance toward "the makers of fables," we would be tempted to conclude that philosophy inaugurates at that moment that which over time will come to be recognized as its most crushing failure. The desire to tell stories, the pleasure of the tale, and the need for history trump all forms of censorship.

In Book X of the *Republic*, Plato declares war on Homer.[1] A target of choice. Homer is surely the best loved and the most respected of all the poets of ancient Greece. To attack the author of the *Iliad* and the *Odyssey* is to take dead aim at the heart of poetry. The magnitude of the adversary, whom Plato also loves and admires, conveys perfectly how high the stakes are: philosophy must establish its supremacy against the loftiest of all poetic talents. Plato delivers his stinging attack against art and poetry at the end of

---

1. Plato, *The Republic*, trans. Sir Desmond Lee, 2nd ed. (London: Penguin, 2003). In Books II (377a–379b) and III (389d–394b), which discuss the education of children and of the guardians of the city, Hesiod and Homer are mentioned as dangerous "creators of stories" or as "fable makers" (377b), whose good stories must be separated from the bad for the edification of the younger generation.

a long peroration devoted to justice. In its relentless quest for the nature of justice, the dialogue of the *Republic* is, from one end to the other, a meditation without concession on how life should be lived. Life warrants being lived in justice, that is, in accordance with ourselves—a requirement by virtue of which the injustices we have suffered are as nothing in comparison to those we ourselves commit and which are, in the deepest sense, injuries inflicted upon ourselves. Only ignorance can so mislead us into a preference for ephemeral pleasure and for worldly advantage over the inner equilibrium that will reveal to our soul the divine world of the intelligible and, when the moment arises, allow us to select a life worthy of such a world. Harmony with oneself is possible only at the price of a tortuous passage that brings us nearer to truth, which is as painful to contemplate as is the day upon emerging from the darkness.

The celebrated Allegory of the Cave, which opens Book VII of the *Republic*, reveals the miserable condition in which humanity, for lack of will to embark on the hard road of truth, languishes. In contenting himself with the glimmering figures projected upon the walls of the cave where he lies chained, in being satisfied by the poverty of the world where his blindness has abandoned him, man lives frightfully beneath his capabilities. The cavern is our mind. The poets and the imitators do little more than spin the wheel of illusion more rapidly; they stoke the fires that project them upon the screen of our idleness. Only the love of wisdom can lead us out of the trade fair of chimeras. So speaks the philosopher.

But lo and behold! He paints like an artist, sings like a poet! By some curious shift, the denigrator of tales has become a teller of tales. Is it because of inconsistency? Has he momentarily wandered astray? Has he forgotten what he himself demands of others? Hard to believe. The tale is the faithful companion of Platonic discourse. In fact, it often becomes, especially at the most critical moments, the tool of choice, the ultimate argument. The fabulation of great poets may well have some utility, providing they are used at the proper time, and that their educational function be strictly subordinated to the greater objectives of truth and philosophy. For philosophy acknowledges stories only on condition of submitting them to its censorship, and of placing them at its service. For all that, the use of stories remains problematic. For a master teller of tales like Plato, the story is a double-edged sword.

The ambiguity that surrounds the relationship between philosophy and storytelling in Plato has totally disappeared with Aristotle, at least in those of his works that have survived. The Aristotle who is available to us tends to be dry, intricate, and elliptical; reading him can be a considerable chore. His style, quite unlike Plato's, stands for us at the antipodes of the conventional narrative. We could even assert that it will constitute, for centuries to come, the prototype of philosophical and scientific prose.

Despite Plato's enormous influence, despite the efforts of his emulators (among whom we find Cicero), dialogue will remain the exception in philosophical discourse. From antiquity down to the present, its preferred mode will be that of systematic exposition, for which the dialogue form is most often a sugar-coating. In Plato, the theatrical flourishes so crucial to certain texts such as the *Symposium* lose much of their breadth in those of his writings where the "dialogue" is little more than an exchange, often an unequal one, which serves only to lend prominence to the words of the master by punctuating it with exclamations of approval, or by seasoning it judiciously with pro forma objections and questions.

Generally speaking, the philosophy that, in the Western tradition, dates back to the pre-Socratics arises from a sharp break with the great stories, in opposition to the founding myths and to the creation epics. For all that, mythology and philosophy have the same object: both offer or seek an explanation of the universe, and attempt to place men and their cities within that universe. But what the former achieves intuitively through mythical representation (*mythos*), the latter seeks to apprehend by means of reason (*logos*). The two terms were almost equivalent in Homer's day, meaning 'story', 'history', 'word'.[2] The opposition between *mythos* and *logos* in distinguishing fable from truthful exposition, absent in the beginning, became sharper and better defined over time, particularly with the development of philosophical discourse, against which myth gradually became suspect, even false, based solely on the fact that it is "invented." Invented by men, that is. Indeed, divine *logos*, as expressed by the Delphic Oracle, lost none of its character as truth. But in the long run it was inevitable that the philosophical word, as testified by the trial of Socrates, for all the pious protestations of the accused, had led to a diminishing of the importance of the divine word and thus, to the "corruption of youth."

The trial of Socrates continues to scandalize. But the scandal is not the condemnation by Athenian "democracy" of the "wisest of men" to a death which he wholeheartedly sought over exile; the scandal is quite simply that this, the most "philosophical" of all societies, showed itself to be so hostile

---

2. The equivalence is partial, but essential to our purposes. In Homeric times, μυθος and λογος referred to both fabulous and historical stories. Nonetheless, the polysemous nature of logos appears to have been much greater than its synonym.

to philosophy. *Philosophy had failed in the cradle of its birth*: such is the conclusion that even today is so difficult for us to accept, and which Plato was the first to deplore. It comes as no surprise that he lashes out at Homer; he knows his audience, and that this audience has not the slightest interest in truth. The people of Athens, who in this respect differ not at all from other peoples, prefer fables and colorful speeches. They worship poets, rhetoricians, and sophists—merchants of illusion all—and send the philosopher packing. The truth is that truth is not wanted, a refusal which philosophy has never stopped fighting, though in a losing cause.

Philosophy's ambition to assert itself as a discourse of truth, or at least as a search for truth, as contrasted to a story that cares little for truth, can hardly stand, as philosophy itself well knows. What is more difficult for it to admit is that it cannot itself avoid narration, for it is in part a story that does not know it. A story, certainly, that *attempts* to lay down relatively strict rules as a way of approaching the truths it seeks; that, in doing so, has drawn up a particular discursive form, a "logical" form distinct from other, more popular forms of discourse (epic, dramatic, religious, mythical, poetic, novelistic); and that has always seemed to lie beneath its aspirations. Philosophy may have failed to attain its loftiest aims, but its failure does not make it any less compelling: quite the opposite is true. The thirst for the absolute preserves in it a tension that lends itself to unease, and to the fertility of the spirit. Philosophical to a fault, this underlying tension pervades art as it does literature. Philosophy is omnipresent wherever man asks questions of himself; it may well be, in the final analysis, nothing but a particular, and particularly demanding, form of narrating the world.

Still and withal, by its concern with truth, philosophy, or at least a certain absolutist conception of philosophy, will have contributed to modifying the sense of the religious. Insofar as it pretends to weld truth to the idea of the One, philosophy undermines the polytheistic, polysemic conception of the world. Monotheism (Christian in particular) is, in many ways, the religious embodiment of the Greek philosophical ideal.[3] But, as we shall see, this monotheism also draws its sustenance from a story: a story no less fabulous than those of Hesiod and Homer, yet which has captured and held in our imagination a totally different stature. One of the ambitions of this book is to demonstrate how Christendom succeeded in imposing a story of truth where, hitherto—to restrict ourselves to the Hellenic universe—had reigned a mythology teeming with meaning and human stories that were utterly

---

3. Greek and not merely Platonic: the desire to grasp Being in its mysterious unity is highly present among many of the pre-Socratics.

"pagan," that is to say, lacking a unifying, revelatory purpose. *The way Christianity employed the narrative form to support the idea of a sole and indivisible truth was to have a decisive influence on what I term the Story of the West.* Our narrative tradition would continue to reflect its influence and would need centuries in order to disengage itself without ever completely succeeding. For, as we will see, the discourse of modernity has appropriated the idea, all the while believing that it is done with God. We can begin to detect the magnitude of what is at stake in philosophy's trial of fable: *nothing less than a vision of the world*, in which the one and the other are at once complementary and competing.

If all philosophy, insofar as it seeks to elucidate the world, contains both an implicit and explicit narrative component, all stories potentially contain a philosophical dimension. Furthermore, every great story, every founding myth constitutes an acting out of our relationship with the world, a dramatization of our origins. Without desiring to conflate philosophy and mythology, we must underline that which they share: the desire to make sense. Certainly philosophy raises questions, but most of the time it cannot stop itself from answering. To the extent that it seeks answers through a process that claims system and rationality, philosophy distances itself from the narrative style. But the attempt at rationalization does not stop it from telling stories, even, on occasion, stories unbeknownst to itself. It proceeds in approximately the same manner as contemporary astrophysics with the big bang theory, a scientific hypothesis which can be seen as a history of our origins, and which borrows perhaps more than we would care to admit from the Genesis story.[4]

There is nothing gratuitous about the comparison: today we expect modern science to create meaning, to describe the world. It is because metaphysics is no longer equal to the task, particularly as a result of its loss of credibility in the face of the dizzying revelations of science, that contemporary philosophy "says" so little to us. Is it so surprising that it has elected to travel along one of the two paths that remain open to it: epistemology and hermeneutics? With the first, it can focus its attention on the conditions surrounding scientific discovery; with the second, it devotes itself to the interpretation of texts. Unable to tell stories, philosophy undertakes multiple readings of texts of all kinds (not only of a philosophical nature). Its reading of the world, today more than ever, proceeds by way of literature or science.

4. Ilya Prirogin and Isabelle Stengers, "Champs," *Entre le temps et l'éternité* (Paris: Flammarion, 1992), p. 154.

In its overweening desire to rationalize the general, philosophy cannot establish itself except as a false science, as rigor without meaning, an extremity that in the twentieth century was most closely approached by Husserlian phenomenology. But the dizzying dance of reason is hardly a recent development; it has always accompanied philosophy. Any explanation of the universe and of our place in it is necessarily reductionist. Experimental science and modern technique are, in this regard, daughters of philosophical reduction, which, no matter how fecund it might be, cannot be achieved without a certain shrinkage of our relationship with the world.[5]

Philosophy has never been able to establish the privileged, not to say exclusive, relationship with truth that Plato claimed for it. But its ambition, propelled by the powerful Aristotelian machine, and expressed centuries later in Enlightenment reason and nineteenth-century positivism, continues to generate an impact down to the present day. Literature and mythology have gained nothing from the disenchantment of philosophy and remain, with respect to truth, in a precarious situation; compared with the achievements of science, they cut a weak figure indeed. Literature enjoys a certain evocative power, to be sure, and contributes in its own way to reveal certain things about life, but as revelation it seems fragile, being both subjective and uncertain in comparison with a science that is constantly demonstrating its objective truth in its spectacular capacity to change the world. Outside of the pleasure it brings us, or in proportion to its power to enchant us, fiction labors under a certain lack of credibility: it teaches us nothing solid. The term "fiction" is an antonym for truth, reality, authenticity, and accuracy.

Yet fiction seems not to have suffered, if one is to judge by the prominence in our societies of the novel and the cinema. It has even inspired a renewed fascination for hermeneutics as a revelatory tool in the social sciences. The problem is that, with the exception of economics and a small number of fields open to the experimental approach, the social sciences are seen as unreliable, tainted by subjectivity, vulnerable to ideological bias. The hermeneutical vogue is hardly surprising in a field as broad and ill-defined as the social sciences, where most researchers have long abandoned the criteria for truth that the experimental sciences claim to respect. Without becoming involved in the ill-considered debate that periodically erupts over the relative qualities of these two great categories of knowledge, let us keep in mind its most stubborn prejudice: that by virtue of their lack of rigor, and of predictive capacity, the social sciences are inconsequential, reduced in

---

5. Henri Atlan, *Enlightenment to Enlightenment: Intercritique of Science and Myth* (in French), trans. Lenn J. Schramm (Albany: State University of New York Press, 1993).

virtually all cases to description and to storytelling. Succinctly put, despite their theoretical pretensions, they amount to nothing more than tall tales! Which brings us back full circle to Plato's critique of poets, with one capital distinction: in our time, fiction no longer poses a threat.

Plato is not so naïve as to believe that stories have no impact. Such naïveté is modern and scientific. It is formulated from a position of certainty about what constitutes true knowledge, whose truth derives from the efficacious. Far more than today's novel, which is firmly rooted in the fictional, the ancient cosmogonies, in their pretensions to explain the world, bring smiles to our faces. But we are quick to forgive their authors. Poor things! They did not have access to the same scientific arsenal we command. The idea that these ancient stories may have *something else* to say does not spontaneously occur to us. We do not realize that their "truth," or rather, their meaning, is situated on another plane. In the same vein, we are ill-inclined to imagine that our sciences and our techniques—in spite of, or because of, their incontestable efficacy—might also be the concrete expression of a vision of the world, that they might contribute to creating a full-fledged conception of life, of man, of knowledge, of the past, of history. All available evidence points to their being at once tributary to, and revealing of, an immense system of representation. Like the philosophy from which it is derived, science participates as well—far more than it imagines—in narration.

The historical persistence of the story in all its forms (theatre, tale, song, novel, film) and its presence in almost all known cultures underline how necessary is history, whether sacred or profane, great or small, "fictitious" or "authentic," to humankind. It constitutes the least restrictive, the liveliest, the most widespread, the most venerable that written texts have preserved for us of human memory. Narration is as old as literature itself; it would be older still were we able to capture from the mouths of storytellers the words that had not been written down. Neither philosophy, nor theology, nor science (in its modern-day meaning) can make such a claim. Stories are for all time; the force that draws us to them has never been refuted. Such attraction is due to the fact that narration has no *a priori* pretension, obeys no rules, and depends upon no system. Though it may frequently be governed by fashion it sacrifices none of its virtual latitude, which is infinite. Stories are self-sufficient. They bow before no external constraints save those of occasional censorship, and may even contradict themselves, as long as they stimulate interest and give the reader good reason to keep reading. This freedom has, as we know, a price. It does not allow stories to lay claim to a well-defined place on the scale of truth, whatever the narrator's own conviction. Herein, however, lies precisely the source of its strength: a formidable strength that poses the inexhaustible question of interpretation.

Reading and Truth

The uncertainty that surrounds a story leads naturally to its *reading*. Uncertainty lends to the act of reading a freedom that, while not absolute, in principle can tolerate no restriction. All stories are by definition open to an unlimited number of assessments, of which none is *a priori* more legitimate than another, up to and including that of the narrator, whose intentions— avowed or concealed—no one is obliged to accept. All stories may, and in certain circumstances must, be read independently of their intentions. This latitude is particularly crucial and difficult to win acceptance for with regard to the stories that have posited themselves as the writ of truth, or which are given canonical consecration. Take the Gospels, which belong to no particular church, and not even to Christendom as a whole. That they form its undisputed foundation does not mean that interpretation must be restricted to their ecclesiastical or priestly functions. A story, "in spite of itself," offers up to readers several concurrent, even contradictory, truths, of which it is not the master. No one can be its master: no more the narrator than the scribe, the wise man than the common reader.[6]

But freedom of interpretation cannot, inversely, be exercised *against* the text, nor can it be used to twist the text abusively to conform to our convictions or our desires. Yet the person who reads is an individual who desires and who, to a greater or lesser degree, has knowingly invested in it a substantial portion of his subjectivity. The limits of abuse are impossible to prescribe, nor can any authority set them forth. The process of demarcation takes place on its own, over time. Every reading will eventually exhaust the text's capacity to support that reading and what it can glean from other readers. As readers turn away from imposture, it will wither away on its own. In the final analysis, my hypothesis is that interpretation finds its value in the turmoil—the joy or the disquiet—that it touches off, by the revelatory power it wields, or by the emotion it provokes among others. Something heretofore shrouded in shadow is illuminated; something that seemed to float in a

6. On the question of reading, and on the relation of the author and the reader to the text, see Paul Ricœur, *Time and Narrative* (in French), vol. 3, trans. Kathleen MacLaughlin and David Pellauer (Chicago: University of Chicago Press, 1984–1988).

cloudless sky suddenly displays infinite shadings of darkness. Nothing more, nothing less.[7]

While the truth of a story remains constantly open to a reading that is always in a position to recreate it, all interpretation, no matter how rich and judicious it may be, can also create a sense of closure. This closure may be provisional, but it may remain in place for centuries, as long as no other reading is able to undo it. Time is not necessarily a source of revelation; it can also act as a reducing agent. From one reading to another, a story risks becoming hardened, impoverished. The danger increases when a civilization appropriates the elements of another culture: the other's story is digested according to the identitarian imperatives of the civilization that has interpreted it, and either rejected into a kind of manifest otherness, or made over in its own image by the removal of its asperities and dissonances. A similar acclimatization takes place over time within the confines of a "same" culture that sees itself as the continuation of those whose heritage it claims, as with our culture in relation to ancient Greece.

Each culture can claim what we might call a *narrative legacy*—or what Ricœur terms, in an expression richer in meaning, *narrative identity*.[8] This legacy not only transmits a given content: unless it is profoundly called into question, it reactivates the suppression of those elements that cannot be made to fit with the recipient culture's image of itself and of the world. In the process of appropriating stories far removed from us by time or distance, interpretation is threatened by the same failing as philosophy's once it attempts, consciously or unconsciously, to reduce all difference, all dissonance, to the tyrannical unity of the identical. Such a unity can nowhere be found, yet it is indispensable. Civilization exists in the utopia of its continuity and its coherence. The diverse materials it uses to speak of itself are like the scraps of fabric used in a patchwork quilt: cut to match the needs of the greater whole. By viewing that whole, by conceiving it as a coherent unit, we forget that it is constructed of odd cuttings. The "interpretation" that conforms to the civilization's unitary vision of itself hardly merits the name. It leads nowhere, reveals nothing: it is nothing but adaptation, confirmation in the service of the same thing, repeated over and over again. Quite the opposite of the reading I propose.

The reading I propose is anything but simple. Ideally, it involves the capacity to step back, a leap that places us in a position to analyse our own

---

7. Marc-Alain Ouaknin, preface to *Lire aux éclats. Éloge de la caresse*, 3rd ed. (Paris: Quai Voltaire, Seuil, "Points," 1992)
8. Ricœur, *Time and Narrative*, op. cit., p. 355.

culture "from without." It goes without saying that such a position does not exist. But taking one's distance internally remains nonetheless possible on certain conditions, the first and most significant of these being the recognition of the difficulties inherent in every attempt at distancing.

Let us examine in some detail what these difficulties hold out for us, in the West. As the self-imagined cradle of modernity, Western civilization, more than any other experiences itself and perceives itself as both clean break and continuity. It locates its roots far from home, in both time and space, in such a way as to confirm itself as culmination and as universality. But this accomplishment is, at the same time, the product of a series of clean breaks without which modernity could not have come about. Modernity is movement.

Movement "outside history"! Wrenching free from the dead weight of the past, liberation from the arbitrary bonds that maintain mankind in the status of intellectual and moral minority.[9] At its far extreme, the emancipation that the Enlightenment prizes so highly aims at nothing less than the abolition of history and, with it, narrative identity, with which the West cannot dispense in order to buttress the foundations of its "age of majority." The groundwork for the break that brought us modernity must have been laid somewhere in history, the same history that modern as "adult" is called upon to cast aside. As a source of both instruction and alienation, history cannot be entirely neglected. Quite the contrary, it should be of concern to us more than ever before as a way of separating the wheat from the chaff, with a view to identifying the earliest markers of the "age of majority" which Kant asserts is "natural" for man. If human emancipation is indeed inscribed in nature, we should be able to observe it, even though as through a glass darkly, at work in the past. But modernity cannot be reconciled with it except at the cost of a purge: the modern form of cultural reductionism, whose effects we have already alluded to.

So it was that with the Enlightenment, according to the Western interpretation of history, a "natural" dividing line was drawn through the events and texts of the past. To one side of this line we assign all that belongs to movement and to progress, which proclaims the advent of emancipatory reason; to the other, that which remains a prisoner of arbitrariness, of custom, of stagnation, which draws its force of inertia from fears and superstitions of all kinds. Since this process of enlightened sorting should have contributed

9. This is the thrust of Kant's famous text "What Is the Enlightenment": an appeal to the use of reason so that humanity may emerge from its infancy and finally accede to adulthood. On this point, see Robert Legros, *L'Idée d'humanité* (Paris: Grasset & Fasquelle, 1990).

to human progress, it could not under any circumstances be seen as "reductionist" by its near-unconscious authors.

As everyone well knows, the history of the last two centuries in the West has cast serious doubt on the emancipatory virtues of reason. Instrumental rationality remains today the most effective component of the program of the Enlightenment. Far from having allowed us to attain the political and moral majority to which the philosopher of Königsberg aspired, the use of rationality as instrument partakes of a dynamic that largely eludes us. Even though technological progress has not slowed, we no longer can justify evaluating the past in terms of the dividing line I have just described, delimiting that which is "progressive" from that which is not. Still, following on the heels of economic and technical development, our conception of the world and our vision of history have hardly changed; year in, year out, they continue to endorse the division instituted by the Enlightenment. It can be argued that we now accept this apportioning process, which no certainty of emancipation can any longer justify, as a form of unconscious censorship. The selective memory of modern reason has become a reductive apparatus that we continue to apply, out of force of habit, or for the sake of security, to our own way of looking at the world.

The invisible filter through which we look upon the past is precisely what a "fresh" reading of the texts that have shaped our narrative identity seeks to make visible, to remove as far as possible from the field of our collective imagination. Truth to tell, the field is not quite so easily "cleansed": the filters are numerous, persistent, and new ones will pop up to replace the old. The lens through which we now view the world and its history is not that which was in use during the Cold War, which itself inspired a radically different perspective than that of the 1930s. We are only too inclined to rush along at the speed with which things change. The frenzy of the new obscures with its brilliance the persistence of the old. Our vision of the world is modified apace, but the underpinnings of our imagination remain and influence us without our knowledge. Our unfamiliarity with them leaves us without reliable moorings as the tempest of transformation rages about us. The few signs that remain are not enough to guide us, either because we consider them to be superseded (hence the frequency of the prefix *post* to characterize our era), or because we are no longer able to read them.

Many are those who know exactly where they are headed, and where the world is headed along with them. This book has not been written for them: they know how to read the signs. Fewer are those who question those signs. But their influence has made itself felt among intellectuals. Today, we are witnessing a veritable outburst of "re-readings"—who will re-read (this or that author, book, era, etc.) in the most inventive, the most profound, and the newest and most radical manner? All things considered, from its very inception our civilization has never stopped re-reading. In the arts and letters alone, the Renaissance saw itself as an imitation of the ancients; the Reformation, a re-reading of the Bible; the century of Louis XIV reinterpreted the classics of Greece and Rome; the nineteenth century rehabilitated the Middle Ages. Beneath our eyes, postmodernism and deconstructionism call virtually everything into question; hardly any aspect of modernity can escape their razor-sharp pendulum.

Seen in this light, this book is inevitably a response to fashion: it is typical of its time and place. On a broader scale, it participates in the incessant crossbreeding of clean breaks and continuities that have so powerfully marked Western civilization. But what can be the use of returning to the past, even via the agency of the great stories, if this is exactly what our civilization has ceased to do? In other words, can the return to the past be accomplished differently, *in another style*?

My wager is that it can. The difference of style here derives principally from the manner in which it approaches time and our relationship with it. The currents of postmodernism have changed nothing of the essence of these relationships: they persist in inserting themselves in the temporal linearity so dear to our civilization. The theory of relativity and quantitative reversibility notwithstanding, we are still all (postmodernists or not) firmly astride time's arrow as it flies in a straight line from the past to the future. On this straight line the future appears to be the most significant time: it guides the arrow. All that matters is what we will experience. All that counts is what is not yet. But the future is pure projection, it has no reality; it is only possible by extrapolation, by anticipation; it only exists in our minds by virtue of the past; the future is always located in what is to come. It is to the future that we offer up sacrifice. As Pascal says, "The present is never our end. The past and the present are our means, the future alone our end. Thus we never actually live, but hope to live ..."[10] The pleasure of writing this book, for example, is constantly threatened by the fear of bringing it to a satisfactory conclusion, to find a publisher, readers, success. Because apprehension about the future is striving constantly to destroy it, the present seems beyond our grasp.

10. Blaise Pascal, *Pensées*, trans. A. J. Krailsheimer (Harmondsworth: Penguin, 1966), no. 172.

Squarely against the logic that governs the development of technique, I would venture that the future is of no interest whatsoever. Contrariwise, the inexhaustible interest of the past resides in the fact that it constitutes our only reality—even more, our only possible guide. The past is to the intellect what clay is to the potter: the only material in which we can work, the only substance to which we can give meaning. If the past was without its significance, the passion for history would be incomprehensible and the past itself, formless. Curiously enough, however, the obsession with the future continues to obscure the significance of this passion. We imagine ourselves fixated on the future, without realizing that there is no other way for us to walk than backwards. And to walk backwards is the exact inversion of the position in which modern man projects himself, for whom meaning can only lie before him, along the path illuminated by reason. The great stories that I propose we read will, I hope, help us gain a fuller understanding of why, for all its triviality, the fascination with the future is so difficult for us to abandon.

To abandon our fascination with encountering our image in the mirror of the past is to give up the search for the meaning of our presence in the world where, rigorously speaking, it should never be: in the non-place of the future. It may well be that meaning is nowhere to be found. There exist powerful possibilities that, as far as the world is concerned, life has no meaning whatsoever. But speaking from a strictly human standpoint, this hypothesis is without interest. All of history indicates in a thousand and one ways that meaning is the last thing human beings can forgo. Even in the depths of physical deprivation, the search for meaning is what keeps life alive. Above all, the most unbearable, calamitous situations of extreme duress (war, famine, torture, sickness) are nothing other than the absence of meaning. If I were not certain of this constant, I could not write—nor read, nor teach, nor love, nor receive, nor give. What is at issue here is not certainty of the metaphysical variety, but a necessity that is altogether human, and all the more human in that on this issue metaphysics provides no answers and possesses no value except as a question. For the question of being remains fundamental and insoluble. Man can only postpone the question of meaning until beyond death, or seek it out in himself—in man, in his own history, in the stories he has already told and continues to tell about the world and about himself in the world.

Narrative Identity

The meaning of which we speak, the meaning man searches for in his past—in what the past has made him and in what he in turn has made of the multiple, accumulated pasts of which he is made—is not a product for instant consumption, given once and for all, but is constantly being reworked, rediscovered.

The effort is by no means self-evident. Far from modifying our conception of the world, our efforts at decoding tend instead to conform to it and to confirm it. For all our civilization's almost fanatical interest in history, the obsession with the future has transformed the interpretation of the past into a kind of instrument for conquest, and the past itself into an annex of our ambitions, a possession to be protected like one's capital—against the other humanities if need be. Reading to devour, to conquer, in accordance with an arbitrary, pre-assigned meaning or a sense that the future alone can reveal, and reading to exploit the past—an echo of the exploitation of the world itself—has bequeathed to us today a history at once rich and deserted, immense and stunted.

Another style of reading, one less self-regarding, humbler, more uncertain, is needed to give us access to a portion of this vanished treasure, and along with it, new possibilities of meaning for our human presence in the world. It is only, I believe, in the telling of stories, that we may hope to achieve this goal. The search for meaning cannot be explained, it can only be told. It is the telling that I undertake here, as I attempt to read as naïvely as possible the stories that humanity has already related to itself, and what Western civilization has made of this story.

No one can naïvely lay claim to naïveté. There is no such thing as a virgin thought. Nor is there such a thing as a path along which the traveller can afford not to look where he walks while ignorant of his destination. The journey that begins here is driven by the conviction that a civilization, like the life of an individual, is a story that has no value, which cannot speak unless it is being constantly reconsidered, constantly re-read.

This conviction found safe haven in me long ago, on reading Proust. Reading and re-reading the famous passage in *Time Regained*, where the narrator, feeling the vacillation of his foot on a paving stone, experiences the infinitesimal disequilibrium that will propel him on his reconquest of time past, never fails to touch off in me a kind of inner upheaval that calls forth a sensation of almost painful truth. "Real life," says the narrator, "life finally uncovered and clarified, the only life in consequence lived to the full, is literature." Taken in isolation from the lengthy passage that precedes it, Proust's exclamation risks reverberating in a vacuum, like a mundane literary provocation. It is necessary to make one's way through the entire work, to experience with the narrator those instants where meaning emerges, confused, and flutters for a fraction of a second before evaporating like a wellspring in the sand, to discover in his company "the greatness of true art" which "lies in rediscovering, grasping hold of, and making us recognize this reality, distant as it is from our daily lives, and growing more and more distant as the conventional knowledge we substitute for it becomes denser and more impermeable, this reality which we run a real risk of dying without having known, and which is quite simply our life."[11]

The danger, the risk of our lives passing us by, threatens not only individuals. It lies in wait as well for communities, cultures, and civilizations—ours in particular. "We, civilizations," said Valéry after World War I, "now know that we are mortal." Overused, the aphorism masks more than it reveals the true extent of the danger, which is not that of dying: all of us, individuals and communities, are promised to death. The danger lies in not having lived at all, in having missed out, in dying without ever having had the faintest idea about the forces that have shaped us and that we have in turn shaped, in dying without having told our story. Many, during the twentieth century, predicted the decline or the fall of the West. Its decline and fall are *etymologically foretold*: no civilization would find it easier to fall while remaining faithful to its name. The fall is our destiny; our civilization possesses the unconscious genius to inscribe itself under the zodiacal sign of its own demise. Let us then abandon ourselves to this magnificent lapse, and cease to fear the inevitable, and instead prepare ourselves for that which we vainly attempt to flee, to forget, to asepticize in a thousand different ways. To avoid death is not the question, but to have lived. To have lived with the greatest possible self-knowledge, just as Socrates invites us to do.

On close examination of individual and collective knowledge, the notion of collective identity stands revealed at its most fecund. For the community as for the individual, "the self of self-knowledge is the fruit of an examined life, a life purified, clarified by the cathartic effect of the stories, historical as well as fictional, transmitted by our culture."[12] But purification is exposed to the very danger it seeks to avoid: that of eliminating dissonances in the

11. Marcel Proust, *In Search of Lost Time* (in French), ed. Christopher Prendergast, vol. 3 (London: Allen Lane, 2002), p. 204.
12. Ricœur, op. cit., p. 357.

interests of acceptable narrative coherence. People inevitably tell stories about themselves for reasons of self-acceptance and self-reconciliation. The impulse to do so—which must surely motivate my own enterprise more than I might care to admit—is most powerful where absence is the most glaring. All by way of saying how necessary it is to take it into full account, *and* to resist it. Once again the Western psyche provides us with a particularly gripping example: the West does not seek only reconciliation with itself, but with the entire world, which it strives to understand and to sweep up in its fraternal, universalistic, and integrative embrace. An embrace that remains perfectly chimerical and negative as long as it is posited upon the expulsion from Western consciousness of all that irritates it, including expulsion of the very past which Western consciousness claims as its own. To assign us the task of reconciliation would be to condemn ourselves to never straying from the highroad I described earlier; it would be to engage ourselves on the long descent into a mediocre, self-satisfied imagination.

If it is true, as Hegel says, that "the spirit achieves its truth only when it finds itself in the absolute tearing apart," all the greater is the need to accept that the wound will remain open, with no possibility of ever closing again. Reconciliation may not be on the horizon. If "the practice of storytelling consists of an experience of thought by which we train ourselves to inhabit worlds foreign to us,"[13] it is all the more necessary to accept that their foreignness will trouble us and that living in proximity to them will be uncomfortable. In these conditions the experiment is well worth the attempt; it is the why and the wherefore of this book. To open ourselves to the stranger, *in the Other and in ourselves*, is surely one of the most difficult and necessary ethical requirements of the day for our civilization. This is the task I take up here, in full awareness that failure is always possible, and with the certainty that a noble failure, a failure acknowledged, always leaves something well worthy of meditation behind.

---

13. Ibid., p. 358.

Part One

IMMORTALITY AND LIFE

BOTH THE *Iliad* and the *Odyssey* sing of life and of immortality, but with differing accents. Ulysses chooses the first; Achilles the second. We find the same contrast, centuries earlier, in the Babylonian *Epic of Gilgamesh*. Above and beyond their differences, these three poems share a common thread: they speak of heroism, of renown, of life itself in all its splendid gratuitousness. Centuries later, at the dawning of an era that has not yet realized that it will come to be Christian, Virgil, inspired by the Homeric prototype, forges a hero whom he places at the service of the state. The epic becomes political, religious. The *Aeneid* is the beginning of a transformation, which the Gospels will soon carry to even more radical lengths.

Early on in the mythology of the Eastern Mediterranean, immortality, which is normally forbidden to man, makes its appearance as an attribute of extreme rarity, accessible only to an exceptional race, that of the heroes. For the common man, faced with ultimate disappearance, there is cold comfort in the idea of biological immortality through his descendents. But such an obscure sense of continuity does not satisfy the hero; he does not agree to his disappearance, to being erased by time against which he struggles with all his energy. For him, anonymity and oblivion are far more odious than death. If man cannot reside in the eternity reserved for the immortal gods, he should at least be permitted, assuming he has the choice, to survive eternally in the story of his heroic deeds. Far from fleeing death, the hero exposes himself to it. It is he who risks death, who deliberately places his life in danger to win immortality and renown. And who has a bard to tell his story.

To gain immortality in the memory of the generations to come is the wish of most of the warriors in the *Iliad*, of whom Achilles is the most powerful, the most extreme incarnation. Achilles stands out above all others, for he alone has the power to choose not to die. His virtual invulnerability puts, in a manner of speaking, physical immortality within his reach. If he does not desire it, it is because immortality would relegate him to oblivion; he is not prepared to pay the price of glory to gain eternal life. Better to live the brief burst of brilliance that immortalizes his name in human memory than to endure indefinitely the obscurity of daily life.

Ulysses' heroism is less flamboyant but more ingenious. He combines renown with the enjoyment of the things of this world. The tribulations heaped upon him as he struggles to return to a normal life, and the intelligent perseverance he demonstrates in recovering the peaceful enjoyment of his realm are what ensure his immortality—what happens to the king of Ithaca once he has slain the suitors and recovered his throne is of interest to no one. The heroism of Ulysses, unlike that of Achilles, seems partly involuntary, and his exploits ultimately accomplish little more than a domestic ambition. If Ulysses achieves anything that surpasses this ambition, it is during the siege of Troy, where he devises the famous stratagem of the horse. Still, this is not the episode that has enabled the *Odyssey* to stand the test of time, even though its gross subterfuge depicts its author as a man who solves concrete problems, and who can untangle the most complex of situations.

But is it accurate to say that the hero makes a choice? Achilles would not have survived his shame had he not avenged the memory of Patroclus. If he had chosen life over glory, Achilles would not have been himself, and his name would be unknown to us. The epic requires its principal characters to demonstrate the continuity and the coherence that are the very conditions of its existence. The *Iliad* cannot be the story of cowardice, nor the *Odyssey* that of abandonment. Yet the need for internal coherence, the contextual unity which the hero provides in accomplishing his fate with the decisive assistance of the gods, cannot prevent each of the Homeric narratives from having its own specific tone. Behind the appearance of continuity that flows from the *Iliad* to the *Odyssey* lies a radical inversion of values. In many ways, the later poem offers a potent rebuttal of the former.

Surprisingly, what Homer tells in two distinct poems can be found together in the *Epic of Gilgamesh*, which distils an unequalled concentration of significance in its general structure. Coming as it does well before the Homeric stories, this tale of heroism rich in meaning sheds light from afar on the tension between immortality and life, posing the problem of choice with even greater acuity.

Later, like a contradictory echo of the *Odyssey*, the pseudo-historical myth of the *Aeneid* weaves a tapestry of collective immortality. Forced to flee his homeland by the devastating machinations of Ulysses, Aeneas embarks, in the wake of his enemy, upon an expedition of an entirely different scope, a founding voyage. His heroism is burdened by a meaning that he cannot comprehend, a significance that towers far above his personal ambitions, even though as a hero he is not entirely insensible to his own glory. Far removed from the spirit of the Homeric tales, the *Aeneid* tells of a sacred mission; it responds to civic concerns, not to say to the loftiest exigencies of the imperial Roman state. Already we have drawn nearer, not without some ambiguity, to the story of truth that will be the subject—after the tragedy of knowledge—of the third section of this book.

Here I examine three moments—Homer, Virgil, and the anonymous author(s) of the *Epic of Gilgamesh*—in what may seem to be a surprising order. I begin with the most "familiar," followed by what seems a Virgilian distortion of the Homeric story, only to return to what can be considered as a point of origin, in the sense that it brings us face to face with the ineluctable.

1

ULYSSES, OR THE HAPPINESS OF MORTALS

THE *ODYSSEY* often speaks of the events related in the *Iliad*. One scene stands out—the brief visit to the Underworld—in which the fates of their respective heroes converge with extraordinary dramatic intensity. There, as the two Homeric narratives cast light on each other,[14] Ulysses encounters the shade of Achilles' glory. The episode is crucial. What can the eternity of fame mean in the realm of Hades? it asks. What is it worth against the value of life? Surrounded by the spirits of his former comrades-in-arms, Ulysses receives the shattering confirmation of what he has known all along. Nothing is more precious than the earth and its light.

The *Iliad* is not a story of the Trojan War, nor the *Odyssey* the voyage of Ulysses. "Sing, goddess, the wrath of Achilles," "Tell, O muse, the man of a thousand artifices," they begin. The Homeric story is centered on the hero. It does not limit itself to telling the story of the hero through his exploits and tribulations; it shows as well the gaping chasm left by his absence: the absence of Achilles from the field of battle, the absence of Ulysses from his house.

The wrath of Apollo descends upon the camp of the Achaeans following the prayer of his high priest Chryses. Agamemnon, in offensive terms, and against the advice of his own assembly, refuses to return, in exchange for a generous ransom, the priest's daughter Chryseis, whom he holds as a hostage of war. Calamity is decimating the Achaeans; Achilles, becoming the interpreter of the common will, calls upon his commander in chief to bow to the obvious: the ravages of Apollo will only cease when the girl has been restored to her father and the offence assuaged. Pride wounded, and

---

14. The interminable debate on the paternity of the texts is of little consequence. The crucial consideration is that they have always been associated in the Greek, Roman, and Western traditions.

'gratification thwarted, Agamemnon seeks compensation for the restitution and avenges himself on Achilles by ravishing fair-cheeked Briseis. Stung by the public affront, Achilles withdraws along with his men and begs his mother, the goddess Thetis, to intercede with Zeus, whom she had rescued from perilous circumstances. She pleads that he tip the scales in favor of the Trojans and drive the Achaeans to disaster, so that the all-powerful Agamemnon, son of Atreus, "may know his madness, what he lost / when he dishonored me, peerless among Akhaians" (I, 410–412).[15] The lord of Olympus acquiesces in spite of the grief his decision is bound to bring him from his temperamental spouse Hera. The spring that drives the action has now been wound. After considerable ebb and flow, the battle transforms the besieged into besiegers. Led by the intrepid Hector, the Trojans battle to within reach of the Achaean boats and threaten to burn them. Although Agamemnon has returned to the straight and narrow, has made more than sufficient amends and has sworn to make good his fault, Achilles' anger, for all the deadly peril, shows no signs of abating. Sent as ambassadors, his closest comrades, Ulysses among them, are unable to prevail upon him. Only the death of Patroclus, the inseparable companion to whom he had finally agreed to lend his arms, can cause him, crazed with grief, to join the battle, repulse the Trojans, and slay Hector. The poem ends with the funerals of Patroclus and Hector whose dead body Agamemnon, forced by Zeus, finally agrees to restore to the elderly Priam, his father.

Nothing in the story, no sudden turn of events, is calculated to startle the reader: all is carefully foreshadowed. Not unlike the gods, who determine the course of events, we know that Achilles will once again take his place in combat and that the Achaeans will be victorious; we know that Hector and Patroclus will die. We know as well what happens before and after the story, which portrays only a brief period, less than two months in all, of the ten-year siege. As we proceed, we learn of the cause of the war, the kidnapping of Helen, the fall of Troy, and the death of Achilles. Far from being reserved for the listeners, this knowledge is often shared by the heroes themselves. Achilles, first among them, *knows* that he will die: this is the price he has agreed to pay for glory. He could well return home and enjoy a long and peaceful life in total obscurity, but he *chooses* immortality by advancing beneath the ramparts of Ilion toward a death whose precise moment—but only that—he ignores. Surely he is ignorant as well of the derisory nature of

---

15. Homer, *Iliad*, trans. Robert Fitzgerald (Garden City, NY: Anchor Press, 1974). Unless otherwise indicated, all translations are from Robert Fitzgerald's translations of the Iliad and the Odyssey. References to the verses quoted are accurate enough to allow the reader to locate the indicated passages in any edition.

posthumous glory that he will encounter in the realm of the shades. The *Iliad*, dedicated to the glory of the living hero, refrains from lifting the veil from his disenchantment. And yet, there is already something present in the *Iliad* that suggests that his glory is not unmitigated.

The hero may well know his destiny, but he is not master of the path that leads him to it. What am I saying! He is not even master of himself. Let us not speak of Agamemnon, an inflated figure who, to explain away his outrageous behavior and his indignities, invokes the "wild distraction" into which Zeus has plunged him (XIX, 85–87). What can the great warrior have in common with mortal men? Human beings rarely fail to attribute to the gods the ill fortune they have brought upon themselves by their own blindness. Achilles himself, a hero among heroes, cultivates his anger beyond all reasonable limits: justified at first, his wrath rapidly becomes painful sullenness when he is offered reparation. He achieves his aim: the illustrious injured party humiliates the proud son of Atreus. Nothing can sway him, not even the friendly sagacity of Ulysses. No, the hero must go beyond the revenge he himself has claimed from the gods. Caught up as he is in his own inexorable obstinacy, the death of Patroclus brings upon him a punishment which prefigures his own. Only the suffering of loss can bring him back to reality. There can be little doubt that his companion must die in order for the hero to lend his energies to the exploits that will immortalize and kill him. Fate has its exigencies, which no one, not even an immortal, can elude. Zeus himself, for all his omnipotence over men and gods, cannot save from death one of his dearest sons, Sarpedon, without undermining the order over which he presides (XVI, 430–460). Nor could he cause Patroclus to die in a different way, in fighting alongside his friend, for instance.

Between the implacable necessity of fate and its workings, the hero enjoys an indubitable yet uncertain room for maneuver. In the image of the world around him, the hero steers a course between men and gods. Son of a goddess impregnated by a mortal, Achilles incarnates the ambivalence that makes it possible for him to trade the prospect of placid happiness for the renown he is fatally brought to choose. Fatally indeed: the mediocre pleasures of life could not hope to satisfy a demi-god. The Homeric hero knows nothing of happiness. Without cease he encounters difficulties, misfortunes, and the thousand perils of adventure, never fearing to expose himself to the violence of premature demise. But though he may put his life at risk, he does not spurn life. It is as though the very danger of losing it that hangs perpetually over his head makes each moment more precious; as though it were necessary to accumulate suffering and hardship in order to taste fully the rare moments of love, friendship, and repose. There can be little doubt that, like the poet, his heroes hold life dear. In his scenes of daily life, Homer deploys a language that is too precise, too subtle, simultaneously too strong and too tender, for us to mistake his intentions.

The love of detail, in cruelty as in pleasure, is probably what moves us most in Homeric poetry. It contains far too much truth for us to believe that we are in another world: this is indeed the world of humankind. But the hero occupies, high above the world, a kind of intermediate level to which the common man has no access, and which lends him wings. He soars above the fray and plunges into it with the savage abandon and the superiority of the eagle, in the image—relatively speaking—of the gods themselves, Zeus first among them, who move without transition between Olympian summits and worldly affairs. Not to join in the battle as Apollo, Ares, and Athena so willingly do—Zeus remains always above the mêlée—but to taste of human pleasures: for all the sumptuous goddesses who populate the heights of Olympus, the son of Kronos does not disdain a night of dalliance with a tender mortal. It would seem that the gods themselves sometimes yearn for earthly beauty, whose fragility makes it all the more precious.

The only serious distinction between gods and heroes is death. Otherwise, both share the same passions, the same excitements, the same access of jealousy; both weave the same webs of intrigue. Heroes often call upon the gods for help, ask from them a guiding sign, and the gods, on their own initiative, often rush to the aid of their protégés to offer them council or to extract them from danger.

The gods are, of course, more knowledgeable; from on high they make sport of men, confound them, guide or mislead them. Homer himself fully exploits the anthropomorphism that transforms the divinities—with the exception of Zeus—into a kind of ethereal double of his heroes. The gods are what we might term their lucky—or unlucky—stars, more rarely their conscience, their inner voices to which the mythological panoply lends familiar human faces. For in Homer the gods are simultaneously the forces of nature that fight and make up under the arbitration of Zeus, and the externalisation of the dreams that men, even though they may be heroes, can attain only by seeking out the surrogate immortality they hope to gain by deeds that remain in the memory of their fellow men. The continuous interaction of higher forces, of inspiration and of earthly tribulation transforms the Homeric universe into a world of dazzling humanity.

The bedazzlement is that of the world itself, where the struggle is magnified, suffused with the gleam of glory, and without mercy. Humanity is present in all its unquenchable savagery, wading literally into the carnage. But it is a humanity that appears even truer in its striking weakness. Bravery, fear, arrogance, fury, wiliness become all the more human in that they change nothing in the long term. Everything has been resolved elsewhere, decided beforehand: defeat, victory, honor, shame. Yet each must bear the weight of his acts. Action is everything, action for its own sake, in the sense that to throw oneself head first into action remains the best way to forget the fate to which the hero must bow. Hector has no sooner confessed to his wife Andromache: "Honor—for in my heart and soul I know / a day will come when ancient Ilion falls, / when Priam and the folk of Priam perish" (VI, 440–442), than he exhorts his brother Paris to march off to war, and to leave his concerns about his reputation for later, that same Paris "who fought best of Trojan horsemen when they fought at Troy" (VI, 518–529).

Action and the manner in which man behaves in the face of necessity are of the highest importance. Whether or not nobility has been inscribed in the hero's fate, it is in action that his greatness or his pettiness will be made manifest. But the stature conferred upon him by his prominent place in the story does not make him immune to meanness, to stupidity, to baseness. Achilles behaves like a spoiled child, snivelling at his mother's apron strings. Hector is far more boastful than valor allows, and when the moment of truth arrives, flees from Achilles like a rabbit. The defects and exaggerations of the heroes are proportional to their stature. But the same stature that raises them up from the mass is indispensable to their visibility. The hero must stand out from the crowd, must always be visible from all directions, even in his absence, in order for the reader, or the listener, to identify with him.

Identification does not mean edification. In Homer—for which Plato reproaches him sternly—even the gods are barely edifying and on occasion go so far as to make themselves perfectly ridiculous, as in the delectable passage in which Ares, god of war, comes whining to his father after being wounded in battle, and complains that Zeus shows no indignation at the sight of "these acts of violence" (V, 871–886)! All the same, however, identification with the hero is necessary, to sustain audience interest, so that each and every one can experience, in full safety, the dream of greatness. And—who knows?—perhaps to savor, as we dream, the quotidian world to which the poet has given such skillful relief and which, in our petty darkness, we are no longer able to see.

The Homeric epic is, in every sense of the term, a dream. The daydream that all of us contrive to repeat tirelessly whenever we imagine that we have overcome the insurmountable or achieved the improbable. It also closely resembles the extraordinarily real, intense, and perfectly unbelievable stories we experience in our sleep, in all their marvellous, trivial, and nightmarish aspect. The hero is in the position of the sleeper: he is experiencing an adventure he is not aware he has created. This is for good reason: he knows, providing he wishes to know, that all has been worked out and set in motion far above him; he even uses his knowledge as a pretext to give himself a clear conscience. Far from being a school for responsibility, the Homeric world has a profoundly amoral cast: it appears to offer full license to the unleashing of the most extreme passions; providing glory will be his, the hero is without scruples. But this very license is accompanied by the glaringly obvious: the hero is the first to suffer for his excesses. Let him heap blame upon Zeus and all of Olympus; his attempts to elude responsibility only add to his misfortune. Ignorance aggravates the evils concealed beneath its veil. In the end, Achilles is a great warrior who owes his exceptional power to his semi-divine birth, but he does not possess, or comes too late into possession of, or possesses to an insufficient degree, an awareness of his acts. His glory shines with a gleam that is slightly suspect. Only the tears he sheds in the company of Priam over the furtively united bodies of Patroclus and Hector lend him, as the poem concludes, an instant of truth that brings him close to men. But his tears may well indicate the cost to man of making his memory divine, to place his renown above all else. In any case, this moment of compassion cannot suffice to make a "model" of Achilles.

Ulysses, whom Homer presents in the *Iliad* as the most vigilant of the Achaean chieftains, is a different story in every respect. Diomedes rejoices in his companionship "for he sees things like no other man" (X, 249). The fact is that he sees things quite differently from Achilles, whom he tries to detach from his resentment by reminding him of the recommendations of Peleus, his father, at the moment of departure:

> Son, Athena and Hera will make you strong if they choose,
> but check your high temper,
> for the better part is in goodwill.
> Eschew vain quarrelling,
> the Akhaians old and young will
> respect you more for doing so.
>
> (IX, 255–257)

Unlike Achilles, Ulysses has no need to take himself for the son of a goddess; he is quite capable of distinguishing between the godly and the human. This knowledge does not insulate him from error, but it does make him a character with whom it is easier to identify. Beyond strength and bravery, everything sets the two heroes apart: one is headstrong and obstinate, the other is thoughtful and bends to necessity; one trades the permanence of fame for the suddenness of death, the other chooses life and the return to home and hearth over the immortal love of a goddess. One is uncompromising in his excess, the other is intelligence in action, who knows how to act and when to wait. We know that the two Homeric epics are focused on waiting, but their heroes' characters lend each of them a distinctive coloration: the *Iliad*, dependent upon the humors of Achilles, is the story of a destructive wait; the *Odyssey*, dependent on Ulysses' return, tells the story of a wait that is no less exasperating but in the end fruitful.

The stage upon which the *Odyssey* is played out is not the "wine-dark sea," no matter how charged with uncertainty its constant presence is, but "bright Ithaca," where all is anticipation. There, Penelope and Telemachus await either the improbable return of Ulysses or the confirmation of his death. The suitors, having taken up residence in his palace, wait for Penelope to choose between them, consuming her inheritance apace. Ulysses himself, physically distant but having returned in spirit, waits for the gods to loosen the chains of his gilded captivity, to free him from the jailer who has long since lost her charm.

Telemachus, in filial imitation that is simultaneously a passage toward maturity, sets out in search of his father. At the same time, the gods assembled on Mount Olympus order that Ulysses be set free. Poseidon, infuriated by the blinding of his cyclopean son, casts our hero into a final sea-storm. As the tempest abates, he is washed ashore on the island of the Phaecians. Its inhabitants are as considerate as they are contented. They show Ulysses every consideration, listen with rapt attention to the story of his tribulations, shower him with gifts and escort him unhindered back to his homeland, taking care to put him ashore in deep slumber, alongside his treasure, in a hidden cove far from the city and at safe remove from prying eyes. Their precautions give a clear indication that his return can by no means be taken for granted, as Athena takes pains to inform her protégé when the two of them hatch an elaborate plot for the reconquest of his lost kingdom. The scheme proceeds as planned. With the assistance of Telemachus, who has returned from his expedition shortly after his father's arrival, Ulysses makes his way surreptitiously into his own palace disguised as an old beggar. Only his old dog, dying neglected atop a dung heap, recognizes him with a sickly wag of his tail. Several episodes follow (his rebuff by the suitors, contact with his man- and maid-servants, the scene of the scar that discloses his identity to the finger-tips of his aged governess, his conversation with Penelope) during which the long-absent master now returned explores the lay of the land and the mind of his opponents. Before his very eyes the insolence of the suitors grows, culminating in the apotheosis of the scene of the bow, which only he can string, and the flight of murderous arrows he soon lets fly against them. Not one will survive. But in killing the suitors, Ulysses has killed off the flower of nobility of his lands, an act that threatens to turn against him. The father of one of the dead men sums up in a few devastating lines the emotions of those who opposed him, and their interpretation of Ulysses' adventure following his departure for Troy:

> Heroic feats that fellow did for us
> Akhaians, friends! Good spearmen by the shipload
> he led to war and lost—lost ships and men,
> and once ashore again killed these, who were
> the islands' pride.
>
> (XXIV, 426–430)[16]

The conflict ends as quickly as it had begun under the auspices of Athena. Her decisive intervention confirms after the fact the opinion of Ulysses' supporters. They maintain that he could not have done what he stands accused of unaided—"When these hard deeds were done by lord Odysseus / the immortal gods were not far off" (XXIV, 443–456)—while the fathers who today lament and writhe in indignation made no attempt to curb the folly of their sons. But Ulysses is neither entirely absolved, nor has he reached the end of his labors. As Tiresias had predicted during his visit to Tartarus, "One trial—I do not know how long—is left for me / to see fulfilled" (XXIII, 248–252). Thus the narrative concludes on a provisional return, which depends upon the success of yet another expedition, as though the hero has been condemned by fate to perpetual wandering in which he must expiate his fault.

Happy ending notwithstanding, there is something astonishing in this violently critical reassessment of Ulysses' acts, coming as it does at the moment of highest drama. The entire scope of the epic vacillates, and along with it, the stature of the hero himself. Suddenly, Ulysses stands revealed as little more than an unscrupulous adventurer who, on pure impulse, sacrifices everything—his wife, his friends, his peace of mind, and the youth of his

16. Homer, *Odyssey*, trans. Robert Fitzgerald (London: Heinemann, 1962).

homeland—to satisfy his vain ambitions. Many are the episodes, which, in the light of this sudden turnabout, gleam with a tarnished lustre. The reader recalls how, on many occasions, Ulysses' companions have paid dearly for his imprudence. In the cavern of Polyphemus, for instance, not only does his curiosity (to see what a Cyclops really looks like) cost the lives of several crew members who have accompanied him into the monster's lair, but he embellishes their escape with a round of boasting that will ultimately prove disastrous.

Instead of allowing Polyphemus to believe that he had been blinded by *Oudeis* (No One), Ulysses, over the strenuous objections of his companions, mocks the monster from the stern of his ship, boasting of his exploit and proudly disclosing his true identity. On Ulysses' words, Polyphemus remembers that the event has been foretold, and invites his erstwhile guests to reconciliation under the aegis of Poseidon, his father, who will provide them with an escort and return to him his sight. But Ulysses redoubles his insults, and proclaims that Polyphemus's eye will not be cured "even by the Earth-shaker!" The Cyclops then

> stretched his hands out in his darkness
> toward the sky of stars and prayed Poseidon:
>
> "O hear me, lord, blue girdler of the islands,
> if I am thine indeed and thou art father:
> grant that Odysseus, raider of cities, never
> sees his home. Laerte's son, I mean,
> who kept his hall on Ithaka. Should destiny
> intend that he shall see his roof again
> among his family in his fatherland,
> far be that day, and dark the years between.
> Let him lose all companions, and return
> under strange sail to bitter days at home."
>
> (IX, 529–534)

This episode functions as the narrow aperture through which the sum of all information contained in the *Odyssey* is funnelled. It takes place during the first two weeks of his return journey and touches off the sequence of misfortunes that follows. Poseidon, son of Kronos, whose standing in the Olympian hierarchy is just beneath that of Zeus,[17] is not to be mocked with impunity. But this act of provocation is to a certain extent necessary, if for no

---

17. Equal in stature to Hades.

other reason than that of plot: something must happen to divert Ulysses far from his route of return and to deprive him of his companions! Divine wrath functions as *deus ex machina*. At the same time, Ulysses' wild-eyed mockery, while he was still under the influence of the monster's all-consuming hospitality, is perfectly understandable. The hero, whose cunning is often compared to that of Zeus, loses control of himself, loses for an instant his principal quality, that of discernment, and along with it his quality as hero. Divine Ulysses ceases for a brief instant to be divine and reveals himself as fully human even in his excesses. One instant of excess is enough for all things to fall apart. The scope of his misstep seems itself excessive, and one might be tempted to attribute it purely and simply to the exigencies of the narrative we have just outlined. But that would be to forget that Necessity itself, not to mention the impotence, which is our lot at the feet of Necessity, also finds expression in the narrator's mouth. Ulysses' weakness, *and* the depth of that weakness, bear witness to human vulnerability: an instant of distraction is sufficient to disrupt an entire life; the hero stumbles and falls because he is human. Were Ulysses still divine, always fully aware of all about him; were he, to put it succinctly, infallible, it would be impossible to identify with him, and there would be no *Odyssey*.

Though he exerts a much greater fascination upon us than does Achilles, and though he is more complete and more complex, he is far from being a model of humanity. This wrecker of cities often displays perfectly revolting cruelty and greed. Not only does he fail to spare a single suitor when they offer him their surrender, submission, and compensation after the first and most arrogant among them has been killed, but he fascilitates as well the execution of the maidservants who in weakness had yielded to their advances.

This is the selfsame man who, shortly beforehand, rejoices at seeing his wife offer herself to the highest bidder: "Odysseus's heart laughed when he heard all this / her sweet tones charming gifts out of the suitors" (XVIII, 278–280). Even if we admit that what Ulysses is admiring here is above all his wife's cleverness, we cannot but be struck by the importance of material wealth to the hero. He seems troubled not in the slightest that the immense pile of gifts that the king of the Phaecians intends for him has been amassed on the backs of the people: "We'll make a levy upon the realm / to pay for us the loss each bears in this" (XIII, 13–15). Not only does the beneficiary not raise the slightest objection, but also the safe delivery of his treasure and its protection become one of his principal concerns. Hardly has he awakened in his hidden landing-place, not knowing even where he finds himself, than he must see and count out his riches: "I shouldn't wonder / if they pulled out with part of it on board" (XIII, 215–217), he says. And of the stranger in whose guise Athena visits him, he begs, clinging to his knees: "Do not feel alarmed or hostile, coming across me, only / receive me into safety with my stores" (XIII, 227–229). Without his booty, the return would be worthless. His greatest fear is to return deprived of his worldly goods, not of his companions.

His legendary caution does not inhibit him from exposing the lives of others to danger. When his flotilla enters Lestrygonian waters, Ulysses allows it to drop anchor in the harbor, with the exception of a single ship that he moors offshore. He then dispatches a search party and stations himself at a safe distance to observe developments, which quickly turn to disaster. The Lestrygonians attack with a volley of boulders:

> and hell's own
> crashing rose, and crying from the ships,
> as planks and men were smashed to bits—poor gobbets
> the wild men speared like fish and bore away.
> But long before it ended in the anchorage—
> havoc and slaughter—I had drawn my sword
> and cut my ship's own cable. "Men," I shouted,
> "man the oars and pull till your hearts break
> if you would put this butchery behind!"
> The oarsmen rent the sea in mortal fear
> and my ship spurted out of range, far out
> from that deep canyon where the rest were lost.
> So we fared onward, and death fell behind,
> and we took breath to grieve for our companions.
>
> Our next landfall was on Aiaia, island
> of Kirke, dire beauty and divine ...
>
> (X, 123–139)

Spice is the narrative's watchword: raw images, a sarcastic shift of fortune in the sword sequence, the juxtaposition of death and happiness, of painful affliction and gratification. Never for an instant does it occur to Ulysses, who in other circumstances never misses an opportunity to point out the errors of his subordinates, to question his own acts. The same tone and the same detachment pervade the account of his confrontation with the Cyclops. For in both instances, it is Ulysses who tells the tale, without a hint of modesty, without the shadow of a regret. And yet, in their benevolence, his

Pheacian hosts seem not in the least offended. Like the reader, they seek only more, and shower the narrator with generosity. Clearly, they make no judgement about the narrative's raw material; they are quite content to take pleasure in it.

Ulysses, in the end, has but one regret, which returns constantly to his lips as he recites his adventures at the court of Alkinous: his departure from his homeland, and the constant postponement of his return. He has entered the end of the tenth year of his wanderings, and has not yet abandoned Calypso to resume his haphazard course. But earlier, ten years of siege had not managed to sharpen his impatience. When he sets sail from the shores of Troy, a speedy return seems no priority. Our hero instead schemes to sack the unsuspecting city of the Ciconians, where he needlessly loses several more of his men. He later spends a month carousing in the palaces of Aeolus. Nor will he need great persuasion to spend an entire year in the bed of beguiling Circe. Patient, faithful Penelope seriously crosses his mind only when his desire for Calypso begins to abate. After seven years in the arms of the same woman, voluptuousness has turned to boredom. Lying with her every night becomes all the more burdensome in that he spends the rest of his time in inaction, that fertile soil for homesickness. It is this sickness, more than the absence of his wife, which gnaws away at him.

But the moment of Ulysses' departure has come at last. Under pressure from the gods, the nymph gives her consent and declares herself ready to assist him. The poet describes the scene thus:

> Now as he spoke the sun set, dusk drew on,
> and they retired, this pair, to the inner cave
> to revel and rest, softly, side by side.

> (V, 225–227)

The imminence of separation is enough to rekindle the flame of desire.

We understand that Ulysses chooses to return home rather than be consumed in immortal boredom, albeit beside the most beautiful woman in the world. But the return, the promise of a long, tranquil evening in the twilight of his life has no appeal unless preceded by an action-filled existence in which the hero has had ample opportunity to taste the joys and tribulations of adventure. Everything in the trajectory of this man is driven, with the help of the gods, by a radical egotism which, taking life as its model, avoids all moral judgement. "Happy the wanderer, like Ulysses, who has come home at last," wrote Joachim du Bellay, whose celebrated formula compresses into a single phrase the power of a dream. Far more than the *Iliad*, the *Odyssey* is a dream, the dream of all dreams that each of us, to a greater or lesser extent, has dreamed: "Dear child, whatever put this in your head? / Why do you want to go so far in the world?" (II, 363–365) Telemachus's governess naïvely exclaims. Discovering his father's fate is merely a pretext; his true wish is to follow his father's footsteps, to sever the ties that bind him to home and hearth, to detach himself from the matrix of childhood all the better to return more aware, more practiced, more wealthy. The treasure that Ulysses so fears being stolen could well symbolize that wealth, but the metaphor does not carry enough weight: that which his travels have allowed him to accumulate is intangible, not something that can be lost or stolen. Such is, at least, the dream of youth plunged by adventure into life. Now he has had more than his share of trials and travels, and from them he has reaped a rich harvest of hardships and emotions in this "great world." The dream has come true, and it has all but become a nightmare. The hero can finally look forward to nothing more than enjoying the material blessings of this world in peace.

As a dream, the *Odyssey*, as distinct from the *Iliad*, consists of an equal measure of familiarity and remoteness. The *Iliad* is bathed almost entirely in the surreality of the warrior ethos, with the occasional nod toward civilian life. The *Odyssey*, always in the same breath, stands astride the real and the unreal. Almost none of what takes place is possible in the waking world, yet all occurs as though in everyday life, exactly as in a daydream. The commonplace and the fantastic are juxtaposed and intertwined on the same level, never to combine, with an equal power of persuasion and in necessarily absolute complementarity, like the colors in a Matisse. No need to seek for references beyond the canvas, nor behind it, nor off to the side. Everything is present in front of our eyes, arranged to perfection. In the *Odyssey*, perfection is a function of the whole, and not necessarily of the absence of awkwardness or of the faultless beauty of each verse.[18] Faultless as well, in the poem as in the work of a painter, is the manner. The world of Ulysses is a two-dimensional one. It provides not the slightest perspective, and possesses nothing resembling a shadow, even less so a hidden face. Ulysses has no soul: no matter how compellingly human he seems, his character is amoral, without mystery, without secrets. In step with the trials of the hero, our emotions as readers follow upon one another in a pure state, unfiltered, without critical distance. This immediacy lends the exuberance of the tale its luminous intensity and makes it almost impossible to interpret.

---

18. Many specialists claim that the Homeric text discloses sharp variations of style that tend to indicate that it was not necessarily written by a single author.

And yet, there is no lack of interpretation. Few stories have been so richly commented upon, copied, enhanced, and transposed as has the *Odyssey*. One after another, Virgil, Dante, Ronsard, Rabelais, Cervantes, Fénelon, Voltaire, Sade, and closer to us, Joyce, Kazantzakis, Hergé, Moravia, and Kubrick, to name but a few, have drawn upon it for their inspiration. It can be said without exaggeration that the *Odyssey* has established itself through the centuries as the prototype of the adventure novel, becoming in the process the generic title of any account of unexpected adventure and of the life of action.

Ulysses, the most celebrated character of all Greco-Latin antiquity, remains today one of the best known and most attractive figures of the West's cultural self-imagination. There is no need to have read a single line of Homer to know him: resilient, courageous, as clever as any two normal men, he stands as the personification of cunning, of adventure, of resourcefulness. He is the archetypal man who always gets out of a tight spot. Though not entirely false, this image bears little relation to the Homeric hero, for the simple reason that it has survived by reconstituting itself in the absence of a reading of the text itself.

We owe our false familiarity with Ulysses to the utter unfamiliarity of the Homeric universe. Outside this universe, Ulysses can be distinguished from modern-day adventurers only by his ancient origins, by his antique livery. Like him, today's heroes of the silver screen and of television, from Tintin to Indiana Jones, via Superman, James Bond, and the cowboys, all contrive to "pull through," to overcome obstacles, to turn the most desperate situations to their advantage—the difference being that these men owe nothing to the gods, and everything to themselves. Ulysses, for all his bravado and cunning, is nothing more than a cork tossed by the waves, a wisp of straw at the mercy of forces whose immensity is beyond his grasp. Our contemporary champions know nothing of Necessity, and have never had to do anything more than to overcome the nastiness of ill-intentioned individuals who vainly attempt to impede their progress.

If Ulysses has any "lesson"—an admittedly incongruous concept where the Homeric corpus is concerned—to learn from his tribulations, it becomes apparent in the greatest possible clarity at the instant when, in his pseudo-beggar's rags, he addresses the most moderate of the suitors who has come to console him in his poverty: "Of mortal creatures, all that breathe and move, / earth bears none frailer than mankind" (XVIII, 129–130). No such considerations trouble the modern-day adventurer; he commits no errors, and always repairs those he does commit; his weakness is merely a passing one.

In the final analysis, he dominates every situation he encounters, masters the world around him, and triumphs over evil. He is a moral being. Such notions are foreign to the world of Homer, though he who imagines himself familiar with that world could easily be confused: Ulysses confronts not evil, but misfortune. He seeks not to dominate the world but struggles to master himself. Ultimately, his fate depends not upon himself. Without Athena's protection, he is at loose ends.

Death hovers constantly around the Homeric hero, not in the form of something that happens only to others, but like an indestructible and constant companion who misses not the slightest occasion to make his presence felt. To call death a constant companion is not to overstate matters. Without the prospect of its end, existence would not have the same value. Death, dark though it may be, is the spice of life. But its premature, sudden onrush deprives us of the chance to drain the cup of life to the lees. In retrospect, Achilles' bargain of death for glory seems an ill-considered one, attributable to youthful hotheadedness, even though it is guided first and foremost by the desire to avenge the death of a friend in combat.

From this perspective, Ulysses' meeting with the shade of Achilles constitutes the culminating moment of the *Odyssey*, to which I alluded at the beginning of this chapter. Forced to descend into the Underworld to consult the shade of Tiresias the soothsayer about his fate, Ulysses encounters as well the shades of his former comrades-in-arms. Some explicitly, others less so, complain of their premature or ignominious departure from life. Then arises the shade of Achilles who, thinks Ulysses, has no cause for grievance, particularly with regard to the worldly tribulations that are his. Recounting his sufferings, the visitor expostulates:

> "But was there ever a man more blest by fortune
> than you, Akhilleus? Can there ever be?
> We ranked you with immortals in your lifetime,
> we Argives did, and here your power is royal
> among the dead men's shades. Think, then, Akhilleus:
> you need not be so pained by death."
> > To this
> he answered swiftly:
> > "Let me hear no smooth talk
> of death from you Odysseus, light of councils.
> Better, I say, to break sod as a farm hand

for some poor countryman, on iron rations,
than lord it over the exhausted dead."

(XI, 483–492)

The confession of Achilles is crushing. The most illustrious of all the heroes of the *Iliad* bitterly regrets the sacrifice of his life for the vanity of glory. In the realm of shades, glory is worth not even a minute of the most humble, the most obscure of lives. Far from being taken in by Ulysses' praise, Achilles knows full well that his old comrade does not believe his own words. Ulysses knows better than anyone the worth of life, and his sojourn in Tartarus can only strengthen his desire to return to the sweetness of daily existence. Seen from the dwelling place of the dead, life shines like man's sole earthly good. Outside of life there is nothing, no above-and-beyond worth mentioning. This moment of light is all the more precious for being so perishable. Still, the *Odyssey* shows in profusion how terrible this "moment" can be; *it is, in and of itself, life in its tumultuous flow*, with all the obstacles that accompany it, and separate us from the well-deserved rest thanks to which we can enjoy it to the fullest. No matter. On the poet's delicate balance our brief sojourn on earth, for all its infinite sorrows, weighs more heavily than the eternity of fame.

The hero of the modern adventure tale clearly knows nothing of the realm of the shades, to which he is quite content to expedite others (*Live and Let Die*) and which, despite all dangers, he never truly approaches. In every sense of the term, he does not know death. Nor old age. Nor, therefore, life. He represents the eternal triumph of the just cause. Ulysses, on the other hand, is neither just nor unjust. His wisdom is an incitement to measure, but there are times when life surges up within him so powerfully that he throws caution to the winds and behaves like a child. He seeks nothing more than the joy of survival and the ephemeral pleasures that this reprieve brings. Ulysses is life in the raw, in all its spontaneity and fragility; priceless life lived in the shadow of death, remote indeed from the modern adventurer, with whom his kinship is ultimately false.

At the opposite extremity of the superficial, ill-considered reading that would cast Ulysses as a modern hero, one can advance interpretations of an entirely different order: complex, subtle, quite capable of attaining the greatest profundity. The ancients themselves had no hesitation in doing so. Early on, from the end of the sixth century B.C., interpretation of the Homeric corpus is no longer restricted to the simple literary pleasure that the human adventure narrative can provide. Scholars sought now cosmological, now physical, political, or psychological meanings. Through his art, Homer "knowingly conceals beneath the veil of allegory"[19] a fully developed science of nature which philosophers were later to restate in more prosaic language. The reservations of Plato would change nothing: those whom he most inspired, the Neoplatonists under the guidance of Plotinus, accorded Homer divine attributes, making of him "a visionary, someone who contemplates intelligible Beauty ... From this most human, and least mystic of all poets, they extracted a treasure trove of mysticism, with the quiet self-assurance and the virtuosity of prestidigitators."[20] No one can therefore plead amazement that, with the triumph of Christendom, the Church Fathers themselves were fated to read Homer in spiritualist terms.

Like all great texts, the Homeric poems are a kind of portmanteau of variable geometry. The diversity and wealth of the readings they sustain are necessarily infinite, and it is tempting to multiply their dimensions. I, like many before me, am inclined to see in the *Odyssey* an inner voyage, not at all as a mystical quest, but from the psychological standpoint. Ulysses travels toward the discovery of his psyche—and we know today how long, arduous and treacherous this road can be. For more than a century now, psychoanalysis has haunted mythology, literature, and, to an even greater extent, literary criticism. Not without reason. If Freud has so firmly seized upon Oedipus that he has all but supplanted Sophocles, what might we accomplish with Ulysses, the precocious hero, unaware of the discovery of the ego (the Freudian *Ich*) and snared by his id and superego! Legitimate and fascinating as they might be, however, one must consider what such readings might sacrifice.

Not all treasures can be buried in the same place. One reading must be chosen, or at least preferred, over others, while bearing in mind that every interpretation has a price. It is not because Freud located in the tragedy of Oedipus a powerful parable of the unconscious progression of sexuality that psychoanalysis has necessarily situated Sophocles's tragedy in its "true" light, nor, *a fortiori*, that a psychoanalytical interpretation provides the master key that opens the great mythological narratives to a deeper understanding. I am the first to subscribe to the idea that correspondences can be established, that psychoanalysis can make reasonably explicit a content latent in the most remote mythologies or, in other words, that mythology has already elucidated in its own manner that which we have

19. Louis Bardollet, "Justifications et opinions" in his French translation, Homer, *L'Illiade et L'Odyssée* (Paris, Laffont, "Bouquins," 1995), p. 710. Bardollet acknowledges his indebtedness to Felix Buffière, *Les Mythes d'Homère* (Paris: Les Belles Lettres, 1973).
20. Ibid., pp. 709, 711 (Buffière quoted by Bardollet).

rediscovered and redeployed centuries later in another language. But in large measure the certainty that such correspondences exist has encouraged me to write this book. Myth and psychoanalysis mutually illuminate each other, but the two never entirely overlap. There exist cases where the correspondence seems weak indeed. To my own surprise, the *Odyssey* proves to be just such a case.

Reading the *Odyssey* as an odyssey of the psyche or of the spirit is certainly possible, but such a reading can only detract from the liveliness of the tale and diminish the effect of otherness that it produces today when heard in the first degree, as an allegory of life in its most down-to-earth humanity, in the worst and in the best sense of the term. There is nothing to be sought outside us, not above, nor beyond, nor in posterity, as the shade of Achilles comes to realize—too late. Everything is played out in the here and now of life. And it is because Ulysses instinctively understands this and, despite certain moments of distraction, acts to the greatest possible extent accordingly, that he is a life-adventurer rather than a hero-in-death. There can be no doubt that fate, death, necessity, and vulnerability combine to weave a backdrop of human tragedy, but the hero himself is not a tragic figure, not only because he ultimately recovers his kingdom, but above all because he accepts his fate and sucks the bone of life to the marrow. Such is not the case, nor to the same extent, with the other Homeric heroes, but it is certainly true, with an exceptional felicity and a rare combination of prudence and insolence, of Ulysses, the man of many wiles. It is a posture, which makes of him and his story a character and a poetic song, far removed from the biblical story and the figures that populate it.

Ulysses is not the character we think he is. Beyond the shadow of a doubt, the Greeks recognized themselves in him. From the standpoint of Hellenic identity, his travels can be viewed as an exploration of the limits of the known, civilized world, and as a lengthy return to that same world. Ulysses learns nothing else. Worse, his only moment of gratuitous curiosity, in the Cyclops's den (Ulysses and his companions have all the livestock they need; no need to steal Polyphemus' sheep), ends in a disaster that sets him off on his wanderings. And when, at the end of his exile in Calypso's chambers, he comes ashore in the land of the Phaecians, Ulysses has already arrived home: not only do these people make him welcome, listen to his tales, heap gifts upon him, and return him to his homeland, but they carouse, sacrifice, and sport exactly like the Acheans. One must tell stories to one's fellows. Among them he begins to rediscover himself, all the more at ease in the knowledge that, contrary to what lies in wait for him in Ithaca, he need not wage a struggle to be recognized. It is enough for him to speak.

To the extent that Western culture claims ancient Greece for itself, and considers it as part of its heritage, we can spontaneously identify with the heroes, real or fictitious, that Greece has produced, among whom Ulysses probably remains the most celebrated and the best loved. But his contemporary appropriation is, as we have seen, fraught with mis-understandings, largely because we do not know his world. Like Greece itself, the Ulysses of our imagination is imprinted with false familiarity. If we were to see him in all the rawness with which Homer depicts him, we could no longer identify with him. Or more precisely, we would see that the identification could only be partial, for the simple reason that the roots of our own imagined world are only partially Greek. In truth, the essence of the intellectual and aesthetic heritage we claim from the Greeks conflicts radically with a morality and a world vision fundamentally derived from the Christian interpretation of the Bible. We will see further on that Christendom represents, in many ways, the impossible synthesis of Hellenism and Judaism. This impossibility, and to an even greater degree the refusal of it, the idea, in other words, that the two underpinnings of our tradition combine in harmonious union, deprive us of the best of the Odyssean poetic universe, that part which recreates it, under death's aegis, as one of the greatest odes ever written to the fragile and powerful beauty of life.

2

THE SHIELD OF AENEAS

A GULF SEPARATES the *Odyssey* from what might, eight centuries later, superficially appear to be its Roman copy, the *Aeneid*.

This gulf owes its existence to more than the simple passage of time. From Homer to Virgil, the material conditions of Mediterranean life had not fundamentally changed. Distances were covered in approximately the same time and under similar conditions. Great builders that they were, the Romans enhanced the comfort of city life and improved road networks; but the means of navigation remained virtually unaltered. In political terms, on the other hand, Rome unified the Mediterranean world around itself. The *Aeneid* is no stranger to this "universalist" purview. Unlike Ulysses, Aeneas carries with him a political project. The ultimate goal of his trajectory is not the celebration of daily life but the foundation of a state. For Virgil, much more is at stake than the composition of a hymn to the fragile beauty of existence; his task is to provide an entire empire with the mythical roots that will ensure its longevity.

Finally arrived at the end of Ulysses-like wanderings in the land destined to be his, not far from the future Rome, Aeneas, a surviving hero of the Trojan wars, encounters among the Latins a fierce resistance that forces him to wage war. As did Thetis for Achilles, Venus asks Vulcan to forge for her son Aeneas a set of invincible arms. On receiving them, the hero contemplates long and lovingly the massive shield, which Virgil says cannot be described. And the description begins:

> The wars in order, and the race divine
> Of warriors issuing from the Julian line.
> The cave of Mars was dressed with mossy greens:

There, by the wolf, were laid the martial twins.
Intrepid on her swelling dugs they hung:
The foster dam lolled out her fawning tongue
They sucked, secure, while, bending back her head,
She licked their tender limbs, and formed them as they fed.
Now far from thence new Rome appears; with games
Projected for the rape of Sabine dames.
The pit resounds with shrieks; a war succeeds,
For breach of public faith and unexampled deeds.
Here, for revenge the Sabine troops contend;
The Romans there, with arms the prey defend:
Wearied with tedious war at length they cease;
And both the kings and kingdoms plight the peace.
The friendly chiefs before Jove's altar stand,
Both armed, with each a charger in his hand:
A fatted sow for sacrifice is led,
With imprecations on the perjured head.
Near this, the traitor Metius, stretched between
Four fiery steeds, is dragged along the green,
By Tullus' doom: the brambles drink his blood;
And his torn limbs are left, the vulture's food.

. . . .

High on a rock, heroic Manlius stood
To guard the temple, and the temple's god.
Then Rome was poor; and there you might behold
The palace thatched with straw, now roofed with gold.
The silver goose before the shining gate
There flew, and by her cackle saved the state.
They told the Gaul's approach: the approaching Gauls,
Obscure in the night, ascend and seize the walls.
The gold dissembled well their yellow hair;
And golden chains on their white necks they wear.

. . . .

Betwixt the quarters flows a golden sea;
But foaming surges there in silver play.
The dancing dolphins with their tails divide
The glittering waves, and cut the precious tide.
Amid the main, two mighty fleets engage:
Their brazen beaks opposed with equal rage.
Actium surveys the well disputed prize:
Leucate's watery plain with foamy billows fries.
Young Caesar, on the stern in armor bright,
Here leads the Romans and their gods to fight:

His beamy temples shoot their flames afar:
And o'er his head is hung the Julian star.
Agrippa seconds him, with prosperous gales,
And with precious gods, his foes assails.
A naval crown, that binds his manly brows,
The happy fortune of the fight foreshows.
Ranged on the line opposed, Antonius brings
Barbarian aids, and troops of eastern kings.
The Arabians near, the Bactrians from afar.
Of tongues discordant, and a mingled war;
And, rich in gaudy robes, amidst the strife,
His ill fate follows him the Egyptian wife.
Moving they fight: with oars and forky prows
The froth is gathered and the water glows.
It seems as if the Cyclades again
Were rooted up, and jostled in the main;
Or floating mountains floating mountains meet;
Such is the fierce encounter with the fleet.
Fireballs are thrown, and pointed javelins fly;
The fields of Neptune take a purple dye.

. . . .

This seen, Apollo, from his Actian height
Pours down his arrows; at whose winged flight
The trembling Indians and Egyptians yield,
And soft Sabeans quit the watery field.
The fatal mistree hoists her silken sails,
And shrinking from the fight, invokes the gales.
Aghast she looks, and heaves her breast for breath,
Panting and pale with fear of future death.
The god hath figured her, as driven along
By winds and waves, and scudding through the thrond.
Just opposite, sad Nilus opens wide
His arms and ample bosom to the tide,
And spreads his mantle o'er the winding coast;
In which he wraps his queen and hides the flying host.
The victor to the gods his thanks expressed;
And Rome triumphant with his presence blessed.
Three hundred temples in the town he placed;
With spoils and altars every temple graced.
Three shining nights, and three succeeding days,
The fields resound with shouts, the streets with praise,
The domes with songs, the theaters with plays.
All altars flame: before each altar lies,

Drenched in his gore, the destined sacrifice.
Great Caesar sits sublime upon his throne,
Before Apollo's porch of Parian stone;
Accepts the presents vowed for victory;
And hangs the monumental crowns on high.
Vast crowds of vanquished nations marched along,
Various in arms, in habit, and in tongue.
Here Mulciber assigns the proper place
For Carians, and the ungirt Numidian race;
Then ranks the Thracians in the second row,
With Scythians expert in the dart and bow.
And here the tamed Euphrates humbly glides;
And there the Rhine submits her swelling tides;
And proud Araxes, who no bridge could bind.
The Danes unconquered offspring march behind;
And Morini, the last of human kind.
These figures, on the shield divinely wrought,
By Vulcan labored, and by Venus brought,
With joy and wonder fill the hero's thought.
Unknown the names, he yet admires the grace;
And bears aloft the fame and fortune of his race.
(*Aeneid*, VIII, 830–975)[21]

Aeneas takes upon his shoulders a destiny he esteems, and which he knows nothing about. No foreknowledge of the greatness of Rome is necessary to make ready for its advent. The hero strives not for himself; he is the instrument of a glory which has been revealed to him, a glory beyond his capacity to grasp, which he will never witness but in which he is already a participant—in which the poet, armed with his knowledge of the prescience of the gods, has caused him to participate. The entire meaning of the *Aeneid* can be found engraved on Aeneas's shield: the symbol of Virgil's own *magnum opus*, which is the writing of his epic. Together, the godly blacksmith, the hero, and the poet will accomplish great things, as they join together the greatness of Rome's origins with its present greatness in the reign of triumphant Augustus.

It should come as no surprise to us that the present needs the past. In this regard, Rome wanted for little: she had a legend, a history of splendor properly reflected in Vulcan's shield. One wonders why Virgil could not make do with the founding legend that seemed to have sufficed until then;

---

21. Virgil. *The Aeneid of Virgil*, trans. John Dryden, ed. Robert Fitzgerald (New York: Macmillan, 1965), pp. 270–274.

why did he feel impelled to enrich it with another ancestry? Though he is not himself the inventor of the Trojan genealogy, he marshals all of his art to invest it with an entirely new substance and significance. In doing so, he demonstrates fidelity to a well-established tradition: to the best of our knowledge, Rome was the first city of Mediterranean antiquity to assign itself a birth date, a year zero (753 B.C. according to Christian reckoning), with which its calendar begins. *Ab Urbe condita* ("from the founding of the city"), thus are the years counted in Rome.

Why then, so suddenly, are Romulus, Remus, and the she-wolf no longer equal to the task? Might it be because the founding act entails, after all, an act of fratricide? After the long years of civil war that preceded the *Pax Augusta*, the Romulean myth symbolized, inopportunely, the fratricidal origins of state power and, along with it, the internal struggles that so many Romans wished the new principality to bring to an end. The hypothesis is simple enough. For all that, Virgil, and the power he depicts, considered it essential to underscore the new departure. Though Augustus has restored the prerogatives of the Senate, all know too well that the Republic is no more. Shortly before his death, Cicero, that ardent and unhappy protector of the republican order, composed his *Duties*, a treatise on ethics and politics dedicated to the future prince. At the same time, Rome's expansion under the republic now demanded a new hierarchy, a new vision of the world.

When he hammered out the shield of Achilles in the *Iliad*, Hephaistos/Vulcan embossed upon it the entire world in its teeming diversity—peace, war, the city, the tilling of the fields—with no other intention than to engrave upon it the beauty of all things; to cast the world as a decorative relief upon the most magnificent, the most unimaginable of shields. The master craftsman's matchless skills gave form to the exploits of the warrior who would bear the shield in battle. Not content simply to borrow the idea, Virgil directly based his scene on the Homeric original. Vulcan's prodigies are no less than those of Hephaistos; Aeneas's worth is no less than that of Achilles. The parallel is painstakingly laid down. It is because of the fame of Achilles' shield, one of the most noteworthy of the *Iliad*, that Virgil equips his hero with the same prestigious arms. The parallels end there, however. Though each of the two shields bodies forth the world, those worlds are quite distinct. The Homeric world has neither a definable time nor place; it is the ebb and flow of life itself. That of Virgil is a specific empire erected to the dignity of *the* world, a historical world to which the Homeric appropriation provides an additional prestige that lifts it up to the plane of the universal.

Homer is explicitly, from the outset, omnipresent in the masterwork of the most admired of all the Latin poets—in its ambition and its overall structure. By relating the wanderings of Aeneas and his Latin war, Virgil quite clearly brings together in a single epic the *Odyssey* and the *Iliad*—while inverting their order. Once he had taken for his hero a character from the Trojan wars, the Homeric reference became inevitable. Still, there was no obligation for the poet to cast his hero in the mould of the *Odyssey*, nor to provide him with a replica of the arms of Achilles. If Aeneas lands on the shore of the Cyclops, and there encounters a companion "forgotten" in Polyphemus's cave by Ulysses three months earlier, it surely derives from a calculated attempt to create dramatic impact, and not from necessity dictated by the hero's Trojan origins. Moreover, Virgil's additions alter the Homeric story in such a way as to demonstrate the magnanimity of Aeneas toward the enemy who had earlier burned down his city: the Trojans welcome and comfort the unhappy survivor, devised for the circumstances. Borrowings abound, as do winks in Homer's direction. Seen as a whole, the Virgilian enterprise, to use the jargon of the American cinema, looks curiously like a remake.

For all its anachronistic coloration, the expression could hardly be more appropriate: often the remake, while remaining ostensibly faithful to the original screenplay, radically alters its spirit. Such is the case with the *Aeneid*. The difference between the shields of Achilles and Aeneas is the condensed expression of that divergence, a divergence visible today in the echo that each of the works (taking the Homeric epic as a whole) touches off in modern readers. Despite the obstacles of translation, Homer brings us a pleasure that we seek in vain in Virgil, a deficit which has nothing to do with the art of poetry: there are, in the *Aeneid*—which moreover is written in Latin—moments of great beauty that summon up on occasion emotions more poignant than anything found in Homer. I am thinking of Aeneas's paternal sadness at the youth of the foe he has just cut down (X, 825–830), of the upsurge of revolt that rises up in him in the face of war: "You beg a truce which I would gladly give," he tells the enemy ambassadors, "not only for the slain, but for those who live" (XI, 165–166). More ruthless than Achilles, the Virgilian hero is capable of surrender to feelings unknown to the son of Peleus (who stops to think on one occasion only, and under the compunction of Zeus, when Priam comes to ask him for the body of his son). This ambiguity, in the case of Aeneas, well illustrates the double mission the poet has given him: to become the friend and the ally of those whom he must fight. Between war and peace, Virgil leaves not the shadow of a doubt as to his preference: just as the Achillean side of his hero rings with a falseness that borders on the grotesque, so his humanity touches us. It is in his compassion that the poet stands forth in greatest veracity.

For all its undeniable beauties, the *Aeneid* lacks the force of conviction of its Homeric model. For all its reputation, it is rarely read today. Its content is ill-known, with the possible exception of the unfortunate love of Aeneas and Dido, who owe their relative weight in celebrity to the opera by Henry Purcell (*Dido and Aeneas*, 1689). Aside from Aeneas himself and his star-crossed inamorata, the heroes of the *Aeneid* have left no trace in the collective memory. Helen, Menelaeus, Agamemnon, Priam, Hector, Patroclus, Andromache, Ajax, Nestor, Penelope, Telemachus, Mentor ... all supremely evocative names that the Homeric epic has bequeathed to posterity, even though it is not always clear exactly who they are, nor what deeds they have done. On the other hand, except for specialists, the names of Turnus and Ascagnus today evoke nothing. Yet they represent for Aeneas what Hector does to Achilles, and what Telemachus does to Ulysses. Since these characters are so little rooted in our imagination, we can calmly dispatch them to oblivion and close the book on their adventures, which add nothing to that which we already know, and which enchant us more.

Let us be quite frank. The *Aeneid* is not a story of adventure. Of course it contains, first and foremost, scenes of flight, peril, storms, loves, and combat; but most of these events have about them the smell of artificiality. Even the taste of adventure, so spicily assertive in the *Odyssey*, is missing. For the principal character himself does not have the soul of an adventurer. Aeneas bores us, and he is himself bored by his own exploits—surely the reason why only his occasional bout of sadness moves us. His great quality is not the inventiveness of Ulysses, nor the combative drive of Achilles. Piety is his principal attribute, even though it occasionally falters. This same piety is at the service of a cause, as Vulcan's shield suggests. If, despite the gradual eclipse of its content, the *Aeneid* still speaks to us today, it is because it conveys something other than adventure, which is nothing more than scaffolding reducible to its simplest expression: it is enough to know that Aeneas flees devastated Troy and, after a succession of unexpected developments, steps ashore in Latium, where his descendants will compose one of the two main branches of the Roman nation. These events serve to confirm what can be clearly identified early on as a mission, and the idea of historical mission has become, for us, a rather banal affair. That Aeneas founds a nation strikes us as no earthshaking accomplishment. Yet it is precisely at this nodal point, in all its banality, that resides all the originality of the work for its time.

The *Aeneid* is remarkable in that it probably constitutes, in Mediterranean antiquity, the first history of origins to present itself as the founding story of a new political legitimacy. It is, at the same time, the first source in which the modern West may *unambiguously* locate an image of itself. We now find Narcissus hard at work. The convex mirror that is Vulcan's shield reflects the greatness of Italy, the Senate, and the people (the famous SPQR—Senatus Populusque Romanus, the military standards), of which the *barbarian profusion* and the *motley arms* of the adversary only serve to underscore the order and unity. This selfsame order will be summoned to meld the diverse and motley mix of Mediterranean peoples like the bronze in Vulcan's crucible. The Western reader spontaneously rallies to the side of Rome. For Rome is incontestably one and the same in the face of the disparate forces of the *Other*. When we consider the distinction drawn by the Greeks between themselves and the Barbarians (originally those who could not speak the same language; their degree of civilization was not mentioned) and between the Jews and the Gentiles (those who did not belong to the Covenant, who did not follow the Law), we can grasp the added connotations of this opposition.

Despite the immense importance we almost unconsciously attach to our Greek and Judaic heritage, they lack a fundamental quality that Rome alone can provide: universality. The Greek, as Aristotle himself reminds us, is universal, through science, in mind alone. Furthermore, it is only by virtue of a quality he believes to be eminently "Greek"—the mastery of the *logos* of rational discourse—that the Greek accedes to the human, of which he probably perceives himself as the most advanced example. But this universality has no concrete political expression—aside from the ephemeral empire of Alexander, whom his compatriots accused of promoting racial mixing and dissolving the Greek spirit in the vastness of Asia. But the Jew, despite having placed his experience at the disposition of all peoples, remains the quintessence of the particular: the Torah contains but the germ of the universal propounded through Abraham, father of the peoples. But the notion of paternity is diluted in the exodus and in territorial conquest, which, in real terms, long remained a more vital consideration than the conquest of the self—even though the Torah illustrates the derisory nature of politico-military enterprises. There exists then, among the Greeks, a pretension to a universality of the mind, and among the Jews, the possibility of a universality of Divine Law. But it is only with the Roman Empire that universality takes the shape of a political ambition. It is Virgil who casts himself as its conscious ideologue, which in turn implies a distinct conception of history.

In its seamless joining of legend to history, the *Aeneid* appears in pre-Western and Western thought as the *proto-type*, in the original sense of the term, of the ideological myth. Aided by the arrow of time, the story is indeed at the service of a single, guiding idea: an idea of Rome, an idea of the world, an idea of history. These are the elements that Aeneas first assembles, and then stitches together with the same thread. Only in this perspective do his wanderings and his trials take on importance. Aeneas leaves Troy in flames, builds a fleet, and sets sail without knowing his destination, though possessed by the sense of having to found a new Ilion somewhere else, in some faraway *Hesperia* of unknown location: to the West. That is all he seems to know. Each of his ports of call, no matter how welcoming, whether populated by the survivors of Troy or not, can only offer him a provisional shelter which must not sway him from his goal. For a brief instant, the Oracle at Delphi seems to have designated Crete as that goal, the great island from which Teucrus, one of the ancestors of the Trojans, had emigrated to found a city on the Phrygian coast. But the Oracle remains obscure, and is badly interpreted. The gods make his Cretan sojourn intolerable, and the Phrygian Penates that Aeneas has brought with him from Troy reveal to him in a dream that the Hesperia promised him now bears the name of Italy: "A land there is, Hesperia called of old, / (The soil is fruitful, and the natives bold— / The Oenotrians held it once), by later fame / Now called Italia, from the leader's name / Iäsius there, and Dardanus, were born" (III, 221–225). The revelation of these origins constitutes the turning point and the *leitmotiv* of the story, the pivot and the spur of Aeneas's progress. The hero now knows where he is going. Stay though he may at Dido's side, his mission is now explicit; nothing more than a reminder from Mercury is needed to wrench him from the embrace of his ill-loved.

Virgil is not the first to identify Dardanus as the founder of the Trojan race, but his masterstroke consists of giving him Italian (instead of Peloponnesian, as in Greek mythology) origins. How can anyone doubt that Aeneas is returning to his roots, and thus to the wellspring of Roman identity? The legend of Troy and the voyages of Aeneas work in synergy to make Roman stock the product of an immense Mediterranean blending process, which locates its center of gravity—Rome—at its very point of departure. By allying with the peoples of Italy (with the Etruscans shortly after his arrival, and with the Latins following his victory over them), Aeneas brings together the diverse ethnic and territorial components which, at the heart of the Mediterranean space—that is to say at the center of the world from the Roman point of view—will be called upon to form the core of the future empire. Aeneas, by virtue of his dual origin, symbolizes both the center and the periphery; in this capacity he incarnates the universal figure that Romulus, being far too "local," could never become.

Aeneas is not, as has been occasionally suggested, a new Ulysses. Ulysses is concerned only about himself and his homeland, and is driven by a zest for living that almost completely expunges the presence of the narrator. Pious Aeneas, on the other hand, constantly concerned with carrying his bard's design through to completion, is busy setting up signposts for posterity. All that befalls him derives from the mission the poet has conferred upon him. If he has lost his wife in the smouldering ruins of Troy, it is because he must be able later to wed Lavinia, only child of the king of the Latins. If he carves out a foothold on Cretan soil in the belief that he has reached his journey's end, it is because a portion of the Trojan lineage comes from the prestigious realm of Knossos. If he comes ashore at Actium and organizes a tournament there, it is by way of celebrating before the fact the battle that will establish the supremacy of Augustus, and of anticipating the quinquennial games that the emperor will cause to be held there in commemoration of his victory. If he bruises the love and pride of the queen of Carthage, it is by way of investing the future Punic wars with significance: just as Aeneas must sacrifice Dido to his mission, so Rome, by destroying Carthage, will sacrifice it to its hegemonic ambitions. If the capable Aenean ship's pilot perishes in a stupid accident before landfall in Italy, it is because the Trojan fleet has at last reached its destination: Aeneas no longer needs a helmsman. Now he stands alone at the helm.

Like Ulysses, Aeneas must carry out the obligatory visit to the Underworld. But even there, resemblances are superficial. Ulysses travels to the domains of Hades to learn from the shades of those whom he has known on earth that which he already suspects: that nowhere else will he find the salt of life. The virtuous Aeneas descends to receive the consecration of his mission and to hear the last councils of his father Anchisus. It is then that he witnesses the eternal expiations suffered by the impious. Tinged with Platonism, the Virgilian Underworld is selective; it is a place of retribution and purification. Certain souls await judgement; others, for better or worse, have achieved their definitive resting place; still others are preparing for a new life. Anchisus points out to his son those who, among the latter group, will create the history of Rome. As the story progresses, the hero will see the meaning of his life take shape in the future of his race, as illustrated by the historical panorama of Vulcan's shield. To this future, which is not even his own, Aeneas will go on to sacrifice his wife, his loves, his peace and quiet, his life. A tragic shadow hovers above the *Aeneid*, and lends it its depth. But the tragedy derives not only from the succession of sacrifices. Taken by themselves, they do little more than illustrate a heroic altruism, which would become boring with repetition. Boredom would be inevitable, in fact, if in the final four books of the epic, the disgust with war did not come bubbling to the surface.

It is easy to understand the political utility of Virgil's disgust. The pious Aeneas can derive no pleasure from massacring those with whom he has been called upon to unite under the roof of a single nation. Still, reduced to this kind of ideological instrumentalization, Aeneas's pangs of conscience would lack any semblance of authenticity. And we would still be mired in justification. But Aeneas is by no means rehabilitated by the final expression of noble repentance. Quite the opposite. Virgil, at the end of the final book, lends the warlike folly of his hero a darker tone, and prefigures a deeper doubt as to the meaning of the epic as it draws to a close: that the poison of war might well never stop spreading, that the reconciliation of adversaries, like the peace of Augustus, might not be anything more than the provisional, fragile suspension of an interminable civil war. The *Aeneid* breaks off sharply (more than simply coming to an end) on a single, terrible event. Aeneas, at the conclusion of a man-to-man combat which will decide the outcome of the war, has just thrown to earth his rival Turnus, chief of the Latin coalition and pretender to the hand of the princess Lavinia. Turnus grants Aeneas victory, Lavinia, and the realm, then begs for clemency: "Lay down your hatred," magnificently declaims the downed man. Overcome by emotion, the victor stays his hand. He listens, and is preparing to consider when, *by ill fortune* (specifies the text) he recognizes upon his opponent the harness of a young companion slain by Turnus in an earlier battle. The recollection of that cruel pain suddenly awakens his fury. Aeneas listens no longer, and covers his adversary with the invective of revenge: how dare he have stripped the corpse of one of his warriors to adorn himself!

> Thus as he spoke, his sword he drave
>   With fierce and fiery blow
> Through his broad chest before him spread
> The stalwart limbs grow cold and dead.
> One groan the indignant spirit gave
> Then sought the shades below.

(XII, 950–952)

Thus ends the *Aeneid*: in the shadows that shroud life as it flees, indignant, before the scorn of men. The hero with whom Virgil leaves his reader is neither magnanimous nor triumphant. There is no apotheosis, no reconciliation, only the spectacle of a warrior blinded by revenge, drowning his rage in blood. Rage at the memory of a friend killed by the blows of the enemy, certainly; but over and above that, the rage of war itself, and this too: the grave disappointment and the furious apprehension of having sacrificed life—his own and others'—in vain. Vulcan's shield has brought with it nothing but false promises. Or perhaps it calls for a second look: how can we fail to see, now, at the center of the tableau, Mars brandishing his fury, and, side by side with the triumph of Augustus, Discord shaking his bloody whip?

Doubts about Virgil's true intentions remain. He died before he was able to complete his work, and on his deathbed he begged for it to be destroyed. Still, we cannot deduct from these circumstances that it would have *ended in any other way*. Everything indicates that the epic was intended to have twelve books and that the twelfth, far from being shorter, is longest of all (its 952 verses exceed the average, which lies at around 800). The poet's will to destruction, insofar as we can determine his motives, can be interpreted in a variety of ways, which we will examine shortly. Still, Augustus showed no fear of violating Virgil's last wishes when he vetoed the poem's destruction.

He had good reason. Virgil had attempted to bestow upon Rome a story that, in the interweaving of history and legend, would provide imperial ideology with a mythical justification for imperial expansion. In this sense, the *Aeneid* prefigures the birth of political ideology. For the Latin poet, the function of the story of origins is not to represent the world, nor to put a face on the elements that make it up, nor to locate man within it. Neither does it seek, as does Egyptian mythology, to link the state hierarchy to the cosmic order, nor to provide power with a new transcendent legitimacy. The Roman state needs no such thing: it has its temples, its gods, its Penates; even more conclusively, its legitimacy stems from its republican tradition and institutions—precisely those aspects of its legacy that have been shaken by the civil war. If the Republic has begun to show cracks, it is only because its constitution no longer responds to the new situation created by wars of expansion that have devolved upon the legions and upon the men who lead them a power that the Senate and the Consuls are no longer able to control. This is what Caesar, the adoptive father of Octavian (the future Augustus), had understood and exploited far better than anyone else.

Caesar does not wage war in Gaul to defend the Gauls from the Helvetian threat, nor to protect them from the Germanians, as he rather too abundantly asserts. Nor is his enterprise necessary to the peace and security of Rome. All the while contributing to the aggrandizement of the Imperium Romanum, his conquests serve first and foremost to increase the prestige and the influence of the man who has accomplished them. It is not for nothing that Caesar takes the trouble to write them down. The account itself is as effective as the campaigns it relates: sober, direct, and accurate. Caesar never boasts; instead, he brings attention to the unstinting efforts of his subordinates, the boundless devotion of his troops, up to and including the valor of his adversaries. By giving the impression of sticking strictly to the facts, the author nearly succeeds in causing the commanding general to be forgotten, while certifying that every soldier must at times risk his neck by joining the fight at the height of battle. His account also gives passing credit to the wise man, the arbiter, the geographer, the engineer, and, above all, to the politician. In both his writing and what it yields, the dominant characteristics are conciseness, moderation, and certainty. Caesar's vision is clear and farsighted. He makes his decisions calmly, and acts without delay. "The style is the man." There are few examples where the adage so totally applies.

Caesar's is the first of a new genre, the genre of "war memoirs," and as a "premiere" it has probably remained unequalled down to the present day. True enough, Xenophon had already, in his *Anabasis*, related the retreat of the Ten Thousand, an exploit as human as it was military: but the event itself is of little historical consequence, and the style of the narrative compels scant admiration. Thucydides' *Peloponnesian War* is of an altogether other caliber, and even today stands out as a model of historical rigor. But Thucydides' importance has only been recognized relatively recently, and we experience some difficulty in understanding why his work did not receive in its own day, and more generally in Greco-Roman antiquity, the appreciation we feel it deserves. Neither Aristotle nor Plato speaks of it. Later, Cicero will find Thucydides complicated and confusing. This same Cicero, however, expresses the deepest admiration for *De Bello Gallico*. His mistrust of the political figure does not stop him from recognizing the greatness of the author. Still, Thucydides and Caesar have something in common: both contribute to the removal of the sacred, to the demystification of history. Though both concede that events contain an element of chance—Caesar himself repeatedly insists on the unpredictable role of Fortune—their purpose is to give an account of human affairs, and to make them intelligible from a strictly human perspective.

Our brief incursion into historical narrative makes it easier to grasp the scope of the work that Virgil composed the better to call attention to the sweeping political changes unfolding around them, and of which the Romans had become aware. A work the issue of which he withheld, which would not be published until after his death—and then done so against his wishes. The reasons remain obscure: poetic scruples, political disenchantment, and personal uncertainty. Whatever the cause, its posthumous publication surprised several of his contemporaries in the literary world: lengthy epics, they claimed, simply were not being written any more. But the archaism, in an author of Virgil's caliber, does not appear to have been involuntary. He could not have been unaware that poetic fashion favored brevity, that the epic as a genre was passé. He had read Caesar (and no doubt Thucydides as well); he knew Titus-Livius, whom no one ever accused of fearing to mix legend with history.

But Virgil does the exact *opposite*: he deliberately *situates* history within *myth*. For him, legend is not an ornament, and its presence even less the fruit of an error of appreciation as to what might retrospectively be seen as "historic" or "legendary"—a distinction which, in our modern naïveté, we often believe can be rigorously established. Not so in the *Aeneid*, where the legend contains the story and is pregnant with it—like the shield upon which it is engraved. The shield itself is the issue of a kind of birth, it owes its nativity to Vulcan's love for Venus—except that here, the roles are reversed: the task of the wife is to fecundate (by her order) and that of the husband, to undergo the labor. It is obviously difficult to know if the author is fully aware of the implications of his metaphors, but such knowledge is not indispensable to our reading. It is enough for it to be possible, for it to hold together, for it to make sense. Even if the sense it makes is surprising. For there is, in the *Aeneid*, something entirely unexpected: its "archaism" opens the door to a perspective that is thoroughly modern.

Is Virgil finally saying anything else but that history is a sub-category of mythology? That *all* history is preceded and impregnated by a mythology that colors it, neither divine nor cosmogonic, but fully human, a mythology created by men for men, the purpose of which is to shed light upon their acts? What is legend but allegory, the fictions that humans tell and retell one another in order to understand what it is that they are playing at, to make sense of the present, and to guide their collective action in accordance with their desires? "Behold, Romans," Virgil seems to be saying, "the uses to which the *Aeneid* may be put: let us strive for the reconciliation of peoples and the unification of the (Mediterranean) world." This very wish quivers, a bit naïvely perhaps, from one end of the *Aeneid* to the other—only to be brutally struck down by Aeneas's final deed, as though Virgil were reproaching himself for having created such a pious wish—and hero. The poet's wish to cast his masterwork into oblivion then takes on a radical significance, calling into question the very conception of history, at once modern and archaic, which the *Aeneid* embodies.

By wielding the forceps at the birth of the legend of history, by creating what we might call "historical myth," Virgil introduced into history a new dimension of time, perhaps not quite as new as one might think for a people accustomed to reckoning time *ab urbe condita*. But, for all that, the *Aeneid* invests the temporal dimension with supplementary power by assigning to history a project. The thread that connects myth to history has a specific meaning; it indicates a progression toward something to be accomplished. Rome, quite exactly like Aeneas, has a mission, time a direction, and humanity a unifying finality. What Virgil fears is that this finality is a chimera. Men will not succeed in uplifting themselves to the level of piety it demands; instead, they will continue to turn aimlessly in ceaseless repetition: wars lead only to other wars, and time has no meaning. There is no great history to be delivered into the world. Myths are useless. Aeneas's sacrifices have been for naught.

Like any work that has stood the test of time, Virgil's continues to make its way independent of its creator. Whatever may have been the poet's apprehensions, the *Aeneid* will have fixed feathers to the arrow of time. Otherwise its longevity is difficult to understand, considering that it has long ceased to be read: of the story of Aeneas's forgotten itinerary survives only the idea that gives it its direction—the master concept of historical finality. The work thus stands revealed as paradoxically "modern"—if not in its intentions, at least in its effect. Even if the bloody tribulations of the empire and the unending repetition of the maneuverings of power and warfare seem to confirm the non-meaning of history, the protagonists of this story—beginning with imperial power itself, the leaders of Christendom after them, and the great powers of the modern West to an even greater degree—continue to invoke historical finality to justify their enterprises. Caesar, despite his obsession with personal ascent, leads us to believe that his campaigns in Gaul were part and parcel of civilization's march of progress against barbarism. The adversary's customs, his institutions, his behavior, and his technique are judged against the achievements of Rome. It never occurs to him that there is any possible sphere in which the Other could possibly surpass Rome—except perhaps that of physical size.

Such feelings of superiority are by no means exclusive to the Romans, but in their case they are combined with the conviction of having a "worldwide" (Mediterranean) mission to accomplish, a conviction we do not encounter among either the Greeks or the Jews. The Greeks were far too concerned with their internal quarrels and the Jews far too obsessed with their survival even to consider assuming any political responsibility whatsoever toward the world. Conversely, the *Pax Romana* takes form as the instrument of the universal civilization, which must transform the entire Mediterranean, *mare nostrum*, into a single world, which can then be projected into the farthest hinterlands. The speed with which most of the "pacified" peoples were to accept Roman citizenship only lends greater plausibility to the idea. When Hegel writes that with Caesar, History itself crossed the Alps, he is expressing not only the *Weltanschauung* of his day, but also the assurance that the Romans, on their own scale, already possessed, and which we find in Caesar himself.

The central idea of the *Aeneid*, that of a world to be unified and pacified, which in the Mediterranean is incarnated by Roman law, would survive the wasting away of the empire in Christian, then Western consciousness. It manifests itself in the present day in the American universalist vision of the world. The connection that is often made between the two empires, Roman and American, far from being either senseless or superficial, has ideological roots the depth of which we tend not to suspect. Universalism has come a long way, and the *Aeneid* is no stranger to its longevity, if for no other reason than the genre it inaugurates, which can be called "historical myth."

Virgil's contribution to the idea of universalism cannot be easily measured. Irrespective of its importance, it bears within it a warning, or is accompanied by at least a reservation, both of which have been lost in transmission. At the end of Aeneas's journey, let us recall, the poet leaves a terrible doubt hanging over the meaning of his work. The taste of blood he leaves in our mouths tells us that there may be nothing else in this world than the mindless brutality of the equations of power, and the hate-filled blindness to which they lead. Humanity cannot emerge as consciousness except at the price of an intellectual and moral piety too lofty for man. One has the impression that Virgil had suddenly come to fear the obfuscatory power of his own myth, had become suspicious of the political uses that might be made of it. If the historical myth, instead of encouraging peoples to surpass themselves, merely stokes the fires of hegemonic ambition, then better depict war and conquest as they really are: brutal exercises in destruction and enforced servitude that no mythology can justify. The universality that believes it can, built upon the relationships of force that it actually helps to mask—be it the force of arms, of technology, or of the economy—is fated to fail; it will never be anything more than the ideological instrument of the dominant. The glory of Aeneas's shield shines with false brilliance. And time's arrow is a murderous one.

In the *Aeneid*, the love of the world is expressed through the hatred of war and of the *raison d'État* that justifies it. If, quite unlike Homer, Virgil abominates violence, it is because its fury is too destructive to belong to life. The empire is not worth all the spilt blood. In the *Aeneid* there occurs something like a last-minute hesitation over the validity of imperial glorification, reflected in Virgil's celebration of life: it knows it cannot equal its model. The appropriation of Homeric deeds in the service of a specific political ideology deprives the story of its gratuitousness and, at the same time, of considerable vitality. Invested with a predetermined meaning, the *Aeneid* is deprived of many other possible meanings. In it we sense the kind of messianism that will later come to characterize Christian-inspired literature. With Virgil, the story has already eluded the pure pleasure of the telling; it no longer responds to the simple imperative: to speak of the human condition.

As we will see, this condition finds its most intense expression in one of the first great stories we have been able to trace: *The Epic of Gilgamesh*.

3

GILGAMESH: THE HUMAN CONDITION

T HE *EPIC OF GILGAMESH* is the most ancient of all the great stories that we
have made a part of our heritage. To claim it as our own is a way of
extending "our" past back to the "dawn of civilization" and to give ourselves
access to that which is unchanging in the heart of man: friendship and death.
For in the heart of *man* lies neither cosmogony nor theogony, but simply *the*
poem of its human condition, made great by the magnitude of the characters
and of their exploits. Seven centuries before Homer, the adventures of
Achilles and Ulysses are given condensed expression in those of Gilgamesh.
No other story from Mediterranean antiquity recounts with such brutality
and, at the same time, with such finesse the inexorable finitude on which the
quest for immortality flounders.[22]

Of its three-thousand-odd verses written in Babylon some thirty-five
centuries ago, fewer than two thirds have been found. Up until the first
century of our era, it appears to have been transmitted via a diversity of
transcriptions and translations before falling into oblivion along with
Babylonian civilization itself. Only in the nineteenth century, in the course of
intense archeological exploration, did clay tablets—sometimes intact,
sometimes damaged—begin to be exhumed; some of them have been
discovered quite recently.

The patience with which scholars reassembled the shards of those
tablets, the persistence that finally allowed them to decipher the cuneiform
characters, put its constituent elements in order, and re-establish the
storyline: the whole achievement itself made for a learned epic comparable
in its sweep to the legend that it had rescued from oblivion. As exploits go,
it reminds one of nothing so much as the great feat it brings us to re-live: the

---

22. For the purposes of this book, Mesopotamia will be defined as a part of the Mediterranean world.

struggle against death. To the fraternal combat that joins Gilgamesh to his double (Enkidu) comes, by way of response, millennia later, the notion of a fraternity beyond time. It is as if fishers of signs had cast their lines back toward the past, and from it reeled in fragments of human immortality carved on pieces of clay. Who can doubt that it is largely a matter of good fortune that we are now in a position to follow Gilgamesh through his adventures and his ordeals? But it is difficult not to see, in the persistence with which chance is appealed to, a sign of the power that binds us to the past and to the desire— which we find in Gilgamesh himself—not to die. To rescue from oblivion our ancient brethren, obsessed with the same fate as we are, is to wish, however confusedly, to safeguard the continued existence of our own memory.

By assigning order to unearthed fragments, by establishing correspondences between the several extant versions, we can, though gaps subsist, form a clear picture of the story as a whole, and of the principal points around which it is articulated.[23] The name of Gilgamesh is well known; his story much less so. We must then begin by laying down an outline.

Gilgamesh, the King of Uruk, justly admired for his courage, his wisdom, and his magnificence, yet given to immoderation, abuses his power: "Lording it like a wild bull ... Gilgamesh would leave no son to his father ... no girl to her (mother)" (I, 66–74). As a chorus of complaints reaches their ears, the gods call upon the Mother Goddess Aruru to shape a model that resembles Gilgamesh in strength and in stature closely enough to neutralize the king and to restore calm to the land. Thus is born, in the solitude of the desert, Enkidu-the-Valiant. "Knowing neither fellow townsman nor country," he grazes and drinks among the wild beasts. A hunter draws the attention of Gilgamesh to the presence of the mysterious vagabond. Gilgamesh, in whose dreams the mysterious individual has appeared as a brother figure,[24] orders the hunter to meet him, along with Shamhat the Harlot, at the well where Enkidu comes to drink with his herd. The harlot's mission is to induce the savage to make love to her. If she can successfully cut him off from the herd, she could then entice him into following her to the city of Uruk. Seduced by

---

23. I am indebted to Jean Bottéro's introduction in his *L'Épopée de Gilgamesh, Le grand homme qui ne voulait pas mourir*, traduit de l'akkadien et présenté par Jean Bottéro. (Paris: Gallimard, 1992). From tablets drawn from a diversity of origins have emerged two principal versions, both written in Akkadian: the extremely fragmentary, so-called "ancient" version, and the "Ninevite" version, undoubtedly rewritten based on the older one, from which have been restituted some two thousand of the three thousand verses it would have consisted of. [Translator's note: For the English version, I have used *The Epic of Gilgamesh*, trans. & ed. Benjamin R. Foster. (New York: Norton, 2001).]

24. The term "brother" is none too strong, for it is Gilgamesh's mother who interprets for her son the dreams that evoke his presence.

his newfound female companion, Enkidu enters Uruk where, at the height of nuptial festivities, Gilgamesh is preparing to exercise his *droit de seigneur* upon the future spouse. Angered by the outrageous privilege, Enkidu bars the king's way. A monumental hand-to-hand combat ensues in the great square before the gathered populace. Gilgamesh is bested. The two adversaries embrace one another and conclude a pact of friendship, which the king calls upon his own mother to witness. The Goddess Aruru's plan has succeeded to perfection.

Having plunged perhaps too precipitously into civilization, Enkidu lapses into moodiness. To snap him out of his gloom, Gilgamesh leads him far away to conquer the Cedar Forest, which is protected by the invincible monster Humbaba the Ferocious. Despite the fears of his entourage and Enkidu's own hesitations, the two warriors march off to do battle with the monster in quest of eternal glory. At the end of a long voyage punctuated by dreams both terrifying and encouraging, they prevail over Humbaba, who begs them to spare him, in exchange for which he will place himself at their service and permit them to cut and carry off as many cedars as they wish. Gilgamesh wavers, but his pitiless companion insists that they kill their foe before Enlil, the chief of the gods, can rescue him. The two friends return in triumph to Uruk with a cargo of cedars (a sign of wealth) and the head of Humbaba.

A second offence against divine order is soon added to the first, the murder of Humbaba. Dazzling in his glory and beauty, Gilgamesh attracts the attention of the goddess Ishtar, the favorite of Anu, tutelary divinity of Uruk. But Gilgamesh spurns Ishtar's advances, citing her lengthy catalogue of ill-treated lovers. In her disgrace, the goddess persuades Anu to deliver to her the great bull which she will dispatch to devastate Uruk. Our two heroes kill the beast to the despair of Ishtar, who comes to lament on the ramparts of the city. Adding insult to injury, Gilgamesh rips off one of the bull's hooves and flings it in her face. Revenge is not far behind: the gods condemn Enkidu to a slow death before the eyes of his friend for refusing to spare Humbaba and for slaughtering the bull. In turn the two friends rue what has befallen them: Gilgamesh insults the giant portal he has caused to be built from the wood of the Cedar Forest; Enkidu heaps maledictions upon Shamhat the Harlot whom he holds responsible for his misfortunes—then withdraws them after one of the goddesses shames him for his ingratitude.

Enkidu's demise plunges Gilgamesh into anguish. Despairing at the loss of half of himself, he is even more distraught at having borne brutal witness to the death of his friend, whom he cradled in his arms until "the worms crawled from his nose." Gilgamesh cares no more for the glory that can bring him such pitiful immortality. Unable to accept the idea of his own death, he goes off on a quest for life without end. To the ends of the earth he wanders, climbs the most forbidding mountain ranges, crosses all the seas, making his way at great risk across the waters-of-death with the aid of UrShanabi, the ferryman, in search of Utanapishti-the-Far, a hero who, with the connivance of the god Enki, has managed to survive the Deluge[25] and acquired immortality. But immortality cannot be passed on, and there is no key to its capture. Utanapishti exhorts his exhausted visitor to accept his condition as a mortal, to return to daily life, to carry out his duties as king and to care for his subjects. Overcome with pity, Utanapishti's wife begs him to reward Gilgamesh for his vain labors by giving him the secret of eternal life, a plant of youth that he must seek out, by dint of superhuman effort, at the bottom of the sea.

It proves to be his last labor, which is as fruitless as all the others before it. On the return journey, a snake surprises Gilgamesh as he bathes in a pool of fresh water, and steals the plant of youth. The loss is irreparable. He had planned to administer it to an old man of the kingdom for effectiveness. Now he would never be able to use it. Gilgamesh no longer possesses the strength to return to the depths of the sea. In any event, he has lost all the signs pointing to the place where he must dive. The hero returns home empty-handed. But his city remains. He proudly shows its ramparts, foundations, and its broad sweep to the admiring gaze of UrShanabi, the ferryman who carried him across the waters-of-death and who has accompanied him ever since in his peregrinations. Thus ends the tale: on a description of Uruk in a few verses repeated from the poem's first tableau.[26]

This short summary hardly allows us to grasp the poem's symbolic richness. Beyond the obvious themes of friendship and death, it is a lesson in life, a complex and difficult lesson.

Enkidu is not only a friend; he is the hero's double. The same terms can be used to describe them: each is handsome, intelligent, and courageous;

---

25. Utanapishti relates in detail the Deluge, and how he, his household and his stable of animals survived in a huge vessel built on the advice of the god Enki, an episode that closely resembles the story of Noah in Genesis.

26. As Jean Bottéro notes in his introduction, the Ninevite version includes a second tableau written later, which gives another version of the death of Enkidu. In it, he descends into the Inferno to retrieve the lost talismans so precious to Gilgamesh. But as he takes lightly the prescribed regulations, Enkidu is condemned to remain there. He will only be authorized, following the supplications of Gilgamesh, to return briefly to his friend, in spirit, to describe to him what happens among the dead, a tale that terrifies Gilgamesh. As Bottéro notes, this addition breaks the cycle of the epic that concludes with the eleventh tablet. As a result, we will not consider it as a part of the story as told here.

each is as powerfully muscled "like a force of heaven" (I, 152). But there is one crucial difference: Gilgamesh is civilized; Enkidu is a savage. Yet there is a certain savagery in the civilized half, who uses his powers to give free rein to his sexual desires to the detriment of the city (and by extrapolation, of his soul). And from the savagery of Enkidu, mollified and weakened by carnal contact with a woman, surges forth the force that subdues the fierce urges of Gilgamesh. In making love with Shamhat the Harlot, Enkidu alienates the pack of wild animals that have till then been his constant companions. Once again, it is the courtesan who weans him away from suckling at the teat of gazelles, and from foraging for wild grasses on the steppe by teaching him to eat bread; it is she who rids him of his hairy coat by rubbing it with a miraculous unguent. In short, it is she who introduces him to civilization.

Love thus stands in opposition to the unending perturbations and pulsations of desire. To win out, it will have need of an equivalent force and savagery, but tinged this time with tenderness. The combat between Gilgamesh and his alter ego is the struggle of the divided soul, which, under female influence, is reconciled with itself. Mother and harlot alike contribute to the initiatory encounter, and its warlike nature reflects the combative dimension of the long, hard apprenticeship that consists, for man, of finding his place in the world. And the apprenticeship has just begun: the fraternal struggle is only the first, that in which the soul tempers itself as it confronts the dangers that lie in wait. Once opened, the fissure will never be entirely closed. When he is finally prepared to channel his energies toward something other than the maids and virgins of the land, Gilgamesh strikes out in quest of riches and glory. Enkidu, who now embodies the voice of his conscience, attempts in vain to dissuade him. Once caught up in action, however, the very same voice prods him, in disregard of divine reason, to go to the ends of the earth.

To kill the Other ultimately serves no purpose; it is an exploit as illusory as it is lethal. By refusing to tame the monster, and by returning instead with its head as a trophy, Gilgamesh-Enkidu sacrifice true wealth to the vanity of renown. The evil which the couple so ostentatiously brandish, and which they imagine having overcome, is within them, invisible. Their blindness (symbolized by an apparent victory in the face of divine will) touches off a series of trials and misfortunes that lead to the death of Enkidu, for all intents and purposes separating Gilgamesh from a part of himself. From that moment on the hero sees, beyond his solitude, only the curse of death. Even before he dies, Enkidu has lost the power to make himself understood: "My friend laid on me (the greatest) curse of all (VII, 183)," he says, with his dying breath. There is no doubt that his funeral will be sumptuous and heart-rending. But what rends most, and what will henceforth give the hero's deeds their motivation, is less the loss of his friend than the knowledge that he is irremediably alone, and powerless, in the face of death.

Gilgamesh will wander far and wide before he can come to grips with his powerlessness. Not only does he rush off to the ends of the earth, he terrorizes the ferryman into transporting him across the sea-of-death where lies the secret he is hunting for. The secret is one of terrifying simplicity: he must return home—and that home is within himself. The quest for the plant of youth offers an ironic illustration: Gilgamesh does not dive to the depths in an attempt to prolong his life—for a brief moment of pleasure and inattention is enough to tear it from his grasp—but for the confirmation that no illusion can deprive him of the only journey that remains for him, the only one that counts: the return to himself.

But this reading simplifies things far too much. It might cause us to think that "introspection" is the path to self-realization. But the story of Gilgamesh stands not simply as a metaphor for the voyage into the self; it speaks as well of the difficulties of the world, of the vagaries of life, and of the whims of heaven. Nor does it map out even the faintest pathway to accomplishment; it depicts an infinite and contradictory apprenticeship which "ends" where it begins with—*perhaps*—a tiny increment of wisdom gained (represented by the discreet companionship of the ferryman, far removed from the flamboyant Enkidu). It is in this absence of clarity that we can locate the resonance that the text touches off in us. Seen from this perspective, we would be tempted to call it "modern," perhaps even "postmodern." The *Epic of Gilgamesh* has no lesson to give, no other certainty to reveal than the brief instant of this earth-bound life symbolized by the city of Uruk and its ramparts, beyond which all is illusion. Man is alone; the gods can do nothing and want nothing for him. On occasion they intervene to bring him back to his senses, but also to provoke him, to cause him to stumble and fall. The only "moral" of the story, if indeed there were one, would be to remind us of our modest dimensions. What can we aspire to when the giants themselves—who are as immense in their physical dimensions as in their courage, wisdom, and beauty—have failed?

Here too, oversimplification lies in wait. The *Epic of Gilgamesh* does not preach resignation, nor can it be reduced to a staged representation of despair. From the beginning to the end of the adventure, beauty surges forth: the beauty of men and of women, the beauty of the world and of friendship.

Each of these beauties conceals a snare, not the least of which is the long, loving glance they call forth. Rare is the element or the incident that can be reduced to a single meaning. So it is with women: the two heroes meet, and their souls find unity through the agency of the courtesan; Enkidu is torn from Gilgamesh, and his soul finds solitude, through the agency of the goddess Ishtar, consort of the god of the Heavens and founding father of the ruling dynasty. Nor is friendship totally free from ambiguity. Though it has brought peace to the city, the new assurance it carries propels Gilgamesh onto the path of glory and excess, to such an extent that the death of the friend becomes, in a certain sense, "necessary."

No deed, no encounter immediately reveals its meaning. UrShanabi the ferryman, who transports Gilgamesh beyond death toward the inaccessible secret of immortality, is also the one who accompanies him homeward. But the hero must still rid himself of the fear of death that has driven him to such extremes. The serpent delivers him by taking from him the plant of youth. Because we have grown accustomed to see the snake as the embodiment of evil, we forget that it is also the symbol of wisdom. Here, it teaches us the value of renunciation. Having abandoned his vain quest for immortality, Gilgamesh must once more forgo the assurance that he can prolong a life he has hardly begun to live, the riches and the limits of which he grasps only at the end, on the ramparts of Uruk, as he displays his realm to his new companion.

Yet even in his newfound wisdom uncertainty lingers. The end of the story leaves everything hanging. It says nothing of what Gilgamesh will make of the life that remains to him. There can be little doubt that his contemplation of Uruk-the-Closed (or Uruk-the-Enclosed) is meant to suggest that it is there, in the strictly circumscribed space which Gilgamesh can encompass with his own gaze, that he must accomplish his destiny: to care for his country, to place his experience at the service of his kinsmen. Disabused of his overweening aspirations, his soul can finally turn friendship to good account (Enkidu has by now been to a certain extent replaced by UrShanabi), no longer with the perspective of great renown but of living more justly. The equilibrium of the soul at last becomes one with that of the city over which Gilgamesh rules. The burden is neither light nor insignificant, and the adventures that have preceded his return to everyday life turn out in the end to have been fruitful: they have tempered the king's soul. Now, one hopes, he will govern more wisely. His wild adventures and his excesses thus have a certain "utility." It is necessary to extend oneself to the maximum, to stretch the limits of one's capacity, to have left the mileposts of ambition far behind, to have known the extremes of passion and despair before facing that most difficult of all ordeals: everyday life in its simplicity and secret beauty. This beauty has existed from the beginning, laid out in the opening description of Uruk, and repeated word for word at the end. But the soul of the hero was blind.

Beyond its multiplicity of themes, the *Epic of Gilgamesh* is first and foremost a voyage of initiation. It would be no exaggeration to describe the hero's voyage as an apprenticeship in justice, in the Platonic sense: to be in harmony with one's self. "One's self" here refers not to the individual, nor modern-day introspection. As with Socrates, the meaning is generic: that of man, in the general, loftiest sense of the term. For Gilgamesh, after all, is not the average man. He is a king, and as such symbolizes the polity over which he rules. Its destiny is inextricably tied up with the fate of his soul. Separated from his realm, Gilgamesh generates no meaning; his destiny can only work itself out within its walls.

There is a danger that the modern reader might misinterpret the symbolic scope of the epic by seeing Gilgamesh as a precursor of Pascalian disquiet, of Kierkegaardian despair, perhaps even as the embodiment of the Freudian unconscious. It seems undeniable that in Gilgamesh, despair finds expression and that it touches us, representing as it does one of the fundamental components of the human condition. It seems irrefutable that the story illustrates in many ways the working of the unconscious, as the significance of the deed—which remains unclear—is given shape outside the awareness of the hero who accomplishes it. But neither the despair nor the unconscious is ours; they belong not to what we call the person (or the individual) but to humanity—perhaps to that prehistoric archaism Freud fearlessly refers to in what some consider as the "damned" part of his work.[27] They belong not to the humanity whose universality we—moderns that we are—believe we have founded, but to that human collectivity which the king can take in with a single glance: his fate cannot be dissociated from the humanity contained within Uruk-the-Closed, and justice has meaning only *within* the city. As long as he is vagabonding about in the farthest reaches of the world, alone or with his double, the only themes are desire, impossible dreams, and trials to be overcome—not justice.

The theme of justice is present from the beginning, in the iniquity of the *droit de seigneur* and the disorders it creates. Reparation of the injustice that threatens the city gives the entire story its impetus, even though the heroes

27. I am referring here to *Totem and Taboo* and *Moses and Monotheism*.

are quick to forget where their paths first crossed. It is only within sight of Uruk that justice, perhaps personified by the ferryman, rediscovers its rightful domain: the community. It is there, within it, that man—the king—can eventually find harmony with himself.

Life, and the life of man in the greater polity, has meaning, but this meaning is not apparent; it must be constructed, built with the same painstaking care as the buttresses and brick walls that ring the city. Their evocation at the conclusion of the epic repeats the verses of the first tablet, but this time it is not the narrator who speaks; *it is the hero himself, who draws his companion's attention to their beauty, to the solidity of their construction.* By placing them in the mouth of Gilgamesh, the narrator is telling us that the king has become aware of something precious, of which the reader has been aware from the beginning, but whose true significance he, like the hero, only discovers at the end of the journey. The city, its walls and its orchards—its very life—are worthless unless they are *recognized* by him upon whom it is now incumbent to carry into the future. Meaning thus lies in the collective task to be completed. Insofar as meaning has not been given from on high, insofar as it must be brought about and invented here and now, the *Epic of Gilgamesh* can be seen as "modern." Insofar as meaning cannot exist, cannot be invented except through the past, through the common heritage that welds men together like the bricks of the city walls, *Gilgamesh* can be seen as "archaic." If we become too attached to the fate of Gilgamesh the individual, we are committing the worst of misinterpretations. The modern myth of the self-made man would have us believe that each of us can make of himself what he wants. But the epic tells us that no meaning can arise from nothing; nothing solid can be built upon the void. To sweep away everything is unthinkable. To imagine such a thing as possible, to take such a pretension seriously, is to condemn oneself to a state of non-meaning.

If we work our way back to the origins of the human species, meaning eventually vanishes in the inaccessible past. "In the beginning, there was non-meaning," Genesis, with its opening darkness, seems to tell us. A god is needed to dissipate that darkness with his light. God or not, meaning is inscribed in what we call *Scripture.* Man has no meaning, nor does his past, until we have traced their markings: primitive paintings, *bas-reliefs*, clay tablets, sheepskin, or paper. *Gilgamesh* comes down to us from a space-time that we consider as belonging to one of the world's most ancient civilizations. The Sumerian-Akkadian civilization possesses its own theogony and cosmogony; an order superior to mankind orders the universe. This divine order intervenes in human affairs, rather in the manner of the heavenly bodies in astrology. But, as the *Epic of Gilgamesh* relates, for us, as human beings, the gods are not sources of meaning. At most, they may trigger the events that compel man to start out on a quest for meaning, perhaps even in spite of himself. A long succession of impulses and impasses not at all unrelated to divine intervention ultimately brings Gilgamesh, physically diminished but spiritually amplified by defeat, back to the one place where meaning is possible. And this place is a human one, entirely of this world. Once we have left our mark upon it, meaning *becomes* possible. It is enough that others have preceded us. In their imprint, civilization is born.

Here lies the radical nature of the Akkadian narrative: man is simultaneously powerless and responsible. Powerless in his cosmic solitude, subjected to the whims of the gods and the spheres; responsible for what he has inherited and for what he will bequeath to future generations, maker of his own meaning. The meaning of life is to be found in the chain that links men—of the same species—together in space and time down through the ages. If Gilgamesh has anything to "teach" us, it is that nothing can be expected from anywhere else, even were such an "anywhere" to exist. Nothing can be expected of the gods. Measured against such a narrative of courage and humility, the quest for the absolute, the hunt for transcendence have all the appearance of a regression, like the story of an aimless wanderer who cannot stop seeking the immortality of glory or of eternal life, like the repetition of an epic whose interminability the characters cannot grasp, whose meaning they cannot stop searching for beyond the human sphere.

Reading *Gilgamesh* underscores a significant aspect of the Homeric epics that our brief excursion into Virgil may have caused us to overlook. In his relationship with life and with death, the stance of the Greek hero is almost a tragic one. Gilgamesh, meanwhile, turns his back on heroism and returns home empty-handed to accomplish that which, from the beginning, the city has expected of him. If his heroic deeds were signposts along the path he had no choice but to follow, they have in the end assumed their rightful place: the lucid renunciation finally accepted by the Babylonian hero clearly identifies everyday existence as the locus where all life, including that of the prince, must be lived. Care for the land of his birth prevails over the call of adventure.

Not so for the Homeric hero. There can be no doubt that Ulysses has no wish more dear than to see his homeland once more. It is indeed probable that, unlike Gilgamesh the desire to return has never left him since the day he set sail for Troy. But having set out, under no circumstances will he return empty-handed.[28] For Ulysses, the return, far from being the renunciation that it has been for Gilgamesh, can only be imagined as a triumph, hence the importance of the treasure he is given by the Pheacians; hence the imperative of his triumph over the suitors.

Thus the heroic exploit invests life with meaning. But at the same time, as the shade of Achilles now so ruefully regrets, life is the sole good imparted to mortals, and it is an earthly one. Now that he resides in the kingdom of Hades, Achilles would almost be prepared to accept slavery in order to return to the light of life. The very life he did not fear to sacrifice for glory he would now accept on the humblest of conditions. The hero, after all, is precisely he who does not hesitate to put in play his most precious and only possession, worldly life itself, for danger is the price of life. Life is only worth living when it is put at risk, and he who is not ready to confront death, and to pay out its full price, does not warrant living; his life is one of indignity. Never, were he to return to the world, would Achilles agree to serve a poor ploughman, and though he declares himself prepared to do so in order to return to the light of day, it is because he knows all too well that, for him, the light is forever lost. The Homeric hero risks his life without ever resigning himself to the idea of loss. He puts it at risk to preserve it, and to preserve it in its full worth; he puts it at risk to give it, day after day, its ephemeral and irreplaceable beauty.

The Homeric hero and Gilgamesh concur on one fundamental point: to flee death is pointless. Flight from death deprives us of the pleasure of savoring the ripe fruits of life. The difference is one of values: for the Homeric hero, the taste of life cannot be dissociated from dignity itself; for Gilgamesh, all is a question of wisdom. Seen in this perspective, the Virgilian hero carries out a second transferral of meaning: he serves a cause. Virgil's genius lies in his ability to understand that—for this reason—Aeneas is profoundly unhappy.

---

28. Ulysses makes his feelings known quite clearly at the beginning of the *Iliad* when the Achaeans, surrendering to despair, seem to want to abandon the siege; he finds the words to dissuade them (II, 276–321).

Part Two

THE TRIAL OF KNOWLEDGE

FROM EARLY ON in the history of literature, myths have sought to explain our origins and have explored man's desire for knowledge. It may well be that this fascination with the birth of the world and with the sources of knowledge is what, in theory, sets myth apart from epic. On the practical level, most of the great stories are a blend of both, in which events are used to construct myth, and culminate in a representation of the world. Hesiod's *Theogony* provides us with an explanatory narrative of the cosmic order, of the place occupied in it by human beings (and particularly of how, thanks to Prometheus, they were given fire) as he retells the titanic epic of the birth of the gods of Olympus.

The Homeric narrative is essentially factual. It is unconcerned either with the cosmos, or with our origins; it tells of events that take place among men, though some may be fabulous in nature. The *Odyssey* seeks neither to understand nor to explain; telling the tale is more than enough. As it does, it speaks of the world in its own fashion, as seen through the poet's eyes. The poet himself must provide the occasional explanation, must respect certain conventions. Surely the narrator is motivated by beliefs, shaped by his culture; he is, to a certain extent, a conscious subject of knowledge. But we also know that all discourse, including the least narrative in appearance and intention, narrates more than it lets on, that it relates what it would rather not explain or demonstrate. No rhetorical form exists in a "pure" state; all is a matter of degree. On the narrative scale, the Homeric cycle occupies, along with the *Epic of Gilgamesh*, the loftiest and at the same time, the most ambiguous place, in that it has no other admitted objective than to charm. And yet, it instructs. But instruction is left up to the listener, to the reader. The fact that the *Odyssey* leaves nothing in the dark does not mean that it cannot be given multiple readings—quite the contrary. Its voice, as we well know, is anything but uniform. If, in comparison, the *Aeneid* does not offer the same openness, the same polyvalence, it is because, despite its author's reticence, it serves a cause, not to say a policy.

With the theme and the texts of this second part, with its biblical stories, theogony, tragedy, and philosophical dialogues, we enter into an entirely different narrative order, one that is much more complex in its ideas and in its intentions. In the Torah, as in Virgil, we find mythical history and the history of a nation. Though not completely ignoring this historical dimension, my reading does not assign it pride of place. The principal interest of the texts I have brought together lies in their thematic unity: the trial—in the sense of ordeal—of knowledge. The trial is manifest in the story of Genesis, in the myth of Prometheus,. and in Sophocles's tragedies. It is a trial that Plato, without attempting to sidestep its difficulties, envisages in the breathtaking inspiration of *Eros*.

4

THE BIRTH OF THE WORLD AND
THE GENESIS OF KNOWLEDGE

To TAKE UP in the same chapter the Book of Genesis and Hesiod's *Theogony* may seem at first glance preposterous. It is difficult to imagine two creation narratives more wildly at odds, two universes more utterly foreign to each other. The futility of the Olympian world stands in violent contrast to the high seriousness of the Torah, which has aged far better. Though we in the West lay claim to both the Greeks and the Jews as our antecedents, we do so without any clear understanding of what precisely it is that we have retained from our two contradictory inheritances. In truth, their union became possible only by expunging from each all that might perturb our ideal assemblage. From our Greek inheritance we claim poetry, art, philosophy; their mythology causes us to smile and, outside a narrow circle of Hellenists, we have come to view it as unworthy of their civilization. Of Judaism, on the other hand, we naïvely believe we have preserved the essential element, monotheism, without noticing how deeply Christendom has altered its substance. To these questions we will return at the appropriate time. Let us simply take up the two texts, Genesis and *Theogony*, with the fewest possible prejudices, as two stories of equal value, each endowed with its own logic and meaning, but also with certain shared concerns.

On the Difficulty of Reading the Bible

Reading the Bible is no small undertaking. Its multiple uses place us before a daunting series of paradoxes. No single book in the West's imaginary past is at once as ancient, as ever-present, and as ill-known; as accessible and yet as difficult, as long-winded and yet as concise. United in its principle—God—the Book is an immense collection of texts that are extraordinarily disparate in form, intent, tone, and source. One's lifetime would not be enough to draw up an inventory of the difficulties presented in reading them all. The question of establishing the texts alone has given birth to an inexhaustible literature. No matter the angle from which we approach them (religious, historical, poetic, philosophic, linguistic, etc.), the Scriptures call into question, in the most acute manner possible, the art of interpretation, scholarly or otherwise.

The Christian tradition, by bringing together under the same roof what it calls the Old and the New Testament has substantially transformed the Judaic tradition which recognizes only the former, which it knows as the Tanakh, the term created from the three great compilations that it subsumes, to wit: *Torah* (the Law, designated in the Christian versions by the Greek title *Pentateuch*), *Nevi'im* (Prophets), and *Kethuvim* or *Ktoubim* (Scriptures). Moreover, neither the order nor the contents of the Old Testament correspond entirely to those of the Tanakh. The Catholic canon of the Old Testament admits the texts that appear in the Greek version completed in the third century B.C. at Alexandria by a group of Jewish scholars whose number legend gives as seventy-two (the version known as the Septuagint), which itself reflects a text much more ancient than the complete Hebraic manuscripts at our disposal. Certain texts contained in the Septuagint version—the books of Deuteronomy—are not contained in the Protestant versions of the Bible, which follow in this regard the Jewish canon as it was established at Iamnia[29] at around the end of the first century of our era.

But these canonical distinctions have not directly influenced our reading, which is limited to the Torah;[30] more specifically, to its first book, Genesis—*beresit* in Hebrew—from its opening words: "In the beginning." But this limitation leaves whole the most fundamental problems, since the chronology of the events related does not correspond to that of their inscription as it has come down to us in its diverse versions. Hence the necessity of providing an overall appreciation of the scriptures brought together in the Torah.

The Torah is the fruit of a narrative compilation apparently carried out between the sixth and fourth century B.C., following the return to Jerusalem

---

29. *Iamnia* in Greek, *Yabneel* in Hebrew (later transformed into *Yabneh*, then *Yamneh*): a coastal town in Palestine which became the spiritual center of Palestinian Judaism following the destruction of the Temple of Jerusalem by Titus in 70 C.E.

30. Taken here in its limited sense: the first five books of Scripture. The term Torah can also be applied to the Tanakh as a whole.

in about 520 B.C. of a portion of the political and religious elite deported from the kingdom of Judah by Nebauchadnezzar from 597 to 581 B.C. The Babylonian exile would be critical for what had, up until then, been the Israelite people and religion. In many ways, both Judaism and the Jewish people are born of exile, and were to be reconstituted in what would later be called the Diaspora. Despite the restoration of the Judean state by the Persians, the Babylonian deportation would leave indelible traces on the collective consciousness, and the Diaspora would assume increasing significance in Jewish history. Exile, and the succession of political and military catastrophes which culminated in it, was to lead to a re-reading of the religious tradition and a spiritual deepening of its message: only the Law (Torah) could henceforth hope to survive destruction and dispersal. It would become the strongest protector of permanence, the indestructible foundation stone of Jewishness.

As a mythical and historical recomposition of the origins of the world and of the people of Moses, the story told in the Torah draws upon four distinct authors whom scholarly criticism has recognized and identified, in order of precedence, as the Yahvist and the Elohist, both of whom are primarily storytellers, and the Deuteronomist and the Sacerdotalist, primarily legislators. Genesis would appear to be the rearrangement by the sacerdotal author of an essentially Yahvist, and secondarily Elohist story. Thus we encounter two successive creation narratives, the most recent of which (Elohist) precedes the oldest (Yahvist). It is easy to discern, on the basis of this example alone, what summits of exegetical virtuosity erudition can attain. Small wonder that the ordinary reader may feel himself disarmed, and hesitate to take up the task.

Nonetheless, he must. A naïve, non-scholarly reading of the biblical stories is not only possible; it is desirable. If there are writings that belong to everyone, despite the immense efforts of the Church to discourage the faithful from using them, these are they. Scientific examination of the texts makes it possible for us to become better acquainted with the evolution of the Hebraic religion, but it cannot cause one particular reading of the Torah to prevail, nor can it restrict its interpretation. In this respect, erudition grants not a single privilege. Here, more than anywhere else, it is the story, as it has come down to us, with all its contradictions and ambiguities, that enjoys pride of place; the story and all the potential meanings it contains.

At the risk of incurring the wrath of Jewish and Christian believers, we must not be afraid to state that neither possesses a monopoly over the scope and the meaning of what they consider as their scripture. Still, as a non-believer, I must grant the believer the right to think that for all the deconstruction of modern criticism the text cannot truly speak with its full force except to him or her who is deeply imbued with the will to believe.[31] But there are several ways of believing, and faith, be it Jewish, Christian, or Muslim, consists of more than a viewpoint; it does not solve the dilemma of interpretation. It is legitimate to ask oneself what notion of fidelity believers feel they must obey. Fidelity to the text does not necessarily depend on a literal reading. Literality of this kind, as we know, does not exist, and its non-existence, here more than anywhere else, rigorously excludes any idea of literal fidelity.

But we know, too, that freedom to read cannot become a pretext for blurting out whatever comes into our head. Each of us is free to read the Bible as though it were a novel—and to enjoy the experience thoroughly: with the proviso that a purely novelistic reading (if such a reading were to mean anything at all) would be of scant interest. For us, the Bible is not simply another book. It is, whether we have read it or not, *the* Book. The book which has more than any other shaped our vision of the world. No possible reading of the biblical texts can ignore the exceptional imaginational charge they carry for us down to the present day, thanks to the continuity of religious tradition. Though I might choose to read Genesis as a myth upon which I have happened for the first time, I cannot forget that this story has been acting upon us for centuries. Openness to the new and attention to memory must be, here more than anywhere else, the attitude we strive for.

Reading the Torah

What story does the Torah tell? Does it speak the anger of God? His almightiness? The infinite patience of his love? Is this God the same throughout? Is he the God of all mankind, or the Lord of a particular people, for whose use alone the story has been written? Does it bring salvation? For whom? For the Jews? For the world? These are but a few of the questions that directly call upon the faith of the reader and cannot be answered outside of that faith.

---

31. We should note here the curious schizophrenia that has afflicted the Synagogues and Churches themselves: their theologians busily deconstruct the texts beneath the microscope of modern literary criticism without calling into question either their divine nature, nor the Revelation of which they are the bearers.

What story does the Torah tell? Such is the question with which we must begin, despite the impossibility of providing an answer that would subsume the diversity of allegiances to which it lays claim. In fact, impossibility itself is our only fulcrum: the meaning of the Torah is necessarily plural, contradictory even *for believers themselves*, if for no other reason than the diversity of its purview: a creation story; the history of a people; the promulgation of a law; an illustration of the role of the prophet as seen in the task accomplished by Moses.

Even to a believer the Torah can occasionally resemble a shaggy-dog story. If we were able to approach the story without prejudice, if we knew nothing of its imaginational weight, we might be able to read it, all things being equal, as we would Laclos's *Les Liaisons dangereuses*, like the adventures of a rather perverse author who enjoys placing his characters in compromising situations. But when we consider the influence of this interminable succession of conflict and catastrophe, if we take into account the passions, the enthusiasm, and the faith this book has generated, and continues to generate, we find ourselves at the edge of a bottomless pit. A perverse tale becomes a history of abysmal horrors. A jealous god pursues his people with zeal as punctilious as it is devastating. He holds them to a goal that cannot be attained, demands of them faultless adoration, and uses every bit of his all-powerful omniscience to cause them to stumble over the insurmountable obstacles that he places in their path. So extreme is his refinement that he trumpets straying from the straight and narrow, and the very faithless he promises to punish. In comparison, the Marquis de Sade is a primer for young ladies of good family. In short, God himself, God the first cause, is depicted as unjust, and to be chosen by him seems more like a curse than anything else. God is an insupportable weight on the shoulders of his people.

But, like the chosen people, the believer cannot exist with the fiery breath of this possessive, vengeful god breathing down his neck. God must be good, and his will unknowable. It is of little importance that the Hebrews, collectively, had proven restive or unsuited to the effort of elevation that God's goodness demands of them, providing that the individual believer may subscribe to it in full knowledge. Where a people, out of wilfulness or ignorance, fails to live up to the desiderata of its chosen status, the individual reader may make a leap of faith. If the goodness that God demonstrates toward his people seems to be linked to the fault to come, and to the threats that will inevitably be acted upon (I shall cause you to triumph, says the Lord, but your triumph will destroy you, remove you from me, and I shall deliver you over to your enemies), the reader is free to believe that his personal fate is not linked to that of the people whose tribulations he follows—especially if he is not Jewish—since he is reading the story for his personal edification. And even if, like Job, his faith is only to be rewarded by rebuke, he knows better than Job himself that it will find recompense in the end. The impenetrable goodness of God is the postulate that makes it possible for the believer to read a story in which everything conspires to turn one away from God and from men.

The Torah cannot be read nor endured except in the light of the salvation it extends to him who understands, or, more precisely, to him who accepts it as true while accepting that he cannot understand everything. But a reading illuminated by the prospect of individual salvation seems to me more evangelical than Jewish—though it is possible that over time Judaism has been contaminated in spite of itself by Christian eschatology. The idea of rewarding the just in the afterlife is not entirely absent from the Tanakh, but it appears relatively late, with the Prophets, particularly in the Book of Ezekiel (37: 1–14), where it can be read as a metaphor for the birth of Israel, then more clearly in Daniel (12: 2–3), where happiness appears to be promised to those who have merited it. However, there is not the slightest trace of such a promise in the Torah. The *Cheol*, which lies beneath the world of the living and serves as a sojourn for the dead, is a place of silence, dry as dust, populated by shades bereft of strength and memory, of which nothing can ever be known.

Naturally enough, any interpretation of the Tanakh claims to fall within the most coherent possible overview of its message. It is by now a commonplace to say that Christians read the Old Testament in the light of the New. Should we be surprised that the Jews themselves, at each of the distinct stages that have left their mark on the style and the choice of stories that make up their mythology, have, through a lengthy process of collection and transmission, interpreted both the events and the most ancient texts in ways that do not necessarily match the intentions of their remote predecessors? The Babylonian exile, as we noted, had made the need to preserve collective memory more urgent, and provided an occasion for painful reflection on the history of Israel. That history, like all history, is a re-reading of the past in the light—a sad light in the event—of the present.

The lengthy saga that runs from the First Man to the Hebrews and to the Israelites, and from the Israelites of Judea to the Jews, resembles nothing so much as an incessant migration interrupted only by a relatively brief period of stability and unity that reached its apogee under David and Solomon (from

1010 to 933 B.C.). Upon the death of Solomon the realm was divided: the history of royal power ends in failure, upon which the prophets do not cease to meditate and from which they continue to draw lessons. Any power, any political entity is obviously fated to perish, but from this inevitable fall Judaism would seem to draw particular instruction, to which we will return once we have investigated the meaning of the interminable peregrination that leads from paradise lost to the desert, from the desert to Egypt, from Egypt to the desert, from the desert to Canaan become Israel and Judah, from Judah to Babylon, from Babylon to Judah, and into the Diaspora.

To begin with, this long voyage must be envisaged as lying beyond any idea of redemption or punishment, in the same manner as we attempted to grasp *Gilgamesh*, with the difference being that here the story tells of the wandering of an entire people. More than that, the migration itself is the act that constitutes that people. The reductions or connections through which the sons of Noah (to begin not with Adam, but with the new beginning offered by the Flood) become sons of Shem and then of Abraham, the sons of Abraham become those of Isaac, the sons of Isaac those of Jacob and finally of Israel take place in successive displacements. With each generation, the story consigns to the shadows first the descendents of Shem and Japeth, then those of Ishmael, followed by those of Esau; countless peoples of which certain elements are later on alluded to by way of suggesting that the multitudes who have not been divinely chosen have not been totally forgotten either. It is as though it were necessary to concentrate on a single, small people reduced to servitude in Egypt—an experience capable of compelling the interest of all humanity, or of the individual human being, whoever he might be.

The process by which the people is chosen does not end either with the exodus from Egypt, the founding moment of the Israelites as a political entity, nor with their settlement in the land long before promised to their ancestors. After Solomon, and to a certain extent by his "fault" (because of the concessions he grants to the idolatric cults of his concubines), ten of the twelve tribes gradually abandon the foreground of the chosen and of the biblical story. Israel is reduced to Judah, itself soon reduced to exile and to a precarious return. The history of this people is one of continual passage through increasingly narrow bottlenecks, the last one being the pitiless military hand of Rome. After this final act of strangulation, the Jewish people can only recreate itself in the Diaspora and sow its seed throughout the world—by finally joining the rest of humanity, really. But this is something that the biblical story, which ends with the reconstruction of the Temple under Ezra and Nehemiah, does not say. The story, like the history of the people which it helped shape, remains unfinished. Strictly speaking, it has no ending: no term, no clearly indicated finality, despite the visions that certain prophets may have had of an Israel to come, to be reborn (for example, in Ezek. 37: 1–14, as mentioned earlier, and in Pss. 16: 10; 49: 16). Neither the Book of Ezra nor Nehemiah, nor the Chronicles presents the reconstruction of the Temple as an apotheosis, but rather as a challenging, danger-wrought attempt to begin over again. Without the Law, the Temple is nothing.

The absence of an ending by no means obviates the question of meaning—or possible meanings. In fact, it poses the question with increased insistence. If, for starters, the advent of an ultimate finality—let us call it eternal life under the eyes of God—seems to hover over the story, the story will, for all its claims to the contrary, be colored by that promise. But as we have seen, neither the Tanakh, nor to an even lesser extent the Torah, makes any such promise. There is no meaning to be discovered beyond the texts themselves—unless other scriptures are added on, quite precisely as Christendom proceeds to do. For all that, a divine promise animates the protagonists of the biblical story and continues to fashion, in a manner of speaking, the people that tells it: that of the land, justly designated as "promised." But even if we were to take the fulfilment of this promise literally, it would soon be reduced to an illusory conquest, for a territorial base can guarantee no loyalty in the heart of the people that receives it, particularly since it has already been proclaimed that possession of the land will not prevent the people from straying from God and from the Law (Deut. 31:14–29). This suggests that the Torah's only finality is the Law itself and its ongoing revelation.

Ultimately, the Torah is its own end. For the word "Torah" does not only mean "law," but also "doctrine," "teaching": another way of suggesting that the Torah has no other end than to teach and be taught.

But to teach what, exactly? That God is vicious and his people mediocre? Scanty fare, as lessons go. To read the Bible as an account of crime and misfortune may, as we have seen, provide some diversion, but it falls short in terms of meaning. It seems quite clear that the Torah can only reveal the richness of its teaching on condition that it is read and re-read at several levels. The story of the tribulations of the people of Israel makes sense only if it is taken as epic, collective memory, founding myth, and allegory all in one. It would be tempting—and all too easy—to consider only the last level, to take everything in the Torah as an allegory. The immediate effect would be to dilute it, to deprive it of most of its flavor and its impact. The power of the biblical story, in spite of its occasional bouts of the miraculous, is that it plunges us up to our eyeballs in the affairs of men, with all their magnanimity, passions and desires, appetites and hopes, deceits and cruelty. Fidelity, treason, repentance, love, hate, courage, cowardice, devotion, hunger, thirst, adultery, war, and peace: nothing is left out.

Before us stands a people forced to seek out its law and its freedom against all odds. Everything seems to have been decided for it. No more than it has chosen slavery, it has not truly sought liberation. It is impossible to strike out onto the hurtful road of Exodus without divine inspiration, not to mention the iron will of Moses, borne by the eloquence of Aaron. One cannot help but notice a judicious division of labor at work, not to mention the political lesson: not only do words alone not make the chief, but they threaten to turn the head of anyone who may take them too literally. We see clearly how disoriented Aaron becomes when his brother confers upon him the guardianship of the people in order to carry on a conversation with God. As if to say that even the chief cannot, without serious inconvenience, spend too much time on the cloud-shrouded summits. The time will always come when he must return to earth, and re-establish contact with crude, cruel reality. The Golden Calf is not simply an emblem of straying, inconstancy, and faithlessness; it testifies to what happens when the power of earthly things and appetites is neglected. To recall this well-known episode brings us back to the question of biblical monotheism: to the status of God—who is "manifest" only when he is never called upon.

And for good reason: Yahweh, or more precisely, YHWH (or YHWH) is, as we know, in a strict sense unpronounceable, entirely ineffable. Which amounts to suggesting that his name must never be spoken, that it must remain, except in exceptional circumstances, unpronounced. By debasing it, by implying that YHWH can be pointed to, as could any other, or by confounding his name with our daily gossip would deprive him of his power. But as the one by virtue of whom all idols must be abandoned must be named, as the prophet and the people are impelled to call upon him, he is given other names: *Adonai* (Lord) or *El-Chaddaï* (God of the Mountains). In spite of everything, the habit of thinking that God can be named and represented has taken root, while at the same time the idea that the taking of his name in vain constitutes a sacrilege has become dominant. To take possession of (the name of) God is forbidden, but this sign of respect does not stop it from becoming commonplace. For if God is "Someone," no single capital letter can stop it from becoming anthropomorphized (if I may be forgiven the barbarism): immaterial though he may be, it is this immortal, omnipotent, superior being who presides jealously over our fates, and passes judgement on our faith in him. And so it is that we are, as in pulp fiction, cast back into the same vicious circle, and the horror story begins all over again …

It would be accurate to say that making sense of the Torah calls for a more radical approach, to erase from our minds every conception, every image, every name, every attribute of the unnameable; to bring about, in other words, what the text itself cannot accomplish unless it ceases to be narrated. God, the Eternal, the Lord, etc., all these overly connoted names, weighted down with twenty centuries of Christianity, must be directly dispatched to the trash bin. "God" repeated one thousand times over obscures by his monumental name any informed reading of the Torah.

The Torah is the emblematic story of men: its writing and its reading form a powerful burst of consciousness. What then of men? They may lay aside their habitual beliefs, may cease worshipping heavenly bodies and idols, may recognize their fundamental nudity against the background of the universe, but there still remains about them something indefinable, more powerful than themselves (which is already saying too much), which impels them with blood and sweat to do more than merely survive. Of course, a certain continuity must be insured, and it is a consideration that invests the idea of 'chosen' with all its meaning: only a group defined by its path through history and its traditions can conceive of itself over time and tell its own story. It is the story that gives meaning, uncertain and perilous though it may be, to those who take it as their own, perpetuate it, and experience the truth of absence. It is, ultimately, a way of confronting, and accommodating, the silence of death: all must be accomplished here, in the continuum stretching from what has been to what will be.

How then are we to interpret the injunctions and incessant interventions of this parlous, exclusive god? Indeed, man is not enough; the people has neither the strength nor the constancy; not yet ripe for silence, it cannot tolerate absence and cannot move forward without a guide. Silence and absence must then be betrayed; the voice of *Adonai* must be taken to tongue-lash the people toward the pitiless freedom against which it so stubbornly balks. If YHWH is, to use Jabés's excellent formula, "the metaphor of the void," it is because the void itself remains insupportable. It must be filled at all cost with something, even those unpronounceable consonants between which the story can do little else than place the vowels that finally make them audible. At the same time, no matter how powerful it may be, the metaphor cannot act in the stead of the people, which it has galvanized. It can even be predicted that its impact will weaken, will shift according to the circumstances. The dream—the Promised Land—fades, evaporates in the appearance of realization, while fall and failure only reawaken its evocative power. For all their weakness, men, and peoples, are the only ones who can make themselves: no god can desire it for them.

Human frailty alone cannot explain the exclusivity the unnameable one demands. Why must divine speech impose upon the people the rigorous unicity of the Law? The prohibition of idols would appear to derive, in common sense terms, from the incompatibility between "monotheism" and "polytheism." Our reading of Hesiod will show us that this opposition is less irreducible than we commonly assume. Keeping only to the Torah, it is easy enough to understand, in light of what we have seen, that the "jealousy" of YHWH is a metaphor for the requirement that represents the repudiation of the fabrication and adoration of signs. As long as we remain attached to the illusory security of the visible, the palpable, and their multiple objects, we can make no attempt to confront absence nor adopt our own law.

Attentive reading of the Torah, without surrendering to our prejudices, must mean ridding ourselves over and over again of the comforting representations that allow us to sidestep the essential. As long as the people flees its responsibilities and its terrifying freedom, no law can hold, no rules can be laid down and passed on to the generations to come. It will be tossed to and fro by its fears and its caprices, and nothing enduring will ever be handed down—because the essential cannot be defined, cannot be named. The cult of the visible and the tangible has conserved its full force of attraction because it places us squarely before what is missing. Void and absence cannot combat this force of attraction on equal terms. They must possess a power capable of making themselves manifest, even at the risk of betrayal. And it is indeed because the unnameable must necessarily betray itself by the obligation to make itself manifest that this power must remain one, without parallel, without rivals. And especially in that it dictates the law destined to regulate social relations within the community. There cannot be two laws for one sole people.

The reading I propose is, of course, a controversial one. Above all, it makes no pretense of explaining how the contemporaries of Moses, David, or Ezekiel conceived of YHWH and their relationship with him. There is no way, in fact, that this can be established. At the most we can postulate that they cannot escape the desire (and the need) for YHWH to possess, even abstractly, a human face. Has the god of Genesis not created man in his image? One cannot move from idol to abstraction without transition, without trauma. The Torah itself provides powerful illustration of just how difficult this passage is, a passage never fully accomplished, always being begun again. But it would not be reading too much into the Bible story to say that it leads us to an abstract conception of that which we have become accustomed to designating by the name of God, to suggest that it presents to us, through the same verbal (or "non-verbal") sign, both *presence and absence*, in short, that it attempts the impossible: to utter the unutterable. If we were to brush aside the inalterability of speaking, the history of Israel, like the entire story, would be reduced to pathetic buffoonery, and "God" an execrable dramaturge. By focusing upon the unutterable, the Torah inaugurates nothing less than literature itself, if by literature we mean any story that cannot be subsumed by its first reading, and which cannot be exhausted by subsequent re-reading. Insofar as it cannot be reduced to any definitive interpretation, writing itself is an act of salvation: the book of the people-which-relates-itself (rather than the "chosen people"), and with it the book of humanity, remains open; it belongs to no one. It is in this spirit that we can now turn our attention to Genesis.

Genesis, or the End of Innocence

The first of the Torah's five books covers succinctly an immense time span reaching from the creation of the world to the death of Joseph. It is a story that forms a prelude of sorts to the emergence of the Israelites as a people. Israel has already derived its name from Jacob's combat with the angel before the settlement in Egypt, but it receives the law only with Exodus, under the inspired leadership of the legendary founder of the Israelites, Moses. If there is no law, there can be no people. Genesis lays down the basic elements of an unwritten law, but it establishes above all the fundamental premises of man's relationship with God, without which the flight from Egypt and the struggle for freedom and autonomy are meaningless.

What is most striking about Genesis, in comparison with Hesiod's *Theogony* but also with the Sumerian-Akkadian and Egyptian theogonies, is its economy: in both versions, the creation of the world is dealt with in a few verses. God is the apparent cause of all, hence the opening's extreme concision. In the story of origins, there is little point in seeking good or evil, happiness or unhappiness, for all their prominence in human affairs. The economy of Creation makes human fallibility all the more difficult to explain: if no antagonism exists in the cosmos, why should it exist among men? Nothing suggests that the night of the beginning symbolizes evil:

> In the beginning, God created the heaven and the earth. And the
> earth was without form, and void; and darkness was upon the face
> of the deep. And the Spirit of God moved upon the face of the
> waters. And God said, Let there be light: and there was light.
> (Gen. 1:1–3)

Following the pattern established by the first act, all the elements lend themselves docilely to the creator's will; not a hint of rebellion darkens the horizon. "Disobedience" or "fault" arises with man, by way of woman, at the urging of the serpent, presented as "more subtil than any beast of the field which the Lord God had made" (Gen., 3:1). The most widespread Christian interpretation makes the serpent the incarnation of evil, the instrument of sin, Satan's intermediary. The serpent indeed stands as the device by which humanity loses its innocence, but there is no explicit statement that the reptile acts with the intent to do harm. The evil commonly associated with it can be derived from the divine curse that condemns it henceforth to crawl upon its belly, and to suffer the enmity of woman (Gen. 3:14–15).

Clever beast that he is, the serpent must be aware of what he is about; thus he sets in motion the wheels of tragedy, with knowledge aforethought. But God cannot be unaware of what his creature is capable of doing. Is he not, after all, the stage manager of everything that is wrought and unwrought under his purview? We can state without exaggeration that he would brook no resistance to a force inimical to his design. At the same time, however, the very docility of the elements is not enough to convince us of the almightiness and omniscience of their creator. It seems clear that some part of his creation eludes him, and without that missing part, the ideas of fault and infraction and the theory of original sin collapse.

Whatever the case, the theory is uselessly reductive. Avoiding, at this stage, any extrapolation upon the nature (infallible or not) of God, of which the text itself says not a word, it is enough to surmise that the Creator allows his creation to follow its course. His pleasure will be to see what happens. But this voyeuristic interpretation plunges us back into the dark hypothesis we raised earlier. No sooner is our attention centered on God than the contradictions appear to become insoluble. Could it be that God has no specific intentions? He presides over the Creation, but once the task has been accomplished our attention shifts from the Creator to his work. Genesis tells not the story of God, but that of man. As in all cosmogonies, it attempts to explain the origin of that which is, but instead of doing so by telling the story of the gods, it seeks to understand through the story of man.

The idea of "original sin" would appear to be justified by the fall to which man is condemned by his expulsion from the Garden of Eden, even though the word "sin" can nowhere be found in the episode that leads to the expulsion. God's wrath, both toward man and toward the serpent, is directed in both cases against that which he himself has created. That they would transgress is all but foretold as being within the realm of the possible:

> And the Lord God commanded the man, saying, Of every tree of the garden thou mayest freely eat; but of the tree of knowledge of good and evil, thou shalt not eat of it; for in the day that thou eatest thereof thou shalt surely die. (Gen. 2:16–17)

Good and evil, long accepted as the exclusive interpretation, can also be translated as happiness and unhappiness. Both are possible, but the former, with its "sinful" connotation, is losing ground even among the Christian erudite. A divine prescription indeed exists, but the order is a warning of what will not fail to happen if ... and this possibility, which Christian tradition insists on naming "sin," is nothing other than man's inevitable curiosity, which, as Aristotle notes at the beginning of his *Metaphysics*, is only "the natural passion to know" (980a). Here, the serpent is merely goading passion on. Adopting a reassuring tone it whispers: "You will not perish as a result," adding that "God doth know that in the day ye eat thereof, then your eyes shall be opened, and ye shall be as gods, knowing good and evil" (Gen. 3:5).

Ambiguity is the mode, rather than untruth. The serpent offers no promise of immortality. The poison of the fruit he invites man and woman to eat is not a deadly one. One does not die from it, but after tasting of it, one sees with greater clarity. It is the drug of knowledge: "And the eyes of both of them were opened, and they knew that they were naked" (Gen. 3:7). The fruit may well be "desired to make one wise" (Gen. 3:6); it may, in other translations, be a key, which in opening the door to knowledge locks that of paradise. Science is incompatible with innocence. And man chooses science. The first thing that he learns from science is that he is naked, vulnerable, and mortal. The serpent did not tell all, for if man had truly known what to expect before acquiring knowledge, he might well have chosen innocence. But everything indicates that he chose curiosity. Moreover, he did so freely.

At the risk of self-contradiction, we might even say "consciously." For to say as much is to suppose that the knowledge of which we speak was already his. But it is only knowledge of the Other: God, and the serpent. Man, strictly speaking, has been warned. But he cannot grasp the full significance of the warning unless he himself can accede to the knowledge whose promise the serpent so enticingly holds out. Here we have a magnificent expression of the richness and the complexity of the relationship between knowledge and freedom. The fruit of knowledge leads man astray precisely because of his innocence: of that which he has not yet tasted. Man "chooses" in total candor, total naïveté—or takes a blind risk. How can we ever know beforehand what will come of the passion to know? Such, from the beginning, is the human dilemma; such, indeed, is what makes us human. Einstein did not know, could not know, in 1916, where his work on relativity would lead. The man of Eden is a happy beast, enjoying the privileges granted by God. Among them is the temptation of discovery and the risk that accompanies it. Man's freedom is real, but he remains unaware of the effect of its exercise. We never understand until after the fact, when, in a certain sense, it is "too late." Once embarked on the road of knowledge, man cannot turn back. One freedom is left to him: to reflect upon the uses to which he may put his knowledge.

"In the beginning," without experience, man knows nothing of the world. From the world of Eden he receives only contradictory messages: one, from God: "Believe in my experience"; the other, that of the reptile: "See for yourself." "Sapere aude! Have courage to use your own reason! That is the motto of the Enlightenment," exclaims Kant, in 1784.[32] At first glance, considering the double language of the God/serpent, the formula seems naïve. But it becomes less so than at first glance, once we realize that Kant is defining what appears to him as the *natural majority* of man. However "natural" it may be in his eyes, it is no less difficult to achieve or to assume, so much so that the minority of man, his attachment to the least-examined beliefs, remains dominant. Such, then, is the choice that confronts the man of Eden: believe or understand. It is a choice that comes as much from God as from his forked-tongued messenger.

It is a message that does not fall lightly from just any tongue. A hoary tradition of venomous calumny transmitted down through the centuries by Christianity to this day obscures the symbolic richness of the serpent, which Bachelard describes as "one of the most important archetypes of the human soul."[33] Like a moving line, the serpent is simultaneously life and

32. Immanuel Kant, *Foundations of the Metaphysics of Morals and What Is Enlightenment?* (in German), trans. Lewis White Beck (Indianapolis: Bobbs-Merrill, 1959), p. 85.
33. Quoted in *Dictionnaire des symboles*, par Jean Chevalier et Alain Gheerbrant (Paris: Laffont, "Bouquins," 1982) p. 868. The dictionary devotes more than twelve pages to the serpent (pp. 867–879), one of its lengthiest entries. No other creature occupies comparable space.

abstraction,[34] conscience and libido; it is stimulating and deadly, primitive and clever, visible and concealed. Once a primordial god, it is rediscovered "at the starting point of all cosmogonies, before it is dethroned by the religions of the spirit. It is that which gives life, and that which sustains."[35] It has only to open its mouth and swallow, and it becomes a womb; rear up, and it becomes a phallus; curl up upon itself and bite its tail, and it becomes the founding circle, impregnating itself, center and basis of the world, passageway from death to life and from life to death.[36] The narrators of Genesis cannot have been unaware of the creative power—in the Mediterranean and in Western Asia—invested in the omnipresent figure of the serpent. I make no attempt to obscure its dangerous, perhaps extreme aspects. For if left to its own devices, the serpent threatens to overturn the very order it has helped create. Hence its reputation for wickedness. But the very threat it bodies forth cannot stop it from breathing life, from inspiring thought, from bringing to life the instincts. Suited to the shadows as well as to the light, the serpent is alternatively visceral and cerebral.

Its dual nature provides an excellent illustration of the deep ambiguity of its advice to woman: the adventure of knowledge is not a garden party, in contrast to what the flavorful appearance of its fruit suggests; and the act of biting—into the fruit and into knowledge—brings with it pain and disenchantment. Yet were it not for their ordeal, the residents of Eden would never have become human; they would never have procreated, never have reproduced. Man would have remained like an embryo in the paradisical uterus. He would have had no name, nor would he have named his companion "Eve, because she was the mother of all living" (Gen. 3:20), a name she receives only upon having departed Eden. Before, she is simply woman (*ishah*, in Hebrew, derived from *ish*, man). The expulsion from Eden is all too clearly an act of birth, in all its pain and violence. Adam and Eve experience directly the pain that surrounds the act of birth of the species. The suffering is more than physical: to be born is not simply to leave the mother's womb, it is to grow up in an inhospitable world; it is to tear oneself away from the mother—a second birth—leave childhood behind, and suffer what psychoanalysis terms castration, the ordeal of which circumcision (and surely excision for girls as well) is the tangible and symbolic manifestation—a mark upon the flesh signalling that our fate is both solitude (nudity) and society (circumcision separates but joins together as well, as all members of the clan must undergo it and recognize, inscribed on their flesh,

34. Chevalier and Gheerbrant, op cit., p. 868. "The Chaldeans had a single word for life and serpent."
35. Ibid., p. 868
36. Ibid., pp. 868–869. Once again, the image has been borrowed from Bachelard.

their common belonging). So it is that the suffering of the flesh and that of the soul are joined, as are birth and knowledge. But if it is raised too often, the connection loses its sharpness: knowledge begins with the initiation into separation, loss and pain. Before man learned anything, he had begun to experience the difficulty of learning and to suffer the slights of freedom.

What injustices this succession of curses brings down upon the head of man after his exile from innocence, now that he has become suddenly responsible for his own ignorance—or guilty of wanting to match God! Would not his creature simply be able, God worries, to "put forth his hand, and take also of the tree of life, and eat, and live for ever" (Gen. 3:22)? It is because of the madness that sets him off in search of knowledge, it is because he consciously desired the impossible, the unthinkable, that is to say, both knowledge *and* eternal life, that man is "punished." Punished for having been lulled by the edifying words of the serpent, punished for not having suspected what his seduction had left in the shadows. For wherever man acts in an imprudent fashion, in his naïve refusal to observe the prohibitions, uncaring of the consequences of his acts, the serpent acts with knowledge aforethought. It knows what man does not; it is the master of the penumbra that accompanies all knowledge, that region of darkness which will henceforth dwell unrecognized within *homo sapiens*.

Knowledge, in order to deploy itself, must forget its penumbra. It cannot be acquired without repressing the sacrifice demanded of it; in a certain sense, it exhibits certain similarities to what today we term the unconscious. Man, driven from his infancy, understands nothing of what has befallen him. To explain what he cannot understand, he constructs, of his ignorance and of his desire to know, a fault, a sin. So it is that he falls into what Kant terms his "minority" (the state of an irresponsible minor). The Königsberg philosopher's "sapere aude!" reverberates centuries later with man's colossal effort to attain his majority and to free himself from the "fault" of attempting to understand rather than being content to believe. Weighed down by centuries of Christian guilt (and in his specific case, the aggravating circumstances of being Protestant), Kant knows that fear is the most tenacious obstacle on the road of knowledge. "Be afraid no longer!" he enjoins his fellow man. By way of contrast, Aristotle, who is a stranger to the tradition, need not free himself from a burden—the fear of learning—he does not know. With him, the passion for knowledge implies no suffering, nothing more than discipline. Above all, it is a desire for wonderment. Of Aristotle we have preserved, or reconstituted, the idea of a naïve, positive knowledge—though we have made of it an instrument for quite a different purpose: that of mastery rather than contemplation. Of Genesis we retain only sin, the transgression of the forbidden. In doing so, we deprive ourselves of hearing what the story of the first human episode of the Torah makes audible: that the transgression it relates is nothing other than the inevitable desire to know through our acts, and the sense of dereliction becomes its first fruit.

The act brings with it vexatious consequences. With Cain and Abel, Adam and Eve have given birth to a veritable nightmare: from God's acceptance, without explanation, of Abel's offering while disdaining his brother's is born fratricidal murder. God quickly heaps inconsistency upon arbitrariness: he forbids that Abel be avenged by promising to avenge seven times over the potential murderer of Cain, whom he marks with a sign "lest any finding him should kill him" (Gen. 4:15). The story can be explained as symbolizing the supremacy of the agriculturalist over the herdsman. The explanation is plausible, in that it prefigures the sedentarisation (however short-lived) of the Hebrews. But the victory of cultivation over pastoralism has no need for fratricide. The initial murder stands, instead, as a sign of the carnage that may be visited upon the group at the slightest pretext. It would have sufficed for Cain to wait a day or two to ascertain whether God would persist in his favoritism or if, sharing his attentions, he would turn his gaze toward the other brother. Thus, in response to God's terrible "what hast thou done?" Cain recognizes that his "punishment is greater than I can bear." Not because God's reproving gaze will follow him to the grave, as Victor Hugo would have it, but because he now *feels* that he is outside the law:

> "thou hast driven me out this day from the face of the earth; and from thy face shall I be hid; and I shall be a fugitive and a vagabond in the earth; and it shall come to pass, that every one that findeth me shall slay me." (Gen. 4:14)

The punishment to which Cain is condemned does not place him outside the law, but places him instead under its governance, which his act of murder has helped to create—and in which God acquiesces to the murderer's demand. Thus divine punishment (flight and the life of the vagabond) takes on its full meaning, the application of sanctions and the setting down of limits: it does not authorize men to kill in the name of God, nor in the name of the Law. The brief episode of Cain is far from a simple consequence of "original sin," but an allegory of jealousy and justice. The murderous jealousy of the guilty one must be punished without setting off the interminable *mimesis* of revenge. If Cain is killed for having killed, there will be no end to the killing. Seen in this light, murder as a motive is unimportant; but that it is at once derisory (a provisional preference of fate for the younger brother) and nodal (the arbitrary overturning of the order that normally accords precedence to the elder brother) is not without significance: the jealous rage that sparks fratricidal struggles lies at the root of the endless, destructive mimesis that can send society spiralling into disorder.

Justice, for all that, does not reign, for as God himself says: "My spirit shall not always strive with man, for that also he is flesh: yet his days shall be an hundred and twenty years" (Gen. 6:3). Faced with the proliferation of evil, God, remorseful at having created man, decides to wipe away all he has wrought. The great cleansing of the Flood is the prelude to a second creation. This time, on the face of the earth, the Ark replaces Eden. Without being necessarily any better than Adam, Noah, "he who comforts," will surely be less naïve. But above all, he is of the lineage of Seth, "the appointed," the third son of Adam and Eve "instead of Abel" (Gen. 4:25).[37] If the substitution is likewise noted, it can only be because we find there the germ of a possible new beginning. This eventuality falls upon Noah whom God has seen as "righteous before me in this generation" (Gen. 7:1); but he is a righteous man aware of the ways of the world, accustomed to wickedness and violence—he has accumulated six hundred years of experience before the Flood. Humanity's second birth takes place in more realistic circumstances than the first: an earth scrubbed clean rather than an idyllic, deceiving garden. Man starts over again, in fuller knowledge of the challenge that awaits him.

There is something illusory, however, about the metaphor of a new beginning. One can never begin again. In the event, Noah is also an illustration of a continuity that can only be understood if man is not unadulterated wickedness, if he is seen to carry within him the desire for justice. The biblical cataclysm is richer in meaning than the version given in the *Epic of Gilgamesh*. The survivor of the flood in the Akkadian epic, Utanapishti (see chapter 3 above) wins immortality almost fraudulently, and has no further connection with human affairs; he has saved no one but himself. Unlike him, Noah shelters himself from the waters and steps ashore on newly dry land the better to rebuild humanity under the eyes of God. The rainbow, sign of the covenant, stands for the tie that binds the world of men to the world of the gods; henceforth, the Eternal Being will no longer attempt to destroy what he has wrought:

---

37. The biblical text adds, significantly: "And to Seth, to him also there was born a son; and he called his name Enos [the Mortal]; then began men to call upon the name of the Lord" (Gen. 4:26).

> "I will not again curse the ground any more for man's sake; for the imagination of man's heart is evil from his youth; neither will I again smite any more every thing living, as I have done" (Gen. 8:21).

God resigns himself to the imperfection of his creation and rebuilds his bridges to humankind, which has been reinvested with its power over all the other species.

So it is that man in Genesis finds himself less at a loss, in religious terms, than man in the *Epic of Gilgamesh*. God—and the serpent—speak to him, give him council, insidious though it may be. Divine wrath does not wipe everything away; though it is imperfect, reconciliation is possible. In the world of the *Epic of Gilgamesh*, the gods are absent as interlocutors, indifferent to the course of human affairs in which they only intervene incidentally, with no general intentions; likewise, we know that the serpent, without a word, steals away the plant of eternal youth that the hero has so laboriously brought up from the depths of the sea. But for biblical man, the sequence of events is entirely different. It is as though he refuses to assume the metaphysical solitude of the Sumerian hero who has resolved to expect nothing from the gods.

For no matter how arbitrary the god of Genesis appears to be, his interventions are never entirely gratuitous. They embody, in a manner that is often curious, a concern for man, and they partake of a secret intention, or of one that is at minimum difficult to make sense of. In the final analysis, this intention, the project that God has prepared for man, is nothing more than a demand addressed by man to his own invisible and lofty self-image. The demand itself cannot be specific, nor can the image be revealed without collapsing; it is enough for man to hope that it resembles him.

We have already seen why YHWH must remain unnameable. We know as well that this absence must be designated in one way or another in order for the law to exist, as the story of Cain testifies. Without fear of exaggeration, it can be said that, from indifferent divine presence in the *Epic of Gilgamesh*, we "pass," with Genesis, to the considered absence of God. This paradox is clearly impossible, however, unless God is seen as pure metaphor: for a principle of a higher, untouchable, unspeakable justice, without which society cannot give itself law, and will fall back into the relentlessly meshing gears of endless violence. Responsibility falls upon man, who has constructed God to care for him. But man cannot admit that he is the author of God without immediately depriving the metaphor of its power. For the same reason, power, though it flows from an all-powerful principle, cannot exercise its vigilance on a permanent basis. Were God always present to watch over man, one could not understand why man so often goes astray and must, like Sisyphus, constantly climb back up his hill.

Finally, God cannot be pure abstraction, nor can he be clear representation. Of necessity, he travels back and forth between the two. It could even be asserted that the wise man, providing he is not so incautious as to say so, can make do without God. He can, and this he owes to his awareness of God's absence. The genius of Judaism lies in indicating, through YHWH, the fundamental defect of any god. But for the common man, such speculation is too risky. It is easy to understand why most believers finally succumb to the need for representation—a need to which Christianity will prove much more sensitive than either Judaism or Islam.

We could continue to read Genesis and the four other books of the Torah, but we would find, fundamentally, nothing more than the illustration—rich, diverse, truculent and turbulent, exalted and painful—of man's ambiguous relationship with the divine metaphor that governs him. On the same occasion, we would behold a constantly shifting tableau representing the relationships of men among themselves. It is clear that these relationships are formed and undone through the story of a people which, from generation to generation, from new beginning to renewal, from defeat to victory, and from conquest to exile, slowly, gradually comes to understand the history that defines it and the task that it must shoulder in the name of a chosen status that weighs down on it ever more heavily, like an overwhelming burden of which it is constantly tempted—and thoroughly unable—to relieve itself. It becomes easy enough to understand why, measured against the rigors of its destiny, the creation of the world is of so little importance that it can be summed up in a few lines. God has seen to it. God will suffice. Genesis is simply not interested in cosmogony. But it is mightily interested in man. And in the people that proclaim, bear, and symbolize him. Yet this man is afraid. Afraid of his own solitude. Afraid of being without God and perhaps, in some obscure way, afraid of finding himself alone with God, alone in the face of the incomprehensible.

From the unavowed desire to know and the transgression implicit in knowledge arises the possibility of begetting. It is only after being banished from the garden of innocence that Adam comes to "know" Eve—*life*—and that the species begins to multiply. Plurality and diversity are the fruits of "wickedness." The story of Babel confirms that God himself drives man to confusion, encouraging differences and dispersion; he does so not merely to stop man from embarking on a course of action that might threaten Him. He,

YHWH, is by definition unattainable and insensible to threats, but, as Marie Balmary[38] has shown, he acts to put a stop to a mindlessly unitarian, totalitarian construct: the wish to connect the earth to the heavens, to bring the heavens down to the earth, to construct the celestial, to give body to that which cannot be articulated. No one can pretend to be the architect of God. The story of Babel bodies forth the idea of the inaccessibility of Principle. Should all humanity come together to construct a tower, or any other ladder reaching toward Him, the enterprise, destined to fail, cannot but flatten man and reduce him to a repetition of himself. Man has been called upon to spread and to disperse himself. In this scattering, a people soon reduced to a fraction of itself (Judah) continues to carry with it the Law. These law-bearers are soon dispersed in their turn to the four corners of the world to bear witness. The Diaspora of the Jewish people symbolizes and accompanies the dispersion of humanity, of which the sons of Noah, the collapse of Babel, the descendants of Ishmael and of Esau are high points, reminders of the human vocation of wandering, of sowing his seed wherever he may go.

That to which the people bears witness is clearly stated in Exodus and in the other books of the Torah. The Law, as we have seen, first takes shape with Genesis. The sacrifice of Isaac by Abraham can be interpreted at face value: faith in God is put pitilessly to the test. Abraham shows that he is prepared to carry out the deed, but the trial itself is enough and God stays his arm, not wanting man to molest his fellow man, whom He has created in His image. It is not solely a question of forbidding human sacrifice, but of much more: the Absolute One refuses that the extreme act (the sacrifice of his only legitimate son) be carried out in His name. The lesson learned is the same as Babel, though from another angle. No act, no earthly enterprise can draw itself up to God's height. No one can possess the Principle as though it were his, even through the greatest act of devotion.

Other episodes, such as the estrangement of Haggar the maid-servant, given in concubinage by the infertile Sarah to her husband, and of Ishmael, son of that union; the paralipsis of Esau, deprived of his right of primacy by his brother Jacob; and the exile of Jacob and his family in Egypt, are more difficult to interpret. Beginning with the first of our examples, the temptation is great to see in it a kind of ethnic selection, to which certain pages of Exodus and Leviticus seem to lend credence: the chosen people must remain pure, and free of any mixing. This superficial reading confuses the meaning of "chosen," reducing it to a "preference" of God for his

38. Marie Balmary, *Le sacrifice interdit, Freud et la Bible* (Paris: Grasset, 1986), pp. 76–87.

people. In the first place, there would be nothing strange about such a preference at a time and in a place where the gods are everywhere protective and specific to the peoples who honor them (even when the same gods can be found under diverse names among different peoples). Seen in this light, the God of the Torah is striking in his abstract quality and in his concern for the other. *Abram*, "father raised," becomes *Abraham*, "father of a multitude," when, following the birth of *Ishmael*, "God listens," God establishes a covenant with him and proclaims that he shall be a father of many nations. (Gen. 17:4). At the same time that he foretells the birth of Isaac (named "He laughs" in that Abraham laughs at the possibility), God blesses Ishmael and his numerous progeny. The text goes to great length to note that father and son (Abraham and Ishmael) were circumcised on the same day, as if to underscore that the covenants entered into are equal: "And all the men of his house, born in the house, and bought with money of the stranger, were circumcised with him" (Gen. 17:27). Circumcision, the sign of the covenant, applies to all the peoples descended from Abraham, and in him "surely all the nations of the earth shall be blessed ... " (Gen. 18:18) Not to be circumcized, for a male, signifies being cut off from his people (Gen. 17:14), he who refuses it violates the covenant and is no longer part of the human race.

Their status as chosen people does not place the Israelites in an exclusive relationship with God; rather it assigns to them an exemplary mission and conveys a lesson that has indirect application for all peoples. Once again, however, the task is a weighty, near-impossible one, and we should not be surprised when the people charged with carrying it out attempt to shirk their responsibilities. Is this not, in the final analysis, the burden that Esau unthinkingly concedes to his younger brother by selling his birthright for a pottage of lentils? In "despising" his birthright (Gen. 25:34), he makes himself unworthy of the responsibility he has renounced. To partake of the continuity of the chosen requires a singular will; Jacob maneuvers cleverly, to the point of deceiving his father, to assume it. His determination does not eliminate the brother, seen as unworthy of the covenant, but frees him and his lineage (just as it does Ishmael's) from the fearsome "privilege" that has fallen upon the chosen people.

It is a fearsome privilege indeed, particularly since Israel does not always rise to the heights God and the prophets demand of it. Worse still is its backsliding in victory or conquest, where success threatens to go to its head, or to soften it. This is the reason why the "stiff necked people" is so often called to order, warned of the misfortunes to which its self-satisfaction and its slacking will invariably lead. It also justifies the length and the difficulty of the journey that leads to the Law. For the Law is not simply given, it must be won. To be chosen exacts a price, and that price is suffering and humiliation. Thus the passage through Egypt is obligatory. The chosen people must experience enslavement before beginning the arduous apprenticeship of *auto-nomy*—in its literal meaning, the capacity to dictate unto itself its own law.

For all that, the relation between the sons of Israel and the other peoples remains ambiguous and problematical. Since they do not follow the Law, God "abhors them" (Lev. 20:23). At the same time, their being put aside is an expression of his will: "And ye shall be hold unto me: for I the Lord am holy, and have severed you from other people, that you should be mine" (Lev. 20:26).

The Torah abounds in similar passages, in which it is difficult not to note a sense of superiority, a sense that becomes inevitable once Israel feels itself called upon to show the way. But such a vocation should, at minimum, motivate it to join forces with others, and we are obliged to note that such mingling is systematically discouraged, even forbidden, by Scripture. There is, of course, a reason for this closing off: obedience to the Law is already a forbiddingly difficult task for the chosen ones themselves; should they mingle, they could not help but become corrupted by the idolatry of others. Which is precisely what took place during the reign of the most glorious and most just of the kings of Israel. Solomon's excessive affection for foreign women leads him to authorize the idol-worshipping cults of their respective nations. Infidelity to YHWH will lead to the irreparable division of the realm and the shrinking of one of the tribes of divine choosing, that of Judah.

We must remember that the Torah, as it has been collated and transmitted, is born of exile, of a situation of extreme precariousness for what remains of the chosen people and its elites. In these circumstances, concern for upholding and transmitting the Law can only be exacerbated, up to and including its projection into the past in the form of a "purity" that had probably never been rigorously observed. From this point onward, it is less important to give an example than to safeguard what is in mortal danger, as though the authors of the Torah had known that henceforth only its writing could cause it to endure and to be passed on down through the generations. It is as if they had sensed that the construction of the temple and the walls of Jerusalem would be ephemeral, and could not of themselves guarantee the survival of tradition. The written text prepares the way for and anticipates a dispersion, which, beneath the hammer-blows of adversity, has already begun. It is the Law, which must be given final form and preserved in time, in spite of the dispersion—or rather, thanks to it, since the realms that preceded it have demonstrated their ephemeral quality. Where the territorial enterprise had failed, the book might succeed.

With the Torah in its final written form, the chosen people no longer need either king or land. The exile to which it is henceforth promised would surely preserve tradition far better than the most powerful of kings. The Jews, everywhere strangers, would cling more fiercely than ever to their identity as it is contained in the book which they carry everywhere along with them. There is no other way, in fact, of preserving the community that bears witness to the Law as it scatters its seed to the four corners of the earth; no finer way of saying that belonging is not necessarily rooted in the soil. That other nations, and perhaps, by way of reaction, more than a few Jews, have not understood this changes nothing of the meaning of the story: it is only in self-preservation, in all its uniqueness and specificity, that the community participates in and contributes to the universal. This is also the surest way for it not to perish. The sense of permanence transmitted in the Torah has no individual quality. Only in the perpetuation of the Law and the story that constitutes it can the Jews seek immortality, which can only be collective. They are indeed the unsurpassed masters of narrative identity.

The trial of knowledge—in the sense of an ordeal—of which Genesis stands as allegory is, finally, far more complex than it would appear at first glance. Its story condenses an interminable process in the course of which humankind encounters at least three types of closely interwoven experience, in which the Other (the serpent) plays an essential revelatory role: the pain of identity, where nudity symbolizes, in the strongest sense, self-discovery; the hostility of the world into which knowledge has cast us; and the irreparable loss that accompanies all knowledge, which has begun with what we forget having experienced when we entered into language.

Hesiod and the Birth of the Gods

Greek mythology has no bible; it is scattered across countless stories contained in contradictory fragments that no ancient narrator, with the exception of Hesiod, has attempted to weave together in a coherent structure. Hesiod's *Theogony* is the principal document at our disposal for understanding the mythical and cosmogonical thought of the Greeks.[39] But it brings together only a portion of the mythology in circulation throughout ancient Greece. Above all, it does not present itself as a canonical *summum* destined to give definitive form to a law or to a sacred tradition. Versions of mythological events vary from one region, one period, or one poet to another. We encounter the same characters everywhere, of course—in particular the world of Olympus, with its dozen principal gods and its secondary figures— but in substantially differing scenarios. The characters themselves are more familiar than the paths they follow, even though certain episodes—Kronos devouring his children, Prometheus bound for having stolen fire—have remained more clearly etched in collective memory than others.

The Olympian universe has a faintly frivolous air about it, reflecting the modern world's long-standing, infantile view of mythology. Even though it has been rehabilitated as a subject of study and reflection, we find it quite normal that the Greeks themselves finally transformed it into a kind of cosmic comedy. The cradle of democracy and of philosophy could not, in our eyes, possibly have believed the fables its inhabitants may have handed down for the fun of it. But the incompatibility is ours; we have attributed it to the Greeks in order that it concur with our stereotyped images of them as inventors of philosophy and geometry, as masters of harmony, balance, and reason—as if the Greeks had been the first and the only ones to have followed such a path, as though their exceptional intelligence had placed them beyond irrational apprehension.[40]

Truth to tell, we have no idea how the Greeks themselves might have read their own myths; at the most, we might surmise that their reading would have evolved toward what Robert Graves calls "philosophical allegory," the term he uses to characterize Hesiod's cosmogony, which, he claims, is no longer a "true myth."[41] But so restrictive is Graves's definition of a true myth that it does not apply, strictly speaking, to any of the writings that have come down to us from antiquity.[42] Be they "true" or "false," we are obliged to reckon with the stories at our disposal. And even though Hesiod, in the prelude to his *Theogony*, tells the muses, "We know enough to make up lies /

---

39. Jean-Pierre Vernant, "Genèse du monde, naissance des dieux, royauté céleste," in Hesiod, *Théogonie, La naissance des dieux* (Paris: Rivages, 1993), p. 7.
40. This is, in a broad sense, the thesis developed by Edith Hamilton in her popular collection, *Mythology* (Boston: Little Brown, 1942).
41. Robert Graves, *The Greek Myths*, vol. 1, (New York: Penguin Books, 1960), p. 12.
42. Ibid., p.12. "True myth may be defined as the reduction to narrative shorthand of ritual mime performed on the public festivals, and in many cases recorded pictorially on temple walls, vases, seals, bowls, mirrors, chests, shields, tapestries and the like." For a broader view, see Paul Veyne, *Les Grecs ont-ils cru à leurs mythes* (Paris: Seuil, 1983).

Which are not convincing, but we also have / The skill, when we've a mind, to speak the truth" (v. 28), we are not dealing here with *the* philosophical truth as defined in the introduction to this book. Hesiod appears to be following faithfully in the footsteps of a certain narrative tradition, without giving us any indication of the significance of his fabulous stories in his own eyes. The question of whether or not the poet "believes his tale" is finally of small importance. What is important is that he considers it appropriate to tell the tale, and to devote all his talent to the telling. As for the rest, we must admit that we are "in the presence of a manner of thought foreign to our habitual categories: it is at once mythical and learned, poetic and abstract, narrative and systematic, traditional and personal."[43]

We do know that Plato did not take this kind of fable lightly; he deplored that the gods were disrespectfully represented and saddled with human defects. Generally speaking, even during classical times, the Greeks took religion seriously, as testified by the trial of Socrates and the case of Alcibiades, who, under suspicion of having mutilated statues of Hermes, was forced to flee Athens to avoid the justice of his fellow citizens despite the fact that they would soon have need of his talents as a strategist. Of particular gravity was his lack of respect for the tutelary gods: to neglect the protective divinities of the city was to neglect the city itself and above and beyond all belief in the "reality" of the Olympian world, to break the founding pact that bound the citizens together, which was bodied forth in the ceremony of sacrifice. In the Greek city-state, religious ceremonies were eminently political in nature. Though it may not be forbidden to find amusement in the misadventures of the gods—to Plato's great displeasure—the sacred itself could not be mocked with impunity; that which held the community together must be respected.

The world of the gods designates the sphere that falls beyond the knowledge and the will of men.[44] The mythological story tells what we mortals, in our certain, rational knowledge, cannot know; where reason recognizes its limits, tradition takes over. Once it has gone beyond this point, the spirit strays into that which the Greeks most abhor: immoderation (*hubris*). In reshaping this tradition to suit itself, mythology illustrates in poetic, even fabulous terms that which reason may attempt to imagine about the unknowable. As it does so, it informs a vision of the world and of the origins of that world which is not without its inner rationality, and which

43. Vernant, loc. cit., p. 8
44. Hannah Arendt, in *Willing*, vol. 2 of *The Life of the Mind*, one-volume edition (New York: Harcourt Brace Jovanovich, 1981), p. 3, goes so far as to assert that the faculty of will does not exist among the Greeks.

makes it possible for humankind to find its place in the world and govern itself accordingly. It is in this sense that we may speak of true mythological knowledge, which reveals a conception of the universe that is not Greek alone but that, beginning with Greece, impregnates to a greater or lesser extent all the cultures that draw inspiration from it—just as Greece had drawn nourishment from the traditions of other peoples.

But to reduce mythical speech (*mythos*) to a particular kind of knowledge, especially one which is "against" or complementary to logical speech (*logos*) is to create skewed perspectives. In Hesiod's day, *mythos* and *logos* were part and parcel of the same expression, simultaneously narrative, religious and poetic, and endowed with reason. In this regard, expression, in the shape of myth and inseparable from worship, speaks the truth and bodies forth the divine, mediating between men and gods. It is the locus of a necessary encounter, whose meaning we moderns are no longer capable of grasping.[45]

It remains to be seen whether myths (the Greeks' or anyone else's) transmit, unbeknownst to those who transmit them, general, timeless verities on that portion of the human soul which for most is concealed from consciousness. Psychoanalysis has long argued that this is so; the reaction of mythologists has been one of overt suspicion. Against psychoanalytical interpretation they invoke several arguments: a considerable part of Greek mythology transposes political and historical events; poets have misread the myths they repeat. Some mythological episodes are little more than pure diversion. But myth is, above all, a way of opening onto the world and onto the divine—*theophaneia*—not the psyche turning in upon itself.[46] None of this can prevent a part of the meaning from eluding the storyteller's grasp and remaining embedded in the narration, right down to the "errors" it may contain. If the stories of the ancients, like those of the so-called primitive peoples, intrigue us to this day; if they are undergoing a renewal of interest to which psychoanalysis is certainly no stranger, it is perhaps because they touch in us, beyond their particular and circumstantial aspects, those more enduring areas of darkness, those half-muffled resonances to which the ancients were probably better attuned than we are.

Our tendency to dismiss myth as mere folklore is a way of relegating to the shadows a considerable part of their wealth. At minimum, we are highly reluctant to reconcile philosophy and mythology because of our reluctance to

---

45. See Walter F. Otto, *L'esprit de la religion grecque ancienne*, Theophania (original German edition in 1975), trans. J. Lauxerois and Cl. Roëls (Berg International, 1995).
46. Graves, op cit., pp. 12, 17. See also Otto, op cit., p. 33.

accept the latter as a narrative capable of transmitting meaning. This most modern of reservations would seem to obscure our reading and to limit its scope rather arbitrarily. It cannot be repeated often enough: every mythological story, "deformed" or not, "well" or "badly" passed on, is intelligible in proportion to the effort extended to read it, whether or not that reading concurs—though we will never know—with those of the Greeks themselves, from one era to another.

In a rousing tale, interspersed with lengthy genealogical digressions, Hesiod relates an "immense myth of sovereignty."[47] The myth itself is preceded by an address to the muses, and opens with a cosmogony antedating the birth of the Titans and the Olympians. First born is *Chaos* (Yawning), then *Gaia* (Earth) and *Eros* (Love), "the loveliest of the immortal gods" (v. 120).[48] Chaos gives birth to *Erebos* (The Covered) and *Nyx* (Night) who, great with her union with *Erebos*, gives birth to *Ether* (Bright Flash) and *Hemera* (Day). Meanwhile, Gaia brings forth *Ouranos* (Heavens), "equal to herself," in such fashion as he may "conceal and envelop her fully" and ensure a "stable dwelling place" for the happy gods, then brings forth *Ourana* (Mountains), *Pontus* (Swelling Sea), *Oceanus* (Deep Whirling) and several other offspring, including Kronos, the youngest, and his sister Rhea, who will become his spouse (v. 116–154). The role of *Eros* is not clear; we do know that he "makes men weak" and that he "overpowers the clever mind, and tames / The spirit in the breasts of men and gods" (v. 121–122). No one can escape him, and everything indicates that Gaia and Ouranos succumb to his power. Too much so. In fact, this outburst of procreation occurs "without pleasant love" (v. 133), insists the poet:

> And these most awful sons of Earth and Heaven
> Were hated by their father from the first.
> As soon as each was born, Ouranos hid
> The child in a secret hiding-place in Earth
> And would not let it come to see the light,
> And he enjoyed this wickedness. But she,
> Vast Earth, being strained and stretched inside her, groaned.
> And then she thought of a clever, evil plan,
> Quickly she made grey adamant, and formed

47. Vernant, loc. cit., p. 8.
48. Hesiod, *Theogony [and] Works and Days, [by] Hesiod; [and] Elegies [of] Theogonis*, trans. Dorothea Wender, ed. Betty Radice (Harmondsworth: Penguin, 1973), p. 27.

> A mighty sickle, and addressed her sons,
> Urging them on with sorrow in her heart.
>
> (v. 154–160)[49]

There can be little doubt that her thoughts are directed at Ouranos, and that the intent of those thoughts is to emasculate him.

The first generation of gods, the Titans, are born to the hatred of the male parent, both the hatred he feels toward his own children, and that which he inspires in them and in their mother. Mother and offspring grumble about the evil, stifling power of an insatiable, possessive, and jealous fornicator who stands in the way of progress. At the same time, this incessant distention has caused the Earth to swell to the bursting point. Kronos, the youngest son, dares to execute his mother's will. He seizes the saw-toothed scimitar and harvests the genitals of a "Father [who] first thought of shameful acts" (v. 171). The blood from the wound is spilled upon the Earth, and its spattering gives birth to the Erinnyes, the Giants, and the Nymphs. Kronos casts the genitalia of Ouranos far out to sea where, mingling with the sea foam, they give birth to Aphrodite.

The castration of the male parent is essential since, by forcing his children to remain within the influence of their mother, Ouranos demonstrates his incapacity to be a father. Far from assuming his paternity, he behaves like a suckling child—he is, after all, the son of the Earth that he has impregnated—who refuses to pull away from his mother's teat for even a moment, who grasps the entire world to himself in a thirst of suspicious possession, preoccupied with all that might threaten him. Ouranos is the first prisoner of his own obsession, yet the filial slash liberates him: henceforth, he may reign and dispose his splendor high above the Earth instead of choking it. Thus from the double conflicts of man-woman and father-son emerge the beginnings of harmony, in which the fundamental elements, Earth, Heavens, and Love, each find their true place. Love, as distinct from possession, must be consorted with at a healthy distance so as not to become involved, nor to involve lovers, in hatred. From this day on, the Earth may breathe freely under the governorship of Kronos, prince of Titans.

For all that, the established order remains, like its new master, unstable. Terrified that one of his children will visit upon him the treatment he has inflicted upon his own father, Kronos devours them one after another, at birth. Only Zeus, whom his mother replaces with a rock wrapped in

---

49. Ibid., p. 28.

swaddling, escapes his father's voracity and finds refuge in Crete. Upon reaching maturity, he brings his father to drink a potion that forces him to vomit his brothers and sisters. Assuming the leadership of the second generation of gods, Olympian Zeus throws himself into a lengthy combat against Kronos, in which he emerges the final victor. Kronos and the Titans who fought alongside him go down in defeat, and are assigned under close guard to the precincts beneath the earth, in the shadowy realm of Tartarus, from which they will never again emerge.

Zeus owes his victory not primarily to his technical superiority, the mastery of lightning, but to his political wisdom. *Metieta Zeus* (v. 56, *passim*), that is, literally, "Zeus, full of *metis* [cunning and intelligence]," promises all those who take his side that he will respect their rank and bestow upon them the honors that they deserve. So it is that he rescues from the dungeons where Kronos has kept locked away the Cyclops and the Hundred-Handed Ones (Gyges, Cottos, and Obriares), who will bring him victory. Perspicacity notwithstanding, the master of Olympus is far from immune to a change of fortune like that which he has himself inflicted upon his own father. The infernal cycle that makes each new generation a threat to the preceding one must be broken.

The threat is made all the greater by Zeus's marriage to none other than Metis herself: Cunning and Intelligence personified. To her he owes his final triumph. Now, suddenly, she is great with a child who may turn out to be a mortal danger. To avoid repeating the cycle of paternal deglutition, Zeus swallows his life-partner, "put her down into his belly, so that the goddess would counsel him in both good and evil plans" (v. 899), and, in so doing, appropriates her intelligence. Athena, with whom Metis was pregnant, springs fully armed from her father's head, and will be his favored child, a chaste warrior goddess, the embodiment of justice, science, and reason. The episode sums up and brings to a close a lengthy course of development, which, in Greek mythology, runs from the all-powerful Earth Mother to the predominance of the father, itself held within certain bounds. For such predominance to be possible, the male must tear himself away from the female; must suffer the castration that tears him from the maternal breast; must take upon himself the properties of his consort. In other words, he must draw a distinction between the nursing mother and the wife whose power he consumes in such a manner as to fear no longer the children he has sired on her. But he must also accept that his domination cannot be absolute. Zeus is neither omnipotent nor omnipresent; thanks to his discernment, he has been able to establish a sustainable order acceptable to the inhabitants of

Olympus, among whom he will henceforth stand as uncontested arbiter. The relationship between the gods has been settled once and for all. Such is the cosmic order under which two closely related questions are laid before men: that of existence, and that of knowledge.

The two questions find an answer in the nature of the relationships established between gods and men. Such is the subject matter of the myth of *Prometheus* ("Forethought," as opposed to his brother *Epimetheus*, "Afterthought"). Curiously, Hesiod places the Prometheus episode before the story of the war between the Olympians and the Titans. The poet had probably intended to illustrate that the two orders, celestial and earthly, are indissociable; or that Zeus, wishing to keep Prometheus (who, unlike Atlas, has chosen the Olympian camp) on his side, has permitted him to act in favor of men, a race Zeus holds in low esteem, and whose advent he will do everything he can to discourage. The human species—creatures of Prometheus—disturbs the Olympian order and comes about under the sign of trickery. After having attempted to allay Zeus's suspicions in a sacrificial arbitration which he falsifies in order to put aside the greater portion of the slaughtered bull for humankind, Prometheus brings them fire against the divine will. For these two successive infractions, he is chained to the rock where the eagle swoops down each day to tear at his liver.

But once again men will suffer most grievously for Prometheus's exploits. Zeus, pretending to step into the trap, chooses only the fatty bones, abandoning to humanity the meat which Prometheus has hidden beneath the offal, for the lord of Olympus has foreseen a way "to punish mortal men in future days" (v. 551–552). Prometheus's division of the spoils allows the gods to draw nourishment from the broth of the grilled fat that better suits them as immortals, and leaves to men the putrescible meat that will henceforth provide them with their mortal fare. Zeus, taking revenge upon men for acquiring the fire which has made it henceforth possible to cook the meat they have been fraudulently given a share of, sends them the most desirable of all women, whose foolishness, mischievousness, and idleness are equalled only by her beauty. From that moment on, the male is forever condemned to unstinting toil in order to satisfy her capricious will. In *Works and Days*, Hesiod gives her a name: Pandora. It is she who opens the jar— the famous Pandora's Box—in which Prometheus had taken such care to lock away all the spites (old age, labor, sickness, insanity, vice, and passion) which, released by feminine curiosity, will henceforth plague humankind. But along with the sad lot, thanks to Prometheus's foresight, we find delusive hope, whose falsehoods keep men from committing collective suicide.[50] The original intention of Prometheus has been nothing less than to give men knowledge (fire) without the unhappiness that comes with it (the jar of all spites). His immoderation lies in wishing to make the human race equal to that of the gods. In opposing divine will, humanity's benefactor is transformed into the unwitting instrument of the curse that will befall it.

The world has no demiurge, no creator. The Earth Mother, Gaia, alone with Eros before the Yawning Chasm, appears to bear within her womb the entire universe to come, since she has brought forth Heaven, and all depends upon her copulation with him. But Chaos, the Yawning, is not pure nothingness: from its depths rise not only the shades and the night, but also the day and the light. From the beginning, opposites act upon one another and mutually give birth to one another. From the confrontation of opposites, Heraclitus will say three centuries later, the most beautiful harmonies are born. Chaos as an idea, as primordial echoing emptiness, is echoed in the notion of the "boundless" (*apeiron*) so beloved of Anaximander, the first Greek philosopher of whom something has come down to us, a fragment of such extreme concentration that, even today, it continues to generate new interpretations:

> (To that they return when they are destroyed) of necessity; for he says that they suffer punishment and give satisfaction to one another for injustice.[51]

All that is defined, all that is engendered, notes Nietzsche, is fated to vanish; only the indeterminate may pretend to the permanence of being, and "all Becoming as a punishable emancipation from eternal 'Being' is a wrong that is to be atoned for by destruction."[52]

We cannot exclude the possibility that Hesiod composed his *Theogony* as the story of a single moment fated to fall back to primordial chaos, outside of time. Still and withal, his poem illustrates, one feels, a certain world order of which Zeus is both the craftsman and the guarantor—though not necessarily the creator. Far from adopting the logic of conflict or of withering away, Hesiod prefers to underline the sterility of conflictual repetition that Zeus, totally at odds with his predecessors, manages to escape. The conflict

---

50. Graves, op. cit., p. 145.

51. The portion following the parentheses is the only fragment of a sentence left by Anaximander himself.

52. Friedrich Nietzsche, *Philosophy in the Tragic Age of the Greeks in Early Greek Philosophy & Other Essays* (in German), trans. Maximilliam A. Mügge (London: T. N. Foulis, 1911), p. 93.

is productive only insofar as it opens onto some prospect other than mimetic reproduction.

In such an organization of the world, men are of practically no value, and appear on the whole as undesirable, as objects, at best, of the rivalry between Zeus and Prometheus. They suffer nonetheless from the overweening self-assurance (*hubris*) of a champion whom they have not chosen, an indication of the rather modest stature that is theirs in the order of things. Against his will, Prometheus indicates to men the limits inherent in their condition, for which they are not responsible. Their only fault may have been succumbing to Pandora's charms. But those charms, willed by Zeus, are insurmountable. Though we may find in her a touch of Eve's seductiveness, there is not a shred of guilt. The curse clearly falls from on high: only after Epimetheus, Prometheus's brother and husband of Pandora, experiences a fainting spell does she open her fateful jar. Subjugated by the desire awakened by beauty, men are little more than the unconscious assemblers of their own misfortunes. But nothing indicates that these misfortunes could have been avoided.

Knowledge is a trap, of which Prometheus and Epimetheus are the two jaws. The first, for all his foresight, takes too great a risk, and the second flings himself forward dizzyingly. In reality, the two brothers are one: in tearing from the gods a portion of their knowledge and power, Prometheus unwittingly opens the doors to evil. The fire he steals from Zeus plays, all things considered, the role of the apple in Genesis; it throws light upon the poverty and the finiteness of men. But his deed, at the same time, is the establishing stroke of the species. By the theft of fire, Prometheus creates humanity, for it is by cooking flesh to eat and learning to know that man distinguishes himself from animals. The knowledge thus acquired is fatal: to be even a small part of the divine plunges man into distress. Man cannot escape the thirst to know, to understand, and this unquenchable desire leads him to his downfall. Knowledge is, above all, the certainty of death, which is unbearable awareness. The only use of hope is to make bearable the terrifying. Stirring this pathetic ingredient into the gruel of Pandorean calamity can only mean, for Hesiod, that man must endure the hostility of the gods.

It is all well and good that man, according to Genesis, has been expelled from the kingdom of innocence and driven just as brutally into that of knowledge, but YHWH does not let him out of his sight. The god of the Torah bears no grudge against man except out of frustration, which is clearly the frustration of man himself at realizing how inferior he is to the Principle that should guide him. Where man, in Hesiod, resigns himself to misfortune, he of Genesis does everything he can to thwart it—unsuccessfully, it must be said. From failure to failure, YHWH remains at his side for as long as he does not abandon the effort: perhaps one day man will no longer cause YHWH to despair of justice. For Hesiod, justice, or more precisely the balance of forces that clash in the world, exists only of and for the gods. Nothing forbids men from drawing inspiration from them in an attempt to avoid, if not conflicts, at least the unending repetition of the mimesis that threatens all societies. Nor can anything protect them from the decrepitude they are wont to paper over with false hope.

No lesson of wisdom can be easily gleaned from Hesiod's tale. As a poetic narrative of the world or as a myth of sovereignty, *Theogony* is quite at the antipodes of the normative rigor and the fixation on identity that runs through and informs the Torah. Like Homer, Hesiod toys with the elements and myths for the greater pleasure of men—Greek men, for the Greeks may well have believed themselves closer to the gods than any other people ... Let us simply say: these men who appear to have had the misfortune of being nothing more than human console themselves in the knowledge that they are Greeks. Measure and excess in the same breath—a representation intended for the use of people well satisfied with themselves and at peace with their origins. The Jews, on the other hand, have written the peregrinations of a people whose origins are marked with pain, and which never rises to its ambitions. Among the Greeks of Hesiod's day, immortality is inaccessible to all but the heroes—by the voice of those who tell the tale. For the Jews, immortality is the law, constant object of ridicule, constantly demanding to be accomplished. The hero is the Book, and it remains eternally unfinished.

There exist, however, two closely related elements in Genesis and Hesiod's *Theogony*: both posit the transmission of knowledge of misfortune via woman; both are gloriously unconcerned by the hereafter; both are rooted exclusively in life itself, Genesis in a much more down-to-earth, much more human manner, in all the rawness of the term; while *Theogony* takes leave of the human world, which Hesiod takes up in *Works and Days*. In it, man is not the master of his fate, let alone the master of the world. We do not find this detachment in Genesis, where YHWH does his utmost to make man responsible for his acts, including making him pay a stiff price for his initial ignorance. This price has its compensation: the responsibility man claims for himself places him in possession of nature, which is henceforth entrusted to his care.

Differences trump similarities. We find ourselves placed before two conceptions of the world, and of humanity, that are almost perfectly contradictory, and which Christendom will vainly attempt to reconcile. Christendom would like to reformulate the Judaic undertaking in terms of the Greek spirit; it goes without saying that this attempt was to give rise to something entirely different. The Judaic undertaking was to emerge altered beyond recognition, transformed by the expectation of individual salvation, which, in the Torah at least, is an utterly foreign concept. From Greece, Christianity would retain the feeling of superiority, but transpose it to the world at large. The Greeks may very well have considered themselves the cream of all peoples, but they also knew that as human beings they accounted for little, and were certainly not the masters of nature. The impossible marriage that produced Christendom is clearly not without consequence for us today. From Hellenism we have taken certainty, but without a sense of measure. From Judaism we have taken the will to mastery, but without doubt. Of the Greek spirit we have abandoned the gratuitous and the polysemic, in the name of an anthropomorphic monotheism in contradiction to all that is most abstract, most demanding, and most "modern" in Judaism: the intricate, virtually inexpressible expression of the Principle by which man makes himself responsible for his own law. If the test of knowledge has meaning, it is this meaning above all.

It remains to be seen whether this is the law that man believes he has been given, or whether it is man himself who is also, and above all, responding to a secret law of which he is not the master. The irremediable fracture that separates mortals from immortals led the Greeks to a wrenching conception of knowledge that was to find its deepest expression in tragedy.

5

KNOWLEDGE AS INNER DRAMA

O F ALL THE literature of antiquity, Greek tragedy (Aeschylus, Sophocles, Euripides) has produced those voices nearest to the modern sensibility. Among them, Œdipus and Antigone, as developed by Sophocles, stand out. Like Homer, Sophocles draws freely from the immense reservoir of mythology. One of the most ancient myths, that of Œdipus, may have illustrated the ritual murder of the king by him who would be named (or would become by virtue of his act) the successor. In this ritual, the new king was considered the son of the figure he was replacing, whose widow he would marry. This monstrous affair, involving parricide and incest, is little more than a "bad" reading of the Greek classics themselves, of a story long separated from the forgotten rite it illustrated.[53] But these are considerations best left to the anthropologists. The Œdipus, who ranges at large through the Western imagination, and upon whom Freud drew, is that of Sophocles.

So powerfully has Freudian psychoanalysis seized upon Sophoclean tragedy that beyond its interpretational limits reading has become virtually impossible. In this interpretation, the Œdipean drama acts out the normally repressed conflict of the young child (primarily male) between the admiring mimesis of his father, whose support he craves, and the unutterable desire to be rid of him to take his place alongside the mother, complete with the anguish that the thought of such a terrifying prospect entails. Freud's Œdipus is not simply the illustration of a theory of infantile sexuality; it makes manifest, at the same time, the universality to which the theory aspires, employing analytical terms to explain a permanent feature of the human psyche already present in ancient mythology. It must be noted here that anthropological denial, which would have the original myth refer to the ritual

53. Robert Graves, *The Greek Myths*, 105:2–3, vol. 2 (New York: Penguin Books, 1960), p. 13.

of succession, cannot be used as an argument against Freud, for it would point to the contrary: that the rite itself, in transforming the murderer into the symbolic son of the murdered king, is grounded entirely in this fundamental structure. It is common knowledge to what extent the father of psychoanalysis was haunted, both theoretically and practically, by the murder of the symbolic father.

Without wishing to become involved in the debate over the *psychoanalytical* pertinence of Freud's use of Œdipus, let us scrutinize what his version, for all its depth, ends up pushing aside, what it ultimately erases from Sophocles's tragedy. Freud's intention, in setting the tragedy within the precincts of the subconscious, was to suggest a deeper reading; so successful was his attempt that today no one, not even the most dedicated anti-Freudian mythologists, can ignore it. But at the same time, this deeper reading threatens to overshadow that which is extraneous or that which undercuts the Freudian concept of infantile sexuality. In the fate that psychoanalysis has assigned to Sophocles's tragedy we find the strongest possible evidence of the reductive impact of any interpretation when it becomes repetitive and fixed, and particularly when it is used to sustain a theoretical position. Examining the tragedy of Œdipus in the light of knowledge allows us to free ourselves of theoretical shackles and to restore the story to its rightful place, without sacrificing what we have learned from applying the tools of analysis.

Knowledge, in Sophocles's *King Œdipus*, turns on the question of the return, which, because it is clandestine, is quite at odds with that of the *Odyssey*. Unlike Ulysses, Œdipus is unaware of his identity, and does everything in his power to avoid returning home. Still, that is precisely where he ends up, without knowing it. Ulysses knows where he is going, even though he is not necessarily going there as he would have wished. Œdipus, believing that he has arrived at his destination, comes to a halt in the very place which he sought to flee. Both are threatened in their positions of king and husband. Ulysses knows it, recognizes his vulnerability, and takes action accordingly. Œdipus seems to be firmly seated atop the throne that he will lose, lulled by a power whose tenuousness he cannot grasp.

As Sophocles's tragedy opens, Œdipus gives every indication of success: his wisdom has led him to triumph over the Sphinx, and to the throne of Thebes which he has freed from the clutches of the monster, and to wed Jocasta the queen. Once again, he is preparing to deliver the city from the evil that has afflicted it. Only one obstacle lies across his path, which will become apparent later: Œdipus has killed, in the narrow defile between Delphi and Daulis, an old man and his servants who, from their chariot, attempted to push him violently from their path and to the roadside. The tragedy opens when, several years into Œdipus's happy reign, Thebes is ravaged by a plague. The king soon learns from the Oracle at Delphi that the affliction will last until the city is cleansed of the "defiling thing," meaning the killer or killers of King Laius, Œdipus's predecessor. Unaware that Laius, whom he had known only by name, had been assassinated, the hero expresses his surprise:

> Œdipus.   But when royalty had fallen what troubles could have hindered search?
>
> Creon.   The ridding Sphinx put those dark things out of our thoughts—we thought of what had come to our own doors.
>
> Œdipus.   But I will start afresh and make the dark things plain.[54]

From that moment on an implacable police investigation begins, in the course of which Œdipus returns unconsciously to his origins. Not only is he ignorant of his own roots, he is unaware that he has set out in search of them. It is only when it appears that Laius may well be the old man whom he killed long ago at the crossroads does Œdipus begin to grasp the danger that the investigation may implicate him, without suspecting that the victim was his genetic father. Furthermore, the two events do not correspond perfectly, for the only servant to survive the incident has always claimed that there was more than one killer. A messenger from Corinth then arrives, and announces that the aged King Polybus, whom Œdipus has always believed to be his father, has died of sickness, and that the people of the Isthmus are now summoning him to the throne as his successor.

Once more, just as everything is about to fall apart, fate seems to smile upon the hero, who stands poised to wear two crowns. More importantly, the good news has undermined the authority of the oracles, to which he need no longer pay heed, and which would seem to relegate the murder of Laius to the background. But Œdipus's impiety is not absolute (in contrast to that of Jocasta, who invites him to mock the oracles). Something is hindering Œdipus from returning to Corinth: the fear of marrying his mother. The messenger hastens to reassure him: neither Polybus nor his wife is his true parent. Once again, Œdipus's world is shaken. The revelation brings him back, in a manner of speaking, to his original starting point: to his youth in

---

54. Sophocles, *King Œdipus*, trans. W. B. Yeats, ed. Balachandra Rajan (Toronto: Macmillan, 1969), p. 59.

Corinth, where a drunken guest had one day cast aspersions upon his ancestry. Despite the indignant protests of his parents, Œdipus had set out for Delphi to consult Apollo. Revealing nothing of his origins, the Oracle had prophesied abominations, which should have been sufficient to prevent him forever from returning home. Now, unwittingly, the messenger has set in motion the implacable mechanism that will lead Œdipus to the discovery of his true, and monstrous, identity.

Beyond parricide and incest, *King Œdipus* lays before us the tragedy of truth. Œdipus travels to Delphi to learn the truth. The Oracle's sinister truth, holding him far from Corinth, sets him in ways obscure upon the path of his true origins. As much as the murder of his unknown father, it is the discovery of the Sphinx's truth, the solution of the enigma, which opens his bed to his unknown mother and places him in possession of the throne of Thebes. The Freudian masterstroke is to have transformed his ignorance into a metaphor for the subconscious. But in Freud, the metaphor has fallen upon the wrong subject. That which the child ignores or represses, in the Freudian Œdipus, is not the identity of its parents, but the nature and the scope of its own urges. As he flees Apollo's dark predictions, Sophocles's Œdipus, supposing that the Oracle has conveyed to him his unconscious desires, attempts to repress them, but his effort fails, for the protagonist mistakes the mortal thrust of the urges that he holds in check.

Because he himself has been ignored, in the most virulent sense of the term, because he has been rejected by those who brought him into the world, Œdipus is unable to recognize them. In sending him to his death, his biological parents have abdicated their parentage. His true parents are those who took him in, made him theirs, and reared him. The unconscious return of the protagonist to his biological point of origin is nothing more than the return of the fault to its source. It is here that the oracle's fulfilled prophesy takes on its full meaning: by the horror his revelation creates, Apollo treacherously enjoins Œdipus to go exactly where he dreads going the most, and to punish his biological parents in a manner he does not even suspect. Far more devastating than the riddle of the Sphinx, which the hero easily solves, is the divine enigma, which thrusts him unknowingly onto the path of an unbearable truth. If the fault lies with Laius and Jocasta, the tragedy is nonetheless that of Œdipus, blinded by the light that, from beginning to end, he has, more than anyone else, helped shed. Beneath the repeated blows Œdipus deals himself with the brooches he has torn from the dead body of Jocasta, it is truth itself which, literally, puts out his eyes as it rips with one fell swoop the veil that protected his borrowed happiness.

The truth, the truth that Œdipus so tragically lays bare, is that he is not himself. Not only is he not the son of his parents, not only has he been, for all these years, a stranger to his own deeds, but his good fortune, his grandeur, his family, his fame, all are imposture, his accomplishments a succession of atrocious misunderstandings which his loftiness of spirit would not permit him to avoid. All at once he finds himself a stranger to his place of birth (Corinth), and native of the foreign land he governs. At his most intimate proximity lies the abomination he was convinced he had driven from his path. Unlike Ulysses, who had never for an instant doubted that the cause of his misfortunes lay outside himself, and who fought atrocity by blinding his adversary, Œdipus discovers the adversary within himself and punishes himself for this terrible discovery by blinding himself:

> Œdipus.　O! O! all brought to pass! All truth! Now, O light, may I look my last upon you, having been found accursed in bloodshed, accursed in marriage, and in my coming into the world, accursed![55]

The light he no longer wishes to see is that which he proudly vaunted in the face of Tiresias's blindness when he rejected the soothsayer's warnings:

> Tiresias.　Though you have your sight you cannot see in what misery you stand ... for do you know the stock you come of—you have been your own kin's enemy, be they living or be they dead.[56]

Truth has no connection with light; it is invisible to the eye. The blind, who are not dazzled by the brilliance of things, know this better than anyone else. Œdipus, that all-powerful solver of enigmas, the man who is greater than himself, has allowed himself to be trapped by the game of intelligence, has believed that he could escape his fate. In his flight a certain fear can be discerned, though, a kind of religious respect for the Oracle, which vanishes at the very moment when, confronted with the news of his father's peaceful death, the hero believes he has cheated it. It is at this instant, at the summit of his glory, that fate finally catches up with him, and informs him by the mouth of this selfsame messenger that he is not the son of those who adopted him. In Sophocles as in Homer, fate is more powerful than man, and that which we moderns call will is powerless. Ulysses, at least, knows it and, in

---

55. Sophocles, *King Œdipus*, Ibid., p. 92.
56. Sophocles, *King Œdipus*, Ibid., p. 67.

a certain sense, acts accordingly. Not simply because he is particularly intelligent (as is Œdipus) but because it has never crossed his mind, not even in the Cyclops's cave, not even in his descent into the dominions of Hades, to doubt himself. Necessity, for him, is that which he must accept and at the same time confront. Œdipus hopes to elude necessity, and it is here, not so much in his flight itself, but in the false sense of security it creates, that he reveals immoderation, or, if we prefer, lack of awareness.

By fleeing his origins, that is to say, that which he firmly believes to be his family and his homeland, Œdipus turns away from himself. Dramatically, he carries out what every person must sooner or later: cut the umbilical cord, leave the family hearth behind. This he does, however, to radical excess. This too, is where he commits the error; the graver error without which, argues Aristotle, he would not be a tragic figure.[57] Rather than delving into the Oracle's meaning, and inquiring into an identity—his own—against which the doubts that motivated his voyage to Delphi weighed so heavily, he could no longer care about his parents. In so doing, he illustrates in dramatic terms what happens to all of us in our ignorance: we forget our earliest infancy.

Such is the state of ignorance in which Œdipus finds himself at the crossroads where the rest of his life is decided, when he meets and kills his biological father: an act of legitimate self-defense against the man who, as he sees it, in a dark return of the repressed, has attempted for a second time to eliminate the son who will bring about his destruction. In wishing to push aside from his path him who has returned, for all his efforts, to haunt him and to claim vengeance, the murderous father brings upon himself the death sentence he once believed he could escape. There can be no clearer way of stating that at the heart of the criminal act lies punishment, that punishment is embedded in the immoderation that has brought it about. Œdipus's fault lies not in having killed the father who has made himself unworthy of the name, but in having acted in such a way as to allow the true dimensions of his act to escape him. *King Œdipus* is the tragedy of ignorance: the fatal error it plays out is the dark desire not to know. The scene of the Sphinx, in which we can detect an encounter no less decisive than that which lays Thebes and his mother's bed before him, now appears in all its contemptible truth: the answer to the enigma is contemptible in light of the knowledge that the hero has concealed from himself, which is of the greatest possible concern to him.

All of us, to a greater or lesser extent, become strangers to ourselves when we lose contact with our primordial experience, a loss that can be

---

57. Aristotle, *Poetics*, 1453a.

attributed to the hardship and tribulations of acquiring knowledge. Like Œdipus, we prefer to leave our memories of it in the shadow. It is as though leaving behind the cradle of childhood has insulated us from the drama that was played out there, and which is more than likely to be played out in other scenes of our lives.

The irremediable distance that Œdipus has ventured when confronted with the prophecy becomes apparent, upon reflection, as the visible manifestation of the fear we all feel at the thought of returning to the drives, the conflicts, and the primordial anguish of our earliest years. But distance itself, flight, and forgetting, instead of rescuing us, transforms us into the most dangerous, most painful, most difficult to solve of all enigmas. Like it or not, the enigma is at work deep within us, deep in the shadows of that which we have forgotten, which Freud calls the subconscious. No sun can shine light upon it. No social success can ever protect us against the return— always a possibility—of that which has been buried deep in oblivion, of that truth which the Greek language so well describes as *alétheia*, meaning non-oblivion, and revelation of the forgotten. Nothing, neither power nor fortune nor even intelligence, can guarantee anyone that one day he will not be forced to undertake Œdipus's terrible journey toward his own dark truth, and to rue the day of his birth.

Sophocles expresses the spectre of an inevitability even more devastating than in Homer, because of its secret nature. Ulysses can easily read the outward signs of the gods. Œdipus is confronted, in the person of the Oracle, with an inner anguish he cannot decipher, but which time and the unpredictable will shortly force him to confront. Freud was not wrong in being fascinated by a myth that displays the full fragility of the ego. But his reduction of it to the famous "Œdipus complex"—whether Freud intended to do so or not—tends to push aside that which a reading of Sophocles leads: a certain modesty before the enigmatic nature of the subject itself. This reduction can be attributed to the general pretension of a certain type of science to install floodlights in the vaults of the subconscious. We moderns would like myth to assist us in curing ourselves of the unknown, and to protect us from the unforeseen. We are like Œdipus before he is driven to blind himself.

The psychoanalytic interpretation—which the reader will have understood, I trust, can be distinguished from a psychoanalytical or psychological practice that claims to be the science of the soul—is clearly not the only one possible. The tragedy of *King Œdipus* is also political: the king can only remain as head of the city-state as long as his personal ascendancy coincides with the interests of his fellow citizens. Œdipus is summoned to govern Thebes because he has saved it. And it is because he neglects the duty of self-knowledge, taken up as he is with his fortune and his reputation, that the plague gnawing away at him from within begins to spread within the body politic, and ultimately forces him to abandon power and the city itself. If his downfall is complete, it is because man can only live with dignity in his capacity as a citizen. Œdipus, precisely because he is king, has no intrinsic worth; his only worth lies in his ties with the polity from which his blindness finally banishes him. His very banishment, despite the atrocity that surrounds it, possesses a noble quality in that, almost without faltering, Œdipus will have fulfilled his duty as first citizen, at the cost of self-sacrifice. In so doing he makes amends for the impiety and the wilfulness of his biological father, King Laius, who has already deceived the Oracle into sending off to death his own son whom, the Oracle had warned him, he could not engender except at the risk of his own end. Œdipus has none of his father's cowardice. Faced with the emergence of the truth that he had for so long attempted to push aside from his path, he no longer hesitates. The more convinced he becomes that the truth he is approaching will destroy him, the more ferocious becomes his desire to know. Surely it is this political integrity, right down to its bleakest misfortune, that will enable Sophocles much later, in *Œdipus at Colonus*, to grant his protagonist, for all the resentment writhing within him, an honorable, near-miraculous end, and to make his tomb a sacred place. In discovering the other identity lurking deep within himself and, even more importantly, in accepting that accursed part of himself, be it at the cost of his eyesight, Œdipus accomplishes an act of immense political compass, which stands forth in its full power only when we read Antigone.[58]

The relations between citizens and the polity are never simple. If *King Œdipus*, politically speaking, seems to illustrate the necessity and the grandeur of individual sacrifice to the common cause, *Antigone* suggests on the other hand that limitations should be placed on what the French call *la raison d'État*. It is not without significance that these limitations find their expression in a woman's determination. Not being a citizen, Antigone probably does not feel herself held to the same level of civic responsibility

---

58. This key aspect of my analysis I owe to the intelligence of Dario De Facendis, who presented a magisterial lecture on *King Œdipus* in a doctoral seminar directed by Isabelle Lasvergnas and myself in 1998–1999 at the Université du Québec à Montréal. A partial version was published in an earlier exposition on the same theme: "La connaissance tragique dans *Œdipe roi* de Sophocle," Université du Québec à Montréal, Département de sociologie, Groupe interuniversitaire d'étude de la postmodernité, Cahiers de recherche, no. 44 séminaire du 15 novembre 1996, pp. 1–44.

toward a community from which she is politically excluded, as would a man. Her marginal status, combined with her stature as a member of the ruling family, gives her both the audacity and the independence to flout the prince's command in the name of a higher justice. Antigone, along with Lysistrata, is one of the rare heroines of Greek literature: of course there are figures like Medea, Helen, Andromache, and Penelope, but as feminine protagonists they are principally the victims of events. In general terms, the Greek woman is an object, an object of struggle, of covetousness (flagrantly visible in the *Iliad*), or worse, an object of misfortune, like their common ancestor Pandora. Antigone is not only an exception; she is one of the loftiest figures of all Greek tragedy, a symbol of courage and justice.

The plot line is one of extreme simplicity. Antigone's two brothers, Eteocles and Polyneices, kill one another in a battle for possession of Thebes. Polyneices has besieged the city at the head of foreign troops. In relying upon the enemies of Thebes to seize power, Polyneices has placed himself outside the law. He is unworthy of the funerary honors that will be his brother's alone, and on Creon's orders is deprived of a place in the burial ground. Antigone defies the royal decree and the death that has sanctioned his trespass by carrying out upon her brother's corpse the funerary rites that will allow him to find his place among the dead. Sophocles brings into confrontation two destructive obsessions, each prepared to stop at nothing to prevail: on the one hand, absolute respect for the laws of the city; on the other, unconditional obedience to the fundamental duties dictated by fraternal love and blood ties. Between the two, the balance is an unequal one. As its title indicates, and as the treatment of the protagonists confirms, the spectator is brought to identify with the heroine and not the representative of power. Where Creon punishes and threatens death, Antigone sacrifices herself and offers her life.

In most interpretations of the drama, Antigone incarnates the superiority of unwritten law and of imprescriptible duties, over and above the respect of the law as promulgated, and even over public order. The polity may not demand of its subjects an obedience that obliges them to violate the most sacred principles even for the best of reasons. Better to die in fulfilling the precepts of divine law, in heeding the supreme voice of conscience, than to live unworthily in submission to the inequitable law of power. Antigone has become the magnificent embodiment of just rebellion, the "anti" *par excellence*, and, in a literal interpretation of her name—"in place of a mother"[59]—has become the emblem of resistance to tyranny.

In the figure of Antigone, Sophocles's "message" has been transmitted intact down through the centuries. The most beloved dramaturge of Athens, birthplace of democracy, has bestowed upon us, with the most successful of all his works, the most moving testament to what today we call human rights. In summing up its essence in these terms, we intuit that Sophocles's tragedy is not only, nor even primarily, a lesson in politics. Nor is it a hymn to fraternity. Like *King Œdipus* (apparently a later work), *Antigone* is first and foremost a tragedy, human tragedy against the untranslatable quality the Greeks called *até*: a combination of blight, misfortune, error, fault, and fatality. In the face of *até*, in the face of the fatal blindness that leads to disaster, Antigone and Creon are equal, absolutely necessary to one another. The balance is not, however, perfect. As victim, Antigone can, without becoming an irritating presence, extend her radicalism well beyond that of her tormentor, which she is quick to do.

Not for an instant does she attempt to persuade, to convince, or to reason with Creon. That is a role that Sophocles takes great pains to entrust to others: to Haemon, son of the prince and Antigone's suitor, then, with even greater force, to the blind seer Tiresias. Not only can Antigone's inflexibility be explained with regard to the tyrant, but with regard to Ismene. Even though she has been lacking in the courage to follow her sister in her challenge, as she herself quite honestly avows, Ismene, when confronted with Creon's fury, will prove her solidarity with her sister, which Antigone repulses in a hurtful way. The hurt is all the more cruel in that Ismene loves her sister to such an extent that she cannot contemplate surviving her. There is nothing for it. Antigone no longer acknowledges that she has a sister: in the course of her ultimate confrontation with Creon, she cries out:

> Thebes, and you my father's gods
> And rulers of Thebes, you see me now, the last
> Unhappy daughter of a line of kings,
> Your kings, led away to death. You will remember
> What things I suffer, and at what men's hands,
> Because I would not transgress the laws of heaven.
>
> (940–943)[60]

---

59. *Anti*, in Greek, literally means "in place of"; *gone*, "the act of childbirth."
60. Sophocles, *The Antigone*, trans. Dudley Fitts and Robert Fitzgerald (London: Oxford University Press, [1930]), p. 62.

Brutal enough as it stands, Antigone's rejection provides an arresting contrast with the words she has used to justify the conclusion of her funereal duty:

> You have touched it at last: that bridal bed
> Unspeakable horror of son and mother mingling:
> Their crime, infection of all our family!
> O Œdipus, father and brother!
> Your marriage strikes me from the grave to murder mine.
> I have been a stranger here in my own land:
> All my life
> The blasphemy of my birth has followed me.
>
> (905–915)

Blood ties prevail over loyalty to the state only insofar as they are irreplaceable. Can Ismene's friendship be any less irreplaceable? Alas, she is only a woman. And for not having quickly enough taken up Antigone's love for her brother, she loses her status as sister. All turns on love, love at its most absolute. To remain faithful to that love, Antigone is prepared to die a virgin, to forgo her capacity for childbirth—what could procreation possibly signify for a family in which the transmission of life seems henceforth accursed? Haemon, his devotion and his feelings, weighs hardly at all in the balance. And yet, it is love that overcomes him, and turns him against his father:

> Love, unconquerable
> Waster of rich men, keeper
> Of warm lights and all-night vigil
> In the soft face of a girl:
> Sea-wandered, forest visitor!
> Even the pure Immortals cannot escape you,
> And mortal man, in his one day's dusk,
> Trembles before your glory.
>
> Surely you swerve upon ruin
> The just man's consenting heart,
> As here you have made bright anger
> Strike between father and son—
> And none has conquered but Love!
> A girl's glance working the will of heaven:

> Pleasure to her alone who mocks us,
> Merciless Aphroditê.
>
> (781–800)

Aphrodite's game plays out to its implacable end: it leads straight to death, toward which Antigone, from the prologue onward, proudly flings herself (72–73), as if a voice deep within her has already been whispering what the Chorus claims on the eve of her torment: "I cannot tell / What shape your father's guilt appears in this" (855–856). Her madness, the *ate* which pursues her, is not hers. A daughter cursed, born of incestuous love, she repeats, invoking the gods; incest unavowed that only death will allow her to fulfil in full purity.

Overcome by emotion exacerbated by resistance to his authority from a woman, Creon ultimately acts out the secret desire of his niece, she who from beginning to end remains the driving force behind the tragedy. Antigone's greatness and his prideful excess combine to diminish him even in his cruelty. Under the pretext of allowing Hades to pass judgement on the young woman's fate, he permits himself to carry out her execution and orders her to be interred alive with food and drink. For all its cruelty, the delayed execution points to a certain hesitation, a secret fear that Tiresias will reveal in its full horror, indicating that the tyrant, contrary to the heroine, is not fully prepared to carry word and deed to their ultimate conclusion. Of the two principal characters, Creon is ultimately the more reasonable. He may violently reject his son's well-reasoned, impassioned pleas, not understanding that he is dispatching him to join Antigone in death. But he finally succeeds, after the fact, and far too late, in proving himself sensitive to the prophecies and to the remonstrance of old Tiresias, who has pitilessly placed him before the enormity of his acts:

> Then take this, and take it to heart!
> The day is not far off when you shall pay back
> Corpse for corpse, flesh of your own flesh.
> You have thrust the child of this world into living night,
> You have kept from the gods below the child that is theirs:
> The one in the grave before her death, the other,
> Dead, denied the grave. This is your crime:
> And the Furies and the dark gods of Hell
> Are swift with terrible punishment for you.
>
> (1066–1072)

Creon, defeated and miserable, reluctantly turns his back on his own intransigence. He does so because, in the final analysis, he has no other debt to expunge than the fault he believes he will be able, *in extremis*, to repair. Where he has simply bowed to the strictures of his position—of *raison d'État*—of which he is at once judge and master, Antigone must answer to a far more rigorous, madder necessity of which she has never been the mistress, but to which she delivers herself with a flawless fervor: this quality we could term "*raison de famille*," more imperious than the exigencies of rule for the simple reason that no one may choose to be born, and that the ties of blood, like those of love, pay no obeisance to reason. Following the example of Œdipus, his lineage is governed by *até*. Ismene is no more immune than her sister, but she is resigned to endure, which Antigone cannot tolerate. Antigone has decided to live her *até* to the full: this is what elevates her to the stature of heroine. Far from simply despairing, she makes herself the protagonist of her own despair. She cannot be silenced, either by Creon, or by necessity. Beneath her pretense of piety she defies the gods and appeals their judgement. Finally, behind the wall that has silenced her voice, she immediately kills herself, spreading death around her as she does: following her suicide, Haemon, then Eurydice, his mother, perish in quick succession. Left alone before the hecatomb to which he has so pitiably contributed, Creon can demand nothing less than to die in turn, but his distress is bereft of courage.

From our vantage point as moderns we see, in the figure of Antigone, an intrepid fighter for the imprescriptible rights of humanity. But this is not where the fascination she continues to exert upon us is strongest. Deeper, more secretly, we are fascinated by her pain at having been born inextricably bound up with the absence of love and the desire for death. No matter how omnipresent this pain and this absence are in our day, they can barely be examined in our civilization which, quite unlike that of the Greeks, attempts in every way possible to conjure death away.

Antigone, more violently than *King Œdipus*, adds something more, something political, to the fundamental question of exclusion. By denying Polyneices his funeral rites, in abandoning him to the wild animals, Creon excludes him even in death, and casts him beyond the human pale. Such a radical measure is not only contrary to unwritten law; it is equally unjustifiable from the point of view of *raison d'État*, if by that we mean not the troubled imperatives of the prince, but the well-being of the polity. Even though political circumstances may require that one of the two brothers— though both are criminals and equally damned—be honored by way of example for the citizens, the difference in the way they are treated cannot be carried so far as to cast the "guilty" brother into such an extreme of otherness as to exclude him from humanity. Creon's failure is not without reason, and it is due not to the obstinacy of his niece. In all its wretchedness, his failure resides in not accepting, in not understanding that the Other, the enemy, also belongs to the polity. Seen from this perspective, the Creon of *Antigone* is quite unlike the Creon of *King Œdipus*. In *King Œdipus*, despite the abominable suspicions levelled against him by his brother-in-law, Creon declines to condemn him and turns wisely instead to the gods to decide the fate of the vanquished king. Even though he later intervenes in the tragic story of Labdacides, the Creon of *Antigone* antedates that of *King Œdipus* in the Sophoclean *oeuvre*. *King Œdipus* thus gives positive confirmation to what *Antigone* has prefigured in the negative: the Other, the enemy, evil itself cannot be cast out from the polity, just as Œdipus himself, caught up in the terrible revelation of his identity, cannot wipe away the otherness that he has discovered in himself. As Dario De Facendis presciently notes, Sophocles opens up the sphere of the political to "the capacity to accept that evil may exist within the field of sameness."[61] Furthermore, such a capacity is one of the hallmarks of the existence of the political as a coherent sphere. We may well ask ourselves whether our modernity, in its anxiety to hark back to the ancient Greeks, has truly understood the full scope of this capacity. The modern democratic discourse displays, for the most part, a rather superficial acceptance of differences: difference is only "tolerated" insofar as it must finally, in the literal sense, be reduced to sameness, that is to say, to the extent that it creates no disturbance. Sophocles, however, illuminates something else: that man, and the polity as a whole, must accept the otherness they bear within themselves up to and including being transformed by it, up to and including calling into question their own view of themselves. Such is the price of self-knowledge, and there is no reason why we cannot find pleasure in it. Seen in this light, tragedy can be understood as the poetic art that finds pleasure in elucidating the process of tearing asunder.

Tragedy is the working out of evil, as it exists in the world. Evil *is*, tragedy tells us. But we can attempt to understand its workings. And this attempt is a source of pleasure. For this reason, insists Aristotle, a good tragic poet must please his audience. To know the wellsprings of that which Ferdinando Camon calls "the human sickness" is probably the most challenging and the rarest pleasure available to man. Man, that "marvel" (*Antigone*, v. 332), cannot escape his fate, but he possesses the means to

---

61. See note 4 above.

understand what is happening to him. And this understanding alone can raise him above his distress. The accomplishment of tragedy, that which purges the spectator's soul, the catharsis so dear to Aristotle, is to frame the action that leads the protagonist from blissful ignorance of himself to painful recognition of his errors, his limitations. Here too, as in Genesis, is established an implicit equivalence between happiness and ignorance, between misfortune and knowledge.

The passion for knowledge is the calamity of man. It is also his only worldly possession. Man is the tragic animal that is able to find pleasure in the knowledge of his evil. Evil, in turn, has been confounded with the desire to know, since we know now that man has no other certain knowledge than that of his own finite nature. Thus is defined the finite nature that the erotic conception of knowledge, in Plato, will attempt to outdo.

6

KNOWLEDGE OF EROS

IN PLATO, the pathway to knowledge is also a trial. But it is Eros who guides us on our journey. This conception of knowledge, which I term "erotic," finds its most vivid expression in the *Symposium*. The reading I propose draws also upon *Phaedrus*, and upon certain passages from the *Republic* and *Phaedo*. But we must constantly bear in mind that our aim is to read a story—the *Symposium*—taken as a self-contained text, and by no means to engage Plato's work as a whole, as I will now explain.

A certain Apollodorus is relating to a group of friends close to the business world how he had recently been approached on the Phaleron road by a wit of his acquaintance who wished to learn what exactly had been said at the famous symposium attended by Socrates.

The man, adds Apollodorus, had obtained his information from someone who had in turn acquired it from a certain Phenix; it was, however, so imprecise that the man now felt impelled to inquire of Apollodorus, who was known to be a member of Socrates' wider circle, about an event that he may have been fortunate enough to attend. The questioner's assumption showed to what extent he had confused his dates, for Apollodorus, who had only become a follower of Socrates over the last three years, would have been a child at the time. For all that, he knew his subject well enough, having heard the story related by Aristodemus, a minor itinerant then quite under the spell of the master, who had been present at the encounter. Though incomplete, the story was plausible: Apollodorus had been in a position to confirm many of the details with Socrates himself.

With the memory exercise undertaken on the Phaleron road still fresh in his mind, Apollodorus feels confident enough in his ability to satisfy the curiosity of his friends. Apart from the teller of the tale's delight at talking philosophy, his story will be of inestimable benefit to his listeners, and will, he says, provide them with considerably more than the base material concerns that are ordinarily theirs. In the face of his friends' irritation, Apollodorus lays it on thicker still: everyone knows how he spends most of his time rambling on! They calm him down, and the story he has heard from Aristodemus begins.

Thus opens Plato's *Symposium*. From the early mists of swirling rumor emerges this jewel of a story. Much, of course, is determined by the circumstances of its transmission. As Aristodemus admits, it contains gaps, but the accuracy of the most important details, those of true import, has been attested to by the principal interested party himself. Over and above the confusion of hearsay, the veracity of the story must be accepted. Such concern for authenticity seems excessive, since the subject at hand is a dinner party that ends in general intoxication, and where the topic discussed may well be little more than a pretext for salaciousness, perhaps a prelude to the interplay of seduction focused on the handsome young man at whose home the friends have convened. These are the intentions which, if we are to believe Socrates, lurk beneath the compliments that Alcibiades, in a state of thorough inebriation toward the end of the banquet, pretends to pay him. But their true purpose is to cause him to fall out with the fetching Agathon. Alcibiades' belated outburst clouds the issue and utterly transforms the nature of the meeting. The guests had come to general agreement, once the meal had ended, to drink in moderation, then to dismiss the flautist the better to undertake a serious discussion of a subject dear to Phaedrus: love. Who amongst them would prove most eloquent on Eros? Each one offered his peroration; Socrates had just completed his when Alcibiades and his escort burst into the room.

It is a providential entrance. Socrates' disquisition, a recapitulation of what he has heard from a woman wise in the ways of love, a certain Diotima of Mantinea, has raised the subject to such lofty heights that no one dares respond. Aristophanes makes a feeble attempt to reply to an allusion to his own earlier argument, but he is fortuitously impeded from doing so by the hubbub of the upstarts. Here, as it is throughout the dialogue, the staging is impeccable down to the tiniest detail: the comic playwright is about to make himself ridiculous in his attempt to quibble. From the summit to which Socrates has elevated the debate, the discussion can only decline into tedium.

Why not then engineer a spectacular fall quite worthy of the ascension that preceded it? To descend from those heights, to awaken from the Socratic daydream calls for nothing less than a brutal outside intervention by merry-makers who are totally unaware of what has been said, and of the atmosphere that they are dissipating. The descent into drunkenness, the joyful slide from beatific contemplation into the salacious jesting of the bodyguards gives the story its salt—and even more, its full compass.

The *Symposium*'s final reversal collides with the Platonic conception that dominates the philosophical literature on Plato. Among his flatterers and detractors, Plato, the founding father of Western idealism, stands as the instigator of a radical break between soul and body, between the world of the intellect and the world of the senses; he finds himself identified as the man responsible for the misadventures this dualism will go on to occasion in Christianity, and which haunts our modernity to this day.

All of this my reading intends quite precisely to put aside. Not to engage in polemics but to put them aside, at least for the time it takes to read the text. The influence of Platonism on the Western metaphysical tradition is undeniable, and I make no pretense of calling it into question. Simply put, Platonism, and all the controversy surrounding it, is not what interests me here. To forestall any possible dispute, I am quite prepared to concede that both idealism and dualism can be found in Plato, and that it is not at all difficult to notice their presence. But I would immediately add that such is the richness and diversity of Plato's thought that it can provide nourishment for almost unlimited argument in a multitude of possible meanings. It is so full of movement, so subtle that its core remains beyond our grasp. More than 2000 years of effort have been unsuccessful—to our good fortune—in giving birth to a Platonic system. The impossibility of doing so is the best possible testimony to the inexhaustible richness of the work. For all that, it has not been able to stop the formation of commonplaces with which Platonic studies are rife. Sclerosis threatens any written text, and Plato is the first to demonstrate his awareness of the danger. Against writing, the writer himself delivers the most serious of warnings.

Plato takes up the theme of writing as poison almost incidentally toward the conclusion of *Phaedrus*. Derrida rather forcefully suggests that the conclusion is the capital consideration, that it shapes the entire dialogue.[62] "There remains the question of the propriety and impropriety of writing, and

---

62. Jacques Derrida, "La pharmacie de Platon," *Tel Quel* 32 and 33 (1968); reprinted in *La Dissémination* (Paris: Seuil, 1972).

the conditions which determine them,"[63] opines Socrates at the end of a conversation on the Beautiful, which concludes with the respective merits of rhetoric and dialectic (274b). Socrates essays an answer, referring to Egyptian mythology: the god Thoth, father of numbers, calculation, geometry, astronomy, backgammon and, above all, inventor of writing, has approached the solitary king and father of the gods, Ammon, to offer him his inventions. The divine ruler weighs the advantages and disadvantages of each of the arts, and when writing's turn has come, expresses serious reservations. Contrary to Thoth's assertion writing, far from being an aid to memory, acts only as a remedy (*pharmakon*) to recollection and, as such, can only favor sloth: "Those who acquire it will cease to exercise their memory and become forgetful; they will rely on writing to bring things to their own remembrance by external signs instead of on their own internal resources" (275a). The *pharmakon*, which is simultaneously a drug, a remedy, and a poison, is a double-edged instrument. Detached from the word and from its author (its father, as Socrates puts it), congealed beyond the bounds of any dialectic, and lifeless, that which is written may fall at any time beneath the eyes of any person. As such, there is a danger of it being seized by readers ill-prepared to receive it, and inclined to overestimate its virtues:

> Then it shows great folly—as well as ignorance of the pronouncement of Ammon—to suppose that one can transmit or acquire clear and certain knowledge of an art through the medium of writing, or that written words can do more than remind the reader of what he already knows on any given subject. (275 c–d)

"*Every speech*," insists Socrates, before taking up the question of writing, "should be put together like a living creature" (264 c) for the very good reason that it is addressed to the mobility of the soul, to that living creature *par excellence*. The only act of speech that can truly imprint itself in the human soul is that which itself is "written on the soul": a living act of speech, animated by him who is its bearer, and who knows how to defend it; who knows as well "those it should address and those in whose presence it should be silent." In the final analysis, these gardens of writing must be seeded "by way of diversion," with the sole purpose of accumulating a treasure trove of recollection for oneself and for those who, as they travel the same road, will take pleasure "to see the growth of their tender shoots" (276 a–d).

---

63. Plato, *Phaedrus, and, The Seventh and Eighth Letters*, trans. Walter Hamilton (Harmondsworth: Penguin, 1973).

Here Phaedrus is the fictitious witness to a trying, even painful confession. The confession, as we suspect, is not that of Socrates who, throughout his whole life, abstained deliberately from any manner of writing. Instead, it comes from Plato, the true father of discourse. In writing, and worse, in causing Socrates to speak via his pen, that is, in giving the word final written form (even though no one is fooled by the procedure), Plato cannot but betray the spirit he invokes. Whatever he says, once he has begun to write, he contradicts himself. Even if it is a simple writing game, not unlike tending a garden, the dialectician has every cause to fear the uses that can be made of the gardens where the writer has sown his words. And yet, he writes. Writes while taking care to introduce surreptitiously into his writings a warning against writing—an operating manual of sorts, veiled from the future users of the *pharmakon*—his *oeuvre*—that he cannot help but leave to posterity. Paradoxically, the discretion of the warning (a few pages in *Phaedrus*) is proportional to its significance: the subtlety of writing and of his warning is the principal condition of his success. It is only to the extent that the written text conserves the fragile imprint of the spoken word and translates with muffled steps its uncertainties and its wanderings that the leisurely stroller may be gently induced not to trample upon the fresh earth in which Plato has planted the seeds of his speech. And never so much so as at the instant in which he shelters his entire *oeuvre* under the aegis of fragility must he make full use of lightness, of finesse.[64]

Everything points to Plato having rather negligently left dissimulated in *Phaedrus* a slender key to reading concealed beneath the mulch of his garden. Such a key, of course, can unlock no lock. Nowhere, and in *Phaedrus* less than anywhere else, does Plato provide anything that might resemble the "key to his work"—an expression so ridiculous as to discourage any self-styled locksmith. *Phaedrus* delivers a warning. Without attempting to affirm that this warning applies to all of Plato's dialogues, we could hardly argue that it is invalid for those composed during the same period; such would seem to be the case with the *Symposium*, which scholars generally locate within the same time-frame as *Phaedrus*, along with *Phaedo* and the *Republic*, writings related both in their choice of subject matter and spirit. There is no need for us to know the specific order in which these dialogues were composed. It is enough to admit—an easier task—that they partake of the same style: a style that betrays, among other things, the intention to lead astray.

---

64. If there is any doubt about finesse, and about what it conceals, I suggest Derrida's subtle analysis in "La pharmacie de Plato," loc cit.

To lead astray is quite exactly the purpose of the story and of its form as dialogue. In the *Symposium*, dialogue itself accounts for little of the work and, until the arrival of Alcibiades, the unfolding of the storyline offers little that might be construed as an attempt to mislead. One speech follows another, learned and pompous, among which Aristophanes' myth introduces an element of good humor, until the point at which Socrates elucidates the truth which he had earlier drawn from Diotima: from those beauties apprehended by the senses, Eros leads the soul by degrees toward the contemplation of the Beautiful in itself, in the kingdom of the Intelligible. The summation is perfect; nothing can be added to it.But, if everything has been said, why does the dialogue not end right then and there, on this note of apotheosis—in the manner of the *Republic*, which concludes on the true essence of the soul and the grandiloquent evocation of its migration; or of *Phaedrus*, which concludes on the crucial question of writing? In short, why does rough-hewn Alcibiades appear? For no other reason than to praise Socrates, of which he has absolutely no need, and which he hastens to mock. It is difficult to see what the triumph of intelligible beauty has to gain at the spectacle of its champion's involvement in the spicy stories of his pupil, even though the master's image escapes unscathed. But let us set aside for the moment the impetuous Alcibiades and his drunkenness, the diversionary effect of which is all too visible. If his intervention were the only one capable of intriguing us, the *Symposium* would have little in the way of surprises to offer.

All the signs are there in the prologue: the fine detail, the circumlocutions surprise us. Then, offhandedly, these little oddities work their way into the story itself, and they merit the most scrupulous attention. On the way to the residence of Agathon, who is holding a symposium to celebrate the triumph his first tragedy has enjoyed, Socrates invites the narrator (Aristodemus) to accompany him even though he, the philosopher, is not among the invited guests (we later learn that he is, but the invitation has not reached him in time). Socrates amuses himself in proving wrong the proverb that holds that "people of quality [*agathoi*] invite themselves to the banquets of people of quality [*agathōn*, the genitive plural; homonym for Agathon]," a way of saying that gentlemen of social standing can easily recognize one another: they no more need an invitation than an intermediary, a position which Socrates offers to assume toward Aristodemus. By way of cushioning the possible adverse effect of his jest on his companion (who is not a person of quality), Socrates hastens to add that Homer has done even greater violence to the proverb by sending the pliable Menelas to take a seat uninvited at the table of the intrepid Agamemnon. At which point Aristodemus observes that he might well find himself, like Menelas, in the situation of a "nobody" forced to invoke the invitation of his master (174 b–d).[65] There is no doubt that Aristodemus, the first narrator, understands that Socrates' humor is intended above all to put him at ease and to designate the social level of the host who awaits them. As the name Agathon indicates, they are proceeding toward "good men," who, upon reflection, bear more than a fleeting resemblance to those who make up the audience of the second narrator, Apollodorus. There is every reason to doubt that the audience notices the connection any more than they grasp the point of the jest, which is that, among "good men," in this gathering of lofty spirits imbued with poetry (Homer's name is not mentioned in vain), the fine and the beautiful may well need to be taken with a grain of salt.

It will not be long before Socrates' ironic insinuation raises its head a second time in the oft-commented episode of the meditative pause. Absorbed by his thoughts, the philosopher allows his companion to move on ahead. Upon arrival at Agathon's, the narrator looks back: Socrates is nowhere to be seen! A servant dispatched to look for him finds him on the neighbor's porch, deaf to his calls. Agathon attempts to have him brought along for fear he will simply go back the way he has come, but Aristodemus dissuades him: Socrates is in the habit of pausing, and eventually he will join the festivities. The guests sit down at the table without further ado as Aristodemus attempts to calm their host, who is itching to send someone off to find Socrates. The meal has thus begun without Socrates, and his momentary absence is a sign. It is the first sign, still tenuous at this stage, of a theme whose underlying presence will continue to expand as the story unfolds. Socrates begins by defaulting (as he had earlier stood up his hosts at the public celebration to honor the poet's victory the previous day), making himself wanted.

"Finally he came …," (175c) and no sooner has the latecomer come into the room than Agathon, who has drunk his fill of wisdom, flings himself upon his prey:

> "Come and sit here beside me, Socrates, and let me, by contact with you, enjoy the discovery which you have made in the porch. You must obviously have found the answer to your problem and pinned it down; you would have desisted until you had."

---

65. Plato, *The Symposium*, trans. Walter Hamilton (London: Penguin, 1951).

Socrates sat down and said:

"It would be very nice, Agathon, if wisdom were like water, and flowed by contact out of a person who has more into one who has less, just as water can be made to pass through a thread of wool out of the fuller of two cups into the emptier. If that applies to wisdom, I value the privilege of sitting beside you very highly, for I have no doubt that you will fill me with an ample draught of the finest wisdom. Such wisdom as I possess is slight, and has little more reality than a dream, but yours is brilliant and may shine brighter yet; you are still quite young, and look at the dazzling way it flashed out the day before yesterday before an audience of more than thirty thousand Greeks."

"Enough of your sarcasm, Socrates," replied Agathon. "We'll settle our respective claims to wisdom a little later on, and Dionysus, the god of wine, shall judge between us; for the moment give your attention to your dinner." (175 d–e)

So goes the first skirmish between poetry and philosophy. The philosopher's irony is not lost on the poet, who does not let himself become flustered. Emboldened by the success of his tragedy, Agathon vows that his verbal skills will prevail in the course of the evening's libations. All the actors are now in place; the game may begin.

We already know what it will consist of: who can sing the most fulsome praises of Eros. It is precisely the kind of program that Socrates, whose only true knowledge is of all things related to love, could turn his back on. His task will be all the more demanding, he grumbles, since he has been assigned last place on the speakers' list. No one is taken in by his coquetry; in fact, his position will turn out to be the ideal one: he will be able to draw on the speeches preceding his and to carry off a spectacular reversal. For none of the speeches that precede his are simply ridiculous, comical, or incoherent: each contains at least one element to which Plato can subscribe.

Having reminded his boon companions that Hesiod and Parmenides situate Eros among the primordial deities, Phaedrus, who opens the oratorical jousting, praises love for instilling strength and courage in lovers who enter side by side into combat: not only do they desire at all costs not to lose face in front of their loved ones, but each is prepared to die for the other. That love is a breath, a powerful source of inspiration, neither Plato nor Socrates can deny. That aside, Phaedrus's tribute to love has the appearance of a sub-coherent display of empty erudition. Pausanias, later on, reproaches him for restricting himself to the narrow register of praise. Like Aphrodite, from which it is inseparable, love is double: heavenly and earth-bound. Here Pausanias makes substantially the same distinction as Socrates does in *Phaedrus*, where the soul is represented as a team of two horses, one docile and obedient to the voice of reason and drawn by beauty in and of itself, the other carried away by the brutality of its instincts and in haste to appease them, against nature if need be (246b; 250e; 251a; 253d; 254a). Socrates' celebrated allegory unfolds in all it splendor, while Pausanias, as he struggles to explain his two Aphrodites, sinks deep into the grotesque. Plato goes so far as to have him say that heavenly Aphrodite owes her elevation to the fact that she "has no female strain in her!" (181 c) He then has him deliver a totally inept panegyric to Athenian customs in matters of love, where all that would, in other circumstances, be condemned, perjury included, is acceptable when caried out under the influence of amorous frenzy (183b). Graver still, the Barbarians, quite unlike the Athenians, condemn homosexual love in the same terms and for the same reasons as does philosophy (182b–c). The connection is a spicy one, anticipating one of the elements of Diotima's discourse by parodying it.

Plato amuses himself by inserting here and there fragments of his own opinions and by making them appear ridiculous, a writing strategy that suggests that isolated or poorly structured reasoning destroys itself: no argument is valid in and of itself, outside "of the methods of division as instruments which enable me to speak and think," of which Socrates terms himself "a great lover" (*Phaedrus*, 266b). But eventually Pausanias, tongue-tied and repetitious, concludes his remarks, upon which Aristophanes, the next scheduled speaker, is overcome with an attack of hiccups, which renders him speechless. This serves as a sign that we are edging into the burlesque, but also a spasmodic reaction to Pausanias's discourse and a wink at the public (not for nothing is Aristophanes a comic): everything indicates that the speech has flopped![66] The interlude prefigures and at the same time postpones the dramaturge's humorous performance, which the speech to follow makes all the more imperious. Pausanias's pettifoggery is thus followed by Eriximachus's medicine. Just as he undertakes to cure his table companion's hiccup, the doctor does his utmost to give his predecessor's performance the nudge it needs: "Pausanias, after an admirable beginning, has not brought his argument to an adequate conclusion; I think therefore that

---

66. In his "Notice" to the *Symposium* (Paris, Les Belles Lettres, 1989), Léon Robin observes, in relation to this interlude, that it is designed to "give the attention respite after a crucial section, and to underline its importance" (p. LI). His commentary follows an earlier remark about Pausanias's speech, which he describes as a "remarkable extract" (p. L). The descriptive is ambiguous to say the least, and remarkable in its dull-wittedness, as far as we are concerned.

it is incumbent on me to try to put the finishing touches to it" (185d). Having heard Pausanias's initial distinction "between the two kinds of love," Eriximachus moves on to medicine, which he defines as "the knowledge of the principles of love at work in the body in regard to repletion and evacuation" (186c). In his overweening passion for science, the wise man gives a lesson in pedantry that sends the audience into the shallowest reaches of the competition. Plato does not let the reader suffer any longer than is necessary, only enough for Aristophanes to recover from his hiccups. At which time the doughty doctor offers a partial apology: perhaps, in spite of himself, he has left certain things unsaid which his neighbor, now that he has recovered from his indisposition, would like to fill in.

Recovered is hardly the word! Aristophanes scoffs at his healer—his recovery is due to a sneeze—and goes on to admit wondering "whether it is the virtuous love in my body which desires such noises and tickling sensations as a sneeze" (189a). Cut to the quick, the good doctor admonishes the scoffer and threatens to administer the same treatment to his speech. Aristophanes seizes the occasion to plead indulgence: not that he fears making people laugh—which is his trade, after all—but because he fears being made a fool of.

What ensues is the hilarious myth (undoubtedly borrowed from the zoogony of Empedocles) that has gone on to become one of the loveliest allegories of love. Originally, human beings were as perfectly round as spheres, fitted out with eight limbs that enabled them to roll at high speed in any direction they wished. These bouncy beings were divided into three categories: males, females, and androgynes. In all their vigor and energy they scaled the skies and attacked the gods. Irritated at their presumptuousness, Zeus sliced them in two as one would a boiled egg, threatening more of the same until they were reduced to hopping about on one leg if they did not behave themselves. He then ordered Apollo "to twist their faces and half their necks toward the cut, so that, having it constantly in view, they would acquire modesty." A process of polishing and finishing that, for all its delicacy, leaves—putting it mildly—something to be desired, follows the surgery:

> "Man's original body having been thus cut in two, each half yearned for the half from which it had been severed. When they met they threw their arms round one another and embraced, in their longing to grow together again, and they perished of hunger and general neglect of their concerns, because they would not do anything apart ... So they went on perishing till Zeus took pity on them, and hit upon a second plan. He moved their reproductive

organs to the front: hitherto they had been placed on the outer side of their bodies, and the processes of begetting and birth had been carried on not by the physical union of the sexes, but by emission on to the ground, as is the case with grasshoppers. By moving their genitals to the front, as they are now, Zeus made it possible for reproduction to take place by the intercourse of the male with the female. His object in making this change was twofold: if male coupled with female children might be begotten and the race thus continued, but if male coupled with male, at any rate the desire for intercourse would be satisfied, and men set free to turn to other activities and to attend to the rest of the business of life....

"Each of us then is the mere broken tally of a man, the result of a bisection which has reduced us to a condition like that of a flat fish, and each of us is perpetually in search of his corresponding tally." (191a–d)

The three kinds of possible unions (heterosexual, homosexual male and female) are placed on the same plane, even though male-female relationships enjoy a supplementary degree of legitimacy due to procreation. Though Aristophanes' words are at sharp variance with all that has been previously said, in which all praise the superiority of male homosexual love, they do not go so far as to place the reproduction of the species as the underpinning of love. It is to be found, manifestly, where the cut has been made, which Zeus's expedient only partially relieves. Neither procreation nor sexual pleasure can replace lost union, and the most insistent desire for union, even between those halves that have located one another, has about it something inexplicable:

"Whenever the lover of boys—or any other person for that matter—has the good fortune to encounter his own actual other half, affection and kinship and love combined inspire in him an emotion which is quite overwhelming, and such a pair practically refuse ever to be separated even for a moment. It is people like these who form lifelong partnerships, although they would find it difficult to say what they hope to gain from one another's society. No one can suppose that it is mere physical enjoyment, which causes one to take such intense delight in the company of the other. It is clear that the soul of each has some other longing, which it cannot express, but can only surmise and obscurely hint at. Suppose Hephaestus and his tools were to visit them as they lie together, and stand over them and ask: 'What is it, mortals, that you hope to gain from one another?' Suppose too that when they could not answer he repeated his question in these terms: 'Is the object of your desire to be always together as much as possible, and never be separated from one another day or night? If that is what you want, I am ready to melt and weld you together, so that, instead of two, you shall be one flesh; as long as you live you shall live a common life, and when you die, you shall suffer a common death, and be still one, not two, even in the next world. Would such a fate as this content you, and satisfy your longings?' We know what their answer would be; no one would refuse the offer; it would be plain that this is what everybody wants, and everybody would regard it as the precise expression of the desire which he had long felt but had been unable to formulate, that he should melt into his beloved, and that henceforth they should be one being instead of two. The reason is that this was our primitive condition when we were wholes, and love is simply the name for the desire and pursuit of the whole." (192b–e)

Here Aristophanes reaches the culmination of his speech. Such is the poetry of the passage that the reader would have almost forgotten the humoristic side of his performance if the playwright had not introduced Hephaistos. No member of the august circle of Agathon's guests, nor of Aristodemus's listeners, is unaware that the gimpy god whom Aphrodite cuckolds with Ares, was the laughingstock of Olympus. Homer, who is constantly evoked in the *Symposium*, depicts the patron of fire and metal working to prepare a trap to chain the adulterous lovers to their beds of passion and to expose their misdeeds in all their nudity to the eyes of Zeus. Hephaistos relies upon the bonds that he has hammered out to dissuade them once and for all from committing their offense a second time and declares that he will hold them as long as necessary to gain reparation (*Odyssey*, VIII, v. 300–320). It takes a powerful dose of irony to transform a notorious cuckold into the spokesman of desire and the blacksmith of love. The irony itself suggests a stratagem: the very one that the lame god has devised to confound his spouse. Could not the amorous quest itself, the very fusion to which lovers aspire, be a trap? If love is nothing more than the search for unity lost, Eros would then be driving us, unbeknownst, into a futile undertaking: to repair the cut before which Zeus has judged it appropriate to place humanity. But to repair it lies beyond our capacity. And if, in spite of everything, we insist on pursuing such a goal, *it is out of ignorance*: to seek to wipe away such a mutilation in full awareness of what it represents would be clear evidence of immoderation and impiety!

Another impiety is soon to follow. At the exact instant when Aristophanes is about to place his audience before the inevitability of loss that grounds the feeling of love, he slips away, ending his speech with a moralizing pirouette: if we ill-behave toward the gods, we are in danger of being sliced asunder yet again; we must take care not to oppose Eros, and to "conduct ourselves well in the sight of heaven, [for] he will hereafter make us blessed and happy by restoring us to our former state and healing our wounds" (193b). Unless of course we bestow upon "our former state" an esoteric meaning that the orator's final remarks seem to rule out, we find ourselves facing a rather bland conclusion, in almost painful contrast with the vitality that has preceded it. The finesse of Aristophanes' discourse holds out the hope of a finer fall. In the guise of a jester, he is the first of the speakers truly to say something: that there is naught to love but absence, and this absence is irreparable.

No, this is quite precisely what Aristophanes fails to say.

There can be little doubt that his failure to do so has a historical explanation. Plato may well have put too much in the mouth of a character whose art he cannot bring himself not to admire but who also, with his comedy *The Clouds*, contrived to turn the Athenians against Socrates. In no wise could the enemy of Socrates be allowed to emerge the winner. To this eminently "political" consideration must be added another, a much more determinant one from the point of view of the inner economy of the dialogue. If Aristophanes were permitted to reveal all, the words of Socrates would necessarily be blunted. Thus it becomes essential, all vindictiveness aside, that the orator skip over the essential, merely brushing it as he goes. Implicit in Aristophanes' speech is that another truth has been unveiled, a truth that Socrates too, though at a different level, will leave unbroached: what love proposes is impossible.

Nothing, however, is impossible for the marvelous Agathon. And once more Socrates cannot resist the temptation to tease him: what could he, Socrates, possibly hope to add after the poet had shone so brilliantly the previous evening before thousands of spectators? Agathon protests: it is much more difficult to address a small circle of intelligent men than a crowd of the ignorant. Socrates could ill-pardon himself for thinking him so unintelligent; he is simply reminding him that the "wise men" who today surround him were, yesterday, part of the crowd. Then he idly speculates, comparing the feelings he would have experienced at committing an error in front of the wise men and in front of the crowd. But Phaedrus, who chairs the séance, intervenes:

> "Don't answer Socrates, my dear Agathon. Provided he has
> somebody to talk to, particularly if that somebody is good looking,
> he won't care in the least what happens to our project." (194d)

All too happy to be called to order, Agathon launches into a surprising
recapitulation of the method which Socrates will soon employ: what are all
these speeches that sing the praises of love without ever having defined its
nature? We must begin by knowing what we are talking about. Far from
being old, as Phaedrus maintains, Eros is the enemy of old age—even old age
continues to pursue him! He is youth and beauty. A beauty that no panegyric
could properly convey. But Eros is not without substance: in him are united
the four cardinal virtues: justice, temperance, courage, and wisdom. Agathon
does his utmost to justify these attributes in a perfectly incoherent morsel of
rhetorical pyrotechnics, which can be read as a crude mockery of the Socratic
dialectic (let us recall that these same virtues are closely examined in the
Republic). Finally, love is poetic, and transforms all those who touch it into
poets, even those who have been strangers to the Muse before; for, continues
Agathon, "how can anyone impart or teach to another an art which he does
not possess or does not know?" (196e)

The remark, let drop amidst a flowery avalanche of flattery, is a banal
one. Or would have been banal in any other context. But since the subject is
Eros, and follows hard on Aristophanes' evocation of amorous
incompleteness, it causes a void, a chasm, an absence to reverberate beneath
Agathon's panegyric. Could Plato be gently deriding the naïveté of the poet
by causing him to utter, in passing and under his nose, a piece of the truth
that is everywhere in abeyance: not even love can "impart that which it does
not possess"? Unless this illusory gift is precisely what the lovers struggle
unconsciously to make of it, as Jacques Lacan, that assiduous reader of the
Symposium, would say in his own way.[67] Otherwise, the mannered and
shallow speech of Agathon yields all too little—except to provide Socrates
with an occasion for the triumph of his dialectic.

The unanimous applause that greets the poet's peroration speaks
volumes of the prevailing mood: the road onto which Socrates must now
guide them will not be an easy one. The philosopher begins by offering his
excuses: he has frivolously entered a contest of eloquence in which he is out
of place. He sees himself as "stupid enough to suppose that the right thing

---

67. Jacques Lacan, "Le ressort de l'amour. Un commentaire du Banquet de Plato," *Le transfert*, bk. 7 of
Le Séminaire (Paris: Seuil, 1991), pp. 29–195. Lacan also suggests that love consists of "giving what one
does not have to someone who does not want it."

was to speak the truth," whereas "the proper method is to ascribe to the subject of the panegyric all the loftiest and loveliest qualities, whether it actually possesses them or not" (198d). Still, he adds, "if it is to be after this fashion; I can't do it. I am quite willing to tell the truth in my own style, if you like; only I must not be regarded as competing with your speeches, or I shall be a laughing-stock" (199a–b).

Socrates' intervention begins with a casual remark that constitutes the sole dialectical moment of the *Symposium*. The philosopher turns once again to Agathon and congratulates him on his initial distinction of "the actual nature of the god, and ... the effects which he produces." The discussion takes a serious turn. From this distinction, Socrates raises several questions, though none more important than this one: "Is the nature of Love such he must be love of something, or can he exist absolutely without an object?" Of something, that much is clear. Or, more precisely, of someone. Whatever its object may be, Love desires that object, does it not? Agathon nods agreement, and Socrates continues:

> "And does he desire and love the thing that he desires and loves when he is in possession of it or when he is not?"
>
> "Probably when he is not."
>
> "If you reflect for a moment, you will see that it isn't merely probable but absolutely certain that one desires what one lacks, or rather that one does not desire what one does not lack. To me at any rate, Agathon, it seems as certain as anything can be. What do you think?"
>
> "Yes, I think it is."
>
> "Good. Now would anybody wish to be big who was big, or strong who was strong?"
>
> "It follows from my previous admission that this is impossible."
>
> "Because a man who possesses a quality cannot be in need of it?"
>
> "Yes."
>
> "Suppose a man wanted to be strong who was strong, or swift-footed who was swift-footed. I labour the point in order to avoid any possibility of mistake, for one might perhaps suppose in these and all similar cases that people who are of a certain character or who possess certain qualities also desire the qualities which they possess. But if you consider the matter, Agathon, you will see that these people must inevitably possess these qualities at the present moment, whether they like it or not, and no one presumably would

desire what is inevitable. No, if a man says: 'I, who am healthy, or who am rich, nonetheless desire to be healthy or rich, as the case may be, and I desire the very qualities which I possess,' we should reply: 'My friend, what you, who are in possession of health and wealth and strength, really wish, is to have the possession of these qualities continued to you in the future, since at the present moment you possess them whether you wish it or not.' Consider then, whether when you say, 'I desire what I possess' you do not really mean 'I wish that I may continue to possess in the future the things which I possess now.' If it were put to him like this, he would agree, I think."

"Yes," said Agathon.

"But this is to be in love with a thing which is not yet in one's power or possession, namely the continuance and preservation of one's present blessings in the future."

"Certainly."

"Such a man, then, and everyone else who feels desire, desires what is not in his present power or possession, and desire and love have for their object things or qualities which a man does not a present possess but which he lacks."

"Yes."

"Come then," said Socrates, "let us sum up the points on which we have reached agreement. Are they not first that Love exists only in relation to some object, and second that that object must be something of which he is at present in want?"

"Yes."

"Now recall also what it was that you declared in your speech to be the object of Love. I'll do it for you, if you like. You said, I think, that the troubles among the gods were composed by love of beauty, for there could not be such a thing as love of ugliness. Wasn't that it?"

"Yes."

"Quite right, my dear friend. And if that is so, Love will be love of beauty, will he not, and not love of ugliness?"

Agathon agreed.

"Now we have agreed that Love is in love with what he lacks and does not possess."

"Yes."

"So after all, Love lacks and does not possess beauty?"

"Inevitably."

"Well then, would you call what lacks and in no way possess beauty beautiful?"

"Certainly not."

"Do you still think then that Love is beautiful, if this is so?"

"It looks, Socrates, as if I didn't know what I was talking about when I said that."

"Still, it was a beautiful speech, Agathon!" (199d–201b)

Socrates goes on to lead his listener to associate the beautiful with the good, and obliges him to conclude that love lacks both the beautiful and the good. Agathon is now nearing total exasperation. Sensitive to his host's self-esteem, Socrates sets him aside to pursue his "pre-recorded" dialogue with the woman who has already taught him everything he knows about love, Diotima of Mantinea.

Socrates thus demonstrates due consideration for Agathon's pride by putting himself in his place, in the position of the young neophyte who responds as best he can to the questions asked of him by the woman who has initiated him. At the same time, reversing roles gives him a free hand to express his conception of love to more telling effect: no one can possibly accuse him of attempting to draw attention to himself (we must not forget that Socrates has withdrawn from the oratorical cut-and-thrust going on around him). Full credit for the discourse lies with Diotima, a woman. This constitutes yet another slap in the faces of the preceding orators: for them, with the exception of Aristophanes, it had gone without saying that the only love worth speaking of is that of men for one another.

The dialogue between Diotima and Socrates begins at the precise point where the dialogue between Socrates and Agathon ended. Convinced by his interlocutor that love can be neither beautiful nor good, Socrates the pupil wonders if it would then be ugly and bad. His knuckles are immediately rapped:

"Don't say such things," she answered, "do you think that anything that is not beautiful is necessarily ugly?"

"Of course I do."

"And that anything that is not wisdom is ignorance? Don't you know that there is a state of mind half-way between wisdom and ignorance?"

"What do you mean?"

"Having true convictions without being able to give reasons for them," she replied. "Surely you see that such a state of mind cannot be called understanding, because nothing irrational deserves the name; but it would be equally wrong to call it ignorance; how can one call a state of mind ignorance which hits

upon the truth? The fact is that having true convictions is what I
called it just now, a condition half-way between knowledge and
ignorance."

"I grant you that," said I.

"Then do not maintain what is not beautiful is ugly, and what
is not good is bad, but rather that he is something between the
two." (201e–202b)

The parallel that Diotima inconspicuously draws between science and
beauty is obviously not accidental. While positing love as an intermediary,
she points to a trail she will return to and expand upon further along: *Eros* is
a matter of knowledge, and knowledge, a matter of beauty. Neither ugly nor
beautiful, *Eros* is no more mortal than immortal, no more man than god, but
always an intermediary, a demon that inspires those whom it inhabits. Here
Love assumes a virtually insubstantial character: it is no more than a breath.
While it may well be essential, it is nothing in and of itself. Existing as a
powerful hyphen, its only power derives from what it joins together.

Diotima uses a myth to illustrate the nature of Eros: on the day of
Aphrodite's birth, as the gods are celebrating, one of their number, Poros,
drunk with nectar, reclines in a stupor on the sidelines. Penia, skulking in the
shadows in the hope of begging a few crumbs from the festive tables, spots
the slumbering god, couples with him in his sleep and becomes pregnant
with Eros. This makes him the son of Poverty (Penia) and of Contrivance
(Poros), himself the son of Invention (Métis). Connected to beautiful
Aphrodite by the day of his conception, Eros is "shoeless and homeless,"
taking after his mother who lives in want. Yet he also takes after his father in
being someone who "schemes to get for himself whatever is beautiful and
good; he is bold and forward and strenuous, always devising tricks like a
cunning huntsman" (203b–e).

Unable ever to grasp fully that which he seeks, nor to attain the beauty
to which he aspires, Eros is in the position of a philosopher who can never
achieve the wisdom with which he is infatuated. Should he do so, he would
cease to philosophize and fall back into the serenity of the ignorant man who,
believing himself to lack nothing, cannot desire what he believes he
possesses. Wisdom and ignorance all but converge in the same beatitude, but
such a convergence remains humanly chimerical: we mortals are far too
vulnerable to fear and to hardship to be able to enjoy the kind of serenity that
must remain the exclusive prerogative of the gods. If ignorance can provide
a short-lived illusion, it cannot in the long run shield those who swear by it

either from the world or from themselves. As it is for Eros, dissatisfaction is our lot. Desire grips us tight in its embrace.

All men, Diotima opines, carry in them, consciously or unconsciously, the desire for fecundity, be it of the body or of the mind. Whatever the level, Love inhabits them. Certainly there are those who are content with the love of money or of games of chance. Others are more sensitive to physical beauty. Love for the Other is kindled through beauty, the reason why we consider it to be the highest expression of love, and why the vocabulary of love belongs to it alone. But sooner or later the attraction exerted by the beauty of the flesh encounters its limitations:

> "The object of love, Socrates, is not, as you think, beauty."
> "What is it then?"
> "Its object is to procreate and bring forth in beauty."
> "Really?"
> "It is so, I assure you. Now, why is procreation the object of love? Because procreation is the nearest thing to perpetuity and immortality that a mortal being can attain." (206e)

"And not only his body, but his soul as well" (207e). Where most people perpetuate themselves through procreation, others seek immortality through deeds or works. The most beautiful offspring of the spirit ensure the longest-lasting posterity and are naturally preferred by those drawn to the fecundity of the soul. Immortal glory is of little interest to the philosopher, however, whom love summons to something more precious, more exacting. Diotima is far from certain that this, the ultimate degree of amorous revelation, is within her pupil's grasp. Still, she takes a chance. He will follow her as best he can.

For some time now, the young Socrates' retorts have been pure form. We have moved imperceptibly from dialogue to a magisterial dissertation, which has now reached an apotheosis. Diotima shows how love, awakened by the beauty of its sensual object, leads to the discovery of beauty in all bodies, and from it to the beauty of souls, from the beauty of souls to that of deeds, from that beauty to the beauty of knowledge to finally discern, "by gazing upon the vast ocean of the beautiful," a science single and unique, that of the Beautiful: "This beauty is first of all eternal; it neither comes into being nor waxes and wanes" (210a–211a). To know is nothing more than to makes one's way toward that supreme beauty which orders the world. This is the reason why Eros, lover of the beautiful, is also the lover of the wisdom that he reveals. He is the first philosopher, or, better still, the demonic breath that inspires them.

So unfolds Diotima's discourse as it proceeds along the pathway to contemplation. The ardor that infuses it and the beauty that it radiates transform its first reading into an unforgettable moment. It leads us into the overflowing sense of exultation that we sometimes experience before a landscape, a face, or when listening to music. But like the landscape, the face, or the music, Diotima's words cannot always create the same effect; we do not always experience the same instant of grace that they first inspire. Upon second reading, a disillusionment of sorts sets in, as with an aria too often heard. Music is no different: the text retains all its richness, but its initial fullness gives way to a slightly excessive satiety. There is an element of excess that is not perceptible on first hearing, something too perfect, too complete. Such faultless, fulsome, glossy beauty leaves something to be desired. By seeking to make itself too beautiful, it has lost something. Exaltation seems to have overflowed its own banks. Perhaps it would have been better to let Diotima continue her powerful ascension towards the meridian of beauty, and be happy to remain half-way up the incline, catching glimpses of the summit through the morning mists ...

Fortunately for us, Alcibiades is waiting in the wings.

His entry is that of truth.

Crowned with a thick wreath of ivy and violets, hung with ribbons dangling askew over his eyes, he staggers toward Agathon to crown the man he loudly declares to be the wisest and the most beautiful. Should he depart immediately after he has completed his tribute, or will he be accepted as a guest, even though he is roaring drunk? A "unanimous cry" invites him to join the assembled company. Embracing Agathon, he places the wreath atop the poet's head; it is only then, eyes unobstructed, that in turning he spies Socrates:

> "Good God, what have we here? Socrates? Lying there in wait for me again? How like you to make a sudden appearance just when I least expect to find you. What are you doing here? And why have you taken this place? You ought to be next to Aristophanes or some other actual or would-be buffoon, and instead you've managed to get yourself next to the handsomest person in the room."
>
> "Be ready to protect me, Agathon," said Socrates, "for I find that the love of this fellow has become no small burden. From the moment when I first fell in love with him I haven't been able to

exchange a glance or a word with a single good-looking person without his falling into a passion of jealousy and envy, which makes him behave outrageously and abuse me and practically lay violent hands on me. See to it that he doesn't commit some excess even here, or if he attempts to do anything violent protect me; I am really quite scared by his mad behaviour and the intensity of his affection."

"There can be no peace between you and me," said Alcibiades, "but I'll settle accounts with you for this presently. For the moment, Agathon, give me some of those ribbons to make a wreath for his head too, for a truly wonderful head it is. Otherwise he might blame me for crowning you and leaving him uncrowned, whose words bring him victory over all men at all times, not merely on single occasions, like yours the day before yesterday." So saying he took some of the ribbons, made a wreath for Socrates, and lay back.

As soon as he had done so he exclaimed: "Come sirs, you seem to me to be quite sober; this can't be allowed; you must drink; it's part of our agreement. So as master of the revels, until you are in adequate drinking order, I appoint—myself." (212d–213e)

Alcibiades may well have turned the rules of the gathering on their head and declared himself master of the revels, but Eryximachus rejects the notion that all should agree to drink "like men do when they are thirsty." Drunk though he may be, the newcomer must come up with a speech as everybody else has. Alcibiades begins by protesting that the game is unfair, but uses his right to speak to ask the assembled guests if they believe a word of the fears Socrates has expressed about him:

"If I praise any person but him in his presence, be it god or man, he won't be able to keep his hands off me."

"Be quiet," said Socrates.

"It's no good your protesting," Alcibiades said. "I won't make a speech in praise of any other person in your presence."

"Very well," said Eryximachus, "adopt that course, if you like, and make a speech in praise of Socrates."

"What?" said Alcibiades, "Do you think I ought, Eryximachus? Shall I set about the fellow and pay him out in the presence of you all?"

"Here, I say," said Socrates; "what have you in mind? Are you going to make fun of me by a mock-panegyric? Or what?"

"I shall tell the truth. Do you allow that?"

"Oh, yes, I'll allow you to tell the truth; I'll even invite you to do so."

"Very well then," said Alcibiades. "And here is what you can do. If I say anything untrue, pull me up in the middle of my speech, if you like, and tell me that I'm lying." (214d–e)

From Alcibiades' succulent portrait of Socrates we learn that, under rather disgraceful appearances, this silenus, this player of the reed pipe, this elemental charmer, this man who drives his interlocutors to distraction, conceals a divine treasure. Socrates behaves like an exemplary citizen-soldier, as impervious to cold as to defeat. But above and beyond all else, even more so than the love he feels for handsome youths, he never loses his self-control. Alcibiades has so proven at his own cost: the ingenious strategy that he had deployed to draw Socrates into his bed proved vain: "In spite of all my efforts he proved completely superior to my charms and triumphed over them and put them to scorn, insulting me on the very point on which I piqued myself" (219c). We can only appreciate the full measure of Alcibiades' discomfiture when we recall that it is incumbent on the elder (the lover) to obtain the favors of the younger (the loved). Alcibiades is reduced to making the very advances of which he should have been the object. If, under constraint, he has had to reverse roles, it can only be because the beauty of the spirit has triumphed over the charms of the body.

Crueller still than the wound to self-esteem is the bite inflicted by philosophy. Socrates is the only man before whom Alcibiades blushes, the only man who causes him shame at the impossible life he leads. The bite is all the more mordant in that Alcibiades knows well that his strategy of seduction had set itself an unattainable objective: the treasure buried within Socrates into which he too had hoped to plunge, as one might search amidst the sileni displayed by sculptors for the *agalmata* or divine statuettes that they conceal in their bellies. The brilliant strategist blushes at having believed he could trade the beauty of his body for the inner beauty of his master. Socrates was quick to deride the intellectual and moral windfall that Alcibiades had hoped to reap on contact with him: the deal that his young friend had concocted at his expense was not such a bad one after all, offering him as it did *dross for gold*.

Providing indeed that there was gold. "But look more closely, my good friend," Socrates had told him, "and make quite sure that you are not mistaken in your estimate of my worth" (219a). Alcibiades' true defeat is not the fruitless attempt at seduction he so smugly relates; it is to have wished to drink from the cup of philosophy as one makes love, to have believed he could take from Socrates something that was never there—not at his disposal, at least—and which he would have been better to seek within himself. Such was the effort he had foregone in exchange for short-lived political glory and the easy pleasures of high-society (a life which Plato's contemporaries knew would turn out badly). If the trial of knowledge must here submit itself to the disappointment of love, the true subject is indeed the desire to know. Alcibiades, for all his pains, has well understood: he has been most bitterly disappointed by himself, inconsolable for having strayed so far away from his own truth.

Alcibiades' speech is only incidentally in praise of Socrates. If it were no more than a testimony to the edifying manner in which the philosopher had put Diotima's principles into practice, little more than a second "Apology of Socrates," it would lose much of its zest. The gritty recitation of Alcibiades' misadventures in love owes its sharpest flavor to the manner in which the subject himself (let us not forget that he is drunk) reveals the depths of his own disillusionment: the incurable bite of a philosophy that far exceeds his grasp. Socrates is little more than a foil for that which Alcibiades has failed to achieve. Worse still, Socrates carries within his person, in a manner of speaking, the deceptive object his young friend seeks. Those marvellous *agalmata* that Alcibiades attributes to him, Socrates *does not possess*. Had he possessed those divine gems, he would no longer be a philosopher but an accomplished wise man: he would not wander about in the company of Eros, *in search* of wisdom and beauty, but would assume his natural place among the gods. Neither wisdom nor beauty is something commonly available in the sense that they can be stored away, or removed.

In *Phaedrus*, Socrates warns against the facility that flows from the *pharmakon* of writing. The illusory transmission of the written word is of the same order as the quest for those notorious *agalmata*: images and idols have taken the place of words. From the earliest moments of the symposium, we have seen Agathon express the same naïve desire: to have science flow into him upon contact with Socrates. Knowing is, however, not substance, nor can it be transmitted, the reason why Diotima hesitates to carry her discourse through to its natural conclusion. What is "transmitted," at most, is the desire to know, hence it is more appropriate to speak of awakening than of transmission. Socrates is constantly insisting on the point, and has never pretended to practice any other trade than that of his mother: he is, in the image of Diotima, the midwife of the spirits. And the truth he helps them bring into the world is a negative one: to deliver them from what they imagine they know in order to make room for the desire to know.

Even Alcibiades' confession is misleading, for the true object of his praise is not truth, but handsome Agathon. Everything you've related, Socrates tells him, had no other purpose than to sow discord between us, Agathon and me, in such a way as to have him only for yourself, and forbid him from approaching me,

> "But we've seen through you; the object of your little play of satyr and Silenus is perfectly clear. Don't let him succeed, my dear Agathon; take steps to prevent anybody from setting you and me at variance."
>
> "You are very likely right, Socrates," replied Agathon; "no doubt that was why he sat down between us, in order to keep us apart. But he shan't succeed; I will come and take the place on the other side."
>
> "Do," said Socrates, "come and sit here, beyond me."
>
> "My God," said Alcibiades, "look how the fellow treats me. He thinks that he must always get the better of me. If you won't be content otherwise, you extraordinary man, you might at least let Agathon sit between us."
>
> "Quite impossible," said Socrates. "You have just spoken in praise of me, and now it is my turn to speak in praise of my right-hand neighbour. If Agathon sits next to you, it will fall to him to speak in praise of me all over again, instead of my speaking in praise of him. Let it be as I propose, my good friend, and don't grudge the lad his tribute of praise from me, especially as I have a strong desire to eulogize him."
>
> "Hurrah, hurrah," cried Agathon. "You can see I can't stay here; I simply must change my place so as to have the privilege of being praised by Socrates."
>
> "That's just what always happens," said Alcibiades. "If Socrates is there no one else has a chance with anybody who is good-looking!" (222d–223a)

As if the truth Alcibiades had promised at the beginning of his elegy could be reduced to a simple affair of sex and jealousy. Everything seems directed toward drowning the theme of love in drink and revelry. With the difference that Alcibiades is deprived of the object of his desire, as Agathon will be of his elegy; for no sooner has he risen to take his place at Socrates' right on the couch than a new interruption of merrymakers overwhelms the proceedings with disorder and transforms the evening into a drinking bout the intent of which is to leave the reader thirsty for more. The principal theme of the dialogue, when all is said and done, may well be neither love nor beauty, for all the space—all too apparent, in fact—they have been given; instead, it may be that ever-present fault line, like a hardly visible vein in the polished surface of the story, which it is necessary not to name in order to preserve the mystery in which Plato abandons us.

The *Symposium* could hardly have ended with the revelations of Diotima without irremediably contradicting her spirit. The words of the woman from Mantinea must be forgotten; if they are not, we are at risk of believing an even more ridiculous, derisory intoxication than that of wine: that we have achieved something that resembles supreme knowledge. The episode of Alcibiades is not intended, as many commentators claim, to bring us "back" from the sphere of intelligible verities to the world of the senses, when we have never even set foot in that world. Diotima's discourse—which takes fourth position in the chain of transmission after Apollodorus, Aristodemus, and Socrates—is a dream, a divagation from which Alcibiades' alcoholic exaltation awakens us.

For all that, her sublime discourse occupies, as do the *agalmata* for Socrates, a central place at the heart of the dialogue. How can we pretend that Plato is not expressing in it the ideas that are dearest to him? That, by virtue of this fact, they are not the most difficult nor the most delicate to grasp? Furthermore, once he has delivered them, he betrays them, attempting to eradicate them from the reader's mind for fear that he will wish to carry them away as Alcibiades desires to carry off the treasure he seeks in Socrates. Fear and desire are intermingled, in Plato, in speaking what cannot be spoken, the clear intent being not to leave matters atop that loftiest of summits. Here indeed is the greatest accomplishment of the art of storytelling in all its magnificence: without this art, which Plato handles so marvellously, none of the great questions raised in the *Symposium*, and least of all the question that winds its way largely unseen through the work, could have been so profoundly and yet so subtly dealt with. Humor, ambiguity, the unexpected, and the narrative flow itself serve the purposes of the narrator as only the art of narration can. Thanks to him, not every seed has yet germinated, even today, in the gardens of writing that Plato has sowed.

Paradoxically, storytelling is for Plato's philosophy the instrument of choice for protection against the inertia and pedantry in which all *written* truth is in danger of becoming mired. The staunchest defender of truth must employ the art of the "fable-makers" to prevent his *pharmakon* from becoming pure poison for the spirit. So true is the injunction that Plato himself is not always able to avoid the temptations of certainty: the same temptation that is at work in the discourse of Diotima, whom Socrates admits "may be very wise" (208c) on occasion, that is to say, she speaks *too well*. Against what we can define as the power of enchantment, the episode of Alcibiades works like an antidote. Seen in this perspective, the *Symposium* in its entirety functions as an antidote to the excesses of truth that burden the Platonic *oeuvre*. Though I have taken pains to avoid examining that *oeuvre* as a whole, I cannot resist the desire to demonstrate the manner in which the *Symposium* functions as a tool for the criticism of certain of its passages, particularly those that touch upon knowledge and death.

Phaedo, *Timaeus*, and, to a much more subtle degree, the *Republic* are permeated with the assurance of him who knows where the truth lies. Plato's whole *oeuvre*, in fact, is permeated with an incontrovertible conviction: that the ultimate reality of the world is beauty, and thought is the surest way of approaching it. But thought, which depends upon the incessant exigencies of the body, remains weak:

> But the fact is we have had it proved to us that if we are ever going to obtain pure knowledge, we must get away from the body, and with the soul itself see things themselves. And then, it would seem, we shall have that which we desire, that which we say we are in love with, wisdom; we shall have it when we are departed, so signifies the argument, and not while we are living; for if it is impossible to have pure knowledge of anything whatsoever with the body present, there are two alternatives. Either we never can attain to knowledge, or we can attain only after death; for then the soul will be alone and by itself, without the body, and before that it will not. (*Phaedo* 66d–e)

So speaks Socrates on the day of his death to those who fear to see him die. If there exists pure knowledge, only death will open its doors to us. A doubt persists: that knowledge "of anything whatsoever" could not exist. But such doubt, in Plato, is minimal, little more than rhetorical flourishes, for during our lives thought enables us to seize fleeting moments, distant glimmers of that truth from which we stand separated: the truth that the maelstrom of the world now reveals, now obscures, but whose existence somewhere above and beyond this world, in the immutable realm of Ideas, is nonetheless certain.

Timaeus is often cited to demonstrate Plato's belief in the "reality" of Ideas. But what reality are we speaking of? Certainly not that which is immediately accessible to our senses. We would be committing a substantial error were we to represent these famous Ideas as perfect corporal objects that furnish the celestial world. What Timaeus says—Timaeus, let us duly note, and not Socrates, who is but a listener for once, delighted at not having to speak—is that the demiurge, the supreme architect, has created the Soul of the world with eyes riveted upon the eternal Model with which it is confounded. This Soul of the world stands revealed as a complex construction, whose details Timaeus spends ample time explaining. In a general sense, his exposition is rather laborious and seeks little more than to provide "a tale suitable to our purpose" of the origins of the world, a reservation that Socrates hastens to approve (29d). Its essence is that within the principle of the universal indeed lies an idea, a model, and an unchangeable form from which the Soul of the world draws inspiration to give order to chaos. To put it more succinctly, intelligence precedes and informs matter, which is itself the organization of chaos. It thus locates the universe half-way between form and chaos, between immutability and movement, between eternity and becoming. But, above and beyond this compromise, the real, the true, the incorruptible—the model—lies Intelligence. The world is the product of a matrix, of which intelligence constitutes the supreme degree of reality. The loftiest, truest, surest possible truth is conceptual perfection—and death, the journey that lays it before the contemplation of our soul. As our souls have already made the journey, each of them possesses a distant remembrance, a sort of nostalgia. For anyone who knows how to look, Plato's ideas can be seen as nostalgia for the intelligible present in the phenomena of the world.

The presence is a virtual one that, for the most part, eludes our gaze. Yet our eyes (and our senses in general) are not entirely without a certain usefulness: "God invented and gave us sight to the end that we might behold the courses of intelligence in the heaven, and apply them to the courses of our own intelligence which are akin to them" (*Timaeus*, 47b). The intelligible is more than simply a memory; it can be partially perceived in the ordering of the cosmos itself (which will cause Galileo to remark that nature is written in the language of mathematics). Its beauty makes itself known to us through the world of the senses. The body is, of course, a prison, but one open to the cosmic rays of the intellect, just as in the *Symposium* physical attraction stimulates a movement toward the beauty of the soul. It is *with* the body that Plato reasons against the body—against the world *in* and *through* the world.

The world is at once transparent and opaque to beauty. Such is the esscence of the tale Plato tells in the celebrated Allegory of the Cave in the *Republic*, which stands as probably the most powerful metaphor for the impracticable path of knowledge ever written. Between the walls of a cavern are seated men with their feet and necks chained, unable to move either their heads or bodies. They can only see the wall before them. From a parapet behind them, puppets are played, illuminated by a distant fire whose source is concealed from the prisoners, who see nothing but the figurines' shadows moving across the screen that constitutes their horizon. They believe that this wall and these shadows constitute the world; that which we unthinkingly label "reality." Let us imagine that one of them contrives to escape his bonds. He turns, sees the contrivance of the cut-out figures, and is startled to see the fire that cast their shadows on the wall. He stands up; the cave has a passageway to the outside into which he haltingly moves, still dazzled by the light he has just beheld. The passageway is long, tortuous, and narrow; he slips, injures himself on the rough surface of the walls, and would have quickly abandoned his ascent had he not been forcibly dragged toward the opening. Suddenly, a dot of blinding light appears, a quickening never before experienced, unbearable. Hands over his eyes, he is drawn upwards into the open air; dazzled, he stumbles. Left to his own devices, he would surely have turned back toward the comfort of the cave, so strongly do his eyes smart. He needs time to realize that the sun of truth cannot be looked upon directly and to be able, progressively, to contemplate that which it illuminates. If by chance he were to return to tell his companions what he has seen, they would not believe him, would take him for a madman, would put him to death (514a–517a).

Not only is the pathway to truth arduous, but truth itself is, in the strictest sense of the word, unbearable. The true (the Beautiful, the Intelligible, the Divine) cannot be contemplated without casting us into blindness, yet its murderous light opens to us a world of which we had been unaware. A world of which the world had been unaware. This world, of which we had had no idea, is, in the final analysis, none other than our world! Coming implicitly full circle, the Platonic metaphor brings us back to our quotidian reality—the sun and the earthly universe it illuminates—to evoke that beauty so far from which we live, chained as we are before the shadows of effigies that we take for reality. But the real, that true reality which the pathway of knowledge allows us to approach, lies there before our eyes, quite like the stars, which, according to Timaeus, trace by their orderly paths the very movements of the Intellect. Which amounts to saying that the cave lies in our mind. The shadows that play upon its walls are our prejudices, our phantasms, our fears, our habits—a constant, indigent repetition of a lesser knowledge that allows no room for amazement.

For us, as mortals, truth remains inaccessible, and the soul, freed from the body, can contemplate it in its purity only in death: a dangerous way indeed of mollifying truth, and of placing in it our hopes. For here the philosopher speaks of none other than *anticipation* (517b). While we await liberation, it is in and through our body, providing that the soul it contains is content to serve only its appetites, that we are also able to accede to beauty in all its manifestations. For though beauty, that of the world of the senses, is available to our eyes, we are unable to see it because, in every sense of the term, we are ignorant of it. We drift on complacently, in the most mediocre of satisfactions, in ignorance of our inner cinema, having first neglected then mutilated our capacity to contemplate the world. To know, to seek to know, means to undertake the effort needed to enter into such contemplation. We must exercise our powers of vision, but this exercise is only possible within the context of a certain equilibrium of the soul that Plato calls justice. To fall in love with a beautiful face is not enough. As mirror of the flesh, it is perishable; its beauty will wane if it does not receive sustenance from other sources. Beauty demands of us the same effort—whether we bear it within us or contemplate it—and by expending this effort, as we live at peace with ourselves, we will be in a position to receive the *reality* of the world.

That the world is *in reality* beautiful, that it is worthy of being contemplated in the intelligence of its reality is Plato's unique postulate. From it all else flows. Particularly that there is no higher, more truthful, more long-lasting happiness than this contemplation. Philosophy, the love of wisdom, and knowledge itself have no other object, no other end. No human enterprise, including and primarily that which seeks to organize life in society, can demand contemplation as a sacrifice. If Socrates unceasingly insists, in the *Republic*, that the justice of the soul and that of the city both obey the same principles, he means that politics can have no other goal than to allow each person, and the community in its entirety, to learn to lead their lives well, to live in harmony with themselves. If the State proves itself to be incapable of doing so, if it deviates from this task, if it is not in the service of knowledge, it cannot erect barriers to such contemplation without a total loss of legitimacy.

How are we to admit that the intelligence of earthly things and of the manner in which we live our lives are worth the effort which Plato invites us to expend if our souls are already pledged, in the hereafter, to the contemplation of the Beautiful in and of itself? Because the soul cannot escape unscathed from its sojourn upon the earth. Death is not pure deliverance. Such detachment would be far too fine a windfall for those who know not how to live: "The soul comes into Hades bringing nothing with her but her discipline and her way of life" (*Phaedo*, 107c–d). Plato's infernal topography and psychology, as they are presented in *Phaedo*, and which were to wield such a powerful influence on Christendom, have little connection with the hereafter of Homer. In the *Odyssey*, we recall, the kingdom of the dead is a kind of non-place where powerless shades wander in regret for the lives they have lived. Plato's Inferno, as later in Dante's afterlife, is highly differentiated: there are abominable depths for incurable souls, rehabilitation zones (the future Christian purgatory) for those souls with the capacity to heal themselves, and places of felicity for those "who have been eminent for the holy lives they lived" (*Phaedo*, 114b). But Plato's eschatology is not a closed system. No sooner has the question of the afterlife and of the undecidable been raised than Plato turns to the mythical form, one which lends itself admirably to all narrative variants, now contradictory, now complementary. Thus, in the *Republic*, Socrates proposes a psychic destiny that is in far greater harmony with the conception he has developed of justice as harmony with oneself. Here too, at the decisive moment, with the myth of Er, story takes over from argument.

Considered dead on the battlefield but with body intact, Er is resurrected on the day of his burial and relates what he has seen in his visit to the afterlife. Irremediably tainted souls suffer the same sanctions as they do in *Phaedo*. But the crowd of ordinary souls, be they from heaven or earth, are called before another tribunal: a tribunal whose sole judge is none other than the soul itself. Summoned to choose freely the life and the person in which it will be reincarnated, the soul exercises its choice in a way that faithfully reflects the judgement, forethought, and wisdom that it had achieved in its previous life. To live a life of injustice, disequilibrium, and inner discord, is to be condemned to repeat the same errors in this new life and in all those that follow. Only harmony with our self can empower us to choose our life, and to guide it, now and later, along the path of knowledge without which the world would remain for us impermeable and its beauty forever a closed book.

Whether in this world or in the afterlife, in this life or another, Plato proposes to set man free by challenging him to mind his soul, to keep alive the breath that inhabits his body and makes it *alive* (*Phaedo*, 105c): to set man free, that is to say, to relieve him of the implacable *ate* of the tragic hero, but also from the tyranny of political ambition, of honors and of wealth, from the derision of ordinary passions, in such a way as to leave the maximum possible latitude for what Aristotle so magnificently calls "the passion to know." But, anticipating what we will encounter in the next chapter, where Aristotle reaps and stows the harvest, Plato is content to sniff the air. Like Socrates (or, more precisely, the Socrates whom he brings to life), Plato sees himself strictly as a philosopher, meaning—it cannot be repeated too often— he is *someone in love with that which he does not possess*, in love with the very knowledge whose poverty he so powerfully senses, taken by the very beauty in which he everywhere discovers the signs of intelligence. Presence and absence cannot be dissociated. They bring the same weight to bear upon the scales of the spirit. Should absence prevail, the spirit sinks into negation: horror and cynicism know no bounds. Should presence dominate and the desire to live be blunted, love, satiated, grows numb. Life has no need of beauty, and even risks being crushed by its permanence. To remain alive, the living being requires that beauty be possible, that it provide a sign unto him.

Unfaithful to the spirit of the *Symposium*, Plato at times allows himself to be overwhelmed by presence. Signs fill him with certainty: the beautiful is not a possibility in this world; the Beautiful *is*. Eros inclines in the face of the truth of Being: a magnified truth upon which Christianity will bestow all power. It should come as no surprise to see the Church seizing upon the Platonic essence to compound its own magisterial *pharmakon*. Plato is reduced in spite of himself—but also because of his excessiveness—to the role of a druggist! On his shelves, the speakers of truth will find all they need. Except for one thing. A thing that we have already refused to name.

Naught but one "thing," a single, subtle, tenacious ingredient that escapes being captured in a bottle, a seepage whose barely perceptible escaping hiss runs throughout the story of the *Symposium*, and which all Western philosophy since Plato, and with Plato, seeks to expunge from its monumental scriptural constructions.

Other merrymakers have burst into Agathon's house. Drunk to a stupor, the guests begin to nod off. Some have already left. The narrator himself has fallen asleep. Awakened by the crowing of the cock, he sees in his somnolence Agathon, Aristophanes, and Socrates still drinking and arguing. Actually, only Socrates is speaking. His interlocutors are experiencing ever-greater difficulty in following him, and one after the other they drop off to sleep.

One is tempted to conclude that philosophy has triumphed over tragedy and comedy. Who could doubt it? But it is a triumph charged with irony, when we consider that the Socratic disquisition, flowing as abundantly as the wine, has lulled its listeners to sleep. Still, the word keeps the one who speaks alive. Comedy and tragedy must both end; the catharsis of laughter and tears cannot last. Man cannot constantly laugh at himself, nor constantly lament his fate. Contrariwise, the faculty of reflection and the capacity for bedazzlement are as inexhaustible within him as is the object of his contemplation. Reflection has no end. It keeps us in a *state of wakefulness*, in love with the world. The philosopher has no truth to offer, but he is the first to affirm that *até* is far from ineluctable, that the world is worth being contemplated, that life can be beautiful, that it is incumbent upon us to lead it in such a way that it becomes so.

As he surveys the choices of reincarnation of souls among the numerous lives offered them, Er finally, with great exertion, contrives to discover with delight that of Ulysses, "lying neglected by the others"—fate has assigned it to the last place, to lead "the uneventful life of an ordinary man" (*Republic*, 620c–d). This tribute to the clairvoyance of the Homeric hero at the conclusion of the seminal work, which Plato has dedicated to the question of knowing how to live, most probably indicates that the adventurer has not suffered his tribulations entirely in vain. In fact, and in a manner of speaking, he has become a philosopher. Rather like Ulysses, but without leaving home and hearth behind, the philosopher finds pleasure in following the hard road along which the passion to know encounters the love of reflection.

7

THE PATHS OF KNOWLEDGE

WITH PLATO we have reached the point where story and philosophy intersect—at which the question of truth must be raised.

It is a meeting of the moment and, to a certain extent, one without a future. Philosophy and story converge and just as quickly diverge, yet of their brief encounter each has contrived to preserve trace elements: philosophy will appear, incidentally, in story and story in philosophy, but the two genres, several notable cases (Augustine, Descartes, Hegel) aside, today remain clearly distinct. In the introduction, I maintained that philosophy, Platonic philosophy in particular, had been constructed against story. Let me be more specific: against a certain kind of story, in which pedagogy is not an end in itself. We have just seen how Plato uses fiction to this end. In Plato, the story is far from incidental, far from ornamental, nor is it limited to "myths" inserted into the structure of the dialogue to evoke that which cannot be expressed in other ways. In many of Plato's writings, story is of nodal importance: that which it evokes of truth derives as much from the narrative structure as that which is expressly declared. We are aware of the underlying reason: the truth may not be spoken, and even less so written, but through the ambiguities of dialogue and stage direction its gleam can be made manifest.

What begins to take on clearer form, at the point where story encounters philosophy, and at the potential cost of great misunderstanding, is the status of truth itself. To which order of truth can thought lay claim? What can man know of the world, of his place in it, and of his death? Plato's postulate is that death, far from being the end point for the psyche, coincides with truth. In death, in separation from the body, the soul finds its truth and, depending upon its state, enters into contact with the ultimate reality and truth of the world where it—the *soul*, not the individual—recommences another cycle of peregrination. Socrates dies without returning, but the psyche upon which he lavished such care continues along its path in a different place. For Socrates, the acceptance of death is part and parcel of the attention that he has lavished upon his soul so that it may contemplate the Beautiful in and of itself. Some go so far as to say that it is inconceivable for Plato that his master die in vain, and that the entire Platonic enterprise can be attributed to the desire for redemption. Perhaps this is so. But what must be redeemed, whatever the case, cannot be the soul (precisely because Socrates has taken such excellent care of it) but the life of the philosopher, the life of philosophy itself.

Plato's greatest concern, in the final analysis, is not to have lived in vain. The ontological speculations that constitute his ultimate justification aside, philosophical heroism joins forces with Homeric heroism: in both cases, the aim is to use, in the most intense, the most judicious way possible, the brief moment given to each person: life itself. The difference is one of content: for the sensorial richness (practical and material) of the Homeric hero is substituted the intellectual and contemplative richness of the philosopher. Just as the Intelligible, in the Allegory of the Cave, evokes earthly light and its source in the sun, in the same way the Beautiful in itself evokes the beauty of the world. Platonic immortality is clearly more than an incidental add-on to the destiny of the Homeric soul, but it is clear that it is *in life*, within the limits assigned to his brief terrestrial existence, that the Socratic hero may delight in the beauties he is in love with. As the soul has forgotten almost everything of its passage through the loftiest spheres, Socrates, as a man, can expect nothing of his term there. All, for him, including eternal beatitude (which Plato desires for him), is played out here below. Above and beyond all considerations of post-mortem retribution, it is essential to have been just, that is to say—at the risk of repeating ourselves—in harmony with oneself, and to have participated in this life, which will never again be repeated, and in the beauty of that which surpasses it. Life itself is the philosopher's recompense. He asks nothing of death. It is enough for him not to fear it, for the *fear* of death and naught else causes us to act against ourselves. In accepting death, irrespective of what may happen beyond it, man accepts the condition that preserves him from unhappiness, from the fate of falling victim to the tragic hero's *até*. The acceptance of death enables loving curiosity about the world.

In Plato, the weakness of this curiosity about the world stems from the fact that it is not entirely satisfied with the world nor with its own postulates, and has set its sights on an ultimate truth instead of self-sufficiency—instead of limiting its purview to the sensibility of the world. Western philosophy has become entrapped in this transcendental finalism, which seeks the truth *outside, above and beyond*, while truth itself lies invisible at our feet, like a hunted animal crouched hidden in the bushes nearby while its hunter scans the horizon.[68] In breaking with the doctrine of Ideas, Aristotle is undoubtedly proposing that we restrict ourselves to the visible world. Paradoxically, beginning with none other than Aristotle, philosophy begins, though not necessarily with premeditation, to stray from the story and more resolutely take up the quest for truth.

The abandonment of the story marks a profound shift in the philosophical project Plato sought to define. It confirms the intention of philosophers to choose a different path from the one which, for all his enormous influence, the man who is considered in the West as the father of philosophy had unsuccessfully attempted to lay down. Before moving ahead with the reading of the great stories that inform our collective imagination, it may be worthwhile to linger for a moment at this decisive parting of the ways. In order to understand that which has been "decided," we must attempt to evaluate, in the light of our readings thus far, the true extent of the break caused by the philosophical project before, with and after Plato. Let us make clear from the start that we are speaking of *Greek* philosophy, without at all making the exclusive claim that philosophy "begins" in the geographical location and in the age of classical Greece. It begins there in the Western self-imagination, which is what concerns us here.

Philosophy sets out with the intent of blazing a fresh trail toward knowledge through a process of inquiry that progressively dispenses with the mythical explanations received from our ancestors. Without being necessarily abolished or held up to ridicule, myth is, at minimum, accepted as a representation worthy of examination. This is probably because myth's power to explain, and its ability to create meaning, had weakened, as witnessed by the liberties Homeric narrative takes with the gods. It is most probable that the celebrated break between *mythos* and *logos*, if one is to judge by the evolution of the two terms (from common to divergent significata), has taken place gradually, beginning quite precisely with Homer. Only in retrospect does the philosophical *logos* appear as the carrier of an intention *sui generis* in opposition to the mythological story. As belief in myth begins to waver, philosophy strikes out in its search for a new cognitive foundation, questioning as it goes.

---

68. By analogy with what Socrates says of the justice he seeks with his interlocutors in *The Republic* (432a–433).

This constant questioning, still in phase with mythology, addresses itself first to nature, to *physis*, to the *cosmos*. What does "that which is" consist of? What of being? What is the world in which we find ourselves? These are, broadly speaking, the kind of questions apparently raised by most of the philosophers labelled "presocratic" or "preplatonic": Thales, Anaximandrus, Heraclitus, Parmenides (considered to be the father of the principle of non-contradiction), Anaxagorus, Empedocles, Democritus. What these giants have bequeathed to us is minuscule: fragments that resist interpretation, and commentaries which may well distort their meaning more than they illuminate it. Still, these fragments testify to a powerful questioning about being, from which the questioner, *man as preoccupation*, appears to be missing—quite unlike what takes place in the *Epic of Gilgamesh* or the Torah.

Preoccupation with the human in the process of philosophical questioning is the hallmark of what is generally referred to as "the Socratic break." Rather than attempting to know *physis*, Socrates investigates the human condition. His investigation leads to the inescapable conclusion that man not only knows nothing of what he believes he knows, but does not even know himself, a requirement that Thales may already have formulated. The first step toward knowledge is therefore to rid oneself of false knowledge, a task to which the Platonic dialogues of the first, or "Socratic" period, are devoted. Socrates brings his interlocutors to admit that they have indeed spoken of beauty, wisdom, courage, friendship, and justice without really knowing what they are saying, with the result that they lead their existence in ignorance of the virtues they pretend to practice. His peculiar form of intellectual midwifery reveals the pretensions and the incoherence of the prejudices, which constitute such a formidable obstacle to true investigation, without which there can be no knowledge worth its salt. Lack of knowledge, in turn, has its practical consequences: when men act badly they do so out of ignorance; when they are unhappy it is because of intellectual sloth. The affirmation is startling, almost revolting. And it is so radical that neither Christian theology nor modern philosophy, with the sole exception of Spinoza, have had the audacity to claim it as their own.

Plato makes Socrates' audacity his own, while seeking to articulate it into a general conception of *physis* that would comfort the philosopher in his decision to assign priority to the care of the soul. Concern for the soul is by no means exclusive to Plato. As Jan Patocka has demonstrated, it is shared by Democritus, Socrates' contemporary. But with Democritus, argues Patocka, the discipline of the soul must serve knowledge, while Plato reverses priorities: "Knowledge is a means for the soul to *become* that which it *can become.*"[69] The reversal is indeed a telling one, and indicates that the entire Platonic conception of the world, with its sense-apprehended manifestations on one side and the sphere of the intelligible on the other, that entire cross-section of his philosophy which was to influence Western metaphysics so deeply, has no meaning except in relation to the question of knowing how to lead one's life. That this question, in Plato's *oeuvre* itself and to an even greater extent in that of his emulators, ends up suffering from his cosmic articulation, that the theory of ideas, to rephrase the proposition, has instead helped relegate Plato's concern for the soul to the philosophical background, indicates that the articulation has not brought forth its expected fruit. Worse: until today, the distinction that Plato draws between the world of the senses and the world of the intelligible has been used as a fulcrum by those critics who locate in Platonic philosophy the origins of the metaphysical tangent taken by Greek, then Western philosophy ever since. That which should have strengthened the existential question has ultimately weakened it.

Aristotle, in abandoning the doctrine of Ideas, may well be attempting to avert the threat of just such a weakening. In affirming that the beauty of the world is visible from Plato's cave, in abolishing the walls of the cave rather than returning to it, Aristotle joins concern for the soul to knowledge more lastingly, and more convincingly, than his master. For him, as for Plato, to know is to direct one's path toward beauty, toward equilibrium, toward the good. We might well say, echoing Patocka, that as the Stagirite moves along this path he develops a loftier conception of human freedom: where, in Plato, the Beautiful and the Good appear as immutably given, restricted to another world, in Aristotle, equilibrium and beauty depend much more upon man himself, in that it is incumbent upon him, here and now, collectively and individually, to lend his life form and consistency, rather than allowing it to be squandered in the formless. "For Aristotle, the problem is not only one of the standard against which man is measured, but that of effective action, in which man must decide and carry out his decision," that is to say, to bring into being "by his action that which does not yet exist."[70] The entire Aristotelian concept of politics leads in this direction: politics is by definition the domain of *phronesis*, generally translated as "prudence," a term ill-adapted to rendering that which might be more plausibly translated as

---

69. Jan Patocka, *Platon et l'Europe*, traduit du tchèque par Erika Abrams (Lagrasse: Verdier, 1983), p. 91. [My translation—FR.]
70. Ibid., p. 211.

intelligence made act. Neither science nor technique, but rather partaking of both, the *phronesis* of this knowledge in action is an open-eyed praxis by virtue of which man may attempt to bring about his aspirations and verify in action their validity and their beauty (*Nichomachean Ethics*, 1140a–b).

Aristotle gives a lesson in politics which politicians and political commentators of today would do well to meditate upon, assuming of course that they seek the common good—and that the expression "common good" has some meaning for them. Circumstances arising from the Aristotelian manner of dealing with knowledge, and more precisely the style of the texts that have come down to us from Aristotle—the majority of which were not meant for public consumption but for himself or for a limited circle of his students—have inflicted upon his thought all the uncertainties to which the written word, which Plato justly mistrusted, is subject. Whether by happenstance or imprudence, Aristotle does not take the same precautions as his master with regard to the written word. Beyond circumstances, the style betrays a difference in approach that flows from a certain purely Aristotelian conception of knowledge, which we could term more pragmatic than Plato's.

This pragmatism manifests itself—almost naïvely, from a Platonic point of view—in the passage referred to above, in the manner in which Aristotle illustrates his admirable concept of *phronesis*. He cites Pericles as an example of a political man who has acted in conformity with it as an exigency. Now, we will recall that in the *Gorgias*, the *Protagoras* or the *Republic*, Socrates refers to Themistocles, Pericles, and their ilk as an example of precisely what must *not* be done: for all their qualities, these great statesmen were unable to advance the interests of the city as they should have; they neglected to care for its soul as they neglected their own; for this reason—their not having strived to make the city a better place and the squandering of their talents—their policies may be considered as failures (*Gorgias*, 515c–516a, 518e). In taking Pericles as his model, Aristotle clearly signals that he does not subscribe to the standards laid down by his mentor.

In a general sense, something in the manner in which knowledge is revealed in the *writings* of Aristotle *as they have come down to us*, differs radically from the Platonic approach. To our misfortune, the Aristotelian dialogues, whose art Cicero so admired, have disappeared. Though we may speculate endlessly about them, they are irrelevant to our discussion. We are obliged to evaluate Aristotle's manner and influence based on what has come down to us from the surviving texts. And, in these texts, the very least we can say is that Eros is no longer a presence, and that his withdrawal can be detected in the very style of the Aristotelian texts. It is a style—little matter whether deliberately or accidentally—diametrically opposed to narration:

> Every art and every investigation, and likewise every practical pursuit or undertaking, seems to aim at some good: hence it has been well said that the Good is That at which all things aim. It is true that a certain variety is to be observed among the ends at which the arts and sciences aim: in some cases the activity of practising the art is itself the end, whereas in others the end is some product over and above the mere exercise of the art; and in the arts whose ends are certain things beside the practice of the arts themselves, these products are essentially superior in value to the activities. But as there are numerous pursuits and arts and sciences, it follows that their ends are correspondingly numerous: for instance, the end of the science of medicine is health, that of the art of shipbuilding a vessel, that of strategy victory, that of domestic economy wealth. Now in cases where several such pursuits are subordinate to some single faculty—as bridle-making and the other trades concerned with horses' harness are subordinate to horsemanship, and this and every other military pursuit to the science of strategy, and similarly other arts to different arts again—in all these cases, I say, the ends of the master arts are things more to be desired than the ends of the arts subordinate to them; since the latter ends are only pursued for the sake of the former. And it makes no difference whether the ends of the pursuits are the activities themselves or some other thing beside these, as in the case of the sciences mentioned.
>
> If therefore among the ends at which our actions aim there be one which we will for its own sake, while we will the others only for the sake of this, and if we do not choose everything for the sake of something else (which would obviously result in a process ad infinitum, so that all desire would be futile and vain), it is clear that this one ultimate End must be the Good, and indeed the Supreme Good. Will not then a knowledge of this Supreme Good be also of great practical importance for the conduct of life? Will it not better enable us to attain our proper object, like archers having a target to aim at? If this be so, we ought to make an attempt to determine at all events in outline what exactly this Supreme Good is, and of which of the sciences or faculties it is the object. (*Nichomachean Ethics*, 1094a)[71]

71. *Aristotle in 23 Volumes*, vol. 19, trans. H. Rackham (Cambridge, MA: Harvard University Press; London: William Heinemann Ltd., 1934).

Thus begins that work which, of all Aristotle's texts, has probably wielded the greatest and most enduring influence on Western thought. Among those ends that can be assigned, says the Stagirite, is one which may be sought in and for itself, and in view of which all others are henceforth subordinate. For Aristotle, the choice is unavoidable in terms of practical necessity, without which ends would all be relative to one another and their pursuit would be without end. No hierarchy of values would thus be possible. But even such a straightforward formulation provides food for thought in a world—ours—in which the hierarchy of ends seems to have become blurred in the fog of individual intentions and private legitimacies which, for all that, partake of a general progress that is at once irreversible and unpredictable, desired and feared. The fact is that our desires are too widely dispersed, too contradictory for them to simply volatilize. But perhaps Aristotle is telling us that it is the collective will that has voided itself of all content, has spent itself. Could there be a better way for us, today, to measure to what extent the civilization that has never ceased to invoke his authority has in reality strayed far from his spirit?

This brief incursion into Aristotle should be sufficient to demonstrate two contradictory movements in his thought, insofar as it sees itself as both tributary to and corrective of Plato. From Plato, Aristotle has kept, as we have seen, the perspective of living one's life well. We also know that this is the outcome assigned to man as a practical goal, in a world where the walls of the cave have been (or can be) demolished. At first glance, this assignment, far from contradicting Plato's intentions, only gives them firmer foundations. But the faculty that may be relied upon to activate it, the *phronesis* we encountered earlier, is distinct from science, whose object is the eternal and incorruptible (1139b). Aristotle thus reintroduces, as the object of the highest category of knowledge, the sphere of the intelligible. Within the field of knowledge, this break, despite being less visible than in Plato, has even more radical consequences. If the Good and the Beautiful are the aims of practical knowledge, which must pass the test of facts, intelligence in action suffices in and of itself. Or at least so it might incline us to believe. In the self-sufficiency of practical reason resides, if only for a fleeting instant, the splendid audacity of Aristotelian thought. Still, it seems all but inevitable that something of the concern for the soul has been lost along the way.

If, for all practical purposes, there no longer exists a link between that which is, out of necessity, the subject of science, and that which *could* come about by virtue of our efforts, the subject of *phronesis*, we can wager with some confidence that the two approaches (not to mention the way in which they are produced) will eventually go their separate ways. It is thus difficult to understand, under these conditions, how the tension of beauty, which keeps the soul attentive to itself, can be maintained. This pursuit has never been absent in a man totally oriented toward the quest that is fated to reveal to him the innumerable facets of the beauty of living beings—and in fact, a significant mass of Aristotle's writings have to do with what today is called biology. But what is at issue here is less Aristotle himself and more his intellectual heritage, which carries a far greater weight than Plato's in the modern conception of science. His spirit of system has clearly been accentuated and partially disfigured by those who have attempted to "put his house in order." Still, the process of putting in order obviously draws some of its inspiration from the very nature of Aristotle's writings, and does so with a subtlety that often hides from the reader what it has concealed beneath an aridity as forbidding as it is elliptical. Aristotle winnows out, classifies, and enumerates the component parts of his subject. More than raising questions, his expositions attempt to establish and to assemble.

Mere ill fortune, or the paths that it has followed, cannot alone explain why Aristotle's writings have given sustenance to scholasticism quickly afflicted with sclerosis, nor why today some persist, at the cost of a substantial misunderstanding of the Greek conception of science, in considering them as the foundation of modern positivism. This misunderstanding is quite understandable: in the Aristotelian project lies latent the aim of a global, cumulative knowledge capable of eventually snaring all nature in its nets. The idea of an ultimately completed knowledge bearing on a finite world, which learned men would over time finally enumerate in all its aspects is totally foreign to the erotics of Platonic knowledge. This omnivorous, spreading conception of knowledge allows us to hope, in the best of hypotheses, for a form of knowledge that might be acquired in this world; it would do no less than suppress the absence without whose tension the love of an intangible reality gives way to the conviction that reality is well and truly contained in a monument the walls of which are unshakable. The Pantheon of knowledge built up over time, like a catalogue of accumulated treasures, has replaced the cave and its effigies. Concern for the soul is now in danger of being suffocated beneath the ambition to create such an accretion. Today, with growing disquiet, we see that it may yet come into being, and to perpetuate itself almost indefinitely—that is to say, within the still ill-defined limits of what we call the ecosystem.

There can be little doubt that in articulating his concern for the soul in the state of dispossession in which we find ourselves with regard to truth,

Plato grounds himself on the deepest underpinnings of our psyche: the irreducible distance that separates the desire for the real from its realization. The real cannot be realized; such is the merciless truth before which Plato's thought places us. That the real may await us in another world in recompense for the care we have taken of our soul is of secondary importance. The essential consideration, for the instant of our presence here, in this world—whether or not another world exists after this one—is that the real exists in our imagination, in the principle of that which makes us living beings. As beautiful as it is pitiless, this truth forbids us from lamenting our condition, for the impossibility of touching the real, to capitalize on beauty, is that which feeds in us the flame that keeps us wakeful. Nothing, in the absolute, guarantees us the certainty of the Beautiful, but something—there must after all be at least one fleeting surge of emotion in a lifetime—bears witness within us to the indestructible desire for beauty. No matter what has awakened it—the curves of a body, the taste of a fruit, the sound of a flute—the love of the world definitively depends upon the work that the spirit has carried out upon itself, and this spirit finds in that work a strength that the world of the senses cannot take away from it: better still, a strength from which the contemplation of this world has everything to gain.

Eros, in Plato, is the tension that transforms into strength the weakness that makes us at once keen for the world, desirous of understanding it, and unable truly to know it. Philosophy will waste little time in dissipating this tension in the legacy of the man it claims as its founder. The disdain with which philosophy sets the story aside is only one of the symptoms of this loss. And the loss in turn results more deeply from the search for certainty which, as it strives toward the absolute, fears to seek answers in the void and in the anguish that lend it its motive force. This void, I believe, is that which Plato intended to keep alive in us as a kind of appeal to being. His most vital contribution, the one most neglected by philosophy, is the idea that the void occupies at the core of our being a fertile place that can neither be ignored nor filled. It constitutes an emptiness, which we must not fear to keep alive. The wish to seal it over, whether by spiritual sloth or by sensual excess, is tantamount to choking off in ourselves the breath without which we can neither live nor die except by diminishing ourselves.

Beginning with that which, in the light of Plato, we can more clearly identify now than at the beginning of the book as the failure of philosophy, it seems fair to raise a question: has the story all along attempted to draw attention, whether deliberately or not, to that which most philosophers leave untouched, to that which they have contrived to obscure with their systems?

This question has already arisen with respect to the great mythical narratives we have studied thus far. To what extent do the *Epic of Gilgamesh*, the Torah, Hesiod's *Theogony*, the *Odyssey*, the tragedies of *King Oedipus* and *Antigone* anticipate, in a manner of speaking, the limits of a reasoned, systematic approach to being?

The *Epic of Gilgamesh* and the *Odyssey* seem particularly eloquent in this regard. The Akkadian hero and the Homeric adventurer, for all their radical differences, have one thing in common: they forgo the other world. The first does so with difficulty, at the conclusion of a series of exploits that brought him no closer to the immortality he so vainly sought, the second almost immediately. From the very beginning, Ulysses seems to have been warned against such a vanity, which is confirmed by his brief visit to Hades. Man has no other choice but to lead his life as though all is riding upon it, as though there were no hope than to seek happiness, no matter how fragile and fleeting, in the here and now. In this view, concern for being need not show itself. The resulting absence lends both stories their striking feel of actuality. They speak, before the fact, of the crippling absurdity of all "metaphysical" enterprises.

Hesiod's *Theogony* moves in the same direction, but along a different path. In Hesiod, the world beyond exists, possesses its history, its hierarchy; it can be told, sung. The gods have things their way, and man, with apologies to Prometheus, must be content with what Zeus is gracious enough to leave him. For some, immortality and pleasure; for others, finiteness and labor. The two worlds are in constant contact, as in Homer, but the contact itself, its extent, and its effect once again are dependent upon the good will of the gods. The presence of the divine world offers man no guarantee whatsoever, neither in this world, nor in Hades. Death leads man toward a world of immaterial shadows; in no way is it a bridge toward immortality, not even for those who have led a meritorious existence. In short, for humankind, there is no transcendence.

It is against this detachment, that is to say, against human powerlessness against the order of the world, that Sophoclean tragedy lifts its voice. Not in the slightest because Sophocles intends to oppose it—the height of immoderation! On the contrary, it gives voice to immoderation as a way of illustrating what befalls the man who believes he is master of his fate. Far from being a protest (in modern terms), the *King Oedipus-Antigone* cycle is in reality a warning: *até* lies in wait for us and will most certainly bring low those who, in defying it, show that they do not know their place in the world. In the case of Antigone, the defiance is deliberate; with Oedipus, it is unconscious. In both cases, however, the order against which the hero forges forward is either indecipherable, or can only be deciphered in retrospect. There is no defense against *até*, and in such circumstances the conceit of viewing being as transcendence seems contemptible. Only the sense of measure and the desire to understand are not. Both partake of the famous precept of the Delphic Oracle, which Socrates makes his own: "Know thyself"—meaning, "take the measure of your ignorance" or "be attentive to the inherent limits of the human condition." Seen in the light of this warning, metaphysics undoubtedly represents the immoderation of the spirit. To the extent that Plato presumes to guide the soul toward a felicity that reaches into another world, his concern goes well beyond that which the tragic heroes— and man in general—may hope to attain. But let us not forget that the Platonic soul has been divorced, in the most definitive fashion, from the individual in which it once resided. Whatever survives beyond our earthly life is little more than the tiny cosmic particle of which we were the bearer. Socrates, yet again, is irremediably mortal.

The biblical story seems to me to be similar, if only from the individual point of view. Individually, man as conceived by Judaism can do little. But he does have the possibility, rather like in Plato, of entering into contact with transcendence with the Unnameable (YHWH). His contact, however, ensures him, as an individual, of no manner of salvation, nor of the slightest participation in eternity. If he can join in transcendence, it is through his imagination, through the collective entity of which he is but one link, and to the enduring nature of which he contributes, year in, year out, in his obedience to the Law. The particular genius of Judaism here finds its fullest expression. The Law shapes the collective identity to which the Jew belongs, and thanks to which he may confirm his spiritual antecedents upstream while projecting himself into the downstream of his life. He becomes part of the great river of the people of whom the Book bears witness; there he finds, in his lifetime, his portion of immortality. Knowledge, which we have seen to be painful, cannot be left to the soul, a concept that does not exist in the Torah; it is a matter of history and has no other dimension than collective. The world is cruel; men do not always clearly understand what is required of them, but together they may attempt to make and to bequeath the Law. Certainly the Law is revealed, and an indecipherable mystery pervades the circumstances of its revelation, even though its authors are men, and no manner of speculation can be admitted at this level of the unutterable. In any event, the Law is brought to earth and locates itself in time, and in time only. It introduces no conceivable manner of metaphysics; no other knowledge than that of the Law and of the history that has made it possible. Ultimately, no other course of study is possible except that of Scripture.

It has by now become clearer at which point the critical encounter with Platonic knowledge, in all its ambiguity, takes place: something in man that Plato names the soul, the breath of life itself, makes it possible for him, drawing on the experience of his senses, to create for himself an approach to intelligible things, of which he may thus gain a glimpse here below. It is the mark of man to possess this possibility within him, and a life that passes it by, that is to say, that overlooks the desire for beauty, that overlooks what is its liveliest aspect, is a ruined life.

This cognitive ambition has retreated to the most distant reaches of Western philosophy, having probably proved itself to be too demanding, too difficult. As we will see in the next part of this book, Christianity has contributed significantly to its retreat: while drawing inspiration from Plato, it transformed the salvation of the soul into something entirely different. Christian salvation depends on faith, upon revelation, upon that which theology calls grace, quite precisely to indicate that it does not depend upon us. Knowledge, in the final analysis, is of no consequence.[72] Furthermore, that which in Plato is a general principle of which all may partake—the soul of the world—becomes, in Christianity, individualized: the Christian must save his individual soul; what is ultimately at stake in salvation is the resurrection of the body to which it is henceforth inextricably bound. To claim that Christendom is "Platonism for the people" is meaningless when we bear in mind the distance that separates Platonism from Plato. Christian theology only accentuates the occultation for which Platonism must ultimately bear the blame.

The Church, taking after Augustine in its dissatisfaction with philosophy, would go on to construct its own conception of the world based on a narrative revelation. The terrible genius of Christianity is to have drawn its own conclusions from the weakness of philosophy and to have founded its own truth upon a myth. Except that—and this changes everything—the myth will no longer be considered as a myth. It will be proclaimed and spread as "good tidings" (the Gospel). Christianity has carried out an exploit that staggers the imagination. It has succeeded in imposing an antinomy: a story of Truth.

---

72. To what extent grace depends on our works, on our actions, constitutes a source of extremely complex theological debates into which it is not necessary to enter. What is essential at this point is to agree that grace does not depend on knowledge.

Part Three

TRUTH OR DEATH

IN CLAIMING TO BE a story of truth, in making itself the messenger of a truth that brings salvation to humanity, the Gospel brings about a sharp break with the narrative tradition that has given sustenance to our image of ourselves. The great literary works of Western Christianity will bear its markings until the Renaissance and beyond. Though Rabelais and Cervantes were eventually to break its spell, the effects of the truth it tells have made themselves felt up to the present.

Concern for truth is by no means exclusive to the literature of Christianity: we encounter it too in Herodotus, Thucydides, and Xenophon. But the historian, though he is never completely free of fabulation, attempts simply to reconstruct the course of human events. The story he has to tell is not one of mystery, even though in its telling he may collide with the most inexplicable aspects of human behavior. Thucydides is not concerned with the gods; he attempts to fathom the Peloponnesian War. What makes the Gospel story particular, when compared to the historical accounts of pagan antiquity, is not that it pretends to speak the truth. Nor that it pretends to speak of the marvellous, which Homer and Hesiod both succeed admirably in doing. No; it is to join the two together, inseparably, and to bestow upon them ultimate finality. It is to assert the following: "The marvellous of which I speak has indeed taken place, it brings salvation, to it I bear witness." At its core lies the conflation of the historical with the miraculous and with salvation. This poses a crucial problem to which we must constantly return.

One need not believe in the *Epic of Gilgamesh* nor the *Odyssey* to read and to take pleasure in them. But with the story of the Passion and the Resurrection, quite the opposite is true: by its own admission it has no meaning except when seen through the lens of faith. To read the life and times of Jesus as fable, no matter how compelling, is to deprive it of its *raison d'être*. It would be a legitimate question to ask what the Gospel story is even doing in this book, since its guiding principle violates the conception of the story as a text open to the inexhaustible fertility of successive interpretations. *A priori*, the Gospel story possesses no mythical quality, and its stature as an act of witness would seem to invalidate any attempt to examine it from that angle. The upshot is that we are confronted with a difficulty of fundamental proportions, one that I do not seek to avoid. Quite the contrary, I have chosen to place it at the center of my reading.

The reading I propose is a deliberately paradoxical one: it approaches the New Testament from the agnostic viewpoint that is my own, while taking nothing away from the power of the Gospel story that it tells. Such is my wager. A wager I feel compelled to make, for such has been its influence on the literature, which, for centuries to come, would follow in its wake. Only in the phenomenal force of the speech of the Gospel can we understand the *Confessions* of Saint Augustine, the cycle of the Holy Grail, Dante's *Comedy*, and the imprint they have left upon our civilization.

8

READING THE GOSPEL

O UR INVESTIGATION begins where it must inevitably end, with a question: can the story of Christ legitimately be taken as myth? Can such a reading be said to have the slightest meaning? The answer seems unavoidable. As the cornerstone of Christian belief, the story of Jesus is presented as revelation. And as such it excludes all that contradicts it. How then can the revelatory nature of the Gospel story be passed over without immediately voiding it of that which, by its own lights, constitutes its essence? To this question there is no simple answer. In fact, it is largely unanswerable.

Though we may take faith as the condition *sine qua non* for the reading of the texts that make up the Gospel, faith alone cannot give us all the keys to the interpretation and understanding of those texts. First, the message of the Gospel cannot be reduced to the written tradition that has given it its form. Nor is the New Testament, in the strictest sense, a sacred compendium. It is not, from beginning to end, the word of God itself. It is only the human manifestation of that word, imperfect and incomplete. Reading the Gospel raises particular, and particularly thorny, problems, which no presumption of naïveté can allow us to sidestep.

The Challenge to Interpretation

No text in the Western narrative tradition poses as bracing a challenge to interpretation as does the New Testament. The breadth of the challenge is equal to the magnitude of the event. But it is also rooted in the near inextricable connection between the texts and their own history, in the history of the first centuries of the Church[73] and in the dogma which, in its essentials, lays down the theological purview of the story of Christ as based on the Creed given final form in 325 by the Council of Nicea: "For us and for our salvation, he came down from heaven; by the power of the Holy Spirit he became incarnate from the Virgin Mary, and was made man;... he suffered death and was buried. On the third day he rose again.... "[74]

The reference to Nicea may seem incongruous. Christians today attach little importance to the theological quarrels that were the hallmark of Christendom in its first centuries. The Catholic Church itself has become less resistant to a symbolic reading of Scripture and more open to interpretation of the mysteries of faith, provided that they are not undermined, and that their reality is left intact. In any event, it is not the *aggiornamento* of the Church that concerns us. How Christian thought, be it Catholic, Orthodox, or Protestant, interprets the New Testament today is of equally little moment. What interests us is the collective imagination, hence the imprint left upon it over time by Scripture. This is unrelated to the current situation of either the faith or of the churches. The imprint we seek is not simply that of the texts; it is, as well, the sign of the spirit that presides over their advent. The Glad Tidings, down to the minutest details of their fabrication, cannot be detached from the conditions of their propagation. Or to put it in a slightly different way: the Gospel cannot be distinguished from the need for truth that it claims to fulfil, and that provides the impetus for its dissemination.

Let us begin by suggesting a definition compatible with the function of truth: the Gospel is the authentic story that announces and promises salvation, the remission of sins and the victory over death, the kingdom of God and eternal life to whomever believes in the mystery of Jesus Christ, Son of God incarnate in a historically attested man, to whom the evangelical narrator bears witness as he reveals his acts, his words, his death, and his resurrection.

This attempt at a definition—an acceptable one, I believe, for most Christians—gives rise at the same time to a series of difficulties upon which theology has focused its attention over the course of twenty centuries. Christian theology has demonstrated inexhaustible complexity and

---

73. Generally, in this chapter, the term "Church" will be used to refer to the totality of Churches and Christian communities, particularly during the first centuries of their existence. The singular is justifed by the unity imposed by Roman imperial power, when Christianity becomes a state religion of universal compass. The term may also designate, more specifically, the Catholic Church, primarily with reference to the modern age (following the Lutheran Reformation). Contrariwise, it will never be used to designate the Orthodox Church following the East/West Schism of 1054, nor the numerous Protestant churches.
74. The Nicene Creed.

incredible inventiveness in its attempts to rationalize, though never quite successfully, that which cannot be rationalized, and at whose core is located the Pascalian mystery or, in broader terms, the double mystery of the incarnation and the resurrection. Any Christian reading of the Gospels must accept the resurrection as "real," even though the resurrected "body" is not, as we will see in reading Paul the Apostle, the same body. In other words, whatever the difficulties raised by the "reality" of the resurrection, it is a reality no doubt can be cast upon. To doubt, to interpret it in a purely metaphorical, allegorical, or symbolic way, is to remove oneself from Christianity. This can be done quite easily; Christianity possesses no hermeneutic monopoly over its founding story. Here I wish to insist only upon what I consider to be a necessary point of departure, to wit, that any external reading, any non-Christian reading must *begin* by understanding, to the extent that a non-believer may believe, Christian truth itself. However, if we are to believe the theologians, the truth of faith does not permit itself to be so easily mastered. Thus we must first briefly examine the limitations within which the Christian interpretation I propose is possible.

The first of these limitations touches upon the texts themselves. Even though, as we have suggested, the texts are not everything, and even though a portion of the truth of the Gospels cannot be located in them, it is they upon which we are nonetheless obliged to rely. They consist, first of all, of the four canonical Gospels themselves (in probable order of composition: Mark, Matthew, Luke, and The Acts,[75] followed by John). These in turn must be viewed as part of the heterogeneous whole that constitutes the New Testament, all the while bearing in mind that the Epistles of Paul antedate the oldest of the canonical Gospels (that of Mark). Many theologians justly consider Paul as the master key to the interpretation of the mystery of Christ. But where Christ is concerned, the narrative dimension is reduced to the essentials, and borders on the terse. This, however, is precisely the dimension that is of greatest interest to us, for it is the *story* of the preaching and the passion of Jesus that has most deeply impregnated the Christian collective consciousness. So, without neglecting the Apostle, I prefer to focus on the four traditional Gospels.

But of what, and of whom, do they speak? Of Jesus the man, the historical character of whom so little is known, or of the incarnate and resurrected Christ, the focus of the faith? Quite obviously, of both. And though theology occasionally draws a distinction between them, they are

75. The Acts is generally considered to be the continuation of Luke, and written by the same hand.

understandably conflated both by depiction and by popular tradition.[76] In fact, it is what is said of Jesus Christ, from the standpoint of our self-imagination, that interests us. I might well be criticized for concentrating on narrative tradition to the detriment of an immense and no less representative iconography. But a choice had to be made. This book attempts to give voice to the texts.

For all that, our difficulties have just begun. It must be acknowledged that the texts themselves, as far as the history of their theological reading is concerned, have been engaged at several levels. The standard Medieval Catholic interpretation lists no fewer than four. A literal or philological meaning, and three levels of spiritual meaning:[77] allegorical, which illuminates doctrine; moral, which enlightens the believer in his behavior; and "analogical," which invokes eschatology, that is, the end of time and eternal life.[78]

To these four possible meanings is added a fifth, which overrides all of them, the "plenary," an expression that embodies the ancient principle by which "the Bible is explained by the Bible in its entirety."[79] This is to say that the New Testament must be understood in terms of its relation to the Old Testament, whose reading it requires. For the New Testament is presented, in part at least, as an interpretation of the Scripture that precedes and proclaims it. Its proclamatory mission then becomes, after the fact, its principal one. Strictly speaking, the Old Testament cannot be said to exist except by virtue and by way of the New. The continuity to which it lays claim takes its form against temporal progression, from most to least recent, even though quite clearly it is meant to be read in the opposite direction, beginning with the least recent. Seen from this perspective, the Old Testament is a thoroughly Christian document; of Judaism it relates that which Christendom wishes to conserve.

---

76. In *On Being a Christian* (Garden City, NY: Doubleday, 1976), the celebrated German theologian Hans Küng affirms that "the Christ of the Christians is an absolutely concrete, human, historical person; the Christ of the Christians is none other than Jesus of Nazareth. And, to the extent that Christianism finds its foundations in the past, the Christian faith is essentially a historical faith." He goes on to add: "From its inception, Christianism was able to overcome the mythologies, philosophies and mystery cults only because it is a historical faith."

77. Here I follow Marc Lienhard in his introduction to the works of Luther, published in *La Pléiade* (Paris: Gallimard, 1999), p. xviii, note 4. For further exposition of the question, see "sens de l'Écriture" (the meaning of Scripture) in the *Dictionnaire critique de théologie* (henceforth *DCT*), ed. Jean-Yves Lacoste (Paris: PUF, 1998), pp. 1083–1089.

78. Theology reminds us that, despite the challenge from certain believers today, belief in eternal life "is a constituent element of the Christian faith" (*DCT*, "Vie éternelle," pp. 1222–1223).

79. *DCT*, p. 1084.

But with regard to the Judaic tradition, and seen from the Jewish perspective, the New Testament appears, contrariwise, as a sharp break, a distortion, even as a betrayal. In discussing the Judaic tradition, we would be better advised to avoid Christian terms in defining its corpus, and restore to it its Jewish denomination: Tanakh or Torah.[80] In its relationship to them, I read the New Testament as the desire to lend continuity to that which, from the Jewish viewpoint, is in effect a sharp break. This is a question to which we will return. Meanwhile, my reading will make every effort to be both literal and plenary, without minimizing in the slightest the eschatological dimension of the evangelical message.

The difficulties I have just sketched out are intimately connected with the very nature of the Gospel; with what, I insist, is the fundamental problem of the Christian tradition: the ambition to found both faith and salvation upon a story, and more precisely, upon a series of eyewitness accounts of ostensibly historical events. I am referring not to the inexactitudes and the incoherencies these accounts may contain, which I consider to be matters of a secondary order. The problem lies not in the circumstances, but in a more general sense in the pretension of arriving at, through the narration of the ephemeral, the historical and the contingent, an essential, transcendent truth in which nothing less than eternity is at stake.

When we are dealing with concepts like truth and eternity, ends may be all too easily mistaken for means. But there is no need for the truth of the Gospel to reveal the enigma of the universe for the believer to partake fully in the living of his life and in his ultimate hopes. Faith in Jesus Christ is more than enough. In this sense, the Glad Tidings are quite unambiguous; they present the Christian with a radical choice: life in the truth of Christ, or death in sin. This exigency lies at the root of any interpretation that would consider itself faithful to the spirit of Christendom, irrespective of church or sect.

But it is not enough for an agnostic like myself to formulate the exigency in order to resolve the nodal question I raised at the beginning of this chapter. The problem of narrative truth that the Gospel claims to represent remains unresolved. Whether I accept this truth or deny it, reading the Gospel story brings me to a kind of hermeneutical impasse. If I take it, simply, as one story among many I am in danger of totally overlooking the truth in whose name it has been handed down; if, on the other hand, I interpret it exclusively in the light of its announced objective of truth, I close the door to all the

---

80. The term Torah designates *stricto sensu* the first five books of the Tanakh, and by extension, the entirety of the Tanakh, which subsumes the Torah (*Pentateuch* in Greek), the Nevi'im, i.e., the Prophets, and the Kethuvim or Ktoubim, i.e., the Scriptures.

meanings that this truth cannot accept without endangering itself. Neither attitude has a median term; neither can accept compromise. The Truth narrative, as a matter of principle, cannot present itself as myth, and refuses to be read as such. To read it as myth is to deny it the status it claims. The impasse appears total.

For all that, it is possible to read the Gospel as myth. Such a reading is both legitimate and necessary, on condition that it does not empty the texts of their substance. It seems to me that this condition has been fully respected by our approach to the other stories touched upon thus far in this book, particularly to the Torah. Seen from this perspective, the scope— inexhaustible—of the story of Christ, like all the great founding myths, far exceeds in its possibilities the intention of its narrators and of its propagators. In this reading, in fact, its scope, far from being reduced, is broadened. It is not my proposal to examine the Gospel "like any other story," which would be of no interest whatsoever. On the contrary, I intend to read it as a myth of such power and profundity that it has gone on to create an effect of truth more powerful, more enduring than any other. The task of interpretation is not to separate truth from myth, but to grasp it in all its power and in its full potential, while at the same time not considering its content, particularly as it has been transmitted by Christian orthodoxy, as the final word. Any interpretation that would reject the divinity of Christ, that would transform Jesus into a simple prophet no matter how great, and take the resurrection as allegory, would overlook completely the central element that has given the Gospel story its immense and long-lasting resonance down through the centuries.

To read the Gospel as myth is to refuse to become captive to the interpretation of the Church (of *any* Church), without neglecting in the slightest its historical impact upon our collective self-imagination. Such a reading presupposes that the texts of the New Testament can be approached from an agnostic position, removed from any allegiance or profession of faith: an attitude that the believer cannot share as such. In adopting it I do not seek his permission, though I respect his faith. I say, quite simply: the texts belong to no one. Everyone may read them, even though for centuries the Church sought to impose its own exclusive reading, including by fire and sword. But they must not be read haphazardly. Any reading of the Gospel, in order to yield up its fruit, must take its thirst for truth as the force that gives it coherence. Even though this truth may subsume one or more latent meanings that tradition either did not wish or was unable to grasp. It is not the least of paradoxes that other interpretations make sense only in the light of the dominant reading.

The power and the specificity of the Gospel lie in the implausible encounter, the fusing of the divine and the human, at an identifiable point in history. *God*, in a manner of speaking, *becomes historical.* An incredible story if ever there was one! But it is a story *believed. Held to be true* by millions of human beings up to the present. Therein lies the miracle. A reading that fails to take this into account is meaningless. Just as the claim that the entire story is false, that it does not have a leg to stand on, is meaningless. Belief, or lack of belief, has, for a long time, ceased to matter. Whether or not we believe will have not the slightest effect on its influence or impact. We will not be able to understand the Christ myth as long as we refuse to ask ourselves how such a stupefying story has come down through the centuries as true. Only by demonstrating how the New Testament has broken with mythology can we attempt to explain its extraordinary mythical or allegorical potential.

Not that all the difficulties inherent in this approach have been laid to rest; far from it. The truth of the Gospel is so inextricably fused with the act of witness that forms its bedrock that no reading can promise to dissociate the two without appearing to attack the story that transmits them. Finally, the question of whether or not it makes sense to read this adventure as myth—as though we could ever make up our minds—can only assume its full dimensions through the reading of the texts that report it, and by the force of conviction such a reading obliges.

In light of the preceding, we can already intuit that, depending on whether we read the Gospel story as truth or as myth, there is a radical difference between the meaning of the connection that it establishes between God and man:

The Truth narrative claims that God has sent his Son, and in so doing, He makes himself—momentarily—man. This is the orthodox interpretation, posited on a literal reading of the texts; it places the emphasis on the resurrection.

The myth—among several possible readings—conveys man's semiconscious desire to be God, to take God's place, in a manner of speaking. This interpretation is symbolic. It places the emphasis on death.

I therefore propose a dual reading of the Gospel. First, as a Truth narrative; then as a myth in which the affirmation of this truth conceals another, unspeakable truth.

The Truth Narrative

The story is so well-known that it has long ceased to astonish. Yet none is more astonishing. To grasp it in all its power, it must be retold as if for the first time.

Under the reign of Tiberius, in Palestine, a man clothed in camel hides bound with a leather belt, who lived on locusts and wild honey, had been baptizing, and preaching the baptism of repentance. It was he of whom it is written in Isaiah that his "voice cries out in the wilderness." Another would soon come, he proclaimed, a man whose power would be far greater than his own, whose sandals he was unworthy to bow down and unloose. He, John, baptized with water, while the one who was to come after him would baptize with the Holy Ghost. And so it was that this man came to John, who baptized him in the Jordan. As the newly baptized emerged from the water, John saw "the heavens open, and the Spirit like a dove descending upon him, and there came a voice from heaven saying, Thou art my beloved Son, in whom I am well pleased" (Mark 1:4–11). The baptized went into the wilderness where he remained for forty days, where he was tempted by Satan. Leaving the wilderness, he went into Galilee, and began to preach and to gather around him his first disciples. Such is the "Beginning of the Gospel of Jesus Christ, Son of God" (Mark 1:1).

Other chroniclers who trace the story further back into the past claim that the Holy Spirit had conceived the child while his mother, Mary, was still a virgin. Matthew reports that an angel appeared to Joseph, Mary's fiancé, to reassure him of the infant's origin and to dissuade him from breaking off their engagement. Luke asserts that the archangel Gabriel himself had come unto Mary. But both find it useful to establish the genealogy of the father by adoption, one tracing his descent to Abraham (Matt. 1:1–16), the other back to Adam, son of God (Luke 3:23–38). It is also said that his birth was accompanied in the heavens by the appearance of a star that guided the three wise men from the East to his cradle. On learning of his birth, King Herod caused all the newborn of Judea to be slain. For naught. Warned by an angel, Joseph fled into Egypt with the mother and child, where they remained until the death of Herod, "that it might be fulfilled which was spoken of the Lord by the prophet, saying Out of Egypt have I called my son" (Matt. 2:1–15). Luke mentions neither the wise men nor the slaying of the newborn, but relates that Jesus was born in a stable upon which shepherds converged, summoned by an angel accompanied by a "multitude of the heavenly host," bearing witness to that which had come to pass.[81] The Book of Luke is likewise the only canonical Gospel to relate an episode of adolescence: Jesus, having gone up with his parents to Jerusalem, tarries there unbeknownst to them. Three days later they discover him in the temple seated among the doctors, hearing them and asking them questions. He responds to their anxiety with surprise: "How is it that ye sought me? Wist ye not that I must be about my Father's business?" (Luke 2:42–51)

On the main aspects of his adult life, following upon his return from the wilderness, Matthew, Mark, and Luke—the so-called "synoptics"—concur. Driven by the unshakable conviction of his divine descent and of the truth of his message, Jesus wanders the land preaching, seeking out disciples from whom he selects twelve apostles, who are given the task of spreading his mission.[82] His miracles, his growing popularity, his contempt for the religious hierarchy, his sense of repartee, his openness to the pagans, his easy-going approach to certain prohibitions, his radicalism—all these factors taken together begin to worry the leading scribes and sacrificers of the Sanhedrin (the supreme council and tribunal of the Jews), who begin to plot his death. The passion and resurrection take place as Jesus himself has predicted to his closest disciples: one week after his triumphal entry into Jerusalem, Jesus is betrayed by Judas (one of the twelve), condemned to death by the Sanhedrin, and upon its petition, crucified by the Romans. On the third day he rises, and, after having appeared before several of his incredulous disciples, he finally convinces the apostles of his resurrection. He calls upon them to go forth into the world and preach the Glad Tidings, and ascends to heaven to sit at the right hand of God where he awaits, at the end of days, his return and the moment of deliverance.

How can such an implausible story have been passed on as authentic, and gone on to enjoy such phenomenal success? No other story, no other individual has exerted upon our imagination a comparable domination, a comparable fascination. The only one, west of the Tigris,[83] with whom we might suggest a parallel, is Socrates: a just man, known by his words alone, condemned to death by those whom he had troubled. But there the comparison ends. All else contrives to separate them: where Socrates asks questions, raises doubts, argues, Jesus affirms, proclaims, promises. Socrates

---

81. None of the canonical Gospels mentions the presence of the donkey or the cow in the manger, yet they have become a commonplace in the nativity narrative.

82. The number twelve is no coincidence: the number of apostles corresponds to that of the tribes of Israel at the time of its unity.

83. A comparable figure, to the east of the Tigris, is that of Buddha, but he does not belong to the West's imaginary image of itself. His influence can be felt, of course, but as a representation of the Other.

is moved by the desire to think, Jesus by the power of conviction. Socrates is moderation; Jesus is immoderation. Above all, Socrates founded nothing; he left his mark upon thinkers, not upon the crowd; his heritage is, at best, a method, a form of intellectual midwifery; on occasion he claimed to be inspired by the demon within him. He is a man to the tips of his toes. In all that is known of his life there exists not an ounce of the supernatural.

His divine nature aside, Jesus' personality is much more flamboyant, much more complex. Neither his words nor his acts make him an easy figure to fathom. What startles us about Socrates is his method of reasoning; what strikes us about Jesus is his behavior. Compassion and severity alternate in him with particular brilliance. But it is an alternation charged with meaning: his compassion flows toward the humble, the lowly, the sick, toward children, the simple in spirit, particularly when such people believe in him without seeking to understand; his severity is reserved for those close to him, the lukewarm (more than the adversaries), the doctors, the profaners of the Temple. Jesus turns his back on his own family (Mark 3:31–35), in the name of the wider family of the faithful. Jesus scolds his disciples, reproaches them for their lack of intelligence, firmness, and humility; they lack confidence in him; they abandon him at the critical moment, and particularly during the terrible long night in Gethsemane shortly before his arrest. The all-too-human weakness of the disciples contrasts with the near-ironclad determination of the master, whose intransigence is essential to the fulfilment of his task, and to the training of those who will be called to carry on with it.

At times, Jesus' severity seems out of phase with the exigencies of his mission. To the disciple who asks him: "Suffer me first to go and bury my father," Jesus replies: "Follow me, and let the dead bury their dead" (Matt. 8:21–22). The injunction not only brushes aside funeral ritual and family piety, but also suggests that only those who follow him are truly alive. The world is indeed a violent place, but Jesus himself does violence to the world in denying—as dead—whatever does not follow his path. His call is a war cry, and at first glance it is incompatible with love for one's neighbor:

> Think not that I am come to send peace on earth. I came not to send peace but a sword.... For I am come to set a man at variance against his father, and the daughter against her mother, and the daughter in law against her mother in law. And a man's foes shall be they of his own household. He that loveth father or mother more than me is not worthy of me; and he that loveth son or daughter more than me is not worthy of me. And he that taketh not his cross, and followeth after me, is not worthy of me. He that findeth his life

shall lose it; and he that loseth his life for my sake shall find it.
(Matt. 10:34–39)

Here Jesus is warning the apostles of the persecutions to come, and
which are already underway even as the Gospels are being written. The
variance they foreshadow indicates that his message may not be universally
well received. For it is a message that cannot be immediately grasped by
everyone, as is illustrated in the parable of the sower: the word will not bear
fruit unless it falls upon good ground; there is nothing to be gained from
explaining to those who hear without understanding (Mark 4:10–13). This
brutal explanation is reserved to the group closest to him—the group to
whom "the mystery of the kingdom of God had been given"—which
excludes "them that are without." Curiously enough, parables are enough for
those without; they will take root depending upon the ground on which they
fall. The enigmatic nature of the parables is necessary, "lest at any time they
['them that are without'] should be converted and their sins forgiven them."
Coming from him who will later be called the Redeemer, the fear is
surprising. Spoken by anyone else, such discrimination would be judged as
cynical. But not when spoken by him, so powerful is the slightly sentimental
prejudice that would cast Jesus as necessarily good. "Why callest thou me
good? There is none good but one, that is, God," he tells the young man who
has knelt before him (Mark 10:17–18). A certain irritation at the man who
desires both material wealth in this world and eternal life in the hereafter is
understandable. But Jesus' frustration goes on to a strange turn:

> And on the morrow [of his triumphal entry into Jerusalem], when
> they were come from Bethany, he was hungry. And seeing a fig
> tree afar off having leaves, he came, if haply he might find
> anything thereon: and when he came to it he found nothing but
> leaves; for the time of figs was not yet.
> And Jesus answered and said unto it, No man eat fruit of thee
> hereafter forever. And his disciples heard it....
> And in the morning [of the following day], as they passed by,
> they saw the fig tree dried up from the roots. And Peter calling to
> remembrance saith unto him: Master, behold, the fig tree which
> thou cursedst is withered away. And Jesus answering saith unto
> them, Have faith in God. (Mark 11:12–14, 20–22)

Faith—which can "say unto this mountain, Be thou removed," as Jesus
asserts immediately thereafter—stands exposed in all its negative power.

Jesus' curse is perfectly gratuitous, a mere caprice: the fig tree is not unproductive, *the time of figs was not yet*. Coming from anyone else, such a gesture would seem demonic or senseless. No less than the episode of the Gadarenes (Mark 5, 1–17): Jesus answers the prayers of the devils he is attempting to disperse by causing them to enter into the swine that are grazing nearby, driving the herd into the sea, to the despair of those that fed the swine, who plead with him to depart their shores. At the marriage in Cana, to his mother who tells him that there is no wine, he directs a cruel retort: "Woman, what have I to do with thee? Mine hour is not yet come" (John, 2:4). Christ's character, as illustrated in the Gospels, has a demented quality; it has become a source of concern for his family (Mark 3:21), a detail that ecclesiastic interpretations have made every effort to efface. This sense of dementia, for both good and evil, quite clearly mirrors the world of men, the world of corruption against which Christ has vowed to fight, as though the just needed a madness no less than equivalent to that of the injustice against which they struggle. His severity is a matter of strategy.

Christ's combat is as paradoxical in its methods as in its aims. Jesus ostensibly preaches non-violence, the corollary of the love for one's neighbor that orders love for one's enemy and deliberate exposure to his blows. Yet he is brutal in his words, his expectations, and exceptionally so in his actions— as with the moneychangers of the temple. Here is another paradox: Jesus is non-sectarian, in that he favors no particular social or ethnic group—which does not stop him from showing the occasional preference for his own kind, as in Matthew 10:5–6: "Go not into the way of the Gentiles ... But go rather to the lost sheep of the house of Israel." As if that were not enough, he himself displays an uncommonly sectarian spirit. Among its essential components are the unconditional love and devotion that the master demands of his disciples. It is as though the world in which they have been summoned to spread the Glad Tidings were, at least for the moment, suspended. The world is thus transformed into a field of action, an object of intervention more than a place to live, to share with one's neighbor. So it is that we find ourselves faced with the paradox of a fraternal mission which begins by isolating those who are pursuing it, on the spiritual level, from the neighbor whom their mission is to convince: the solidity of faith that binds the community of the earliest believers is the overriding concern. For the same reason, the sheep that has gone astray must always be found at all costs, and brought back into the close-knit flock of the believers. No worldly deviation is permitted to him who would serve Christ, to him who would enjoy the privileges of secrecy, of sharing his mission, and of walking in his footsteps.

On the religious level, it was not to be without a parallel in the militant behavior of certain nineteenth and twentieth century revolutionary movements.

On the eve of the martyrdom for which he has prepared both himself and his entourage, Jesus reassures the apostles: he will return to take them along with him after having prepared for them a place in the house of his Father. But at this point, Thomas expresses a doubt: "Lord, we know not whither thou goest; and how can we know the way?" Jesus replies: "I am the way, the truth and the life: no man cometh unto the Father, but by me.... he that hath seen me hath seen the Father" (John 14:6–9). Here the master speaks directly, and reveals his nature: he has come from the Father and to the Father he will return. His disciples reply: "Now we are sure that thou knowest all things ..." (John 16:28–29). In this passage John raises, more radically than the other canonical Gospels, the ambiguity of both Jesus' personality and of his message. Up until this point, Jesus has appeared to be torn between public notoriety and secretiveness. He asks some of the disciples to bear witness to what they have seen him do, while others he asks to keep silent. He performs miracles in public, but insists on performing others with one or two disciples as his only witnesses. After having asked his disciples, shortly after causing the loaves to multiply, "whom say ye that I am?" and having heard Peter's answer, "Thou art the Christ," Jesus "charged them that they should tell no man of him." It is upon this occasion that he begins to teach them that he must be rejected, put to death, and resurrected. On hearing the words, Peter begins to rebuke him. Jesus immediately exclaims: "Get thee behind me, Satan: for thou savourest not the things that be of God, but the things that be of men" (Mark 8:29–33).

Six days later, at the top of a high mountain, where Jesus has brought with him only Peter, James and John, the transfiguration occurs: the disciples witness Christ's garments take on an unearthly whiteness as he converses with Elias and Moses, who have suddenly appeared at his side:

> And there was a cloud that overshadowed them: and a voice came out of the cloud saying, This is my beloved Son; hear him....
> And as they came down from the mountain, he charged them that they should tell no man what things they had seen, till the Son of man were risen from the dead. (Mark 9:2–10)

The perplexity of his closest disciples sheds light on Jesus' own apparent hesitations, his peculiar mixture of audacity and caution, his desire simultaneously to reveal and to conceal his true nature, to evoke and to veil his destiny; in short, all that which in his life and in his message remains, up until the passion, purposefully ambiguous. Without ruling out that Jesus himself may have momentarily experienced doubts about the ultimate significance of his mission, and whatever the strength of his own convictions, we see that the master understands, and realizes when faced with the incredulity of his disciples, that the truth is simply unbelievable, even to his first and most faithful companions. This truth, the divine nature of his person and the resurrection are too much, scandalous even, beyond the grasp of a man's spirit no matter how devout he might be, as in the case of Peter. The miracles, and even the transfiguration, are not enough. Only the incontrovertible fact of the resurrection enables him to prove to the apostles his divinity and the truth of his mission. Jesus would have revealed it to the apostles in order to strengthen his hand at the crucial instant: *he had foretold it!* All turns on the advent, on the reality of this stunning miracle. But, like his disciples themselves, the readers must be carefully prepared.

Call it the necessary marrying of contradictions (a theme to which we will return) or surpassing skill, the narrators must make the resurrection—the determining moment of the Christian faith—plausible. Their approach, one of increments, of tiny touches, of parables leading toward the impossible revelation; their winks at the unbelievable always grounded in the worldly order; their deeply human manner of incrementally revealing the superhuman lend the supernatural an immense reserve of power and of credibility. As if that were not enough, the verisimilitude of the implausible requires that the hero himself be riven by doubt. In the course of the night in the garden of Gethsemane that precedes his arrest and passion, Jesus reveals to his closest friends, Peter, James, and John, his mortal despair. For the first time—for the duration of a prayer—he falters. "Father," he says, "all things are possible unto thee; take away this cup from me." And, promptly pulling himself together: "Nevertheless not what I will, but what thou wilt" (Mark 14:36). His moment of weakness is reported by the three synoptic Gospel writers, but does not appear in John, where the certitude of truth overcomes all hesitation: a certitude that makes John's version a less convincing *story*, even though John's writing possesses a power that the other evangelists do not. John declaims more than he relates, but his declamation, for all its beauty, suffers from the absolute quality of all that it relates.

Jesus' second and ultimate lapse appears only in Mark and Matthew, at the hour of his death. In the climactic moment, the evangelists place upon the lips of the crucified the terrible words, the magnificent words, the most heart-rending words that can be imagined for him and for all men, at the crucial moment of death: "My God, my God, why hast thou forsaken me?" (*Eli, Eli, lama sabacthani?*) Here the story attains an authenticity of staggering intensity, more intense even—which is certainly no overstatement—than Peter's renunciation. For an instant of doubt, anguish, and pain, the entire truth of the Gospel hangs suspended. In this supreme instant upon which everything turns—the word, truth, salvation, eternity—the Son of God is alone, fully and only a man: fragile, perishable, mortal. For *he dies*, and at the moment of his death, all in which he had believed so unshakably during his life, all that for which he had given his life—God, grace, resurrection— all of it collapses, and vanishes in the nothingness that carries him away. Abruptly the entire Gospel is tainted by that tragic moment into which floods the underlying disquiet of the human condition: no one, irrespective of his convictions, can ensure beforehand that he will not falter in the face of imminent death. Nowhere is the Gospel story as powerful as it becomes at that instant. If there were only one reason for believing in Jesus and in his story, it would be this one, because of the resonance of his words in us at that moment.

Perhaps it is because they did not feel the need for suspension, because they did not understand the importance of doubt to the truth of the Gospel itself, that Luke and John substitute words of reassurance and calm:[84] "Into thy hands I commend my spirit" and "it is finished." No, nothing is finished. In fact, everything may well be turned upside down. For if, at the height of his torment; if, at the decisive moment of his death, all is for the best; if Christ's spirit is in safe hands and his mission accomplished, then the resurrection is to a certain extent already upon us, it can be taken for granted, and the intervening three days are pointless. If all unfolds as had been foreseen, without a hitch, then the ease and the normality of the resurrection work against it, and its insipidness makes it even less believable. It is already quite difficult enough to believe in the resurrection in and of itself; but it is utterly impossible to acquiesce in its banality, to accept it as an inevitable outcome. There must be doubt, anguish, pain, *and loss*, in order for the miracle to take place. There can be no resurrection unless there has been mourning, time for suffering, in the absence of which Jesus cannot have been truly dead. The calming effect, the quiet certainty of Luke and John weaken, and nearly annihilate the truth that they perhaps believe they serve in silencing uncertainty.

---

84. The idea of substitution is clearly a hypothesis, but one supported by the fact that Mark almost certainly antedates Luke and John.

The resurrection, which the Gospel story expends so much energy in authenticating, establishes beyond doubt the divinity of Christ, even though his nature remains a matter to be treated with utmost precaution. None of the Gospels truly says the same thing, except *with regard to the essentials*: all report the disappearance of the body, that necessary absence upon which the very possibility of the resurrection rests even though it provides no proof; all speak of the apparitions of him who has risen. But the reality and the circumstances of these apparitions vary. Jesus is not believed, not recognized, at least not immediately, and not by all. Only Luke and John insist on the corporal, physical nature of the resurrection. The latter does so indirectly: Jesus says to Mary Magdalene, "Touch me not, for I am not yet ascended to my father" (John, 20:17). Contrariwise, he invites Thomas to touch him, but it is not said whether Thomas does so, perhaps to see (out of modesty?) is enough for him. Yet even that is too much to ask. "Because thou hast seen me, thou hast believed; blessed are they that have not seen and yet have believed," Jesus tells him (John, 20:29). The weight of faith is greater than that of the senses; in fact, it alone is of any account. The crowning ambivalence of the Gospel story is this: Jesus takes pains to manifest himself, at least through his voice and his image, but his manifestation seems more like a testing than a proof. The solidarity and the faith of the apostles must be put to the test, and not as a demonstration of the material impossibility of the resurrection. Does Christ live within them? That is all that matters. And that is why Thomas seems so disappointing.

Still, the resurrection of Jesus must be seen as far more than a simple metaphor. Paul, whose writings antedate the composition of the Gospels, sums up the matter with remarkable clarity: "But if there be no resurrection of the dead, then is Christ not risen: And if Christ be not risen, then is our preaching vain, and your faith is also vain" (1 Cor. 15:13–14). Having laid down what is at stake, the apostle then turns his attention to the believability of the event:

> But some man will say, How are the dead raised up? And with what body do they come? Thou fool! That which thou sowest is not quickened, except it die. And that which thou sowest, thou sowest not that body that shall be ... So also is the resurrection of the dead. It is sown in corruption; it is raised in incorruption; It is sown in dishonour; it is raised in glory: it is sown in weakness; it is raised in power. It is sown a natural body; it is raised a spiritual body. (1 Cor. 15:35–37, 42–45)

The resurrection is real, corporeal. But the resuscitated body is not of the same nature as the dead body; it is spiritual. Paul's innovation is an extraordinary one; through it, the phenomenon of the resurrection can be taken literally while its mystery is preserved fully intact. The metaphor of the sowing gives only an image of process while taking away nothing from the veracity of the event. Moreover, the resurrection is not amenable to reason except insofar as it produces something that we cannot entirely grasp from the earth-bound viewpoint that is necessarily ours. It is of little importance to have seen the body of the resurrected Christ when he may just as well appear to anyone, at any time, as Paul himself testifies by virtue of having experienced it on the road to Damascus. Neither sight nor touch is of any import; only grace, and faith (1 Cor. 15:8–11).

Paul's innovation is valid only for Christ's resurrection, and excludes those accomplished by the master himself on several occasions, the most compelling of which is that of Lazarus. It cannot be a simple matter of curing, nor of awakening, as in other instances where "death" (coma, extreme lethargy) has occurred.[85] In the case of Lazarus, the text makes it quite clear that he has lain for four days in his grave and that his body "stinketh" (John 11:39). Now, such a body may only be resurrected in its earthbound form. It provides an excellent example of the nearly insurmountable difficulties of interpretation that threaten stories held to be true. The resurrection of Lazarus, like all the other miracles, is nothing more than a sign of Jesus' power, which we may either accept or reject.[86] But the Easter resurrection is the very subject of faith, it can neither be doubted nor reduced to allegory. It must be real. And mysterious. But we have not yet come to the greatest of all mysteries.

The greatest enigma, and the true miracle of the Gospels, no matter what we might think of them today, is to have succeeded in imposing itself down through the centuries *as historical truth*. Or to put it more precisely, *as religious truth attested by history*. On our rapid reading of the *Aeneid*, we noted that one of the innovations of the Virgilian narrative, and probably its greatest innovation with respect to the epics preceding it that have come to our attention, was to interweave the history of Rome with its legend. Legend and history encounter one another in full consciousness: the events engraved on Aeneas's shield are historical while the shield itself is legendary: a fact about which neither Virgil nor his readers entertain the slightest confusion. It is of small matter that the hero himself has one foot in legend and the other

85. See Mark 5:33–43 and Luke 7:11–16. See also the resurrection brought about by Peter (Acts 9:36–41).
86. The Lazarus episode appears only in John, the most extreme of the canonical Gospels.

in history, that the borderline between the two ways of being (historical and legendary) is indistinct; it is enough for us to admit that a difference sets them apart: even if Aeneas had really existed, what the poet says of him is a conscious fabulation, since no identifiable source can provide access to that aspect of him which might be historical. The canonical Gospels, on the other hand, offer themselves as sources; they have been received as direct and indirect eyewitness to what truly took place at such a time and in such a place. Seen from this perspective, Luke is the most explicit; he is the only Gospel writer to undertake, in the manner of Thucydides, what we would today term a criticism of his sources:

> Forasmuch as many have taken in hand to set forth in order a declaration of those things which are most surely believed among us, even as they delivered them unto us, which from the beginning were eyewitnesses, and ministers of the word; It seemed good to me also, having had perfect understanding of all things from the very first, to write unto thee in order, most excellent Theofilus, That thou mightest know the certainty of those things, wherein thou hast been instructed. (Luke 1:1–4)

Luke does not give us a first-hand account of events. His story, based on "perfect understanding of all things," is the fruit of a historical inquiry. Or at minimum, of a compilation. The critique of sources, to speak frankly, remains rather rudimentary. The narrator claims accuracy, but does not appear to have differentiated among the eyewitnesses at his disposal, nor to have evaluated their degree of reliability. About concordance of testimonies, about connections between them, about contradictions he says not a word. Nor does he attempt to distinguish between the legendary, the fabulous, and the real. In Luke all is real, all is certain, all is true. In this regard, the four Gospels closely resemble each other: all share the same tone, that of certainty. It is not enough for them to tell a story. Nor do they limit themselves to telling a life story, a "true" story. Through the telling of that which has authentically taken place, they speak *the* truth. Not just any truth, but the final, definitive Truth of which Christ is the bearer and which he will return to establish throughout the world.

As if that were not enough, this Truth posits itself as the direct descendent of the Old Testament. Such is the function of the genealogies contained in Luke and Matthew. On several occasions, Jesus integrates into his preaching expressions and passages from the prophetic texts. Even when he is on the cross: his cry of abandonment repeats word for word that of

David (Ps. 22:2), a borrowing that would tend to weaken the impact we earlier attributed to his lapse: his words of despair cannot be, all things considered, anything more than a final indication of Jesus' descent from David. It is true, however, that their spontaneous return, in circumstances of supreme agony, underscores the tragic nature of the moment. Whatever the reason, such a reference at such a moment would surely have been noticed by those Jews who knew even the rudiments of their own Scripture. The concern for continuity sometimes expresses itself quite openly: in his first four chapters, Matthew insists at least five times that events have taken place in fulfilment of *that which was spoken by Jeremy the prophet*. This naïve insistence, which reverses the link of causality between the event and its prediction, awakens suspicions of the lineage it is meant to certify— precisely because the lineage itself cannot be taken for granted.

Nothing in the texts upon which the Old Testament is founded, nothing in the Jewish sources themselves (the Tanakh), in other words, clearly foretells the coming of Jesus. On two occasions there is talk of a messiah, of an anointed one to come: one, whose identity remains obscure, in Daniel (9:25), on the occasion of the reconstruction of Jerusalem following the Babylonian exile; the other in Psalms (2:2), in which the psalmist speculates about why the kings and princes of the earth have taken counsel together "against the Lord and against his anointed," whom the Christian tradition recognizes as its own. This same tradition sees in the Twenty-second Psalm elements that prefigure Christ's passion (of which the most troubling is most certainly "they pierced my hands and my feet" from verse sixteen, as though the literal meaning of "they pierced" were not "as a ravening and a roaring lion") and the prefiguration of his advent in Psalm 110, in which the LORD invites the Lord to sit at his right hand. In a similar vein, Isaiah (7:14) is said to foretell the birth of the Lord: "Behold a virgin shall conceive and bear a son, and shall call his name Immanuel (God with us)"; but many commentators, some of whom are Catholic, view this passage as announcing the birth of Ezekias.

Though there are numerous references to the Old Testament in the New, the correspondences between them remain tenuous. What indications do exist testify above all to the scriptural knowledge of the authors of the Gospels, and quite lack the imperative character these authors would like to read into them. Whatever the circumstances, the Old Testament is always in a position of receiving from the New the illumination, which, paradoxically, the latter needs. For all the efforts of the evangelists, the Tanakh is not pregnant with the New Testament. The distance that separates them is so great that one might almost speak of incompatibility—which only the long tradition of the Christian churches and force of habit keep us from noticing. Revelation is, of course, central to both, but they differ radically in both spirit and subject. The huge composite story of the Tanakh is not the history of God but the story of his people, throughout which YHWH makes tangible his presence and his absence, his discontent, and his expectations. The deeply human story it tells unfolds beneath his gaze, and on occasion benefits or suffers from his interventions, and only to this extent does it receive here and there a nudge from the supernatural, an illumination that reveals.

What stands revealed above all are the Law, and the unceasing difficulties that surround its establishment; but not YHWH. Even when he makes himself manifest to Moses on Mount Sinai, he takes care not to appear: lightning flashes and clouds are all the prophet is allowed to witness; in a subsequent encounter, it is said that Moses and those who accompany him contemplate the God of Israel, but they see only that which lies beneath his feet, "the body of heaven in its clearness" and a "devouring fire on the top of the mount" (Exod. 24: 9–18). YHWH makes his presence known only by his voice. YHWH is power of speech, path, principle, Law. Only the weakness of our own power of abstraction makes him a "character." The unique genius of the Torah, and that which distinguishes it from all the other mythologies of Mediterranean antiquity, is not so much its monotheism, as is often claimed, but rather that it strives to establish the presence of YHWH without giving him a form. The effort is not wholly successful. At the beginning of Genesis, the Creator makes man in his image: a case of anthropomorphism that indicates how difficult it is to conceive of God without imagining him, without representing him to ourselves, even if indirectly. This does not stop the Torah from leaning toward an abstract, non-figurative conception of YHWH. It cannot be said often enough: YHWH, in his essence, is *words, speech.*

However, the Gospels stand this formulation precisely on its head. John makes it expressly and magnificently clear:

> In the beginning was the Word, and the Word was with God, and the Word was God. The same was in the beginning with God. All things were made by him, and without him there was not anything made that was made....
>
> And the Word was made flesh, and dwelt among us, full of grace and truth.... (John 1:1–14)

What we are witnessing is a breathtaking fusion between the account of Genesis and that of John, who, in his attempt to craft continuity, brings about instead a final break. *Was made flesh*: exactly what the word of the Torah does everything possible to avoid. *Was made flesh*: such is the aim of the God of the Gospels. The two approaches could hardly be more antinomian, more irreconcilable. It is as though the word of the Gospel were forcing its way into the tiny opening created at the very beginning of Genesis to reverse the movement: man makes God in his image. In this regard, the evangelists had invented nothing; the Greeks had been doing the same thing for centuries. And the Gospel is Greek—as much as it is Aramaic or Judean. Greek anthropomorphism subverts, in effect, Judaic revelation: such was undoubtedly the price of winning the Hellenized world to monotheism. In the popular imagination, Zeus, the father of the gods, could with relative ease become the Father and nothing else. God (in Latin, *Deus*, etymologically formed from the possessive of Zeus) sends the Holy Spirit to impregnate Mary just as Jupiter penetrates Danaë with his golden rain. All well and good for the pagans. But not for the Jews.[87] Once God has become incarnate, the story of the incarnation can only be that of God on earth, the story of the earthly tribulations of God. There is nothing surprising in the Jews' stubborn refusal to accept the incarnation. From their point of view, it is wholly offensive.

The God of the Gospels is not and cannot be the YHWH of the Torah.[88] The Gospel story reveals what must not be revealed: the face of God. John knows this all too well, when he reminds us "no man hath seen God," before immediately adding, "the only begotten Son, which is in the bosom of the Father, he hath declared him" (John 1:18). In attempting to develop through Jesus knowledge that proves to be in radical opposition to the continuity, which it claims for itself, Christendom plunges into an adventure that can only be described as schizophrenic. The Word of Christ is an extension of the Word of God, but it is now fraught with an image that transforms it. That which cannot be represented suddenly represents itself in the world, steps into history. And in the world, in history, the divine Word cannot be anything but human. It can be no accident that despite the iconophobia of certain of the Fathers of the Church, Christianity would soon be awash with images. So much so that images would almost come to supplant the word.

---

87. With the exception of those communities that accepted the Gospel, but by virtue of which would lose their Jewishness in the long run.

88. This opposition between the two Testaments would be given theoretical form in the second century by Marcionism, and fought by the Church as a formidable heresy.

Far be it from me to point to some hypothetical congenital defect that would transform Christianity into a simple case of a path not taken, or into a monumental blunder in the interpretation of Judaism. Not at all; my intention is to shed light on the breadth of the challenge offered by the Gospel in its attempt to reconcile the irreconcilable: the carnal humanity of the Greek gods and the indescribable non-humanity of the divine breath and word of the Torah. In this near inconceivable torsion resides the greatest genius of the Gospel story: its ability to stretch a tightrope between man and the unutterable. The prodigious success of the New Testament can only be explained by the fact that the truth and the revelation of salvation have assumed the face of a man located in history, of a man prepared to die in their name. But this success carries with it a substantial risk: in bringing truth down to earth and giving it a human face, we remove from it that which had been unutterable. It then became possible to speak in the name of Christ. Thus, in the name of God. Few would restrain themselves from doing so. Seen from this perspective, the Resurrection, that most unlikely of all events, appears as little more than a restraining device.

The temptation of repetition being as strong as it was, the resurrection became the lock that would bar access to any repeat performance. This is why it must have truly taken place. Had it been purely metaphorical or symbolic (as if to say, "great minds never die"), a clever charlatan would have easily manipulated it; any rhetorician can come onto earth and speak the truth to mankind. For all the precautions taken, truth-sayers have continued to poach in Christ's preserves. But none among them could acquire his authority—not Paul, not even the Church that he helped found. The resurrection of a man-god is probably the kind of event in which a given civilization can believe only once in its history. But what can be made of this unprecedented event remains, for better or for worse, inexhaustible ...

What lends the Gospel story its specificity is not only that it tells the authentic history of a real yet divine man—literally the Son of God—come to speak the truth to the world, but also that it presents this Truth—eternal life—as a finality, as a goal to be sought after and attained. The unbreakable tie between earthly life and eternal salvation established by the truth of the evangelical message transforms the latter into the finality of the former. The principal *raison d'être* of life in the here and now is located outside itself, in an afterlife that is no longer hypothetical but certain, a matter of assurance at least to those who have made it an article of belief. Piety is no longer its own reward, a way of helping us live out our mortal lives. Instead, this life, and the way in which it has been lived, becomes the currency, the hard-earned currency with which each of us must purchase his place in Eternity. When the Gospel sets itself this objective, it takes on a revolutionary quality. One might object that Plato had already formulated the idea of finality. Perhaps, except in the manner of its formulation. And manner makes all the difference. Plato has no truth to proclaim; he abstains from any revelation whatsoever. He expresses his conviction as a man that beauty *is*, that it governs the cosmos, that it warrants being sought after here below, and that the more deeply in love with beauty the soul has been in this life, the better it will be able to choose its subsequent lives.

Plato's reflections on the manner in which life should be led draw on an intimate certainty, but he holds out no definitive truth. Truth exists, for him, in connection with the Beautiful and the Good, but it remains beyond our grasp, beyond our ability to transmit. At most, and at the risk of being misunderstood, the philosopher may attempt to let others know of the love he feels toward truth, but certainly not to sacrifice himself in its name. Socrates accepts death, not at all to save the world, nor to provide a lesson for his fellow citizens, but to remain faithful to himself. If the concrete perspective of death shakes our convictions, argues Socrates, it is because those convictions were worth little. Death is the moment of truth that puts to the test the manner in which we have led our lives. But this moment of truth does not unalterably seal our fate. The question of the afterlife remains open.

Of all the stories that have come down to us from Mediterranean antiquity, that of Christ is the only—or the first, in any event—which dares so peremptorily to seal off the question of death and eternal life. That the kingdom of God, as proclaimed by Jesus, is already among us by no means cancels out the promise of eternity to come: indeed, this presence creates the continuity that allows us to strive in the here and now for our salvation, and to look forward to the advent of a final Redemption. All cosmologies set up in one way or another a correlation between life and death, between the present and the afterlife, between the mortal and the immortal, between the earthly and the heavenly. The particularity of the religious spirit lies in its attempt to institute coherence between the world of human beings and that of the gods, between the earth and the cosmos. Despite the need for coherence, most of the great founding myths leave prudently open the question of what happens after. For them, the access of dead souls—if there is such a thing as a soul—to transcendence and to eternal life is anything but a foregone conclusion.

For the Greeks, the realm of Hades, which closely resembles the Hebrew *sheol*, is a kind of grey, neutral zone where the dead, be they good or bad, are nothing but shadows of what they had once been; it is a realm that holds out neither promise nor retribution. The order of the cosmos may well govern that of men, but it guarantees them nothing, and certainly not immortality. Life after death does seem to have been one of the great preoccupations of Pharaonic civilization. Its mythology and its funerary rites provide for an extraordinary passage between the here below and the above and beyond. The passage is an exceptional one, in that it involves only Pharaoh and his entourage. In the Egyptian conception of the universe, the two orders, the earthly and the heavenly, come into contact (like two circles tangential to one another) at the apex formed by Pharaoh himself, simultaneously king and god, earthly and heavenly. Insofar as he provides an indispensable link between the two worlds, he cannot die. Behind the apparent succession of Pharaohs, he who appears under different faces is always the same. Pharaoh is immortal. Here, immortality is not, any more than in other cosmologies, a promise made to men in general, but a necessity associated with a function, the mainspring of the two worlds. And in any event, fate itself is collective in nature.

Fate and survival are also collective in nature, as we have seen in the Tanakh, at least in its first part, the Torah. With the prophets, and to an even greater degree in subsequent writings, the idea of an individual fate timidly raises its head. In the Sixteenth Psalm, David praises YHWH for giving him counsel, for being always before him; he exults in that "my flesh also shall rest in hope. For thou wilt not leave my soul in hell, neither wilt thou suffer thine Holy One to see corruption," a hope that we encounter once again in the Forty-ninth Psalm. These are perhaps the first, frail signs of the desire for eternity felt by the man who is no longer satisfied with survival through the intransigence of the group. But David is not just any man. Suspended from this slender thread we can retrospectively detect the questionable continuity between the Hebrew Scriptures and the message of Christ.

The thread is a false one. Christ comes open-handed with an offer of immortality to all men, combining this tempting proposal with one exorbitant condition: unreserved acceptance of the truth he brings. *Truth or death.* On condition that the believer accepts Truth, death will be overcome. Failing that, death will irremediably strike whoever has not believed. Here death stands both as punishment and as curse to be overcome—a cause whose torch modern medicine seems all too inclined to carry. Because the sense of collective belonging has been worn away, and individuals can no longer find meaning in collective life, they must be told a story that will encourage them to find meaning in themselves, and better still, that will certify it for them. To so certify, Christ gives his life. And to prove that his gift has not been in vain, he rises from the dead. All that is needed is belief. The price may seem a small one to pay, as Pascal attempts to persuade us via the logic of his famous wager. And in a certain sense, Pascal is right: very little is lost in wagering on God. But much is lost in excluding all other paths to the divine.

The story of Christ is both rich in a beauty that we are far from having exhausted, and impoverished by its Christian interpretation, which exacts a price that is impossible to pay. We cannot so easily put uncertainty behind us. To name certainty is to take out insurance against the fear of nothingness; to attempt to fill, at all costs, the void left by the death of Christ. There is no other way to transform his failure into victory, to transform doubt into truth. There is no way by which this victory can be assured, but it has come above all to represent—as we will see—a formidable weapon in the hands of the civilization that wields it.

If it were possible to sum up in a few words the historical importance of the Christian revolution, I would put it thus: Greek mythology represents the world, the Hebrew Scriptures enunciate, or better, teach the Law. But both address themselves to the world as finality. But the Gospels proclaim to this world a truth that is not of this world, and which overturns the relationship of the believer to life. Whatever stories man might contrive to tell about himself outside of this truth are no longer of any great moment.

As the truth of the Gospels is presented as both definitive and universal, so the story that sets it forth reduces the possibilities for interpretation. In the broadest sense, quarrels of exegesis aside, from the Christian point of view there is only one possible reading of the New Testament. This singularity of voice might seem without consequence, for it is subsumed in a message of peace and love. But the effect of its message is to cast into blindness, alienation, and war all those who desire neither this particular peace, nor this particular love. Just as those who rejected the benefits of civilization under the *Pax Romana* were consigned to barbarism, so the peace of Christianity, having invested that of Rome, was to surpass it. The Gospel, the Good Tidings, was to triumph where the *Aeneid* had failed, for its truth is absolute and its universalism without limits.

But its Christian meaning is not the only one possible. And its exorbitant quality only becomes clear in the light of other readings.

The Story of the Death of God

The resurrection need not have actually taken place for it to acquire its extraordinary standing. Quite distinct from the question of its reality, the story of Christ incontestably holds within it immense symbolic power. If this account has echoed as it has down through the ages; if it has been propagated in space and in time with such effect, it can only be because, despite being confiscated by the Church, the story it tells far exceeds in scope the ecclesiastical hierarchy's use of it. The first and overwhelming reason is because the life and word of Christ together answer an inexhaustible need for consolation; second, because they link together and condense ancient myths, which well antedate Christianity; and finally, because the declared intention of Christ along with all that flows from it correspond to an aspiration both unspeakable and sublime. That aspiration is, in fact, a superhuman one that can be brutally expressed in three words: to become God. Or, in what boils down to the same thing: to suppress God.

René Girard has taken a significant step in this direction.[89] In Christ he sees a man who wishes to surpass the ordinary condition of his fellows and is prepared to put his life at risk to do so. In Girard's view, men alone—and not men as unconscious instruments of divine will—have killed Jesus. His being put to death is the logical outcome of his refusal to accept the push and pull of force in a world where force reigns supreme. Taken to its extreme, this refusal leads Christ to suffer the blows of others, and to die of the violence of the world. The power and the beauty of this interpretation stem from the fact that Jesus is a simple mortal whose resurrection becomes pure symbol: he lives on as a deathless model in the hearts of men. Of Christianity, Girard preserves only the moral while suppressing the marvellous. There are no miracles; there is no absolute truth. Thus we gain access to a mythical reading of the Gospel story, which I would like to attempt here to advance a bit further by showing that it may be read as the expression of an audacity long considered inconceivable: as the scarcely conscious effort to make God human, and to make man God—to transcend the strictly human. Far from diminishing the impact of the myth, the reading I would like to suggest enlarges it: it relocates its field of meaning, while depriving it of none of its power.

I will not deal with the consoling dimension of the myth, for it cannot be mistaken. Its beauty plays a significant role in the longevity of the Gospel

---

89. René Girard, *Des choses cachées depuis la fondation du monde* (Paris: Grasset & Fasquelle, 1978; Le Livre de Poche [biblio essais], 1986) p. 300.

narrative. It will endure as long as men cannot forgive themselves for being what they are: victims and executioners in turn. I will instead direct my attention to the fraternal virtues of the myth, in all its ambiguity. There is more than a charitable aspect to this sense of fraternity, something deeply fearsome, something impossible.[90]

God, says the myth, makes himself man and dies on the cross. Let us attempt to evaluate this symbolic incarnation to the fullest—for it is immense. The Father offers himself up for sacrifice in the person of his Son. God is simultaneously executioner and victim, he who sacrifices and he who is sacrificed, a duality expressed by the father/son dichotomy—one which rules out any possibility of interpreting the sacrificial act as mere suicide. The Father orders or, at minimum, authorizes the death that the Son has accepted to endure for him. One kills, the other dies. But if one is the other, if both are of the same substance, as John writes ("the Father is in me, and I in him," 10:38) then God indeed dies through Christ and with him on the cross.

But it is the Son who proclaims what is to come, who speaks for the Father, from and in his place. More precisely, a chain of narrators has reported what the Son has affirmed. Men, by which we could say the sons, are the tellers of the tale. Men are the intermediaries through whom we are able to glean some faint idea of what the Son has said and done. But, as this selfsame Son has declared, men "know not what they do." They surely know nothing more than what they transmit, or what they invent—for the disciples often admit that they do not understand. The Son meanwhile asserts superlatively that he, more than any other, is from God, but is like any other man as well. Christ personifies to the highest possible degree the mortal condition, which is also that of Adam. Adam, the first man, and all of his descendants—that is to say, we—are sons and daughters of God. It is as quintessential Son, to such an extent in God that he claims to be one with him, that Christ speaks. And what he proclaims quite simply boggles the

---

90. The interpretation that follows derives from a passing remark by Jacques Derrida in "Foi et savoir," *La religion*, sous la direction de Jacques Derrida et Gianni Vattimo (Paris, Seuil, 1996) p. 20: "In his definition of 'faith as it reflects upon itself' and of that which indissolubly binds the idea of pure morality to Christian revelation, Kant employs the logic of a simple principle, that which we have just quoted in his letter: '[T]o behave in a moral manner, one must act as though God did not exist or as if he had no concern for our salvation....' Is this not another way of saying that Christianism cannot respond to its moral vocation and to the morality of its Christian vocation, than by enduring, here on earth, in the history of phenomena, the death of God, and well above and beyond the characters of the Passion? That Christianism is the death of God as proclaimed by Kant, and as he reminds the modernity of the Enlightenment?" This reflection impelled me, even as I had already begun work on this chapter, to write a short article on "The Evil Genius of Christianism," *Conjonctures, Revue québécoise d'analyse et de débat*, no. 28, *Les Écritures et la vie*, Montréal, hiver 1999, 99–108, from which I borrow certain elements, sometimes in their entirety, without so indicating in quotes.

mind: through him, Jesus, God is summoned to die and to be reborn, so he says, as Son for all sons, and by extension for all brothers.

But what the Son says is far too enormous for his brothers to follow. What is really taking place is nothing less than an act of self-emancipation from the Father, the symbolic murder of a symbolic father. And the founding, upon this act of extreme audacity, of a new brotherhood. A brotherhood for which Christ is prepared to pay with his blood, as though a true sacrifice were necessary for the new covenant to be sealed. The power of symbolic murder has its price, and that price is the murder of him who has proposed it.

Objections will be raised, I am sure, that this reading cannot be justified by the texts. Indeed, it cannot, and for good reason: their drafters are *a priori* resistant to the other possible meanings of the message they bring. They hold fast to the only truth acceptable to them and to their community. Their choice is perfectly understandable: all things considered, the resurrection of the body is less difficult to admit and above all less blasphemous than the death of God. Nonetheless, the manner in which they present the truth that lies closest to their hearts is not entirely free of contradictions that find voice despite efforts to muffle them. They are indicators, if nothing else, that the single-voiced nature of the truth they proclaim has been imposed only with difficulty.

Let us use the question, which I believe to be central, of the kingdom of God, as a way of elucidating the ambiguity of the Gospel story. To the Pharisees who ask him when the kingdom (or the reign) of God will come, Jesus answers: "The kingdom of God cometh not with observation: Neither shall they say, Lo here! Or, to there for, behold, the kingdom of God is within you" (Luke 17:20, 21). This was precisely what the Pharisees, from whom Jesus himself was not too far removed, could not bear to hear. But they are not the only ones who are deaf. For all their good will the disciples fare little better. Time and again, the telling of the story indicates that something essential has eluded them; something, according to the evangelists themselves (or to those who have reported their account), that has continued to be misunderstood. Peter, who has just recognized Jesus as the Christ, rejects the idea of the sacrifice foretold and is sternly rebuked by the master for savoring "the things that be of men" (Mark 8:29–33). Something of the divine radically escapes him. The violent reprimand ("Get thee behind me, Satan!") is in tune with the truth as the evangelist sees it. But immediately thereafter, Christ gathers about him his disciples to tell them:

Whosoever will come after me, let him deny himself, and take up
his cross, and follow me. For whoever will save his life shall lose
it; but whoever shall lose his life for my sake and the gospel's, the
same shall save it. For what shall it profit a man, if he shall gain
the whole world, and lose his own soul? (Mark 8:34–36)

Few passages have been more frequently commented upon than this one,
which expresses a near-Platonic concern for the soul—but with the addition
of the cross. The nuance is a crucial one. For he who speaks, *even now*, is the
Crucified One—though I should have said "whom the narrator causes to
speak" at a time when both death and the resurrection have long since been
accomplished. The ambiguity fairly breathes with anticipation. If the
kingdom of God is "within us," it would suggest that the soul being
expressed is fully that postulated by Plato (in Luke, the most "Greek" of the
evangelists) and the death of Christ the true end point of his adventure,
irrespective of what might become of him thereafter, and which in any event
escapes human comprehension. If, as the four evangelists never tire of
repeating, the kingdom is that heavenly one to which Christ ascends on the
third day, then his martyrdom can only be a passage toward eternal truth, for
which his disciples need not mourn. They should instead rejoice. This, in
fact, is what Peter, incapable of understanding "that which is from God,"
appears unable to fathom.

There is a touch of the incomprehensible about such incomprehension on
the part of the most faithful of the disciples. Which of the two following
hypotheses is, for a believer, more painful to accept? That which has Christ
die once and for all? Or that which has him rise from the dead? Everything
would seem to point to the first: for the disciples, it is totally inadmissible
that their master, considering the powers he has made manifest, die passively,
ignominiously;[91] that his death be "for naught"—quite like that of any other
mortal—to such an extent, in fact, that the Gospel story itself can be read as
a myth that seeks to drape the infamous with glory and to make sense of an
unacceptable death.

The effort cannot entirely sweep aside the doubts that must have
occurred to Christ's companions during his lifetime. Here, Peter, as he does
in other circumstances, reacts in a perfectly human way. But he does so
before the death of the master, a death he rejects, in his understandable
inability to believe that the master can rise again. But his inability finally

---

91. Today one tends to forget that the ordeal of the cross was not only agonizing, but that it was, for the
Romans, the most degrading way of putting a man to death.

gives way beneath the weight of mourning: once death has been administered, accomplished, the faithful follower can only offer his final farewell at the price of the very resurrection that he had earlier denied. For that which he had refused to countenance was, in fact, death itself, and with it the end of Christ's mission. The reality of the resurrection, if one is to believe the New Testament, is that it allows the disciples, and more specifically the apostles, to free themselves from the despair into which the execution of Christ had plunged them, to recover their faith and to propagate the Glad Tidings. To put it bluntly, the resurrection is transformed, *horribile dictu*, into a functional necessity for the propagation of Christ's message. It becomes a question of morale, of survival. But this functional necessity weighs heavily upon the message itself, conferring upon it that single-minded meaning, that sense of intangible truth from which it will never extract itself, and which stands as a barrier against any other interpretation.

And so we have come full circle, back to our point of departure, though in such a way as to propel our reading further forward. The spirit of survival, which in the texts coalesces around the truth they claim to embody, need only appear as the *sine qua non* of the community of believers and of its growth and development; the simple *hypothesis* need only be *plausible* for the myth to be freed from all that binds it. And that is not all. Once set free, the ambiguities of the story can be better explained: with the salvation narrative that follows and justifies Christ's death are intermingled elements of the events that occurred during his life. Among them figure prominently the enigmatic words with which the master announces his death and resurrection. But their meaning is not necessarily that around which the Gospel texts themselves seek to create agreement.

Christ knows that he will die at the hands of men. They, up to and including his own disciples, cannot bring themselves to accept the enormity of that which he proclaims and which, two thousand years later, has hardly been absorbed: the knowledge that God is called upon to die. The death of God is both inevitable and necessary; henceforth it must be faced squarely, for nothing, when all is said and done, can possibly prevent it. Martyrdom and crucifixion are the prices Jesus must agree to pay in order to take to their ultimate conclusion the difficult truths he wishes to transmit to his human brethren. Among them is the most disagreeable of all: that men are themselves responsible for what befalls them even though they know not what they do. For the brethren to be emancipated, the Father must die; but ultimately they need not invoke his authority for their self-enfranchisement; it will be accomplished out of mutual respect. Sooner or later the idea of a heavenly Father, of divine providence, of supreme justice will exhaust itself, and men will discover that they are alone. Their inability to face ultimate solitude will prove to be their one true distress, their unique and terrifying punishment.

If Jesus has accepted that he must sacrifice his life, it is, as we have seen, out of respect for the most imperative of all the commandments, "Thou shalt not kill, " that he prefers to suffer death rather than be forced to inflict it, even in self-defense. But he has probably also done so because sacrifice has always played such a central role in religion that the sheer amplitude of the fraternal reversal he promises us cannot but be accompanied by the greatest of all sacrifices: that of oneself. So imperative is the acceptance of such sacrifice by each and every one that Christ is prepared to burn the image into the minds and memories of future generations by sacrificing his body, as magnificently symbolized in the scene of the Crucifixion. But his sacrifice must be the last. It must perpetuate down through eternity the message of Him who accepted it. The message will be reborn from the act of martyrdom as the Phoenix from its ashes. But to an even greater extent the myth draws its sweeping power from the crucifixion itself, translating into deed the death of God that the Gospel dare not foretell. God, says the myth, is nowhere else but in man, in each and every one of us. When we execute Jesus, it is indeed he whom we kill. An act of murder, as exemplary as it is unspeakable, must open with dreadful finality the eyes of those who have perpetrated it, or have allowed it to be perpetrated.

Murder kills in the murderer all divine potentiality. The murder of Christ, for it not to have been in vain, must therefore be the last. It is a burnt offering that foreshadows the resurrection, not of the crucified body, but of the undying love born by the Crucified One above and beyond his mortal flesh. God must indeed survive, but as that which he truly is: a metaphor for the unspoken need for men to accept one another. But at the last minute, the hero is overcome by an appalling doubt: that love might not survive his death. That his sacrifice might not be understood.

Almost in spite of itself, the Gospel provides the most convincing evidence of how well founded the doubt is. It speaks above all of the incapacity of the faithful to accept as definitive the death of him who so powerfully inspired them, mingled with a sense of guilt at having allowed him to be put to death. The resurrection redeems the cowardice of the disciples, and in a more general sense absolves men of the assassination of God. It expunges the most heinous of all crimes. Beyond its inability to confront the death of Christ, the Gospel embodies another, more substantial, almost insurmountable difficulty: the impossibility of accepting the highest aspiration of him whose death we mourn, the refusal to entertain the hope of human emancipation—that man might ultimately be able to live without the Father, that he accede by himself to that which is virtually divine within him.

The call for the emancipation of man indeed runs through the Gospel story from end to end, but it collides with the ancient idea of a heavenly father seated atop his throne far above a world awaiting the final judgement and in the end founders against the imperative of the resurrection of the body, brought on both by the rejection of death and the denial of the murder committed. Fear and guilt combine to recreate a god of flesh with a human face at precisely the moment when Christ might have been perceived, like a new Prometheus, as the mythical figure struggling to abolish all forms of divine terror. Despite its message of love (at its strongest in Paul), the New Testament reinvigorates the fear of God. That Jesus was a misunderstood— and disturbed—figure are part and parcel of what the texts report about him, of that much we should have no doubt. That in their ambiguity the Scriptures surreptitiously narrate the death of God and yet recoil from the thought need not be seen as unthinkable. For in all myth, what counts is the thinkable: that which myth, its narrators notwithstanding, allows us to think.

The Path of Truth

The Christ myth can be interpreted in a multiplicity of ways; the one sketched out above, for all its deep-rooted conviction, is not offered as *the* best reading of the Gospel story, but only as *one* possible reading. A reading I hope will be fruitful, if for no other reason than by virtue of what it allows us, by way of contrast, to adduce as evidence.

Myth is, by definition, to use Lévi-Strauss's splendid formula, "the endless succession of its versions."[92] The unfinished nature of the mythic illustrates *a contrario* what I term "New Testament closure." The New Testament not only brings to an end the interpretation of the founding story upon which it is based, it also brings to a close that of the Old, in whose wake it expends considerable effort to place itself—an effort that confirms the Jewish origins of both Christ and his message. Those origins have, to this day, left Christianity inconsolable. The way in which it imposes its reading as the sole and only possible one means that the Christian narration—which

92. Quoted by Dany-Robert Dufour, *Le bégaiement des maîtres* (Paris: Éditions François Bourin, 1978), p. 15.

quite naturally refuses to consider itself as mythological—brings about a historical break in narrative style.

It may well be that forcing the truth in this way, to a level just below that of consciousness, is the product of a kind of pessimistic wisdom concerning the mental and moral faculties of humankind. Men—yesterday no less than today—probably lacked the strength to abide the death of all gods, the abolition of all the transcendental or supernatural bases of the religious impulse, the loss of respect in the presence of the unutterable, of wonder at our presence in the world; in sum, to endure what constitutes a radical suppression of the celestial. Such has been the reasoning of many a pastor, many a theologian, whose intelligence I by no means underestimate. Nietzsche himself suggests nothing less, when in his celebrated passage on the death of God, he causes the Madman to say:

> How shall we console ourselves, the most murderous of all murderers? The holiest and the mightiest that the world has hitherto possessed, has bled to death under our knife—who will wipe the blood from us? ... Is not the magnitude of this deed too great for us? Shall we not ourselves have to become Gods, merely to seem worthy of it? ... This prodigious event is still on its way, and is travelling—it has not yet reached men's ears!" (*The Gay Science*, III, no. 125)

My aim is not to assess the perspicacity of the theologians, but to call into question the impact of the Gospel discourse on our narrative self-imagination, the impact of what I term, paradoxically, the Truth narrative. The contradiction in terms is obvious. All narrative that presents itself as the sole and indisputable truth forfeits that which in my eyes constitutes the essence of narrative: its incessant plurality of meaning, and its perpetual openness to new readings. Seen from this perspective, the Gospel, in setting for itself the truth as its end, constitutes the most insidious of all narratives and, without admitting as much, assumes the ambitions of philosophy. But philosophy, at least until the advent of Christianity, lays its cards on the table: it argues for its discourse of truth and submits it, *nolens volens*, to the critique of reason. And when its argument has reached the point of exhaustion, it turns to myth, as Plato so clearly demonstrates. But its methodological recourse is explicit, and makes no pretense at anything more than what a myth can express. For myth is allegory, metaphor; it is, in a word, open to interpretation.

Introducing to the story the appeal to authority in order to impose a truth exclusive of all others would have the effect of robbing the narrative of its fundamental freedom. It would entail serious consequences for the course that Christian, then Western literature was to follow. Christianity did not of course kill all narrative freedom, and to suggest as much would come down to proposing the thoroughly absurd notion that it forbids all fiction. I am simply stating that with the expansion, then domination of Christianity in Western Europe, the nature of the great stories, and particularly the most influential among them, undergoes a radical shift. Neither Saint Augustine's *Confessions*, nor the *chanson de geste* (from the *Song of Roland* to the Arthurian cycle), nor Dante's *Divine Comedy* is thinkable outside the truth of the Gospel. Even works of "pagan" inspiration, like the *Roman de Renart* or the *Roman de la rose* play themselves out in a world overseen by God. Certainly divine supervision was often less stringent than we imagine it today, and medieval literature is frequently surprising in its audacity. But our concern is not to characterize a vast and prolix literary era, but to reflect upon the magnitude of the rupture brought about by the truth found in the Christian *geste*.

This rupture touched not only literature; it impacted upon philosophy, history, science and even today influences our conception of the world. To assume that its influence has been so reduced by the secularisation of our societies and institutions that it has today all but ceased to exist would be the greatest of errors. The idea of truth, and the need to believe in it have been less affected by the decline of the Church and the Christian faith than is generally supposed. Both idea and need have shifted, along with the need for the religious itself. The shift has taken place principally toward the sciences. Today, for all our scepticism and our relativism, it is from them that we stand in expectation of salvation. An expectation that is Christian to the core.

To examine our civilization without taking into account the ineffaceable imprint of the evangelical spirit upon our collective memory would be to risk failing to understand the importance of the question of truth for the West even today. The worst of all misconceptions would be to believe that we could henceforth take upon ourselves collectively, the death of God, which the story of Christ had unwittingly proclaimed and which, two thousand years later, gives no sign of lessening its grip. Even had God's death been as widely accepted as some contend, I am far from certain that the sense of guilt that has for so long been a part of the Christian faith would vanish along with it. It may well burrow so deeply into the darkest reaches of consciousness that we will no longer be able either to touch or to comprehend it. As Elias Canetti writes:

> The image of the unique being whose death Christians have mourned for nearly two thousand years has penetrated the consciousness of all vigilant humanity. He is a dying man, and he must not die. (*Masse et puissance*, Paris, Gallimard, *Tel*, 1993, 497)

To believe that we can rip up our religious roots would be to condemn ourselves to never understanding the essence of that which rules over us, and to allow Christianity to rule over us in our ignorance. That which it rules over is nothing less than our relationship with truth. In our day and age, we are convinced that this relationship is governed by science, and has thus been expunged of belief. But faith in science overlooks the debt owed by science to belief. Science thirsts for truth, an ambition that remains tributary to our relationship, be it positive or negative, with transcendence. Transcendence can be affirmed or denied, but it haunts our imagination and conditions the way in which we think, the way in which we look at the world. The negation of transcendence (the death of God) weighs more heavily upon us today than its affirmation—of which we now believe ourselves relieved—once did. The guilt that all but overtly accompanied the adoration of Christ has only withdrawn a bit deeper into the depths of our collective consciousness.

God perishes slowly, endlessly in front of our eyes. But the idea of his murder has fallen gradually into oblivion. Our unquenchable thirst for truth grips us darkly. We exhaust ourselves in the pursuit of fleeting truths, but we cannot admit that our frantic chase has another objective: the absolute, the nostalgia for which we cannot relieve ourselves of, the ultimate truth that we cannot forgive ourselves for having sacrificed. If we postulate that the dark achievement of Christianity is to have planted in our civilization the lethal seeds of the idea of God, it is altogether probable that the seeds have been sown (again and again down through the centuries) at the price of a strange, mute terror: man, that wavering murderer of God, is guilty of not knowing the truth; nothing he can do will ever be great enough to absolve him of this sin.

9

THE SIN OF IGNORANCE

N O ONE rails with greater acrimony than Saint Augustine against the sin[93] of ignorance, against the disgrace of being constrained to live outside truth. Augustine exemplifies to the fullest possible extent the price a Christian must pay for not reading the Gospel as though it were myth. Yet at the same time he can achieve the fullness he yearns for only in the Gospel's "all or nothing" pronouncement: truth or death.

The Gospel proclaims the truth; it does not bestow it. The truth that Christ incarnates, the truth that he has come to proclaim to humankind must be grasped, piece by piece, by each and every one, on his own; there is no certainty of either attaining it, or preserving it, once attained, for faith is a gift of God. The will to truth alone is not enough. Grace is needed, and grace depends not upon us. To will with all our strength, even though will alone can achieve nothing: such is the paradox of Augustine's *Confessions*, the story of a long battle the aim of which is revelation.

The man whose contribution, above and beyond any other after Paul and before Thomas Aquinas, would shape the theology of Latin Christianity relates how, after innumerable deviations and vacillations, the thirst for truth led him, with God's help, to embrace the Catholic faith. To say that he relates would be an understatement; he declaims, rants, and waxes indignant at the memory of his own itinerancy, as though having finally reached the truth of Christ was not enough, as though it could not entirely redeem the time lost. He chastises himself, "O beauty, so ancient and so lovely, how belatedly I

---

93. Sin is here understood in the Pauline sense, as interpreted by Augustine, that is to say, as a form of slavery. It is persistent and guilty submission to error that holds man far from God, far from truth, and leads him to death. It is most certainly not a simple, passing, nor occasional fault. We must remember that Augustine is the author of the expression "original sin," based on his reading of Romans 5.

loved thee ... thou was with me but I was not with thee" (10, XXVII, 38).[94]
Written at the dawn of the fifth century, at a time when the Church was not
yet certain of its triumph,[95] the *Confessions* is the story of a tearing asunder
that may well be without end ...

From the beginning to the end of his narration, Augustine addresses
himself directly to God. God accompanied him, step by step, in the darkness
of his suffering, along a road of convoluted twists and turns that he, God, had
known well beforehand. God knows the truth with which he is one, and to
which only he may lead.

God had been present in his mother's milk. Augustine's mother Monica
was intensely Christian, but as a child he remained untouched by her faith.
His life *infans*, before acceding to speech, Augustine remembers only by
proxy: by what he is told and by what he can verify among the infants he
observes. Like any infant, Augustine early on is brought up sharply against
the limits of will and wields the weapon of the weak:

> Then, little by little, I realized where I was and wished to tell my
> wishes to those who might satisfy them, but I could not! For my
> wants were inside me, and they were outside, and they could not,
> by any power of theirs, come into my soul. And so I would fling
> my arms and legs about and cry, making the few and feeble
> gestures that I could, though indeed the signs were not much like
> what I inwardly desired and when I was not satisfied—either from
> not being understood or what I got was not good for me—I grew
> indignant that my elders were not subject to me and that those on
> whom I actually had no claim did not wait on me as slaves—and I
> avenged myself on them by crying. (1, VI, 8)

The recollection is indistinct, a retroactive projection of adult memory
onto infancy. At the outset, Augustine provides us with the key to the drama:
to want, and yet to be unable to attain what he wants. What we might call
man's original and permanent inadequacy, the powerlessness of will
experienced by the infant upon entry into the world, does not fade away in
adulthood; it simply changes places. What the infant Augustine experiences
in his body and in his primordial needs, the adult Augustine will discover
much later in his soul. The possibility of such a discovery remains beyond

94. The *Confessions* consists of thirteen books. The version quoted throughout this chapter is translated
and edited by Albert C. Outler (London: SCM Press, 1955).
95. Christianity became the state religion of the Roman Empire in 391, ten years before the writing of the
Confessions, which can be dated to approximately 400. Born in 354 at Tagaste, in North Africa, Augustine
was elected bishop of Hippo Regius in 396; he died in 430.

the child's grasp even after he has begun to speak, for by acquiring language he finds himself thrust into the social universe of adults. At home as at school, others grant themselves the right to tell him who to believe, who to read, what to think.

Yet when it comes to the most crucial questions, the youth remains alone: "In pity tell a pitiful creature whether my infancy followed yet an earlier age of my life that had already passed away before it?" (1, VI, 9) At most, he would have been told certain things concerning his mother's womb, and he himself would have seen pregnant women. We hear nothing more of the mysteries of sex and the carnal appetites that were later to torment him. His mother's Catholic influence, though far from negligible, is rapidly offset then overcome by the rhetorical exercises imposed by his masters. Primitive speech is punished even more vigorously than any moral lapse. The pupil obeys his mentors in order to "flourish in this world and distinguish myself in those tricks of speech which would gain honor for me among men, and deceitful riches" (1, XI, 14). Augustine condemns his literary education, and the great enjoyment of it that made him "a boy of good promise" (1, XI, 26). Seen in retrospect, the fables of the great poets are worth little, and call forth commentaries whose severity reminds us slightly of Plato: Homer is an empty wheedler, who has the impudence to believe that a lesson in debauchery—Jupiter descending in a golden shower into Danae's womb—can possibly have descended from heaven! The schoolboy is still unaware that he will soon devote to the service of God the rhetoric he has mastered. For the moment, it is an artifice that turns him away from the essence of things.

For the youthful Augustine, God is little more than an invisible, helpful force toward which he can turn and pray to avoid being beaten for his grammatical errors. For the frivolous occupations that adults term "business" take precedence over the little lad's innocent game of ball. How curious, notes Augustine, that through the innocence of infantile pleasures, the infant commits sins (laziness, minor deception) by disobeying rules which are themselves flawed, in that they prepare him for an experience of the world which, far from God, is already "fornication" (1, XIII, 21).

Suddenly, something serious happens: Augustine falls gravely ill and calls for baptism with an infantile fervor worthy of his mother's faith. But his rapid return to health postpones the sacrament. "So my cleansing was deferred," writes Augustine, "as if it were inevitable that, if I should live, I would be further polluted; and further, because the guilt contracted by sin after baptism would be still greater and more perilous" (1, XI, 17). The deferral may well appear to be a subtle manifestation of divine grace that will allow him later to arrange his baptism to coincide with his entry into the new life of the believer. But would it not have been of greater worth to have been cleansed of all sin at his tender age, and made to submit to Christian discipline? Unless, even in the baptized state, he would not have successfully negotiated adolescence without yielding to temptation ... Augustine wavers, he knows not for what purpose his baptism has been deferred, nor whether or not it was for his good; but, more than ten years after his conversion, he is still torn by regrets. Better than any other, this episode evokes the obscure nature of the paths by which God guides his servant toward the light. There can be little doubt that Augustine must experience the long trial at the hands of the truth that "any soul in disorder" is itself its severest punishment (1, XIII, 20); and in itself, the most troubling enigma:

> Is any man skilful enough to have fashioned himself? Or is there any other source from which being and life could flow into us, save this, that Thou, O Lord, hast made us—Thou for whom being and life are one, since thou thyself art supreme being and supreme life together. (1, XI, 10)

With the *Confessions* arises, as though it were new, the question of individual identity. Who makes us? What part of us is shared with another, what part can we claim for ourselves, what part is God's? Augustine feigns leaving the matter unresolved: God is outside of time, ever identical to himself; thus, it is unimportant to know whether or not we will ultimately be joined with him, nor how we have sought him, in the event that we have found him, whether consciously or unconsciously. But this kind of detachment is only possible after the fact. If then! The mechanism seems too obvious. Augustine's evasiveness cannot deceive us: "who am I?" has become indissolubly connected with "who do I want to be?"—the double-barrelled question of identity and will leaves him no respite.

For Augustine everything begins before adolescence, with a raging fire that none of the literary vanities can calm, and with that elemental certainty that, early on, he feels possesses himself:

> For I existed even then; I lived and felt and was solicitous about my own well-being—a trace of that most mysterious unity from which I had my being. I kept watch, by my inner sense, over the integrity

of my outer senses, and even in these trifles and in my thoughts
about trifles, I learned to take pleasure in truth. (1, XIX, 31)

Over and above the pleasures of truth, Augustine cherishes the integrity,
the unity of his inner being. As a source of internal strength, it will prove
priceless. It is exactly this sense of integrity that is threatened by the
"Babylonian" debauchery of adolescence. With the eruption of puberty, the
shifting alluvium of carnal lust sweeps him along, depositing him at the foot
of the passions that overwhelm him. On the pretext of satisfaction "with
worldly things" (2, I, 1), the adolescent dissipates himself in the bitter
displeasures of lust under his father's indulgent gaze and despite his mother's
discreet exhortations, which, having failed to discern as the voice of God, he
sees as nothing more than the advice of a woman which he would blush to
accept.

Though he never describes his past wickedness, Augustine revels in
lashing out at the carnal infections of his soul, at the treacherous paths taken,
at the illicit gratifications, as though thirty years later he still bore their
ineffaceable stigmata. Being neither a believer nor having been baptized at
the time, he could hardly, as an adolescent, have lived in a sinful state of
which he was ignorant. Doubtless he experienced the emptiness of his
mindless quest for carnal pleasures that his lack of experience and judgement
had condemned to failure. His behavior, notes the narrator, is as much a
response to the social pressures of his cohorts as to his own desires: burning
memories of being caught up in the vulgar sweep of camaraderie, of being
swept away by the social whirl rather than obeying his inner requirements.
But there may well be more: the insistence with which the Bishop of Hippo
Regius revisits, in violently deprecatory terms, the infamies of bygone days
would seem to indicate that the battle has by no means ended. His repeated
fulminations against sin are probably an indication that, years later, he is still
obsessed by temptation.

For Augustine is, in every respect, a man of excess. The fire of his faith
blazes today as brightly as the ardor of his carnal loves, or his sudden passion
for philosophy, once did. Indeed, an intense passion sweeps over the young
man when he reads Cicero's *Hortensius*:

Now it was this book, which quite definitely changed my whole
attitude and turned my prayers toward thee, O Lord, and gave me
new hope and new desires. Suddenly every vain hope became
worthless to me, and with an incredible warmth of heart I yearned

for an immortality of wisdom and began now to arise that I might return to thee....

How ardent was I then, my God, how ardent to fly from earthly things to thee! Nor did I know how thou wast even then dealing with me. For with thee is wisdom. In Greek the love of wisdom is called 'philosophy', and it was with this love that that book inflamed me....

Only this checked my ardor: that the name of Christ was not in it. For this name, by thy mercy, O Lord, this name of my Savior thy Son, my tender heart had piously drunk in, deeply treasured even with my mother's milk. And whatsoever was lacking that name, no matter how erudite, polished and truthful, did not quite take complete hold of me.

I resolved therefore to direct my mind to the Holy Scriptures, that I might see what they were. And behold, I saw something not comprehended by the proud, not disclosed to children, something lowly in the hearing, but sublime in the doing, and veiled in mysteries. Yet I was not of the number of those who could enter into it or bend my neck to follow its steps. For then it was quite different from what I now feel. When I then turned toward the Scriptures, they appeared to me to be quite unworthy to be compared with the dignity of Tully. For my inflated pride was repelled by their style, nor could the sharpness of my wit penetrate their inner meaning. Truly they were of a sort to aid the growth of little ones, but I scorned to be a little one and, swollen with pride, I looked upon myself as fully grown. (3, IV–V, 7–9)

Cicero, along with philosophy, inflict upon the young Augustine the bite of truth. But the bite remains incomplete. Whether "the name of Christ" is truly what is lacking, or whether the name acts as a signifier under the narrator's pen is of secondary importance. Reading the *Hortensius* has merely given him an appetite for truth and wisdom, an appetite that reflects all the impetuosity of youth, rather than revealing a lack of humility. The apparent inability in his eyes of biblical Scripture to attain the loftiness of Ciceronian dignity must be sanctioned as the mark of sin: of the disdain and self-importance of him who persists in ignoring the presence of God close beside him. Given that God already—and secretly—occupies the future believer's thoughts and deeds, the account of his early years cannot but be colored by a kind of latent grace. As Augustine so judiciously puts it, the terms of his narration were "quite different" from his feelings at the time. For all that, as a writer he cannot help stigmatising them in the name of the truth to come. Does he do so for the reader's edification? Or out of necessity, in pursuit of the inner struggle?

In either case, the events related *already* contain their explanation, and the narrator is unconditionally convinced that his existence is predestined. The incomprehensible needs no explanation; divine grace sheds its light over all. Above and beyond the question of faith, the Augustinian narrative introduces, quite unlike anything before it, the irresistible power of finality: the *Confessions* are totally subordinated to it. It is not enough to know, as in the *Odyssey*, how the story will end nor the details of its conclusion. The reader must feel that the end dictates each and every episode, which is simultaneously the culmination, the advent and God's design. The same pre-determination sustains the organization of the *Aeneid*, which Augustine knew well, but Virgil's pre-determination operates on the level of legend and in the service of history. Augustine places himself entirely within the truth of his personal experience.

When it comes to truth, the weight of finality also determines the Scriptures, by whose spirit Augustine is content to abide. But the author of the *Confessions* adds yet another dimension to biblical finality. We know now how different the finality of the Tanakh is from that of the Old Testament. The latter derives its meaning from the New Testament, whose advent the Old is now claimed to have "made ready." To this day the Tanakh remains open, subject to a diversity of interpretations. Judaism, let us recall, is in a process of ceaseless construction and ongoing discussion with itself; alongside it Christianity has all the appearances of a closed system, carrying a finished message. But the finality of the Gospel is that which God, through Christ, has assigned himself. Augustine takes a further step along the road toward truth: everything happens as though God were watching over him, a simple mortal, up to and including his withdrawal and his silence, and waiting to bring forth within him, Augustine, illumination. At first he is a secret interlocutor; then he stands revealed in his search for truth. God, for all intents and purposes, is the narrator's *alter ego*. His presence, even unseen, is such that in its constancy and interiority we can no longer distinguish *in the narrative* between God and his servant's consciousness. The question arises: who, in fact, serves whom? Is it not God, in the final analysis, who serves Augustine?

Anthropologically speaking, it is a commonplace that man invents God to express his needs, his fears, his hopes and aspirations. But from the perspective of the believer, the revelation and its story transcend the human, and only transcendence itself is of moment: for him, it is real; man has not created it, but received it. So it is with Augustine, precisely because he finds the truth of reason and philosophy unsatisfactory, uncertain—deeply flawed, in fact. Only the mystery of a revealed transcendence can slake his thirst for truth. Truth and believing, truth and grace are indissociable. His humility and submission to God are thus perfectly sincere; without them, belief would be quite impossible.

Like all the great narratives, however, Augustine's exerts certain effects and bodies forth currents that far outstrip its author's intentions. It is difficult today not to capture, from a close reading of the *Confessions*, in the passionate story of the relationship woven between God and the soul, a truly unprecedented manner of presenting one's self as an individual. It would never have occurred to Plato to address the Creator directly, or to speak to Beauty in intimate terms. Humility notwithstanding, Augustine had progressively transformed himself into the conscious interpreter of a new sensibility of the self, in an era when communal solidarity was dissolving in the immense and confusing identity that Roman citizenship conferred upon the inhabitants of a declining empire. Even though it makes itself manifest within the confines of a small community of believers, the attachment to God binds the individual directly to Him. In the political context of the age, the importance of this personal link grows in inverse proportion to the weakening of traditional collective ties. It provides, in short, a substitute for identity, for security.

Seen from this identitarian perspective, Augustinian humility is not enough to make us forget that, by the narrator's own admission, the point of departure of his spiritual journey is the feeling of his own individual integrity (see above, 1, XX, 31); a feeling that will soon be threatened by his dissolute life, and that the Ciceronian love of wisdom seems powerless to restore. From adolescence onward, we recall, Augustine is torn between the desire for an inescapable truth and for self-dissolution in worldly pleasures, between the need for inner coherence and the wilfulness of the flesh. Female sensuality has a stronger grip on his soul than does the spirit. And in this unequal battle where spiritual will-power ceaselessly capitulates before the urgings of the flesh, neither Manicheism, which he has come to follow for want of a better alternative, nor philosophy, can lend him the weapons he needs to bring about the triumph of the spirit. Augustine's humility arises from the fact that, for all his intellectual accomplishment, he is never quite successful in forcing himself to obey his own orders; in both his will and his intelligence, he is brought low. He fancies himself a master, but he learns that he is a slave. His revolt draws all its nourishment from this searing internal contradiction:

> And I especially puzzled and wondered when I had remembered how long a time had passed since my nineteenth year, in which I had first fallen in love with wisdom and had determined as soon as I could find her to abandon the empty hopes and mad delusions of vain desires. Behold, I was now getting close to thirty, still stuck fast in the same mire, still greedy of enjoying present goods which fly away and distract me: and I was still saying: "Tomorrow I shall discover it; behold it will become plain, and I shall see it; behold. Faustus[96] will come and explain everything." Or I would say: "O you mighty Academics, is there no certainty that man can grasp for the guidance of his life? No, let us search the more diligently, and let us not despair. See, the things in the Church's books that appeared so absurd to us before do not appear so now, and may be otherwise and honestly interpreted. I will set my feet upon that step where, as a child, my parents placed me, until the clear truth is discovered. But where and when shall it be sought?...
>
> While I talked about these things, and the winds of opinions veered about and tossed my heart hither and thither, time was slipping away. I delayed my conversion to the Lord; I postponed from day to day the life in thee, but I could not postpone the daily death in myself. I was enamored of a happy life, but I still feared to seek it in its own abode, and so I fled from it while I sought it. I thought I should be miserable if I were deprived of the embraces of a woman and I never gave a thought to the medicine that they mercy has provided for the healing of that infirmity, for I had never tried it. As for continence, I imagined that it depended on one's own strength, though I found no such strength in myself, for in my folly I knew not what is written. "None can be continent unless thou dost grant it." (6, XI, 18–20)

Even the acceptance of Scripture as a source of truth is not enough to extract Augustine from his indecisiveness. His tardy conversion to the Church's Holy Writ is still too intellectual. Then, something takes place that cannot deceive us: he notices that these books speak to the humble and to the ignorant as much as to the cultivated elites. "The uninstructed start up and take heaven and we—with all our learning but so little heart—see where

---

96. A highly regarded Manichean bishop encountered during Augustine's stay in Carthage, and of whom he expected much (5, III, 3).

we wallow in flesh and blood" (8, VIII, 19). To this hard lesson in humility is added an even more ominous obstacle, the ultimate ordeal. Sure enough, it is hardly different in nature than that which had been his throughout the years of struggle, but the narrator, with his infallible dramatic sense, formulates it far better than it had ever been before, in a stunning foreshortening that precedes the pivotal point of conversion. Augustine's indignation at being unable, so close to his goal, to accomplish the decisive step here reaches its apex:

> But it must be a strong and single will, not staggering and swaying about this way and that—a changeable, twisting, fluctuating will, wrestling with itself while one part falls as another rises.
>
> ... Thus I tore my hair, struck my forehead, or, entwining my fingers, clasped my knee, these I did because I willed it. But I might have willed it and still not done it, if the nerves had not obeyed my will. Many things then I did, in which the will and power to do were not the same.
>
> How can there be such a strange anomaly? And why is it? Let thy mercy shine on me, that I may inquire and find an answer, amid the dark labyrinth of human punishment and in the darkest contributions of the sons of Adam. Whence such an anomaly? And why should it be? The mind commands the body, and the body obeys. The mind commands itself and is resisted. The mind commands the hand to be moved and there is such readiness that the command is scarcely distinguished from the obedience in act. Yet the mind is mind, and the hand is body. The mind commands the mind to will, and yet though it be itself it does not obey itself (8, VIII–XI, 19–21).

This remarkable passage calls for an attentive reading. Not only because it so forcefully expresses the tragedy of will, the divorce between wish and deed, which we have already found in Paul (Rom. 7: 14–20), but because it lays before us in a manner at once violent and ambiguous, the impossibility of the object of Augustine's quest, and of his nostalgia, which is for the unity of the self. The very self that Augustine, more than anyone else of his era, has succeeded in placing at the center of his spiritual concerns, now appears weakened by an irreparable fracture. As a division it does not, unlike so many other moments of the *Confessions* or Paul's Epistles, draw a line of separation between the spirit and the flesh. Augustine demonstrates, instead, with what ease the body bends to the command of the mind. The fault line passes through the mind itself. Ten years after his conversion, the narrator has not yet received an answer, and appeals for the compassion of divine illumination. What can be the reason for such an anomaly? It can only be, he says, because "the will does not will entirely," nor does it "command totally." Could it be that, when all is said and done, the anomaly is not as great as it seems, that it is simply an "infirmity of mind"? Anomaly or infirmity, the scandal of its powerlessness remains whole: "I neither willed with my whole will nor was I wholly unwilling."

And yet, Augustine immediately puts forward a kind of solution, a pious explanation:

> And so I was at war with myself and torn apart by myself. And this strife was against my will; yet it did not show the presence of another mind, but the punishment of my own. Thus it was no more I who did it, but the sin that dwelt in me—the punishment of a sin freely committed by Adam, and I was a son of Adam. (8, VIII, 22)

"Thus it was no more I who did it, but the sin that dwelt in me ..."—Augustine has no sooner discovered the dislocation of his being than he explains it away, attributing it to sin.

Sin may well indicate—for Augustine—"infirmity of mind": Christians call "sin" that which Plato terms disequilibrium, discord, injustice; and that which Freud would much later attribute to the subconscious. Mere questions of vocabulary, we are tempted to conclude. Hardly! If Plato speaks of injustice or discord, it is because he believes that the lover of wisdom is able to acquire the means of understanding that which torments him, and find the strength to live in fuller awareness of himself—the same task that psychoanalysis was later to undertake. To speak of the division of the self as the outcome of sin implies, on the other hand, that outside divine grace no remedy exists. Plato, in locating the question of justice within the boundaries of the human sphere, may seem pretentious, especially when contrasted with Christian humility. But his pretension is based (in the *Republic*) on a closely reasoned, nuanced analysis which concludes that justice, partially at least, cannot be found. The Platonic requirement is conscious of the limits within which it must remain, but it makes no appeal to an outside power.

Following in Paul's footsteps, Augustine—who speaks from experience—does not believe that man, in and of himself (and without God's help), can possibly work toward inner justice, toward the equilibrium of the soul. With Augustine, the break is a radical one, almost as sharp as the famous *Spaltung* that splits the Freudian *Ich*, had it not been transformed into punishment. By presenting sin as a perversion of will and as a disgrace, the Bishop of Hippo Regius snaps shut the fault-line he had just caused to open at his feet: no, he says, there is no other nature in me, only the presence of sin, which God alone can erase. In his rush to discard the Manichean concept that makes evil a substance, Augustine reduces it to a sinful perversion. But in the same breath he pushes aside the ultimate implication of his analysis: that in the ego, at the heart of that most intimate of beings, there exists the other. *Not the presence of another mind, but the punishment of my own*: the passage rings out like an attempted exorcism to expel his own otherness from consciousness.

Even as he names him, Augustine refuses to admit the existence of the other, the stranger that Oedipus paid so dearly for having ignored in himself. No sooner named, otherness is dismissed as the feeling of guilt that inhabits us, and of which only the Lord may dispose. God, who is both within us and outside us, emerges as master of our unity and our identity (our sameness). Abruptly, the ego assumes a consistency radically different from its earlier weakness. Initially a sign of humility, the appeal to grace now tends to relieve the ego of the ambiguity that had made grace necessary in the first place. It is easy to see why it has been suggested, sometimes rather broadly, that the Augustinian ego is the distant precursor of the modern sense of individuality and of its oneness.

If by grace was meant the unutterable, the Judaic YHWH, a door to absence would have remained open. But Augustine, whatever his intentions, speaks from within the context of evangelical anthropomorphism. This he does ever so slightly in spite of himself, since one of the main reasons for his acceptance of the Scriptures was precisely the idea, in Genesis, that God has made man in his image. While in Milan, under the influence of Ambrose, the narrator discovers that what is at issue is not that man's body has been modelled upon God's, as the detractors of the Catholic faith claim, but that conformity with God is spiritual in nature (6, III, 4). But if, by Augustine's own admission, the soul is the locus of determination, God is indeed the creator and guarantor of our spiritual identity. By giving himself a human face in the person of the Son, he has made a powerful contribution to reinforcing the sense of identity. Its disclaimers notwithstanding, Christianity humanizes God as do neither of the two other Abrahamic monotheisms. Such is the framework within which Augustine's thought takes shape and, to an even greater extent, expands: the Savior, in cleansing us of our sins, saves us from our secret otherness, from the *Unheimliche* that, centuries later, Freud was to formulate, but with no cooling balm.

If the beauty of Augustinian (and Christian) submission to the mystery of the divine seems tarnished, choked by the swollen ego in its relation with God, we need look no further for the reason. But the swollen ego is Augustine's adversary. He struggles against it by belittling his literary knowledge and deprecating the narrow-minded insolence of the jurisprudents. The strength of the Christian message, as Paul so eloquently puts it, lies in its madness: "Let no man deceive himself. If any man among you seemeth to be a fool, that he may be wise.... For the wisdom of this world is foolishness with God" (1 Cor. 3:18–19). Augustine's conversion is Pauline to a fault, not only because it is brought about by his reading of the Apostle, but also because what sets it in motion, as well as the content of the reading itself, seem irrational and arbitrary. Of course, the narrator's state is such that anything can happen:

> and weeping in the most bitter contrition of my heart, when suddenly I heard the voice of a boy or a girl—I know not which—coming from the neighboring house, chanting over and over again, "Pick it up, read it; pick it up, read it." Immediately I ceased weeping and began most earnestly to think whether or not it was usual for children in some kind of game to sing such a song, but I could not remember ever having heard the like. So, damming the torrent of my tears, I got to my feet, for I could not but think that this was a divine command to open the Bible and read the first passage I should light upon....
>
> So I quickly returned to the bench where Alypius was sitting, for there I had put down the apostle's book when I had left there. I snatched it up, opened it, and in silence read the paragraph on which my eyes fell: "Not in rioting and drunkenness, not in chambering and wantonness, not in strife and envying, but put ye on the Lord Jesus Christ. And make not provision for the flesh to fulfil the lusts thereof." [97] I wanted to read no further, nor did I need to. For instantly, as the sentence ended, there was infused in my heart something like the light of full certainty and all the gloom of doubt vanished away. (8, XII, 29)

There is nothing in the passage from the Epistle to the Romans that Augustine himself would not have repeated one hundred times over. This time, however, circumstances are such that the exhortation seems to issue directly from heaven. The double coincidence—the voice of the child crying out in a moment of supreme despair; our narrator opening the book to a

---

97. Rom. 13:13–14.

precise page—this tiny miracle is, in fact, a sign. God, at long last, has responded to his servant's constant supplication. A sign, and not simply the workings of chance; for Augustine's soul, in his yearning for a direct connection with God, is stretched to the breaking point. Had he not been convinced of a personal linkage, there could have been no miraculous coincidence; the narrator would surely have scoffed at such childishness, and would certainly never have attempted to interpret it. Augustine bows before the irrational in the deep conviction that there must be a privileged relationship, one whose advent he implores. It could only be a privileged relationship, for grace is not given to all men, not even necessarily to those who most desire it.

In the weight it lends to individual fate, the *Confessions* stand, in the wake of the New Testament, as a major turning point in the sensibility of Latin Christianity. Though carefully circumscribed and defined by the Church, faith and choice have now become personal considerations. Not that the individual is absolved of his responsibilities by the ecclesiastical and secular authorities, but because the individual is now, after Augustine, as naked as Job before the power of God. Job, in the Tanakh, incarnates not only human weakness and the poverty of intelligence before the unfathomability of creation; he ultimately turns his back on the reward of his piety and justice. Where Job no longer expects anything from God, the Christian anticipates that his faith will be recompensed, if not here on earth, then in the hereafter. Having reached the farthest boundaries of his revolt, Job accepts that he cannot understand. The Christian, on the other hand, wants the truth; he wants his measure of the "secrets of God" to which Job can never hope to accede (Job, 15:8). The Christian's expectancy of eternal life, his anticipation that grace will become certainty, lends his nudity a provisional quality, while Job's return to his earthly prosperity, even twofold more than he possessed before being brought low, gives him no such assurance. For this pious man whose only happiness is his piety, nothing is assured. It is written of Job only that he "died, being old and full of days" (Job, 42:17).

But whatever assurance the Christian enjoys cannot be absolute. Of the reality of the hereafter there can be no doubt, but access to it (or to its positive part) remains forever conditional. Catholic grace in itself is certain, but it can never be taken for granted by him who receives it. The *Confessions* is written in the burning heat of temptation. But its peculiar intonation, its sense of unease suggest that conversion has not entirely caused the duel with the will to vanish. For the narrator, to live by the dictates of the flesh exercises still an attraction that every indignant page betrays.[98] The images of the past remain fully alive in his memory, a cruel reminder of the duality, and of the infirmity of his ego. From there, it is but a short step to holding any sensual pleasure suspect. In the "examination of conscience" that ends his penitent's confession, Augustine evokes his response to religious music; that his emotions might be affected more by the music than by the words torments him: "See now what a condition I am in ... in whose sight I am become an enigma to myself ..." (10, XXXIII, 50) The beauties and the diversions of the world keep alert the senses, those permanent guests in the house of joyousness and curiosity where the soul lies in constant danger of perdition.

The believer may well have touched upon the truth, but that does not mean that he possesses it as an inalienable good. The victory of faith remains brittle, and I am tempted to say that its brittleness is its saving virtue. It makes Augustine's story, for all the exhausting repetition of the invocations that punctuate it, a truthful, compelling act of witness. The truth of the *Confessions* is not faith, but the inner battle of faith. The outcome of the battle is uncertain, as God alone ultimately decides. God and truth are, but their mystery remains whole, intact. Though transparent to God, Augustine's soul remains in part obscure to itself; its quest leads not to knowledge but to belief. There is, of course, "knowledge" of God in the joy of his presence, but there is nothing either explicable or rational about this immediacy. Not that rationality has been banished from the Augustinian discourse—"believe in order to understand and understand in order to believe," he wrote—but because without belief rationality leads nowhere, and ends in an impasse. The desire for and the experience of humility in Augustine are authentic, though humility, in the relationship it seeks with God, is under constant threat of inflation.

To a certain extent, the question of humility goes farther than Augustine suspects. It is noteworthy that the story of Augustine's spiritual journey ends shortly after his conversion, in Book Nine of the *Confessions*, with the death of his mother, who is at peace now that her prayers have been answered and her son returned to the faith. The narrator's trajectory is also, for all intents and purposes, a voyage toward his mother, and his entry into the Church a kind of return to the maternal bosom. Augustine abandons the woman of the flesh, the prostitute, for his spiritual mother, the saint. Monica discretely prefigures the role that will later be assumed in Catholicism by the Virgin Mary. Not only do the gift of faith and the return to the original womb

---

98. In Book Ten (XXXIV, 51), Augustine writes that the temptations of "carnal appetite ... still assail me (me adhuc pulsant)."

coincide, but this coincidence meshes in turn with the primacy of belief over reason: in God as in the maternal bosom reign security, warmth, and a truth that is invisible but palpable, and that no obscurity can diminish. In his examination of conscience in Book Ten, Augustine crouches beneath the outspread wings of God: "I am insufficient, but my father liveth forever, and my defender is sufficient for me. For he is the Selfsame who didst beget me and who watcheth over me; Thou art the Selfsame who art all my good" (10, IV, 6). Father and mother are reunited where he was begotten, in the safe haven that awaits him always. The movement is the opposite of that in Genesis; a return to paradise.

Under God's maternal wing the uncertainty that flows from the things of the world is no longer a cause for heartbreak. The assurance of truth, even though it is incomprehensible, makes doubt bearable and the importance of knowledge relative. At the same time, our sense of incompleteness testifies to the necessity of God and of his mystery. Were mystery not a certainty, reason would be everywhere wounded by its inability to understand and its appetite for knowledge, deeply troubled. With God's help, man need not understand, and can, within the bounds of his comprehension, learn the ways of the world with greater serenity. The sin of ignorance has nothing to do with the inadequacy of our worldly knowledge, and nothing to do with our inability to know God; as sin, it is the absence of concern for God, the deliberate ignorance of his presence.

The three final books of the *Confessions* (9–13) deal with several fundamental questions concerning the capacity for knowing. Augustine touches on certain pages of Genesis and Exodus without attempting to give them a definitive interpretation. To the Scriptures must be left their enigmas, their silences. The mystery of the trinity, or the question of what God may have been doing before he created the world, for example, are as enigmatic as the question of time, which normally is of no concern to us in our daily lives yet which, on reflection, carries with it a full share of insoluble problems. Augustine's celebrated thoughts on time are breathtaking: "Let us then, O human soul, see whether present time can be long" (11, XV, 19). The most familiar, most banal things can plunge us into bottomless perplexity. God and his mysteries are just as fascinating, just as difficult to accept as the abyss.

Ultimately, the dangerously swollen ego that demands a personal relationship with God is deflated when it is exposed to the enigma of creation. The unfathomable exposes us to our infinite tininess. The man who is held up as the precursor of the modern sensibility fears nothing quite so much as the "evil arising" from those who "please themselves in themselves" (10, XXXIV, 64). Wholeness belongs only to God; man can partake of it only by proxy, and remains subject to incompleteness. Augustine has involuntarily planted the seed of ego, of an individual subject who, should he stray from the divine metaphor, might well claim wholeness for himself instead of leaving the matter in God's hands; he might well even conceive disproportionate pretensions and ambitions. If there is no more transcendence, then our identity has no other point of reference than itself. The tautological definition of YHWH, "I am what I am," has become man's. Man, against his own failings, can no longer turn to the spiritual. He can turn only to his own knowledge, itself caught up in a dynamic of unlimited expansion, for whatever limiting factors once existed do so no longer. Henceforth man's sole resort will be his own continuously expanding knowledge. No longer does anything stand above it to limit its reach.

Platonic knowledge had no other ambition than the achievement of internal equilibrium. By entrusting God with man's weakness, the Church paradoxically released man from external constraint and allowed him to redirect his power toward the world. By making the temporal linearity of the Old Testament its own, and by decreeing an end point of history (the Second Coming), Christianity in the same breath established an expectation and a finality against which the faithful may henceforth measure their prayers and their actions. Derived from divine essence, Christian finality began by reducing earthly finalities to almost nothing, and even cultivated suspicion of scientific curiosity. But at the same time it set out a direction, which, as mystery was reduced to a commonplace and faith corroded, was soon to leave its imprint upon the affairs of mankind. What he could no longer expect from God, the modern man came to expect from his own enterprises. The earthly future, and not the heavenly future, dominates the present. From that day hence, the ego, both collective and individual, was to invest itself in what we unthinkingly term the meaning of history. Jewish and particularistic at first, the idea took on a universal dimension under Christianity: all men and all cultures must from now on, on pain of death, make this perspective their own. Such is the immense paradox of a doctrine that prefers the above-and-beyond; a doctrine whose greatest contribution is to have helped produce a civilization that seeks to master nature and construct a material paradise on earth. The *Confessions* may appear today to contain the seeds of something resembling modernity; the subject, for all its debt to Augustine, could hardly be more un-Augustinian.

Augustine intends, by confessing his erring ways and his hardships, to convince men of the necessity of faith. But he illustrates at the same time man's distress when deprived of faith. All things considered, distress is better than indifference. Better the uneasiness of faith, even the anguish of disgrace, that the tranquillity of disbelief. Better to despair of truth than to forgo the search for it in the revelation of Scripture. In his struggle to overcome his despair, Augustine passionately affirms, like none other, the inseparability of truth and salvation.

Tradition ascribes to Augustine the primacy of certainty over doubt, of the general over the particular. The price has been a serious diminution of our understanding of him. What makes the *Confessions* extraordinary is less its end point, more the path taken. The narrator's greatest accomplishment is not to have encountered the truth—an occurrence that by his own admission is conditional upon God alone—but to have searched for it so long and so ardently. But the encounter itself risks obscuring the path, a danger heightened by a spiritual sloth, which, with the benediction of the Church, remains quite content with a ready-made reading. The triumph of the truth everywhere overwhelms the intensity of the drama experienced by the narrator as an individual. It is apparent on every page of the *Confessions*: Augustine's words are incarnate, his flesh cries out, his soul is an open wound, and all that is so apparent is threatened by oblivion. Something in the *Confessions* itself leads inexorably toward oblivion, something closely connected with the narrator's ultimate intentions.

As he narrates an individual experience, Augustine makes himself the agent of universal truth. He incarnates the ultimate goal of the Gospel message. To the supernatural incarnation of the Truth in Christ is added the first-hand account of an entirely human, individual incarnation. What has been added is anything but paltry and insignificant. On the contrary, it explains the immense impact of the autobiography, which has proven to be an unending inspiration for Western literature. The New Testament restricts itself—if I dare say so—to the story of a man who has himself left not the slightest trace, not the slightest written record. This proviso is a critical one: for all the Church's efforts, it leaves room, no matter how slight, for a mythological interpretation of the Gospel. If the story of the Passion, despite its pretensions to authenticity, can be read as myth, it is because the story of its hero, Jesus, is related by others.

Augustine is, in the fullest sense of the word, the author of his own story. And with regard to its central core—his long march toward revelation—his tale leaves practically no latitude for interpretation. His *Confessions* is nothing less than the direct narration of a subjective encounter not simply with truth, but with Truth; a truth which is not only that of the narrator, but the universal Truth proclaimed by the Gospel, which thus becomes indissociable from the narration that bodies it forth. Subjectivity and objectivity are fused into one. Specific experience becomes one with universal experience and in the same breath lends it gravity or, at minimum, reinforces it. Truth exists; I Augustine have encountered it, and I attest that there is none other. The experience of Christ, as it has been related to us, is by definition unique; it remains distinct from common experience. The same holds for Paul's overwhelming conversion, itself also unique. As recompense for his perseverance, Augustine's conversion is offered, for all its hardship, as something accessible to all, and particularly to those least inclined to accept it: it can be replicated, and it is desirable. There exists only one Christ, only one Paul, but there are millions of possible Augustines. The multitude is necessary, and is the best possible proof that there exists, with or without anguish, but one door to salvation through which all successive generations must pass.

We cannot be too attentive to the contradiction Augustine exemplifies, in spite of himself. He has founded a general (though revealed) truth on individual experience, yet the truth he has propounded leads to eternal life. In placing the emphasis on the individual, existential dimension of this contradiction, which becomes for each and every one of us a question of life or death, Augustine reinforces the closure placed by the Church upon interpretation of the Gospel story. More than ever, truth and the salvation that depends upon it forbid any pluralist reading. The possibility that the believer may escape death is transformed into a duty. This possibility and this duty have now become the ultimate *raison d'être* of faith. Such a belief, to sustain itself, can only be blind to the subjectivity upon which its universality is constructed. Without it, anyone could see that which, from beginning to end of the *Confessions*, stares us in the face: that the truth of Augustine's grace is necessarily of the same order as the experience that has led him to it: fundamentally subjective—which does not stop thousands of others from sharing it with him. Anything, in other words, that depicts the affirmation of faith as being indissociable from the terms in which it is uttered and from the conditions that make it possible, is incompatible with revelation.

Saint Augustine is an immense paradox: almost in spite of himself, he, the entranced witness to the division of the soul deprived of truth, confirms and embodies the particular kind of schizophrenia that lends his desire for truth its inimitable contours. Divine revelation only repositions or papers over the breach that has been opened. The subject of the truth—literally subjected to it, in fact—has been unconsciously divided. It is impossible to tell whether in moving from the slavery of sin to the slavery of truth, Augustine has not attempted to trade painful for comforting ignorance. Saint Augustine may not have entirely succeeded, but his greatness is none the lesser for that. His *Confessions* echoes down through the centuries like a victory; a victory that ignores the occultation that has made it possible.

Western thought up to the present day remains profoundly influenced by this triumphal, willed blindness. It derives its force from the hermetic barrier that implicitly separates truth from him who utters it. The idea of a universal revelation and, later, of a scientific truth would not only have been impossible were it not for this impassable barrier; had it been conscious of the schizophrenia that enables it to exist, it could never have perpetuated itself, let alone transmitted itself. If Saint Augustine is indeed a far-distant precursor of modern subjectivity, then that subjectivity can be said to have begun its journey in the ignorance of that which divides it. Which is as much as to say, in the subject's self-ignorance. Not that the subject is unaware of conflicting forces (good and evil, or flesh and spirit) but because it knows nothing of the force of attraction that pulls it, inexorably, toward what it holds to be true. It does not know what it ignores; it is closed off to Socratic ignorance. Seen through the Augustinian prism, Plato becomes incomprehensible. Platonism and Neoplatonism have no other dimension than that of "preparation" for Gospel truth, and metaphysics enters into the service of theology. Even when the serving maid no longer desires to serve her mistress, as in Descartes, the Augustinian subject casts a long shadow across her meditations.

Today, as the emergence of the modern subject appears in retrospect, and given our awareness that the line of division that runs through it has been a deep misunderstanding (even though this awareness is far from being shared by all), it is possible to seek the source of the misunderstanding as far back as the Bishop of Hippo Regius. One thing seems certain enough to me: this misunderstanding still holds us in its sway; it has become one of the foundation stones of Western philosophy's search for truth, the driving force behind the flowering of the experimental sciences. There lies, perhaps, an indication that we owe the exponential curve of our scientific and technical achievements in part to modern man's subconscious need for self-ignorance.

Part Four

HEROISM AND TRUTH

SOCRATES, CHRIST, AND AUGUSTINE: each one, in his own manner, is a hero of truth. The first two lay down their lives for it; the third sacrifices the pleasures of the flesh in its name. For Socrates, however, death is not something whose truth can save us. Death is inevitable; the question is one of knowing what the state of our soul will be as we enter into it. Socrates elects to die at a time of his choosing in the integrity of his convictions, rather than to prolong, in self-renunciation or in exile, a life that is drawing to an end. He does not die for truth, but with it, happy in its excellent company.

But for Christ the truth is a conquest, culminating in his sacrifice and resurrection. Augustine's sacrifice is a lesser one, but its spirit is the same: the ephemeral present is offered up in exchange for the eternal, the sensual for the spiritual; the world is left behind for the sake of faith. This prospect, as we have seen, introduces into the narrative the fundamental break by which multiplicity of meaning is in turn sacrificed to the oneness of the True. With the consolidation and expansion of Christianity, the literature of Western Christianity was inevitably to bear its markings.

But the pleasure of storytelling cannot be extinguished. Adventure and epic were to remain popular. The difference being that henceforth they would develop under the influence of Christian truth, which would, in turn, be adjusted to its new circumstances. For heroism and truth create unlikely bedfellows. These curious couplings were to be called tales of chivalry, and included such masterworks as the *Song of Roland*, and the sublime and mind-boggling quests of the Arthurian knights in the epic cycles known as the Matter of Britain. There is yet another, more singular tale of adventure, a spiritual epic, a sort of oneiric, chivalrous expedition in which love and truth call out to one another, and ultimately embrace: the fabulous voyage of Dante.

10

THE SUBLIMATION OF HEROISM

T HE CHRISTIAN epic heroes, in their ardor, are pagan antiquity's true heirs. But they differ from their predecessors in that the truths they are expected to serve give form and meaning to their struggles and ordeals— while at the same time they place these truths at the service of their own renown. The pursuit of glory and service to God reinforce one another. Roland is a Christian Achilles. Seen from the Christian perspective, Roland carries heroism to its loftiest point: he makes it sublime.

What causes Charlemagne's nephew's wits to forsake him is not some venal division of spoils, or the loss of a fine capture. His valiance, not to mention his boldness, has won for him the immortality of fame. But his exploits take place under the gaze of God. Eternal life is his ultimate conquest. Still, Roland brims with pride, a cardinal sin. Against Ganelon, against his peers, against even the king himself, he stands for war to the extreme: the peace offers of King Marsilies, that crafty foe of God, must be rejected. What follows cannot fail to bear him out: the "pagan" prince has no intention of pledging allegiance, and even less of converting.

A large contradiction lurks: the warlike ideals of chivalry have no apparent connection with the love of Christ. Jesus bears the sword, of course, and God only knows that the tellers of the Arthurian legend abuse the metaphor to illustrate the victory of the New Religion over the Old. But Christ's sword is his *word*, and the love it preaches wages war on war, the proud clashing of worldly powers: that which belongs to Caesar can be left to him without even an afterthought; it is entirely derisory when compared to the debt we owe God. There is violence to be found in the message of the Gospel and we know it, but the violence that Christ demands is directed first against oneself and those nearest to us: leave behind your family, turn the other cheek ...

Nothing could be more remote from the chivalrous ideal, which tolerates not the slightest offence. All affronts against oneself and one's own must be pitilessly avenged. The relationships between men woven by feudal society make loyalty and the word of honor the essential condition of their viability. The oath may well be sworn to Christ, the city of man may well place itself under the symbolic aegis of the City of God, but the men who serve the first city, the knights, pay obeisance to a distinctly non-Christian logic. Augustine accepts war only in the most extreme circumstances, and with the greatest reluctance: "The wise man, it is said, draws his sword in the name of justice. Indeed! If he should remember that he is a man, should he not bitterly deplore the necessity that has placed arms in his hands?" (*The City of God*, XIX, 7)

The two dominant orders of feudal society, the Church and the knightly establishment (to put a label of convenience on the politico-military hierarchy) were in constant conflict. Around 1000 C.E., amidst the political fragmentation that in Western Europe followed the disintegration of Carolingian power, the Church played the role of moderator with regard to warfare within Christianity. Its strategy was to win respect for the Peace of God, while pursuing a policy of incitement outside the faith.[99] It helped channel the warlike energy and the spirit of pillage of the military class away from Christianity. The campaign against the infidel was economic and political well before it became a holy war.

The Song of Roland is part and parcel of the compromise between the two orders, and reflects their warlike reorientation in heroic terms. In a conflict between two Christian princes, Roland's hot-headedness could only have been condemned. This is precisely the reason why the action involves the army of the Emperor Charlemagne and the multitude of pagans then occupying Spain. The Carolingian reference is largely a fictitious one; it provides the distance necessary to any epic tale and lends it the brilliance that remains associated with the glorious memory of the emperor. Probably written in the ninth century, the *Song of Roland* more likely mirrored the spirit of the Spanish Reconquista, and prefigured the Crusades. Projecting into the past a vital concern of the present, and transforming the Carolingian era into an exemplary legend, it lays before us the only war that Christianity

---

99. In "Les trois ordres ou l'imaginaire du féodalisme," Georges Duby reminds us, with regard to Urban II's call to Crusade: "The sermon of 1095 first proclaimed, and let us not forget it, the Peace of God and extended it to all Christianity so that Christ's faithful of an age to bear arms could join the Holy War" (Duby, *Féodalité*, Paris: Gallimard, Quarto, 1996, p. 661).

could tolerate. In so doing, it lent Christian truth a new aggressiveness. The battle for the faith had become militarized.

The historical incident upon which the structure of the epic rests is tenuous: in the spring of 778, Charlemagne did indeed cross the Pyrenees to come to the aid of a Muslim prince; called back across the mountains by the revolt of the Saxons in August of the same year, his rear guard was in fact slaughtered by Basque mountaineers (either Christians or in the process of conversion to Christianity).

The time elapsed between the composition of the chivalrous epic and the events it describes is thus substantial: for seven years, Charlemagne has been waging war in Spain against the pagans; the only city that remains to be captured is Saragossa, whose sovereign, King Marsilies, feigns submission. Dispatched to the holdout city as an envoy at the instigation of Roland, Ganelon, a partisan of peace, vows to take revenge for a mission in which he risks death (other ambassadors have already been massacred at Saragossa). He seeks his revenge by proposing that Marsilies wipe out Roland and his men, whom he, Ganelon, will arrange to place at the rear of the imperial army. If this warmonger and his liegemen could be eliminated, Charlemagne would be deprived of his right arm and forced to sue for peace.

The traitor's machinations move implacably forward, facilitated by the mad zeal of his designated victim. Roland, who is neither willing nor able to keep away, decides to undertake the rear guard with his forces alone (twenty thousand men) and rejects the massive reinforcements that Charlemagne proposes to dispatch (fully one half of the imperial army). Even in the presence of danger he persists in his rejection of help. Alerted early enough to the size of the enemy force to summon help, he stubbornly refuses. The entreaties of his friend Olivier, whose bravery is no less, but more cautious, than his own, are to no avail: Roland will not sound his Olyphant. Or, to be precise, he will sound it only when it is too late, to summon his suzerain not to his aid, but to the spectacle of his heroic end. Having repulsed, at odds of one against twenty, the successive assaults of the pagans; having sacrificed the lives of all his men, Roland dies, undefeated, of ruptured temples, as the brain matter oozes from his ears after he has sounded the Olyphant too violently and for too long.

But he has enough strength remaining to make his way back across the battlefield in search of his closest companions, the twelve peers, whom he lays before the only other dying survivor of the battle, Archbishop Turpin. He has enough strength, too, to crush the head of one last foe that, having feigned death, attempts to take away his sword as he lies dying, ready to give up his soul. In fear that someone else seize it after his death, Roland attempts to break his precious Durendal on the rocks, but they are cleft through and Durendal remains intact. The sword of God cannot be broken, nor even blunted. His servant dies lying atop it, facing the enemy, so that Charlemagne and his men may say that "he died a conqueror" (I, 174),[100] master of the battlefield.

Meticulously, Roland sets the stage for his own death. Death with honor is more important to him than the fate of his troops, whose eradication he could have avoided by taking the advice of his best friend. Pride in him has become so extreme that it could well have angered God. Nothing remains but for him to gain God's pardon, not explicitly, but by wrapping that pride in the broader cloth of all his sins:

> "Mea Culpa! God, by Thy Virtues clean
> Me from my sins, the mortal and the mean,
> Which from the hour that I was born have been
> Until this day, when life is ended here!"
> Holds out his glove towards God, as he speaks
> Angels descend from heaven on that scene.
>
> (CLXXV, 2370)

God sends his angels to take the dying man's glove, and in so doing signifies that he grants pardon. Roland will gain the paradise promised by Archbishop Turpin to the combatants in the heat of the action. The assertive presence of this high dignitary of the Church in the heart of battle is more than symbolic. Not for him merely to bless the troops, "a thousand blows come from the Archbishop's hand" (110). The narrator is at no loss for words of praise: "Such shaven crown has never else sung mass" (119). The entire epic is draped in the cloth of religious sanction, and the parallel with Christ, at the peak of the battle, verges on blasphemy.

It is midday. The French, taking heavy casualties, are on the point of overcoming the first wave of assailants: one hundred thousand men of whom "not two thousands now" remain (111). King Marsilies prepares to engage his main force, three times larger than the advance guard. For Roland and his companions, death is now certain. But it will be a victorious death, which the armies of Charlemagne will not be slow to avenge, and which the story prefigures as storms and tempests lash France. The entire land is shrouded in black mists rent by lightning flashes. Hearts are struck by terror; "the end of

---

100. Translation by Charles Scott Monkreif, London, 1919.

time is presently at hand" (110). No, "twas the great day of mourning for Rollant" (110). Only the veil of the temple was not rent in twain. It is a fresco worthy of the crucifixion, one that speaks more eloquently than Roland's entire combat. He fights for God. And as if that were not enough, he almost becomes Christ in arms offering up his life for the one true faith.

God then bestows upon Charlemagne a miraculous grace: he halts the course of the sun in the sky to allow him to pursue the enemy and to take his revenge (1, 179). What would he not do for him who carries, embedded in the golden hilt of his sword, the lance-head that pierced the side of Christ on the Cross? (1, 183) The lance-head, symbolically turned by the champion of Christendom against those who reject truth, is prolonged in a macabre fashion after the final victory.

> Passes the day, the darkness is grown deep,
> But all the stars burn, and the moon shines clear.
> And Sarraguce is in the Emperour's keep.
> A thousand Franks he bids seek through the streets,
> The synagogues and the mahumeries;
> With iron malls and axes which they wield
> They break the idols and all the imageries
> So there remain no fraud nor falsity.
> That King fears God, and would do His service,
> On water then Bishops their blessing speak,
> And pagans bring into the baptistry.
> If any Charles with contradiction meet
> Then hanged or burned or slaughtered shall he be.
> Five score thousand and more are thus redeemed,
> Very Christians; save that alone the queen
> To France the Douce goes in captivity;
> By love the King will her conversion seek.
>
> (266)

The narrator seems unaware of the black humor of the sequence: if the queen is an exception, it is because the "very Christians" are those whose conversion owes no debt to love! It is a slip of the tongue that, better than anything else, reveals exactly what the *Song* would prefer to conceal: that the chivalrous order it glorifies "christianises" in ways foreign to Christian love.

All literary merit aside, the epic of Roland is not only remarkable for the absence of humor, a quality found infrequently enough in the epic genre, but to an even greater extent by the blindness with which it proposes to serve truth. But it may well be that such service is not its chief objective. Perhaps it has merely borrowed from the spirit of the age to tell an altogether different story. The war against the infidel would then be little more than the familiar backdrop against which deeds, characters, conflicts, and violent emotions are depicted.

It cannot be ruled out that the *geste* was written above all for pure pleasure, and for the pleasure of those who would make up its audience. Listeners could not but be captivated by the felony of some of its protagonists, the courage of others; by the recital of chivalrous camaraderie; by the exposition of the inner conflict between wisdom and bravery. The two friends, Roland and Olivier, can even be considered as two faces of the same character, torn between two conflicting duties: the honor that condemns any appeal for help, and the strategic effectiveness that requires it. Once the moment of that requirement has passed, the roles are reversed. Now it is Olivier who, becoming in turn the staunch defender of knightly honor, grows angry at Roland for having sunk so low as to sound his horn, *when it is too late*. Archbishop Turpin cuts off the discussion, allowing that Olivier is right in principle, while agreeing with Roland that Charlemagne must be alerted in order that he may at least avenge the dead.

What we have then is a drama of friendship, in which God plays a small role, even though His representative (Turpin) acts as arbiter. Just before he dies—and he is among the last—Olivier, dazed by the blows he has suffered and blinded by blood, strikes Roland by mistake:

> At such a blow Rollant regards him keen,
> And asks of him, in gentle tones and sweet :
> "To do this thing, my comrade, did you mean?
> This is Rollanz, who ever held you dear;
> And no mistrust was ever us between."
> Says Oliver: "Now can I hear you speak;
> I see you not: may the Lord God you keep!
> I struck you now: and for your pardon plead."
> Answers Rollanz: "I am not hurt, indeed;
> I pardon you, before God's Throne and here."
> Upon these words, each to the other lean,
> And in such love you had their parting seen.

(149)

Of the entire *geste*, this is surely the most moving scene. Touched by friendship, Roland for an instant wonders if he has not warranted the blow.

Perhaps his friend has struck him in the heat of the anger that had touched off their violent quarrel; perhaps he did so on purpose. But in that event, he should have defied him. The answer dissipates all concern: Olivier cannot see him. Though the explanation reassures the fighter, something about it leaves the reader sceptical. Is Olivier not blinded by blood like Roland by pride? Has he not struck as Roland enters combat, unthinking, blindly? "May the Lord God you keep!" he hastens to add. Not only in the sense of protecting his friend, but of *understanding* him as well; that God understand the madness in Roland which Olivier cannot. In the face of death, friendship reasserts itself and has no need of understanding: at the instant of final separation, Olivier and Roland love one another above and beyond all that separates them. But what of God? In this singular moment of tenderness the story sets the stage, with great finesse, for the pardon that Roland will soon ask of God. His prayer will be meaningless unless the hero accepts, at least in part, the reproach levelled at him by his double, and his *alter ego*. But is the request truly directed at God? To surrender one's gauntlet is a gesture made from one man to another. Up to and including the way he repents, Roland reveals himself to be more chivalrous than Christian.

God, faith, and Christendom may well be little more than elements in an obligatory decor, that of a social class that holds war in the highest esteem, and prizes honor above all else. Turpin himself exhorts his peers not to flee, "lest evil songs of our valor men chant" (1, 115)—that no worthy may speak ill of them. God is continuously present, as he is absent. At their inner core, the knights are most emphatically not Christian, but they must fight for a noble cause, for the sole acceptable, honorable cause. The *Song of Roland* could not have permitted itself to sing the hero's wrath, as the *Iliad* does that of Achilles. The war he wages could not have as its aim the reconquest of an unfaithful woman; it must bring about the triumph of the true faith. If for no other reason than that the Church wills it, proclaims it, particularly in the celebrated sermon of Pope Urban II at Clermont, in 1095, at which he launched the Crusades. The *geste* was recited in the same spirit as the Crusaders set off for Jerusalem: in the name of adventure and conquest more than of God. But it was unthinkable that God be against them.

By declaring Holy War, the Church enabled the knights, who hungered for fiefdoms and glory, to fight and conquer in its name. It permitted, even encouraged, the practice, on condition that these things be done *in the other's land*. The Church could not reconcile itself with the chivalrous order except if it directed its bellicose energies to the cause rather than to the detriment of Christendom. The function of God, in the *geste* as in life, is not a secondary one: God delimits the boundary between that which is like us, and that which is other. Hence the Muslims as idol-adoring pagans. Not only in the eyes of Christians, but pagans in the absolute sense, as the *Song of Roland* is at pains to establish by placing the epithet in the mouths of those upon whom it falls. "My pagan tribes adverse / Battle to seek, canter ye now ahead!" the Muslim chieftain orders his troops, brought up to relieve Marsilies (1, 238). If the other recognizes himself as a pagan, it is because the difference is one of nature, and not simply of circumstances or of viewpoint.

Self and Other now appear as two incommunicable essences that can only meet in the violent clash of swords (the only form of "communication" *the Song of Roland* allows us to attend, Ganelon's embassy to Marsilies being an act of treachery). In exchange for the authorization to survive, the other must expressly abandon his otherness: such is the ultimate meaning of Charlemagne's ultimatum of "believe or die" before Saragossa, a motif we find again and again in Latino-Germanic Christianity. There is little doubt that the *geste* of Roland owes a good measure of its repute to the feeling of identity it helped establish or create in western Christendom. To have God on one's side is to know who one is.

To have God on one's side is to grant oneself superior legitimacy. To need God in this way is also a sign of inadequacy. It was enough for the Acheans to know that they were Acheans, the Trojans, Trojans. The Frankish knight must know that he is, and desire himself to be, Christian. Honor seeks its own justification in truth. But the sanction is purchased at a cost in blood: the truth that gives eternal life kills. To truth Christ offered himself in sacrifice; to it Augustine sacrificed his sensuality. Henceforth, the death of the Other must bear witness to the justice of faith. Roland expires (in God) only upon having murdered them all, to the last man. From sacrifice we have moved on to massacre.

11

THE TRANSFER OF HEROISM

Perceval, or the Mythical Transfer

IN THE SONG OF ROLAND, both the narrator and the audience know that the hero is on the side of truth. Truth is the condition, the indispensable framework within which his heroism thrives; it is a given. Roland serves truth, and that is enough; there is no need for him to set out in search of it.

The quest for truth and the pure pursuit of self belong to another cycle, that of the Arthurian legends, which form an essential component of a much broader field. Commonly known as the Matter of Britain, this corpus subsumes the Arthurian legends, including those of Tristan, Merlin, Arthur and the Holy Grail.[101] Here, from the twelfth century onward, the Celtic cycles fuse with the adventure of Christianity. The innumerable tales of the Round Table and the Grail share one overriding objective: the Christianization of Celtic myth. For all its ambiguity, the combining of the two leads to the appropriation of "true" Christianity by its westernmost wing. The Celtic tale thus brings about a mythical transfer, which, though now obscured by failing memory, has never ceased to wield a strange, subversive power. What better evidence could there be than the recurring fascination with chivalrous tales in Western cinema?

To venture into the Arthurian world is rather like penetrating into the mythical forest of Broceliande itself. One never knows when, nor how, one

---

101. "No strict equivalence can be established between 'Matter of Britain,' 'Tale of Brittany,' and 'The Legend of Arthur.' The first is broadest in scope, however, as it encompasses all tales of Celtic origin, those of Tristan as well as those relating the figure of Arthur," writes Danielle Régnier-Bohler in her preface to *La Légende arthurienne, le Graal et la Table ronde*, édition établie sous la direction de Danielle Régnier-Bohler (Paris: Laffont "Bouquins," 1989), p. viii. [Translator's note: unless otherwise indicated, all citations in this chapter have been translated from T. Hentsch's French text.]

will emerge. For it is a forest of signs—some obscure, some luminous—in which each apparition, each happening is swollen with a Gnostic or mythic charge whose diversity, whose multiplicity of correspondences our modern minds must struggle to distinguish. The mysterious profusion of the symbolic forest, to which Baudelaire alludes in his *Correspondences*, to this day draws us to it, sends up our spine a shiver that our rationalism has not entirely contrived to extinguish. Hence our attraction for the mysteries of a lost world into which the cinema today has fraudulently reintroduced us. The price—an ingratiating oversimplification—is high; the mystery has been reduced to the magic of "special effects." The Grail cycle has become for us a sub-variety of the Western in chain mail, the donjon has replaced the ranch house and the forest the plains. The modern resurgence of the helm and the broadsword, which the Monty Python troupe held up to such splendid ridicule, has in itself a signification to which we must attempt to return.

We are lost in the forest of Broceliande not only because of its immensity and the complexity of its labyrinthine paths. We are even more baffled by the apparent fact that there are as many forests as there are narrators, as many heroes as there are stories. The same figures assume different characters from one storyteller to another, the same exploits pop up in story lines that cannot be superimposed upon one another. There is not *one* story of Lancelot, of Gawain, or of Perceval with relatively minor variations between versions, but a multiplicity of stories which are barely compatible and in some cases nothing short of irreconcilable. The further we penetrate into the Celtic legends, the more we encounter different and even contradictory Lancelots (or Gawains, or Percevals), who have little in common except that they belong to King Arthur's entourage, and who, were they to meet, would undoubtedly be forced to fight it out amongst themselves.

The image is by no means as absurd as it seems at first glance. Those whom the Arthurian heroes must confront in the guise of the evil adversaries and the perilous circumstances that they encounter in their solitary wanderings, are none other than themselves. The ordeals and the dangers that lie in wait along their path can be seen as belonging without distinction to both the inner and outer worlds. The obstacle to be overcome is often, and explicitly, presented as a chimera: the bridge that Gawain must cross in order to gain entry to the Fortress of the Grail proves to be so narrow as to be inaccessible, yet the knight need only embark resolutely upon it for it to become "broad and easy to cross" (B, 189).[102] No matter the number, the frequency or the nature of his encounters, the hero moves inexorably forward alone—an ancestor of the lonesome cowboy. Companionship is never more than fleeting, provisional. The knight is not a commander on the field of battle. He may lead expeditions to distant lands, but such ventures are rarely described, and more often merely evoked. No Roland, no leader of men, canters across the moors and through the forests of Britain. Not that he who would mete out justice scorns glory, but he is, first and foremost, alone with himself.

Among the numerous heroes of the court of King Arthur, one figure stands out as more worthy than all others who finally come upon the Grail: Perceval (*Parzifal* in German), also known as Perlesvaus or even Parluifet, so named because he has literally made himself.[103] The most ancient Perceval is that of Chrétien de Troyes. Chrétien, who to this day must be counted as the greatest classical author of the chivalrous tale, occupies a nodal position in the transmission of the Matter of Britain and of the Arthurian legend. He was to inspire throughout Western Europe a vast literature that both continues and breaks with his work.[104]

Chrétien relates how the son of the Widowed Dame of the Desolate Forest—who does not yet know his own name—while riding through the woods, happens upon five splendid knights whom he mistakes for angels. Dazzled by the apparition, the lad leaves his weeping mother, travels to the court of King Arthur to be dubbed a knight, is instructed in the rules of chivalry by a wise freeholder, discovers chaste love, and accomplishes his first exploits which, in a succession of episodes, lead him to the mysterious castle of an infirm lord, reduced to fishing in the river and thus named the Fisher King. A strange scene then occurs, whose importance the young knight fails to grasp: during the meal to which the Fisher has invited him, two things pass three times before him, borne by young men: first a lance from which continuously drips a drop of blood; then a Grail of purest gold whose

---

102. "B" refers to *La Légende arthurienne, le Graal et la Table ronde* in the "Bouquins" collection (See note 98), which presents fifteen tales in verse or prose written by primarily anonymous authors between the late twelfth and late thirteenth centuries. Numbers refer to the pages of this 1200-page work.

103. In French, *par lui fait*: "by himself made."

104. Chrétien wrote a *Marc et Iseult*, of which no traces remain—not to mention his adaptations of Ovid. He borrows a part of his canvas and the majority of his principal characters from Wace's *Brut* (1155), "adaptation en langue romane de l'Historia regum Brittanniae" by Geoffroy de Monmouth (1138), "qui s'ouvre sur la fuite d'Enée de Troie, se poursuit avec la naissance du Brutus, ancêtre éponyme des Bretons, et l'histoire des rois qui ont régné sur l'île jusqu'au-delà du roi Arthur" (C.T., 16). The letters C. T. refer to Chrétien de Troyes, *Romans* (Paris: Librairie Générale Française, Le Livre de Poche « La Pochotèque », 1994). The quoted text is from the introduction by Jean-Marie Fritz. The letters are followed by the page number; those which cite verses are indicated with a "v."

use, purpose, and contents escape him. Thrice, in accordance with the virtue of discretion taught him by the freeholder, the knight without a name declines to question his host about the significance of the objects that have been paraded before him. The following morning he awakens in a deserted castle; all the doors, except those leading to the outside, are closed. Departing without taking his leave, the knight encounters a maiden who criticizes him for his silence of the previous day: it will prove to be the cause of great misfortune for himself and for his host, who could have delivered him of the questions he had been expected to ask but were not forthcoming. When the maiden asks his name, he intuits that his name is Perceval of Galles. You shall henceforth be known as Perceval the Unfortunate, replies the fair maiden, who rapidly informs him that she is his cousin, that his mother has died of the pain of parting, and that it is because of his sin of abandoning her that he could not ask the questions he should have.

On his return to Arthur's court, Perceval is once again criticized, by a passing bully, for not having spoken while he was a guest at the castle of the Fisher King. The hero then swears to depart in search of the mysterious castle to find the bleeding lance and gain knowledge of the Grail. Five years later (during which the tale relates the adventures of Gawain), Perceval, from peril to challenge, has strayed so far from the object of his quest that he has lost even the memory of God. Penitents he meets on a deserted road shame him for carrying arms on Good Friday, and lead him to a hermit who turns out to be his maternal uncle. The holy man teaches his nephew that the Grail contains a host that is being carried to another of his uncles, whose son is the Fisher King. The host itself has the property of prolonging the life of him to whom it is ultimately destined, one so pure of heart that he needs no rich victuals. In his distress at having strayed from the path of God, Perceval consents to do penance, and to relearn religion in order to rediscover the virtues that had been his so long ago. The narrator allows Perceval to take Easter communion from his hermit uncle, and informs us that he will return to him after having related the tribulations of Sir Gawain. But the story breaks off 2500 verses later, still taken up with Gawain. Perceval never reappears. Chrétien has died before he could complete his work.

The fact that the work has remained unfinished may not be due to the author's death alone.[105] The story unwinds as though the narrator could not make up his mind to bring it to an end, as though it were impossible for

---

105. Though unfinished, *Le conte de Graal* is far and away the lengthiest of the Arthurian tales written by Chrétien de Troyes: 9066 verses compared with 7112 for *Le chevalier de la charrette*.

Perceval to return to the Castle of the Grail to redeem his lost speech.[106] The interminable adventures of Gawain, now forced to follow, without either conviction or great success, the trail of the holy lance, accredit the idea that the very essence of the Grail is to remain unattainable. The quest for it may continue, may be forgotten only to recommence *ad infinitum*.

The impossible nature of the quest accentuates the mystery surrounding the holiness of the Grail, which at first seems to be curiously lacking in definition. Only after Perceval has visited his hermit uncle does the myth take on a clearly Christian coloration. By christianizing itself, the myth initiates a turnabout, which, one supposes, will profoundly alter the meaning of the quest. For it has thus far evolved quite lightheartedly; the protagonist himself has all but forgotten his original motivation. But when the story returns to the deeds of Gawain, it plunges once again into pure chivalry, and makes it impossible to ascertain what significance the author meant to assign to the symbolism of the Grail and its Christian dimension. Like the entire tale, this dimension has never been thoroughly elucidated.

Many, if not most, of the later tales promote christianization more vigorously, in particular two prose accounts from the early thirteenth century to which I will be referring: *Le Haut Livre du Graal*, better known today by the title *Perlesvaus*, written by an anonymous author; and a trilogy, *Joseph, Merlin et Perceval*, attributed to Robert de Boron, himself the indisputable author of *Le Roman de l'Estoire du Graal*, written in verse at the end of the twelfth century.[107]

Perlesvaus (or *Le Haut Livre du Graal*) takes up Chrétien's tale where it left off, while lending it a different tone. King Arthur appears as a figure lost in a world consumed by war, thrown into a state of melancholy and decline by the silence of a certain knight at the sight of the Grail and the bleeding lance during a visit to the abode of the wealthy Fisher King. Gawain and Lancelot travel each in turn to the castle of the Grail, but neither is able to repair the fault of their mysterious predecessor. The Fisher King dies, and his evil brother, the King of Château Mortel, seizes control of his estate, with the result that the Grail no longer displays itself to anyone. But a mysterious knight, who is none other than Perlesvaus, will ultimately reconquer it.

---

106. Several later authors attributed the quest for the Grail to another, even more irreprochable knight, Galahad, son of Lancelot.

107. *Perlesvaus* and a portion of the trilogy attributed to Robert de Boron, *Merlin and Perceval* (combined by the publisher under the title: *Merlin et Arthur: le Graal et le Royaume*) have been published in part in *la Légende arthurienne*, op. cit., of the "Bouquins" collection, herein identified by the letter "B."

The story proper is preceded by a two-page prologue that unequivocally locates the origin and the general framework of the tale: the narrator is simply translating a text (from Latin?) written by a certain Joséphé "upon dictation by an angel, in order that his testimony might be known on the truth of the knights and the holy men who have consented to suffer pains and torments to glorify the religion which Jesus Christ wished to institute by His death upon the Cross" (B, 123). Joséphé well intends to celebrate the memory of a good and chaste knight of the lineage of Joseph of Arimathea, the uncle of his mother, who by failing to speak at the right moment, has plunged Great Britain into misfortune. *The essence of the quest stands sharply revealed*: the great nephew does nothing more than recover the relics preserved by his great uncle after he had lowered the body of the Savior from the Cross: the lance is that which pierced His side and the Grail, the cup that received His blood. Hardly has the story proclaimed itself an apology of Christendom, and explained several of its bloodiest episodes as allegories for the triumph of the New Law (or religion) over the Old, than the mystery comes to an end. It was to destroy this Old Law, explains an elderly friar to Gawain, "that God consented to be struck in the side by a lance; it is by that lance blow, and by his ascent to the cross, that the Old Religion was eradicated" (B, 186). In striking their adversaries with a lance, the good knights are merely continuing a battle begun long before. They turn against the enemy the iron received by Christ in his flesh. The marvellous aspect of the Arthurian legend here meets the spirit of the *Song of Roland*.

In the trilogy attributed to Robert de Boron (probably prior to the tale of *Perlesvaus*), the myth of the Grail takes on its full "historical" dimension. It crystallizes at the intersection of three contradictory yet complementary genealogies. One, which we already know from *Perslevaus*, ascends via Joseph of Arimathea to the house of David, King of Israel. A second, drawn from Wace's *Brut*, joins Arthur and his realm to Rome through Brutus the Trojan, descendant of Aeneas and ancestor of the Britons. The Roman lineage of the British kings will legitimize Arthur's claim to the imperial crown when he is forced to fight the Roman emperor. The third genealogy establishes the character of Merlin through a detailed narration of his origins, which reads like a parody of the Immaculate Conception.

Irritated that a "man born of woman" could have escaped his ascendancy and that, in conformity with the word of the prophets, he has come to earth to deliver sinners from the torments of hell, the Devil and his demons dream of producing a man gifted with such memory and intelligence that he can thwart Jesus Christ's work of redemption. One of the demons, which have the power to impregnate women, does his best to carry the task to a successful conclusion. At the end of a complicated intrigue, he contrives to anger an irreproachable virgin, then takes advantage of her in a moment of distraction—in an ephemeral state of sin—to impregnate her against her will. No one, clearly, believes that she cannot possibly know the author or the circumstances of her fecundation—a backhanded insinuation that the dogma of the Immaculate Conception cannot stand. Arrested and condemned for lust, the maiden owes her salvation to the intervention of her confessor, who suggests to the judges that the child has not sinned, and that it would be more appropriate to await the birth, or better, the weaning of the child. Once weaned, the infant Merlin demonstrates prodigious precocity. He confounds the judges and saves his mother. In the knowledge that the mother cannot be held responsible for what has happened, God decides to spare her and to foil the schemes of the evil one. Since the Devil has bestowed upon Merlin the memory of things past, God goes one better and gives him knowledge of the future. "Now the decision is his to take: should he wish, he may chose the Devil's portion, or that of Our Lord" (B, 331).

Merlin without hesitation takes the part of Christ. From the demons he keeps only the knowledge of their ruses and magical ways, but will not use these things to their advantage. "The vessel that received me," he tells his mother's confessor, "was too pure to have been theirs, and my mother's virtue brought upon them great misfortune" (B, 340). The inversion has been accomplished, and the Devil's confounding complete. The parable of the Devil is thus transformed into a veritable immaculate conception, which ultimately resembles, at one remove, the Annunciation of Mary. Merlin is a kind of underground Christ who lacks only that essence which is purely divine. Knowing as he does the past and the future, Merlin alone knows the entire tale, in all its ins and outs. Thereupon he relates to the confessor the story of his mother, whose historiographer the confessor becomes, taking the greatest care to make it clear to Merlin that the book he is now writing in the form of dictation—for like Christ, Merlin does not write—"will have no authority for you are not, you cannot be an apostle" (B, 341), meaning he, Merlin, is not Christ; he has not suffered on the Cross nor has he been resurrected. He restricts himself to reconstituting the true sequence of events, of the mysteries, from their spatial and temporal origins up until the British realm of Arthur, to whose birth and advent Merlin will nonetheless lend a substantial impetus.

Like Merlin, Arthur is born of a subterfuge: not through the machinations of an incubus this time, but of a great lord enamored of

Arthur's mother, whom Merlin causes to assume, as Zeus impersonates Amphitryon, the appearance of her spouse. As a "fatherless son," Arthur is the worldly replica of him who is the true author of his conception and who desires to remain in obscurity. "As I am in darkness and so shall I remain for those whom I would not wish to reveal me," Merlin tells the scribe who is recording his story, "so too this book will remain hidden, and rare will be those who will laud you" (B, 341). Proportionally speaking, Arthur is to Merlin what Merlin is to Christ. Both are earthly representatives: one wise, secretive, and mysterious (that of the Devil's portion that remains in him), the other a crowned freeholder, radiant defender of the New Religion. In wrenching Excalibur from the anvil from which no other man could extract it, Arthur stands revealed to all as the only knight worthy of carrying Christ's sword and to be proclaimed king: "When our Lord brings about justice in this world," proclaims the archbishop who presides over the rite, "He will body it forth by the sword with which he has invested the chivalry when the three orders were established" (B, 345).

As the unseen artificer of this apotheosis, Merlin the Wise succeeds by giving rise to Arthur in joining earthly genealogy to divine, and thereby in harmonizing intervals of time that cannot easily be reconciled: the long lineage that runs from Aeneas via Brutus and the British kings contrives to compress itself, by the magic of Merlin, into the short period of no more than three or four generations that separates Joseph of Arimathea, and thus Christ, from Perceval. Merlin accomplishes the connection between mystical and "historical" by which the Grail makes its journey from East to West. He establishes the way stations that, from Jerusalem to Britain (Great and Small), by way of Rome, transfer the blood of Christ from Orient to Occident. That which is so transferred constitutes the very essence of the New Religion, since the Grail, the instrument of the Last Supper and of the Eucharist, carries the most sacred of all substances: a veritable transfusion that transforms Latino-Germanic Christendom and its chivalry into the true heirs of Christ. The Arthurian legend by no means restricts itself to reconciliation of the two orders, the military and the ecclesiastical; it carries out a thoroughgoing *displacement of Truth* to the advantage of Western Europe.

The commingling of Roman, Celtic, and Christian mythologies now takes on its full meaning: it symbolizes both the Christianization of northern and western Europe (which, in the twelfth century remained more superficially Christian than is generally believed), and the occidentalization of Christianity—nothing less than a continuation of the *Aeneid*, in Christian form. The combat that Merlin entrusts to the Knights of the Round Table (who quickly reduce their number to the apostolic figure of twelve) has, as its principal aim, beneath the symbolic veneer of struggle against the Old Religion, the question of the legitimacy of, and belonging to, the New. The true defenders of Christendom, and with it, the ultimate homeland of Christ, must be identified. Judaism is not alone at issue; the transfer of legitimacy also sets its sights on Byzantine Christendom in the aftermath of the Great Schism of 1054. In all times, goes the legend, Christian truth (and truth, period) had been destined to migrate westward—a movement that today confirms the ideal of the solitary American in pursuit of justice, the one true legatee of western chivalry and bearer, in its Protestant version, of the Christian missionary spirit.

Robert de Boron's *Merlin* carries out this transfer with a breathtaking simplicity: in the *telling* of history, Merlin *makes* it. It would be difficult to express more succinctly to what extent history belongs, both literally and figuratively, to those who make it. Arthur makes history first hand, carelessly, often chaotically, which explains the reverses of his court and of his realm. But he is ultimately little more than a strong arm. Merlin, the veritable brain of the narrative, makes history in a much more decisive way by relating it, that is, in assigning to it its meaning. One would have to be blissfully modern, convinced of the hermetic barrier that separates history from myth, to be startled by all this. Hegel's method differs hardly at all. His philosophy of history repeats Robert de Boron's achievement in relating Merlin's tale. In both instances, it is incumbent upon the stage director to bring forth the truth, to ascribe meaning to the events of the past and those to come, and to make Western Christendom (and then the West itself) master of this meaning.

Among the points of divergence that separate Hegel and Merlin, the most significant is that the magician, by his own admission, does not speak the whole truth, and takes himself less seriously than does the philosopher. Not only can Merlin's narration not be taken for the word of the Gospel, but the ingenious stage director refrains from revealing all the secrets his tale conceals: he cannot and must not, he tells his biographer, disclose "the secret words spoken between Jesus Christ and Joseph" (B, 341). The same can be said, in *Perlesvaus*, of the explanations Gawain receives from the old monk he consults before entering the castle of the Grail. After revealing the meaning of several scenes the knight has witnessed, the old man refuses to explain an allegory that seems to refer to the enigma of the Trinity (of which Augustine wrote that it was easier to drink sea water than to understand): "My lord," says the monk, "I can tell you no more, and you should consider yourself fortunate indeed for the mysteries of the Savior must not be revealed: those to whom they have been vouchsafed must keep them secret" (B, 187).

To this explicit discretion we can add a certain restraint, a touch of mystery that pervades the narration itself. We will never really know, for instance, why Gawain, oft instructed as to what he must do when he sees the Grail pass before him, remains open-mouthed in astonishment in its presence. The scene is one of high and mysterious power: the knight, having reached the goal of his profoundest quest, watches the Grail without truly seeing it. Gawain is seated alongside the Fisher King and his knights when two damsels emerge from a chapel, one holding the Grail, the other the lance "from whose tip blood drips into the holy vessel":

> My lord Gawain looked upon the Grail and thought he beheld within it a candle burning, like such in those days few could be seen: and he beheld the tip of the lance from which dripped vermilion blood, and he thought that he could see two angels bearing two golden candle-sticks alight. And the damsels passed before him and entered into another chapel.
>
> My lord Gawain, entirely absorbed in his thoughts, was overcome by joy so intense that he forgot all, and turned his mind toward God alone. The knights looked upon him, sad and afflicted. But at that moment one of the maidens emerged from the chapel and passed once more before Sir Gawain: he was sure that he had seen three where before there had been two, and he thought that he beheld in the Grail the silhouette of an infant. The noblest of the knights hailed my lord Gawain, but he was staring straight ahead, and saw three drops of blood fall upon the table: full taken up in contemplation, he uttered not a word. The damsels moved away and the knights, alarmed, looked at one another. My lord Gawain could ill turn his gaze from the three drops of blood, but when he reached out his hand to touch them, they fled his touch, for they could not be touched, neither by the hand nor by any manner of means.
>
> And lo! The damsels once again passed before the table: My lord Gawain now beheld three, he believed: he raised up his eyes, and before him the Grail seemed as if suspended in the air. And above it, a man nailed to a cross, a lance piercing his side. This my lord Gawain contemplated and was overcome with the profoundest compassion for him; and his thoughts were of one thing only, and that was the suffering endured by the King. The

noblest of the knights once more exhorted of him that he speak, and said that should he further hold his peace he will never again have such an occasion. But my lord Gawain held his peace. The knight he heard not, and directed upward his gaze. And the damsels returned to the chapel bearing the most Holy Grail and the Lance; the knights caused the table settings to be taken away and departed the table, then withdrew to another chamber, leaving Sir Gawain alone.

He looked about him and beheld the closed doors; he looked toward the foot of the bed: two chandeliers were burning before the chess-board, and the pieces, fashioned of ivory and of gold, were disposed atop it. My lord Gawain began to play, using those fashioned of ivory, while those of gold moved against him and twice placed him in checkmate. The third time, seeing that they had once more gained the upper hand whilst he had hoped for his revanche, he transposed the pieces: a damsel emerged from a room adjacent and ordered a manservant to remove the chess-board and the pieces. My lord Gawain now felt the fatigue of the long journey that had brought him to the castle, lay himself down and fell asleep until morning of the following day, at the rising of the sun when he was startled by the sound of the horn. Rapidly he donned his coat of mail and sought to take his leave of the Fisher King, but found the doors barred in such a manner as to prohibit him from entering into the other chambers. He could hear solemn mass being sung at a nearby chapel, and great was his despondency at being unable to attend. (B, 192–193)

The scene brims over with meaning—quite independent of the narrative imperative that obliges Gawain to keep silent in order to enter fully into the mystery and thus allow Perlesvaus to complete his task. But it leaves us perplexed. The allegory is troubling in its audacity: the very thought of God, the very blood of Christ, the very sight of the Crucified Christ and none other have divested Gawain of his speech and caused him to fail in his highest duty—the duty for which he had so painstakingly prepared himself. Unlike Lancelot, whose all too earthly love for Guinevere makes him unworthy to attend the passage of the holy relics, Gawain not only possesses the requisite purity, but also perceives, beyond the objects themselves, that which they represent. And because he sees the deepest meaning of all he beholds, he is incapable of speech: in the presence of the unutterable, nothing can be said. Such, at least, is one of the possible meanings of this particularly dense passage, for which the reader himself must find the key. For its ultimate meaning is not given; instead, the story leaves it open.

The openness is striking for a story redolent with the absolute, one that hardly takes its subject matter lightly. In *Le Haut livre du Graal* (or *Perlesvaus*), even more than in the trilogy of Robert de Boron, and contrary to the *Song of Roland*, religion cannot be posited as a simple, conventional framework for the action. Firstly, the religion in question is constantly described as "New," as though it was still at a considerable remove before overcoming the Old; secondly, the necessity of its triumph and the transfer implicit in it gives shape to the entire narrative. Love and the service of Christ demand of its champion exclusive devotion. Perhaps Gawain loves life, adventure, and women all too well, though his behavior toward them is irreproachable. Lancelot, we know, is more heavily burdened still, for the absolute he must serve has not the Savior but woman as its object. Exhorted by a hermit to confess his sins before entering into the Castle of the Grail, Lancelot agrees to repent of all, save his love for the Queen. But to repent thus would be to abjure his very self, and to forfeit the strength that makes it possible for him to carry out his exploits. "That which is best in me comes from this love," he humbly tells his confessor (B, 212). It is therefore with knowledge aforethought that he renounces the Grail. Between God and Guinevere, Lancelot chooses Guinevere. His gesture is magnificently human, but it places him below Perlesvaus.

The superior knight has an inhuman cast. Chaste to the last, he exists as a law unto himself, a seeker after justice in the pure state. After a series of exploits and turnabouts, after having found and avenged sister and mother (who in this version has not died from her abandonment at his hands), he takes the Castle of the Grail by storm and dedicates himself to re-establishing the New Religion there where it had been abandoned, taking "life from those who refuse to believe in God" (B, 251). His evangelizing mission accomplished, he returns to his most holy castle where, until the death of his mother and sister, he lives a monastic life dedicated wholly to the Lord. Then, obeying a heavenly voice that has called him to a new departure, Perlesvaus entrusts the Grail and the Lance to forest-dwelling hermits, and shortly thereafter, sets out toward an unknown destination with the bodies of his mother and the Fisher King, on a ship with a white sail emblazoned with a vermilion cross. Since that day, no one knows what fate has befallen him. His castle has crumbled into disrepair—the chapel alone still stands—and none of those who sailed off with him have ever returned, with the exception of two young Welsh knights who make their way back after a long absence to lead the lives of hermits. And in response to those who ask why they live in such dire need, they say: "'Go where we have been, and you will know the reason'" (B, 309).

The mystery that hangs heavily about both the hero's destination (it could be death, another crusade, or yet another, more secret quest), and the fate that awaits those who might stray amongst the ruins of the castle blunts, though only slightly, the sharpness of the truth for which the good knight does battle. Were it not for this final uncertainty, which reminds us of the enigmas that the story leaves hanging here and there, *Le Haut livre du Graal* would amount to little more than the fanatical representation of a chivalrous order dedicated entirely to God. It is that, of course; and more. God and the New Religion themselves appear as metaphors for an inner objective that cannot be spoken, and which constantly escapes all who would attempt to draw near it. Let us recall Gawain, absorbed, silent before the apparition of the Grail: the pain of Christ on the Cross is his pain, an almost instantaneous anticipation of the knight's grief at passing truth by just as he felt he had grasped it fast ... Until the bitter end the Grail radiates an all-pervasive ambiguity as to its very nature, for it is simultaneously a material recipient historically determined by the Last Supper and the Crucifixion, and an evanescent, untouchable object, a locus of mystical images and projections, a barometer of the morality of the age, disappearing and reappearing as circumstances warrant.

The density of the mystery attenuates the absolute quality of the battle for Truth. It is a battle as radical as the quest for Truth is ephemeral: a paradox that the uncompromising piety of Perlesvaus, in *Le Haut Livre du Graal*, takes to its extreme conclusion. Perceval, in the trilogy attributed to Robert de Boron, is a more human figure; like Chrétien de Troyes's hero, he falls in love, cherishes combat for its own sake, is easily diverted from his quest, and for seven years fails to remember God. Such is his passion for tournaments that Merlin the demiurge must intervene to take him to task and to return him to the path of the Grail (B, 404–405). Contrary to the account in the *Haut livre*, the sacred vessel has remained in the hands of the Fisher King; Perceval need not capture it by force of arms. He becomes its master simply by asking the question that came into his mind during his first visit, thus causing all the spells cast upon the realm of Arthur to vanish. The Fisher King (in this case his grandfather rather than his uncle) initiates him into the secret of the relics before taking leave of the world. Perceval succeeds him, abandons the knightly order, and devotes his life entirely to the Creator. This vision is more humane and less fanatical, a vision that ends without mystery. One that brings the mystery to an end, in fact.

But the most humane of the three Percevals whose careers we have traced remains the first, that of Chrétien. He is, at the same time, the most disconcerting. The narrator looks on with tender benevolence as he blunders forward with all the obduracy of a headstrong child. The young man who knows nothing of the world, who hardly even knows his name, sets out in search of his fate, and in search of his identity, under the influence of a sudden illumination that is anything but magical or divine. The all-too-real knights he encounters in the forest create the occasion for a spicy parody of an apparition: Perceval believes he has encountered angels, and takes the handsomest among them for God. He is not God? Not to worry; he is certainly more fetching than God. "Ah, how whole-heartedly I would like to resemble you, to be as brilliant, as well-made as you!" (v. 174–175, B, 9) Perceval exclaims, so overwhelmed by wonder and curiosity that he pays not the slightest heed to the knight's efforts to obtain information from him: "Were you thus born? —Nay, valet, 'tis impossible. No man could be thus born. —Who then dressed you thus? You really wish to know? (v. 276–283, B, 11) —Certainly. —You will find out." Nothing more is needed for the valet to decide to "travel to the king who makes knights!" (v. 458, B, 13).

This first, decisive scene tells us what we need to know of the character: his ingenuity never abandons him, and he continues to behave with concern neither for the niceties nor for the wishes of others. He interprets everything using the concise code of courtesy that his mother, between two sobs, attempted to convey to him before his departure: he throws himself upon the first damsel he encounters and against her will kisses her on the mouth. His behavior at King Arthur's court is violently impolite. But it is expressed with a candor for which none can blame him (only Keu, the cantankerous seneschal, upbraids him, but then Keu spends the better part of his time deriding all present). The freeholder who initiates him into the mysteries of chivalry makes a sincere attempt to instruct him in the elements of comportment, but the only time he obeys the rule and respects the niceties, it works against him. He holds back the one question that his natural curiosity ought to have driven him to ask. The reversal is ironic: the crucial fault that he must devote his energies to mend originates quite precisely in this world. Up until the instant of the fatal "fault" which will reveal to him in short order his name and his misfortune, Perceval is the soul of innocence: an innocence as awkward as it is engaging, which, in response to Blanchefleur's love, is enriched by a sense of tenderness and lucidity. It is a pure, probably chaste love—impossible to be certain—but also a sensual, carnal love about which Chrétien writes with ironic delicacy.

Blanchefleur, whose side the hero leaves only briefly to seek out and bring back his mother, enters the narrative prior to the first visit to the Castle of the Grail; we will never know the outcome of the gentle passion she awakens in him, and encourages with all her charms. Even the revelation of his fault and the death of his mother are not enough to turn Perceval's mind from his amorous intent. The experience of love, followed immediately by the experience of failure and of mourning that go hand in hand with the realization of his identity, lends his innocence a new gravity, which Chrétien evokes in what is undoubtedly the most touching moment of the story. Witnessing the attack on a goose by a falcon, Perceval hurries to the place where the bird, wounded in the neck, has fallen. But the goose flies off, leaving three drops of blood on the snow:

> When Perceval saw the trampled snow
> Where the goose had lain
> And the blood that stained it now;
> Resting upon his lance
> He saw, as if in trance,
> How snow and blood together
> Were like the whiteness
> Of his beloved's face
> And so absorbed forgot himself.
> And likewise upon his face
> Was the scarlet against the white,
> Like the three drops of blood
> That lay upon the snow.
> He could only stand and stare
> Such pleasure did he draw
> From seeing the new color
> Of his fair friend.
> Of these drops dreamed Perceval
> As dawn broke. (v. 4128–4147, C.T., 1065)[108]

Perceval is so deeply immersed in contemplation that he does not hear the calls of Arthur's knights who, one by one, challenge him in the name of the king; he returns to reality only at the sight of the lance bearing down on

---

108. Translated from the author's comparative rendering of the original based on a modern French version by Charles Méla.

him—only to reassume his posture of meditation immediately after having unhorsed the upstart. Only the exquisite courtesy of Sir Gawain will finally put an end to a reverie whose object has already begun to vanish in the snow. This is the last, strong scene the narrator devotes to his hero, before returning briefly to him, five years later, all the better to abandon him a penitent in a hermit's lodge. Since we cannot witness the consequences of his conversion, the Perceval bequeathed to us by Chrétien is, for all his purity, a knight without God, a man obsessed with love and glory, who has naïvely set out in search of himself. Only his naïveté and his rashness make his egocentrism bearable. Only because he knows not who he is, because he knows not what goal goads him onward, does this knight with the arms of a giant and the mind of an infant work such a powerful charm—unbeknownst to him—on those around him. Perceval is the bright prism through which, long before Cervantes, Chrétien was to magnify and at the same time decompose knightly matter. Perceval is, before the fact, a young Don Quixote.

Through the guilelessness of his eponymous character, the narrator places the entire world of chivalry at a distance. The breaking off of the story leaves us in doubt about the poet's intentions. But its gentle irony is also at work in *Le Chevalier de la Charrette*, by this selfsame Chrétien de Troyes, a full-formed work in which we look on as Lancelot the protagonist embarks upon a quest of a different kind which, though as rich as ever in multiple symbols, is not at all religious and ceases even to be Christian in its finality. Of Christianity it preserves only the social framework.

Lancelot, or the Amorous Transfer

Lancelot, whom Chrétien de Troyes calls the "Knight of the Cart," is the best known of all the adventurers of the Round Table, despite his minimal involvement in the quest for the Grail.

As a character he owes his popularity to *Lancelot du Laik*, a prose tale by an anonymous author of the early thirteenth century (posterior to Chrétien), that relates his life from earliest childhood. An orphan taken by a providential fairy into a lakeside paradise inaccessible to mere mortals, the child prepares himself, with the loving care of his second mother, to enter into the world and to conquer his name, driven on by the love he has received from the queen. Lancelot is a symbol of continuous change. Several times he is born, and reborn: by the mother who abandons him at a tender age and whom he will never know; in the dominions of the Lake, his second womb, from which he emerges into the world of adulthood; in the desire of the queen who brings him alive to the beauty of love. The narrator lingers (for more than one third of the tale) upon the misfortune of his natural parents and upon the hero's childhood up until his arrival at the court of King Arthur. The remainder is devoted to his exploits, intermingled with those of Gawain, in a progression that leads him first to discover his identity then, while struggling to keep it secret, to gain recognition by the queen. The spiritual quest begun by Perceval becomes, in Lancelot, an identitarian and amorous one.

Though prior to the prose tale, the Lancelot recounted by Chrétian de Troyes in the *Chevalier de la Charrette* is already an accomplished knight, though absent when the tale begins. It is a curious, almost discordant, even grotesque, beginning, in which we see an insolent knight challenging Arthur to release the prisoners he is holding not far away in the woods. The king, he shouts before turning back on his tracks, has not a single knight of sufficient confidence to entrust the queen as pledge in combat against him. Struck by the apathy of Arthur and his court, Keu the seneschal swears that he will abandon the king's service unless the king blindly acquiesces to his demands. Arthur agrees. Keu then insists that he proceed with the queen, to meet the arrogant knight's challenge. Sick at heart, and to the despair of his wife, Arthur is forced to honor his undertaking—a display of cowardice and bewilderment that makes him doubly unworthy of her. At least, protests Gawain, we should attempt to learn her fate! Delighted by his nephew's good graces, the king bids him go.

As he draws near to the forest, Gawain spies Keu's warhorse in a sorry state, without its rider, followed by an unknown knight astride an exhausted steed. The knight, who appears to recognize Gawain, calls out to him to ask for one of his horses, and vanishes without explanation on his fresh mount. Gawain gallops off after him, and soon comes upon the vestiges of a violent combat in the midst of which lies the body of the horse he has just given to the strange knight. A little further along, the knight himself, alone, is marching ahead fully armed, and approaches a cart driven by a dwarf, whom he asks if he has seen his lady, the queen. The villainous dwarf will inform him by the following day whether he will allow him to climb into the cart— a sign of the vilest loss of rank, since the cart is used for the transport of criminals and reprobates:

> The knight hesitated only for a couple of steps before getting in.
> Yet, it was unlucky for him that he shrank from the disgrace, and
> did not jump in at once; for he will later rue his delay. But common

sense, which is inconsistent with love's dictates, bids him refrain from getting in, warning him and counselling him to do and undertake nothing for which he may reap shame and disgrace. Reason, which dares thus speak to him, reaches only his lips, but not his heart; but love is enclosed within his heart, bidding him and urging him to mount at once upon the cart. So he jumps in, since love will have it so, feeling no concern about the shame, since he is prompted by love's command.[109]

Gawain catches up to the cart, stunned at the sight of the knight seated in it, and asks in turn after the queen. "If thou art so much thy own enemy as is this knight who is sitting here, get in with him," the dwarf responds. Gawain abstains from what would be pure folly, and falls in behind the cart. The two knights soon learn that the queen's abductor, Meleagant, son of King Bademagu of Gorre, has taken her to his father's realm, which is accessible only by two paths—each one more dangerous than the other—the Water Bridge and the Sword Bridge, which is as sharp as a razor's edge. Gawain chooses the first bridge, and the knight of the cart sets off toward the second, henceforth accompanied by the general scorn that his decision to ride in the ignoble vehicle deserves. Never revealing his identity, he overcomes all obstacles, accomplishes several additional feats, and crosses the Sword Bridge, badly wounding his feet and hands in the effort. For all his exhaustion and his wounds, he confronts Meleagant in lone combat and forces him to concede defeat. The defeated knight's father, King Bademagu, who disapproves of his son's behavior, welcomes Meleagant's defeat and receives the victor as a guest of honor. In revenge, Meleagant orders his men to seize Lancelot through treacherous means. Released under oath by his jailer so that he may participate incognito in a great tournament, Lancelot returns and resumes his status as prisoner, only to be walled up in a lonely tower built to that sole end. But he makes good his escape with the aid of a maid whom he had earlier rescued, and who reveals herself to be Meleagant's sister. In a final joust at Arthur's court, the queen's champion once more confronts her abductor and this time—a rarity in Chrétien's duels—cuts off his head after having unhorsed him, bringing to an end his evil deeds, as well as the tale itself.

There is nothing terribly surprising about the ending. Reparation is exacted, as it must be, for the original affront. But the reparation will have been bought at a grievous cost: the "avenging" knight obtains in recompense

---

109. Chrétien de Troyes, *Arthurian Romances*, tran. W.W. Comfort (London: Everyman's Library, 1914), v. 361–377.

the queen's offering of her body. The public affront to Meleagant, who owes Arthur nothing and has abducted his wife in full respect for the rules of chivalry, is followed by a veritable felony: Lancelot violates the allegiance he owes his suzerain. That the king has forfeited the queen's esteem cannot make Lancelot her legitimate possessor and in no wise justifies adultery, which remains unpunished only because it has remained secret. The narrator provides the adulterer no justification whatsoever beyond the mutual attraction of the two lovers. Chrétien carries the irony so far as to make Lancelot the champion of him who is, in his stead, accused of having slept with the queen. Keu, still not yet fully recovered from his wounds, has been ordered by the good king Bademagu to stand guard over the queen and, to this end, to sleep in her chambers. To join her in her bed, Lancelot injures himself on the bars of the window and, unknown to him, leaves bloodstains on the sheets. Meleagant then asserts that the blood points to the seneschal, and Lancelot offers to prove Keu's innocence in a legally sanctioned battle against the accuser, from which he emerges victorious. His second victory has all the appearances of a laughable replica of the first. But it proclaims the queen's innocence in the eyes of the world, and that is what counts.

Ultimately, Lancelot makes no attempt whatsoever to avenge his king for an affront, which the tale takes pains to avoid having him witness. Lancelot has never wanted but one thing: that his love be recognized, and that the queen return it. His love is quite unlike that which we know as courtly, and can be defined, quite apart from its allegorical dimension, as a respectfully amorous devotion, placed at the service of the chivalric institution and the relations between man and suzerain: in braving all dangers for the love and the glory of his lady, the young knight pays homage to her husband and lord. His love must hence remain chaste, for the function of courtly love is to strengthen social cohesiveness. Lancelot's love for the queen is a powerful dissolvent; it inverts his relationship to the chivalrous order by making it subordinate to himself. Such is the meaning of the critical episode of the cart: the very act that brings general condemnation upon the knight—sitting on the bench of infamy—exposes him to the queen's glacial silence, but for a diametrically opposed reason: *she cannot forgive him for having hesitated.* For an instant the chivalric code of honor has come close to emerging victorious over his unconditional love for her ("it was to be for him but a source of greater sorrow," the narrator had warned). The same inversion of values once more arises, in broadly comic terms, during the tournament in which Lancelot, who has just been released from confinement, participates anonymously, clad in a scarlet tunic. The queen, once more alone among those present in suspecting his true identity, confirms the accuracy of her suspicions by sending a message calling upon him to fight "his worst," that is to say, as badly as possible—to which the scarlet knight responds by a series of clumsy maneuvers and attempts to flee that make him the laughingstock of the tournament—if only in the short term. Who but he could demonstrate such obedience; who but she could hope to gain it? The world's greatest knight can breach the rule for none other than his lover.

Chrétien de Troyes adroitly evokes the contradictions between individual passion and the coded violence of the social order. With his Lancelot, we are far indeed from the Holy Grail: the individual, and *the lofty view of himself* to which the chivalrous order disposes him, takes precedence over the oath of allegiance, over the sacred authority of the king, over God. That which Perceval places at the service of the Lord, Lancelot devotes to his earthly love, for it is to this love, as he says, that he owes that which is best in him. In the mirror of his beloved he seeks himself; in the eyes of his lover his identity is confirmed. If the knight of the cart obstinately refuses to speak his name, it is because only his lady may reveal it, for she alone can recognize him by his acts. The *Chevalier de la charrette* creates no enigmas, and the allegories we encounter there seem to me far less rich than its human content. Because its hero becomes himself through the fusion of adventure and the amorous quest, even to the disdain of the conventions of the day (as the title of the tale itself indicates), he becomes the archetype of the modern hero who will stop at nothing to satisfy his ambitions.

For all that, the word "ambition" rings hollow. One cannot even speak of ambitions where Lancelot is concerned. Lancelot becomes himself in the course of a daydream, which he is able to pursue precisely because its object remains beyond his grasp. Never will he possess the queen. The only night of love he spends with her will never recur, and will never even be seen to have taken place except by the two of them. Arthur himself has not been truly betrayed—or if he has, it is to a depth he does not suspect, as the frivolousness of his conduct proves. That which the two lovers have taken one from the other is the soul; the carnal love that has united them for one fleeting night is the seal of the secret they share. It cannot, must not, happen more than once. For Lancelot, no boundary exists between the real and the imaginary; the idea of the queen inhabits him, fulfils him utterly. The thought of her or her presence, like the drops of blood for Perceval, puts him beyond the world. Beyond the world and nearer to himself, for, contrary to Perceval, Lancelot imagines no truth, no quest that lies beyond. Lancelot is a happy dream, which Chrétien unfolds with a sense of amused tenderness. The hero needs only know that only one person shares his dream, she who stands as its unique object. His love, no matter how mad, now matter how tainted by melancholy, is possible, perhaps even beneficial. This may be why the traces Lancelot has left in our self-constructed imagination are less serious, and thus perhaps less profound, than the despairing love of Tristan.

Tristan, or the Mortal Transfer

Tristan is the incarnation of impossible love. Love as tragedy. As malignancy. Love to the absolute degree, which is consummated only in death. Tristan's truth, which Iseult shares with him until the bitter end, is farther still from Christian truth than that of Lancelot. Such at least is the case in the version I have chosen to draw upon. Tristan, it must be said, has many authors, from the most anonymous to the best known. The Tristan who comes most naturally to mind has been, for the last century, Richard Wagner's, in which the passions of the night triumph over the vulgar forces of the world of the day in the annihilation of the body, which transforms the death of the lovers, as in *Romeo and Juliet*, into the locus of their supreme and veritable fusion. Wagner has invented nothing of course: from the most ancient versions of the myth known to us today, the relationship between death and truth has undergone a shift from divine to passionate love. This movement has in turn created a new relationship with the hereafter, the ambiguity of which is now fully open to question.

There exist so many variants of the story of Tristan that we must relate it as we would draw a tree, with countless intersecting and diverging branches, taking care to place at each fork the conjunction "or": Iseult loves *or* loathes Tristan, or loves *and* loathes Tristan; Brangwein pours the potioned wine inadvertently *or* quite purposely; Iseult knows *or* is unaware of what she is drinking; King Marc sends Tristan to Ireland to be rid of him *or* so that he will find the maiden with the golden hair. Our choices are necessarily arbitrary ones, for no particular version can speak with authority; the diversity of sources, of vestiges, sequences, copies, and fragments does not allow us to trace the text back to a single source that can be identified with any certainty. There exists no "original" text in terms of precedence. Thus I have chosen to employ a modern translation of the celebrated reconstitution carried out by Joseph Bédier working from a late version, dating from the fifteenth century.[110] This sequencing process is in itself open to discussion, and I do not propose to dwell at any length on the arguments that justify it. Quite simply, of the several versions translated into modern French that I have read, it seems to me to be the least ornamented, and also the least "Wagnerian."

Wagner's version is probably the most powerful, and also the simplest. It is also the one that is most likely to speak to us today, even though our ears may have become hardened to its serious tone. All the more reason, then, to turn toward the version that seems at furthest remove from it, not for reasons of an authenticity which must be assessed with extreme caution, but *to take the full measure of the gap*. Of the legend, Wagner has certainly captured that which has best met the test of time (though despite his genius, he cannot remove himself from his own era). But the legend of Tristan and Iseult's timeless quality lies in precisely what seems most familiar to us moderns, that of its absorption with the superficial, if nothing else: the archetype of passionate love and its by-products, which has become the principal food of our literature and cinema, a fare so absent from our daily lives that we can never obtain enough of it.

Tristan and Iseult tells not only a tale of forbidden love, the dark love of the two eponymous protagonists as they confront the hostility of their entourage. At the core of the tale lies a constellation of five characters: Tristan, his uncle King Marc, and three Iseults. Three women share the same name: Iseult the Blond, lover of Tristan and wife of Marc; Iseult the mother of Iseult the Fair; and Iseult of the Snow-white Hand, who will eventually become Tristan's spouse. As though to compensate for his mother's death while giving birth to him, Tristan is ensnared in a web of women, which, in addition to the three Iseults, includes his stepmother (his father's new wife) and Brangien, servant and companion to Iseult the Fair.

Charmed early on by the young Tristan, his stepmother grows jealous and quickly comes to hate him with deadly passion. In order to escape, the seven-year old child flees the paternal castle with the master to whom his

110. *Tristan et Iseult*, mis en français moderne par Pierre Champion, Paris, Presses Pocket, 1979. Unless otherwise indicated, numbers in parantheses following citations refer to the pages of this volume. The text is a modern French version based on Joseph Bédier's celebrated reconstruction, which is in turn based on a prose tale of the fifteenth century, itself considered as derivative of a thirteen century text faithful to *Tristan et Iseult*, by Thomas, of which we possess only fragments (2,300 verses out of an original estimate of 13,000). The thirteenth-century transcriber has integrated pieces of the Arthurian legend into his version. Champion judiciously eliminated them from his modern French translation. (For a critical summary of the oldest extant texts in various languages dealing with the legend of Tristan, see *Tristan et Yseut*, Bibliothéque de la Pleiade, sous la direction de Christianne Marchello-Nizia [Paris: Gallimard, 1995]. Hereinafter indicated by the letters "PL.")

father had entrusted him before dying: Gouvernal. Reared by him under the protection of a French lord, the lad has grown up amid the amorous attentions of the damsels and ladies of the court until the day when, ripe for adventure, he takes his leave, flanked by the faithful Gouvernal, to place himself at the service of his uncle Marc, King of Cornwall. Tristan gains the king's affection, all the while contriving not to reveal the blood ties that bind them. But soon enough he must reveal his true identity, after being knighted by the king and sent off into combat with the fearsome Morhoult, brother-in-law of the king of Ireland. He has come to claim the yearly tribute of two hundred young men whom Cornwall must surrender to Ireland as long as no man can best the Irish envoy. For all his distress at sending his nephew to a certain death, King Marc cannot go back on his undertaking; the battle must take place. Tristan deals his adversary a deathblow. So violent is the impact that his sword is chipped, leaving a fragment in the head of the Irishman who, though dying, returns to his ship where he finally expires. But the victory is a costly one: the poisoned sword of his enemy has inflicted upon Tristan a suppurating wound that seems incurable, and which inexorably drains him of his strength. Tristan, placing his fate in the hands of God, causes himself to be put out to sea alone, with only his harp and his sword, in a small boat loaded with provisions which, fifteen days later, will come ashore at the foot of the king of Ireland's castle. Drawn by his singing, the king and queen (who is none other than the sister of Morhoult) take him into their court and entrust his care to their daughter Iseult, who knows the powers and properties of plants, and the arts of healing.

A first cycle is thus completed, which, with his first flight from his stepmother's hatred through a tainted release (the victory over Morhoult), leads Tristan to the very root of the venom that is draining his life from him. Both poison and remedy share the same source, from which will also spring the fatal philter that will forever link him to Iseult.[111] From that moment on, Tristan becomes captive to the feminine *pharmakon*, and is fated to be healed by women and yet to suffer at their hands—until death.

Once healed, Tristan leaves Ireland before he can be recognized as Morhoult's slayer. But a terrible dragon is laying waste the land, which Tantris (prudent to a fault, the hero has transposed the syllables of his name) cannot resist the temptation to slay. This he does, but not without suffering another poisoning, from which he is once again saved by both Iseult the

---

111. In other versions, Iseult herself is queen, and possessor of knowledge of plants, and who, in caring for Tristan, recognizes the poison from which he suffers, for it is the same substance which she had prepared for the sword of her brother, Morhoult.

mother and the daughter. But the queen discovers soon thereafter that the hero's sword is chipped, and that the fragment which she had earlier removed from the head of her brother corresponds perfectly to the chipped section of the damaged blade. She cries out for vengeance, which the king seems prepared to allow her. However, before his assembled court, he changes his mind: Tristan is a valorous knight; it would be treasonous to put to death a guest who had been brought back to life under his roof; but the killer must nonetheless depart the realm immediately and never return, on pain of death.

Upon his return to Tyntagel, in Cornwall, Tristan is welcomed amidst general rejoicing. But the king, jealous of his nephew's growing influence at court, begins to hate him and to cast about for ways to rid himself of him. The insistence of his entourage that he marry gives him the opportunity. By way of encouraging the marriage, Tristan pledges under oath to find the king the wife he wishes. The king then reveals that he desires the only maiden whose beauty Tristan has praised: Iseult the Fair, daughter of the king of Ireland. "When Tristan heard these tidings, he believed that his uncle was sending him to Ireland to die, rather than to possess Iseult" (69), but he cannot betray his solemn vow; to Ireland he must go. This time, the poison is his uncle's hatred, which sends Tristan back to women and the danger they embody, all the while insisting that he conquer for another man the only beauty to whom he is himself attracted.

Many versions either pass over or minimize the king's ill will toward Tristan, attributing them instead to his barons, who, in their jealousy of the king's favorite, scheme to eliminate him. The innocence of Marc dictates the episode of the golden hair: holding up the hair of a swallow, the king declares that he will wed only the maiden to whom it belongs, quite certain that no man can find it. But Tristan, who has far from forgotten Iseult the Fair, declares that he knows such a maiden and offers to seek her out. The first version is harsher, and more powerful. But above all, it lays the ground for Tristan's "betrayal," which corresponds unconsciously to that of the king: since he is being sent off not for Iseult but to his own destruction, he may as well claim the lady for himself. Here lurks, in spite of the philter (we will soon turn to its meaning), a coiled spring of revenge, which drives the hero far beyond what he could have ever imagined: still toward the death to which the king has assigned him, but along totally different paths. From that moment on, Iseult ceases to be the cause, or even the main object of the conflict between Marc and his nephew; she becomes instead the means through which the two men torment one another. The source of their opposition seems an enigma—unless we simply read into it the classic father-son confrontation.

Tristan sets off to carry out his mission, but a providential storm washes his ship ashore in the lands of King Arthur, where, without transition, the tale depicts him joining the retinue of the king of Ireland, whom he rescues from great peril. Thus are the two reconciled, and along with them, their two lands. Tristan accompanies the king to Ireland, where yet again Iseult heals his wounds. Shaken by Iseult's beauty, Tristan vows "that he shall ask for her for himself, and for none other" but ultimately decides that he "prefers to safeguard his honor" and asks her hand for King Marc. As though he is able to read his heart, Iseult's father answers: "I give her over to you, for you or for your uncle" (73). The choice the hero now faces is explicit: between betrayal and love.

During their passage to Cornwall, Tristan and Iseult slake their thirst with the love potion that Iseult's mother has prepared for her daughter and her spouse-to-be, which has been in the safekeeping of Brangwein. The text reads thus:

> In his thirst, Tristan asks for wine. Gouvernal and Brangwein go off to seek some, and find the "love potion" amongst the numerous cups of silver. If they have erred, it is certainly by accident! But Brangwein took up the golden cup and into it Gouvernal poured the potion that was like clearest wine. (76)

So, they have not misled him on purpose! The clumsiness of the denial, which seems to reflect the consternation of the characters themselves, is more eloquent than any confession. The substitution may well have been fortuitous, but the narrator believes not a word of it, despite his disclaimers. If we are to view the two accomplices as the doubles of their master and mistress (a hypothesis their marriage will in the end confirm), it is almost impossible to overlook the fact that they *jointly* cause the secret desire of the two lovers to become reality. In certain versions, Brangwein's duplicity is clear, and Iseult could not possibly mistake it for anything else—which would explain why Brangwein couldn't refuse to take Iseult's place (another substitution) on the wedding night to deceive the king with regard to his wife's virginity.

Whether in complicity or as gesture gone wrong, the potioned draught both justifies and reveals. On the one hand, Tristan is no longer responsible for the passion that drives him on. On the other, fatality corresponds all too well with his desire. Even before he tastes of the philter, Tristan has desired Iseult. He has even admitted it to himself, but repressed his impulse in the name of honor and the code of chivalry. Tristan is torn by his sense of duty to King Marc, who stands in for his father, and his reprehensible lust for Iseult, whom he cannot possess without committing, in addition to lying under oath, an act of near incest. The taboo is a powerful one, but under the influence of the drug it is set aside. Liberation is marvellous, without limits, fearsome:

> Oh! God, what a draft!
>
> Thus did they enter upon the highroad from which they will never depart, the day of their lives, for they have drunk of their destruction and their death. How sweet, how tasty did the beverage taste to them! But never had sweetness been purchased at such a price. Their hearts changed, and moulted. For no sooner than they had drunk, the one looked upon the other in astonishment. They thought of those things, which they had done before. Tristan thinks now of Iseult. Iseult thinks of Tristan, and lo, King Marc is forgotten!
>
> For Tristan thinks of nothing else but the love of Iseult, and Iseult, of nothing else but the love of Tristan. Such is the harmony of their hearts that they will love one another for all their life. (76)

Their hearts have *moulted*, sloughed off the enveloping layer that had prevented them from entering into the truth of their desire. Suddenly, desire knows no barrier; the two lovers give themselves to each other without reserve, immediately. And, because their passion is not merely a simple moment of ecstasy, because it is not a brief moment of distraction from which they might recover, it will pull them down into a whirlpool of destruction. Bottomless indeed is the passionate love that knows only the insatiable call of the flesh. Such love cannot survive quotidian reality, and even prolonged intoxication is not enough to keep it alive: the proscription that the philter has undone from within must be preserved from without; passion draws its nourishment from the obstacles it must overcome, and requires constant renewal, up until the moment when these obstacles, having become insurmountable by virtue of the physical distance that society imposes on the lovers, separate them too conclusively for them not to die.

Clearly enough, the tinctured wine is not a marriage draught, for everyone knows that marriage is incompatible with passion.[112] Iseult's mother has brewed it not for King Marc, but for her daughter, whose inclination for the handsome, young, and valiant Tristan she has easily detected. Unless of course she has concocted revenge for a murder that *she* has never forgiven. What is certain is that, like her two homonyms, she is well aware of the power of plants, and is capable of using that power either to cure Tristan or to cause him to perish. The meaning of the philter becomes clearer. Far from being a long-acting aphrodisiac, it is a fatal formula for that love that totally unites, of which limitation and liberty are the complementary and contradictory ingredients. The mixture that the lovers drink is an explosive blend of their mutual desire and its prohibition: "They have drunk of their destruction and their death." Their magical love, the terrible *pharmakon* with its double composition, lofty yet malevolent, is at the antipodes of Platonic Eros and, in a more general sense, quite far removed from the ancient conceptions of love. In Greek terms, the originality of the "British" concept of love could be found in the indissoluble amalgamation of *Eros* and *até*[113]— of love and calamity.

This dark love, this love unto death, will be lived out in chaotic fashion, in the course of struggles, plots, and betrayals. According to the courtly ideal, the heroes, though victims of a fatality that dominates them, must be above reproach; Tristan must appear to be constantly torn between passion and loyalty, uncle and nephew must be reconciled, the philter must lose its power and the story its obscurity; the untameable carnal attraction of the lovers must be transformed into spiritual love, and this love must become placid and licit. This process of sublimation is symbolized by the famous episode of the sword: Tristan and Iseult have been living in hiding in the forest for two years when King Marc happens upon them asleep, separated by Tristan's sword laid between them. Touched by this sign of chastity, the king replaces Tristan's sword with his own and goes away, leaving behind a sign of confidence and forgiveness, from which point reconciliation and the restitution of Iseult will become possible.

The episode of the sword does not appear in the version I have used. Instead, Marc surprises Iseult in her forest retreat while she is alone, and takes advantage of Tristan's absence to have her abducted by his henchmen. Such brutality fits in better with the preceding episodes and, in a general

---

112. The incompatibility was once much clearer than it is today. The idea of marriage based on passion is a typically modern one.

113. For a discussion of these two notions, see my analysis of Sophocles's *King Œdipus* (Chapter 4) and of Plato's *Symposium* (Chapter 5) above.

manner, with the severity of relations between men and women, in which women are by no means the mistresses of courtly love devoted entirely to them, but are instead coveted objects of exchange and combat which males (fathers, husbands, feudal lords) trade and steal among themselves. In his cuckold's fury, King Marc does not hesitate even to deliver Iseult over to the lepers, from whose clutches Tristan will forthwith wrench her, thus gaining the right that his lord has forfeited. Iseult henceforth belongs in full legitimacy to him who has rescued her. In recapturing her two years later, by force, King Marc has committed nothing less than an abduction. Tristan does not hasten to deliver her because he has been wounded by a poisoned arrow. But since Iseult is now imprisoned, and inaccessible, he must travel far away to another healer.

The Other is a double: Iseult of the Snow-white Hands, whose name and beauty cause the wounded man to hope that he may find consolation beside her for the loss of his beloved. But when time comes for the marriage to be consummated, all is for naught. For all her sweetness and her perfection, the copy cannot replace the original, and the memory of the only true Iseult prevents Tristan from acting. He had believed that he could escape the torments of separation in a sham that, on the contrary, serves only to revive them. Worse still, despite the power of their love, the distance that now separates the two has worn away their mutual confidence: the idea of infidelity (which Tristan's engagement only tends to bear out), torments both.

Tristan, who has departed on a short journey to Cornwall, must literally play the fool, and transform himself into an abject, unrecognizable being— the total opposite of himself—in order to approach the queen and be recognized by her, not without enormous hardship. Their mutual recognition, their fleeting and final reunion, cushion the last days of their estrangement. Yet estrangement is force enough to prevent Iseult from arriving in time to heal her friend of a wound she alone could have cured. By convincing her husband that the Iseult he is expecting is not aboard the ship that carries her (the famous lie of the black sail), Iseult of the Snow-white Hands—the double, jealousy—obscures their reunion. The tale could have had the two lovers die together. But on this point, all the texts concur: they die one after the other.

Another kind of reunion takes place, it is true, in their tomb, which most versions represent in the form of two plants or two bushes that intertwine as they grow. But the image in our text is much more vigorous: a fine, leafy green bramble bush rises from the tomb of Tristan, then bends over to penetrate that of Iseult, to the chagrin of King Marc, who cuts it off three times. Three times it grows again, more vigorous than ever, one last gesture of defiance toward the husband who looks on impotently at the act of love he has devoted his full energy to emasculate and yet does not cease to haunt him. The irony is splendid, but hardly compatible with the myth of mortal fusion that would join together in death that which life has torn asunder.

In the richness and variety of its transmission, the tale of Tristan and Iseult vibrates with contradictory resonance. It oscillates continuously (oftimes within the same version) between the terrible, the all-too-human, and the sublime, between the earthly and the heavenly, between the finite and the infinite. The pagan miracle of the bramble bush, in the harsher version I prefer, might well even be interpreted as a parody of the Christian idea of redemption. But I cannot avoid the thought that its function is to attenuate the sense of the irremediable. How difficult it is to accept what the tale so brutally relates: that men struggle without mercy for the possession of the poison that kills them; that passionate love cannot be lived; that death is separation.

The Tristan myth is a harsh one, even in its gentler versions. What is all the more striking is that it emerged at about the same time as the tales of the Holy Grail. Its pitiless character, and the near-sordidness of several of its episodes, brutally confirm what had already begun to emerge in the Arthurian cycle, creating a thorny paradox: *the dechristianization of narrative fiction.* Taken as form, it appears to discard Christianity as rapidly (and at almost the same time!) as it had taken it up in the first place. It is as though the knightly *geste* (Lancelot, Tristan) were hastening to abandon the religious framework of which it had pretended to make itself a part. As if, in other words, the desire to tell a story, to relate the innocence of man in his happiness or in the nudity of his unhappiness, had regained the freedom (which had certainly never been entirely lost) that Christian truth had sought to deprive it of, and for which the bramble bush sprung from Tristan's grave provides an insolent metaphor.

Freedom has indeed been regained. But not to the extent of wiping away all traces of Christianity. The liberty of the chivalrous hero and his peculiar relationship with death are not those of the Greek heroes. What Christianity seems to have unalterably transformed, with respect to the pagan era of antiquity, is the question of fate: Christianized heroes, unlike Achilles and Ulysses, reject the truth of death in all its irremediability. They may well expose themselves to it, may even openly seek it, but they do not do so only for glory, for the immortality of their name; for them, death is the ultimate hope, a passage toward deliverance, toward another, necessarily finer world. "Ah! Death, come upon Tristan and put to an end his pain" (98), exclaims the hero when the king catches him in the act of love and treachery. His cry of despair is transformed, in the final mingling of the lovers in the afterlife, into the act by which all is accomplished.

Denis de Rougemont, that great lover of love and of the West, expresses the highest regard for this accomplishment. Evoking the meeting of the soul with its heavenly self in the Mazdaism of ancient Iran, de Rougemont[114] opines:

> It is difficult not to imagine that this "auroral encounter" with the heavenly self in the form of an angel, and woman, informs the conclusion of the Tristan myth: all occurs three days after the death of love. Is not Iseult an evocation of the light that one encounters only in the above and beyond, and which would have been, on earth, the veritable object of Tristan's desire, his far away Princess, and his "love of afar", in the phrase of the troubadour Jauffré Rudel? Tristan's apparent narcissism could then be interpreted in spiritual terms....
>
> And would it not, in turn, throw new light upon the Christian tradition of love of one's neighbor?[115]

In attempting to reconnect the Tristan myth to the truth of the Gospel (as his text goes on to confirm), de Rougemont appears to wish to narrow the gap that, I believe, separates the love of Christ from narcissistic love, the love of one's self in the gaze of the other. The Christian idea of the afterlife persists—of this there can be no doubt—but in the case of Tristan, it is the ego that must not perish. The persistence of the ego in death seems to have become detached, independent of the content of Christian truth.

Death and truth are henceforth juxtaposed in another dream, in which earthly love, passionate love, lends the ego the strength to deny death and to live eternally—with or without Christ, who has become secondary. The negation of death, as an irremediable end, ceases to be Christian only. It is as though we were witnessing a pagan desire for infinite survival, which harks back to Gilgamesh's aspirations to a life without end. There is one crucial difference: Gilgamesh finally renounces his aspiration, while in the myth of Tristan passionate love becomes, at the same time it reveals to the hero his

114. The celebrated work of Denis de Rougemont, *Love in the Western World*, trans. Montgomery Belgion.(New York: Schocken Books, c. 1983) [*L'amour et l'occident*, Paris: Plon, 1939] devotes its first book to a now-classical analysis of the Tristan myth, an analysis which acts as a focal point for the entire work. For de Rougemont, the myth is the first model upon which the foundation and the evolution of passionate love in the West can be understood.
115. Denis de Rougemont, preface to *La merveilleuse histoire de Tristan et Iseut*, restituée par André Mary (Paris: Gallimard, Folio classique, 1973), pp. 18–19. [My translation—FR]

true identity, the means to avoid death. Far from being accepted, death continues to be refused, but this refusal is no longer necessarily related to Christian expectation. It has become paganized. Human love, in all its ambiguity and its connection with the divine, now stands as a new truth that magnifies the ego and keeps it from death. Which explains why this truth can still touch us so deeply today, in a world in which Christianity has become faded, enfeebled.

In the *Odyssey*, Homer depicts Achilles as disabused of his love of glory, and Ulysses as a tired man, impatient to return home laden with riches. There comes a moment when the cup is full, and the adventure must end. The hero can think of nothing else but rest, and intends to enjoy what he has amassed.

No such thing occurs in the *geste* of Christian chivalry. Its heroes never tire, are never deluded, and are only rarely sated by their exploits. Never will they have done enough to win recognition from their liege lord, from God, from their lady, and, ultimately, to win the approval they crave most, of themselves. They may join the battle on the side of truth, like Roland, or to take possession of their innermost secret, like Perceval; they may win the reward of a single glance, like Lancelot, or they may struggle and scheme mercilessly to possess the other body and soul, like Tristan: the combat itself never ends. It concludes only in a death, which is itself provisional—or exceptionally, in the asceticism that sometimes precedes it. Never in sensual pleasure. Driven continually onward by the fear that their name—their renown—will never be secure, that God will never be sufficiently served, love never exhausted, recognition forever inadequate, feeling forever threatened by erasure, the chivalrous hero is possessed by loss, obsessed with inadequacy. His endless quest for that which he seeks to accumulate—self-esteem—can come crashing down from one moment to the next, as much in his own eyes as in the gaze of the other. Love, friendship, piety, honor: none of what he seeks can be safely stored away for safekeeping. Tristan attempts to do so, in vain: tracked down in the depths of his forest, he cannot possess the treasure that is his love. The knight, unlike Ulysses, has no dwelling place (a prerogative of kings, which makes them more vulnerable and less chivalrous). He is condemned to be continuously setting out, always farther afield. But the object of his quest, assuming that he knows, remains unchanging: a self-image that is at once acceptable and fleeting. The idea that here may remain more to conquer (or to reconquer) returns always to haunt him.

Curiously, this never-ending cavalcade toward the rejection of all accumulation leaves in abeyance that which, in the reality of social relationships, makes it possible to go on: money. Georges Duby has demonstrated the role played by the "sinews of war" in the tournament system of the twelfth and thirteenth centuries. Money, in this system, was both means and object. Pecuniary gain was not in itself the sole motive, but without it, without the circulation of material wealth, tournaments simply could not be staged. The tournament (and the hope of the combatants) was propelled by prizes: horses, weapons, equipment, and above all, of men, with ransom as both moral incentive and payment. The chivalrous literature we have surveyed does not pass over the fact, but with the following, fundamental proviso: in it, the reward is always gratuitous, and brings nothing but self-esteem; the victor offers his lady the horse he has won, or sends the vanquished to submit himself to the king as prisoner. Not to purchase his freedom, but to relate the exploits of his victor.

The absence of money is a clear indication that the chivalrous narratives deliberately locate themselves outside the world. Of it they retain only the codes that are understood to order relations among men. But only the imaginary hero can respect the letter of the code. The "world's finest knight" need not concern himself with money. So it is that he may devote himself entirely to his honor, to God, to his love, and pursue unstintingly the quest for his identity in a world where there is no need to lay down the borderline between the real and the imaginary; where the absence of all borderlines leaves free reign to the inexhaustible play of symbols. Yet at the same time, the imaginary realm in which honor accumulates is the mental expression of a closed universe, in which the process of accumulation has become never-ending, unrestrained.

12

THE HEROISM OF THE POET

H ERE WE MUST set all haughtiness aside. Here all self-certainty must perish. We stand before the poet as the poet stands before God, "outside of time and space," in a spiritual precinct where human measure no longer applies, where pride and humility no longer pertain. And yet, the teller of the tale is a mortal man. What he tells is what no one before, and no one since, has ever dared: the story of the long, arduous road that he has travelled up from the horrors of the Inferno through the ascension into Purgatory, and onward into the supreme Truth of Paradise.

The poets of the Celtic *geste* sing the deeds of knights. Dante tells the story of himself. In the *Divine Comedy*, hero and poet are one and the same. Augustine has already taken himself for the subject of his spiritual epic. But where Augustine reveals his youth as he remembers having lived it, trapped between the lofty exigencies of the spirit and the temptations of the flesh, Dante becomes a participant in his own fiction. Though he speaks of the past, Dante tells us not what has happened to him: what has happened is what he asserts has happened. The *Comedy* has no epic to sing; it is, in its writing, the Epic. As both creator and the protagonist of his story, Dante moves forward and decodes it at the same time as we do, encountering the same difficulties that we do. Like his reader, the poet is immense and tiny, miserable and glorious, essential and contingent. He takes the greatest of all risks, that of fully realized grotesqueness: to bear witness to the abyssal depths and to the sublime heights he himself invents.

To be precise, Dante invents only the stage props, the itineraries, the places, and the interconnections, but the truth toward which he makes his way under the guidance of the great Virgil is that of the Church—which must here be understood not as an institution but as the community of believers, and, concomitantly, the sum total of the dogmas that have accreted around it. To Dante alone belongs the state of spiritual impoverishment in which he finds himself at the beginning of his tale: "Midway upon the journey of our life I found myself in a dark wood, for the straight way was lost" (*Inferno* I, 1).[116] He is obviously not alone on his journey; many others, all of Italy in fact, share with him the pervasive state of degradation. But, for all its exemplary qualities, the sense of being lost is also his own. The eternal glory toward which he advances in fits and starts, sustained by his guide, in no way belongs to him, and remains outside himself—at least up until the moment when, come the very end, the narrator dissolves himself in a kind of obliteration of the ego and of the earthly world.

As the poet has become witness to his own fiction, the frontier between the real and the imaginary is even less clearly defined and more porous than in the Arthurian legends. The very idea of a frontier becomes inconceivable. Be it to relate the misfortunes of Florence or the siege of Lucifer, the turpitude of the Roman Curia or the heavenly rose, Dante's writing is constantly shifting, with constant vigor. For him there exists only one reality with its thousands of components; from the earthly world to Hell, and from Hell to Paradise, there is continuity. With the same steady pace the poet proceeds from one discreet moment to another in a world in which his traveller's spirit recognizes no partitions. Yet little could be more compartmentalized than this universe criss-crossed by towering walls, riven by ditches, hierarchized to a multiplicity of degrees, from the most throat-gripping horror to the most sublime beatitude: jealously protected circles in which souls, for all their immateriality, are, with few exceptions, imprisoned. These prison regulations are applied in their full force only in Hell. Purgatory, a place of passage (more often than not long-lasting), erects barriers which have more in common with the ordeal than with imprisonment: no matter how long the period of detention, their aim is purification, not confinement. Paradise, where traffic flows more smoothly, appears to possess its own curiously inorganic yet palpable spiritual hierarchy.

In his descent into the depths of Hell, which is also the center of the universe, then in his ascent to the uppermost reaches of Heaven, which constitutes its supreme envelop, the poet transgresses the law that separates the the two spaces. His pretension is a disproportionate one: to accomplish, under Virgil's wing, a voyage that no other mortal has ever made, nor has

---

116. Dante Alighieri, *The Divine Comedy*, translated with a commentary by Charles S. Singleton, Bollingen Series LXXX (Princeton: Princeton University Press, 1970).

ever boasted of making. Yet Dante is not boastful; there is nothing spectacular about his progress. His is a stumbling silhouette, driven by forces beyond him: he follows along behind those who have guided him, who have raised him up and propelled him forward. His sole exploit is literary: apart from the beauty of his language (which is difficult to appreciate in translation), he performs the *tour de force* of contriving to exist, at the core of his own poem, only in the form of hesitations, fears, and questions. As he vacillates and moves reluctantly forward through arcana that never cease to astonish him, we forget that he is, when all is said and done, the author of the tale he tells. His apparent modesty conceals an exorbitant privilege: that of testifying to ultimate reality.

Such a privilege owes nothing to his personal qualities, and everything to his art. It is the singular privilege of language. Only language can lead man, a man like Dante in his *Comedy*, outside of time, outside of space. Only language can transgress the law, break through the walls of the maze through which scurry the tiny intrigues of human life. They—these intrigues—possess the same weight as divine things, and the poet, no matter how high he may climb, never loses sight of them. Grandeur and pettiness permeate the *Comedy*. In it, Dante brings them together with an artistry that we will later encounter—with perhaps greater freshness and truculence—in Shakespeare. But his art cannot but begin to falter as it approaches the summits, for which the poet repeatedly begs our pardon. That which he sees from on high "exceeds words" and cannot register in his memory:

> As he who is dreaming sees, and after the dream the passion remains imprinted, and the rest returns not to the mind; such am I, for my vision almost wholly fades away, yet does the sweetness that was born of it still drop within my heart. Thus the snow unsealed by the sun; thus in the wind, on the light leaves, the Sibyl's oracle was lost.
>
> O Light Supreme, that art so far uplifted above mortal conceiving, relend to my mind a little of what Thou didst appear, and give my tongue such power that it may leave only a single spark of Thy glory for the folk to come. (*Paradise*, XXXIII, 55–72)

The narrator literally finds himself and returns to himself, in precisely the place where all that he has been contemplating vanishes under the influence of an inexpressible spell. Human speech is not totally ubiquitous; its mobility cannot quite reach God, who alone possesses Speech in its plenitude. But the poet draws close enough to this plenitude to submerge himself in it, to be impregnated by it, as his final verses testify:

> Here power failed the lofty phantasy; but already my desire and my will were resolved, like a wheel that is evenly moved, by the Love which moves the sun and the other stars. (*Paradise*, XXXIII, 48)

His immense poem comes to a paradoxical close by inducing within him a state of ecstatic felicity that he cannot articulate. Indescribable though it may be plenitude, *he says*, has been attained. No epic can dream a loftier dream than the total fusion of the self in divine love. As he climbs, borne by the power of speech, up the ladder of the real, as an acrobat climbs his rope by the strength of his wrists, the poet cannot resist the temptation to proclaim victory. He takes his leave of us at the summit of the absolute he has just attained, pushing away the ladder of verse we believed for an instant we might climb along with him. We will never know if he has awakened from his dream, or if he has awakened from the nightmare of life to reach the eternal truth of his story. For, along with the narrator's ecstasy, it is the story itself which, despite his flaws as a narrator, becomes one with the supreme truth it evokes: the truth by which Dante, like none other before or since, dares to *provoke* us.

The entire *Comedy*, in fact, can be seen as provocation: to modern readers, and to his contemporaries. But the ways in which it provokes, I believe, are different.

The elasticity of his speech was probably less surprising in Dante's day, when readers had not yet "learned," as Foucault has demonstrated, to distinguish words from things. The people of the Middle Ages were not so simple-minded as to believe that things existed separately from words, or that words carried less weight than things. Metaphor and allegory were for them means of locomotion as ordinary as the helicopter and the airplane are for us. Perhaps they would marvel—though even that cannot be taken for granted— at our ability to transport ourselves from New York to Rome in a few hours, but they would not understand our modern repugnance at travelling from Florence to Purgatory, chatting with the dead along the way. Dante has become literally unreadable for us today. It is as though, under the influence of the scientific stringency that allows us to construct rockets, our imaginations have lost the mobility we have gained in the realm of matter.

It may well be that science, as it gives every indication of doing, will obligate us to reconsider the real, will cause us to understand that metaphor is not simply the golden billhook with which the poets reap their laurels. Still, our relationship with literatures, and with fiction in particular, has remained virtually unchanged: we cannot stop compartmentalizing them, arranging and rearranging them, while looking askance at that which we dismiss with a pejorative gesture, as the "mixing of genres." At the most, literary jargon sets aside an ambiguous space for the "indefinable" when, for example, the mixture is intriguing enough to capture, if even for an instant, the critic's attention. Such is the purgatory to which we would surely assign Dante's *Comedy* today if it had not long become a classic, that is, an item catalogued and assigned once and for all to the paradise of deathless works no longer read, except by a handful of librarians. Dante no longer provokes us—or provokes only by virtue of his "archaism"—for the down-to-earth reason that we have ceased to read him without ceasing to use him. We appreciate the *Comedy* as an inexhaustible source of quotations, of passages whose overall meaning leaves us quite cold: Hell and Purgatory no longer concern us, and the Empyrean is an abandoned railway station for which even transcendence—all that is left of it—has no use.

Or to put it differently, the poet's contemplative purposes aspire to heights that inspire scant confidence, and even less hope, in our day and age. In the contemporary scheme of things, God is little better than an outdated remedy against death, which we store, for any eventuality, in the bottom drawer of our consciousness. God no longer stands for the name of heights to be scaled, for the metaphorical locus of some fundamental aspiration. Yet such aspiration feeds into the Arthurian legend, which has made a curious comeback on our motion picture screens. The dreams of a Lancelot or a Perceval are as lofty as Dante's, but their lances have maintained a greater power of fascination than the poet's pen. The victory they seek provides us with all the satisfaction we desire: the elevation we experience when we bring about the other's fall. Such satisfaction, as we all know, is short-lived, but the emphasis laid upon martial accomplishment in the chivalrous *geste* makes it plausible.

Unlike the knight, the poet wields none of these flamboyant arms. Naked, boasting neither coat of arms nor fine livery, with fear itself as his only adversary, he sets out on a quest utterly bereft of gallantry. Brilliant in his exploits, the Arthurian knight seeks himself in the long-awaited gaze of God or of his lady. Of his lady, Dante expects nothing less than Lancelot, but he does so through the advancement of a modest penitent who offers the reader no distraction from his slow progression toward the transcendence she embodies. That which remains largely concealed in the Arthurian legend, hidden primarily beneath the clash of combat, becomes in the *Comedy* an objective—to become one with the glory of God—whose clarity and ingenuity today bring smiles to our faces. The *Comedy*'s most troubling paradox stems from the fact that this mountain of metaphors heaped one atop the other quite explicitly gives birth to the unutterable—which, given its poverty of means, it can barely express. What lends Dante's paradise both its weakness and its provocative power is its very accessibility.

Today, Dante all but fails to convince us of the existence of Paradise. If, despite this disappointing conclusion, we still catch a faint glitter when we read him, it is surely because we can detect, in his improbable spiritual voyage, a tremor that still touches our sensibilities.

Clearly, we are not talking about the Florentine's "patriotic" vibrations, for all their omnipresence. The naked eye can easily detect the political vein that winds its way through the strata traversed by the poet. The thread of his argument is easy enough to follow: diverted from its primary tasks by the management of its temporal dominion and by the struggle for power such management entails, the papacy has come to conduct itself like a whore or a conspirator, prostituting itself to the highest bidder to achieve its aims, which are harmful both to the Church and to Italy. Only an emperor truly committed to restoring the grandeur of Rome (as Henri VII of Luxembourg had indicated since his election in 1309) can restore the unity of ancient Italy and return Christianity to the path of righteousness. Only by fully assuming the political destiny of a restored empire could the emperor enable the successors of Saint Peter to extract themselves from the muck-filled ditch into which they have fallen, and to carry out their spiritual mission with dignity. One need not be aware of Dante's political predicament to understand that the poet, all the while taking the high ground with respect to the political struggles in which he has been a participant, has accounts to settle. Of this there is aplenty; but there is much more.

One might think that political quarrels would flow as if by gravity into the appropriate places: Hell, and secondarily, Purgatory—which is mostly what happens. But the narrator cannot resist the temptation to drag scraps of these conflicts from the time and place where they belong, up into the Empyrean: by invoking (through the voice of Beatrice) the empty throne henceforth reserved in the heavenly court for the "lofty Henry, who will come to set Italy straight," Dante casts a final dart at his sworn enemy, the Duke of Alagna, alias Boniface VIII (*Paradise*, XXX, 137). This ultimate outburst of rancor when the highest felicity is so near at hand is more than simple revenge; it represents the unity of the heavenly and earthly worlds of which we have already spoken.

In writing of politics, Dante reminds us that Heaven forgets nothing of man's doing. Forgiveness, along with the forgetfulness that accompanies it, is granted only to those souls which have repented and returned to the bosom of the Church, or better yet, have strived for that goal in the course of their lives. Purgatory, after all, is accessible only to active, repenting believers. Without the combination of these two qualities (faith and repentance), the most just, most upright souls, those who have known neither the Christian faith nor the Jewish faith before it, like Socrates, Plato, and Aristotle, are relegated to Limbo, which in Dante's topography is assigned to the outermost, relatively clement circle of Hell. Only by virtue of an exceptional and altogether provisional favor is Virgil authorized to accompany the narrator to the highest ramparts of Purgatory before dropping away to return, his mission accomplished, to Limbo, where he belongs. This system of preferential treatment has, as we shall see, a vital function in a thoroughly muddled political system.

The economy of earthly relations with the hereafter is, for Dante, no simple matter. At first glance, it seems to conform fully to the dogmas of the Church, particularly to the theology of Thomas Aquinas. In the lower circles of Hell, the narrator encounters souls which would clearly prefer to have been elsewhere, such as Farinato and Thegghiajo, those "once so worthy" men (*Inferno*, VI, 28). Men like Brunetto Latino, Dante's master, suffer eternal condemnation to the seventh circle for an unspecified fault that his classification among the "violent against the spirit" has defined as an intellectual sin, perhaps even excessive liberties taken with the teachings of the Church; unless of course punishment here symbolizes the supremacy of revealed knowledge over reason—one cannot be sure. For all that, the poet is saddened: "Are you here, ser Brunetto?" he exclaims, recognizing the man whom he will thank soon thereafter for having been his precious guide, "the dear kind paternal image" (*Inferno*, XV, 30; 83). In the broadest sense, penalties seem to be meted out quite independent of the narrator's affections or personal judgement.

But such is not always the case. Some of the retributions handed out betray the narrator's preferences and prejudices, as we have observed in the places assigned to Emperor Henri VII and Pope Boniface VIII respectively. Far from being completely arbitrary or purely emotional, his partiality conforms to a clear-cut political logic. Insofar as it does not openly challenge church dogma, the Dantean hierarchy rewards those souls that have toiled for the grandeur of the two Romes, and punishes those who have plotted against them. By the two Romes, we mean Christian, spiritual Rome, and ancient Rome, whose power Dante wishes to see restored. Only nostalgia for the imperial order can justify Caesar's eternal repose in Limbo while Ulysses, as an adversary of the legendary ancestors of the Romans, suffers all the torments of the eighth pit of the eighth circle of Hell for having contributed to the destruction of Troy.

Virgil's paternal presence can be explained not only by Dante's literary admiration for the author of the *Aeneid*. It points with stark clarity to the importance the narrator attaches to the connections that unite the temporal and the spiritual, that joins history to his political hopes and dreams. As the mainspring of the narrative, Virgil, the bard of Aeneas and herald of the origins of Rome, is better placed than anyone else to ratify the linkage leading from Augustan Rome to the Eternal City. The rocky trail along which he leads his acolyte is not merely the itinerary the narrator must follow to attain his personal salvation, it is also the pathway which—like the one that led Aeneas to Rome—both Italy and all Christianity must follow in order to carry out their historic mission and bring about at every level the transmission of the New Law.

From beginning to end of the *Comedy*, ancient mythology and Christian theology intimately intertwine to form a single, tightly braided cable. Minos becomes the dispatcher of souls condemned to Hell, and Cato of Utica, guardian of the gates of Purgatory. The damned cross the Acheron on Charon's ferry while the repented gather on the banks of the Tiber, as if to associate Roman geography with the path of salvation. The interpenetration of the two mythological corpuses sometimes takes a surprising twist: among those who practice "violence against God" and who burn in the seventh circle, we encounter Capaneus who, while besieging Thebes alongside Polyneices, had challenged Zeus to defend the walls: the insult to Jupiter is equated, with no other justification, to a crime against God.

Such amalgams, and they abound, illustrate the fusion that Dante's writing brings about, in the most natural way, between Greco-Roman cosmogony and Christian evangelism, and they naturally bring to mind Robert de Boron's genealogy of Merlin. But that fusion occurs at the cost of a veritable highjacking of scriptural meaning: a biased lineage is set up, one that sets the Old Law aside. Certainly the poet has an obligation—almost in spite of himself—to allude to the continuity he seeks to play down by setting aside places in Paradise for a certain number of Old Testament figures (Adam and Eve, Moses, Joshua, Judas Macchabeus); but they appear strictly as extras, with no significant role to play, confirming that they no longer have a contribution to make. Their silence and effacement contrast with the eloquence the story lavishes upon the Roman eagle in canto XIX.

The narrator hardly hesitates before setting up a pagan military ensign as representative and defender of inscrutable, blind justice! The emblem of imperialism sings the mysteries of salvation, chastizes the behavior of Christian princes, and pleads for the impenetrable will of God whom it had fought so bitterly before adopting his Law. The Roman Empire, in Dante's hands, receives a grace that illuminates and justifies all its enterprises. It is the miracle of Pauline conversation raised to its loftiest historical power: like Paul on the road to Damascus, it bears witness to the secret, majestic avenues that have transformed it retroactively into the likeness of divine justice on earth. Far more is at stake than a simple settling of accounts. Spoken in the heart of Paradise by the herald of Roman power, Virgil's fervent declamation resonates with a political passion for Italy that we will encounter a century later, driven by the same hatred for the papacy but stripped of its Christian attire, in Machiavelli.

For all the significance it may have held for Dante and his contemporaries, and for Italy during the centuries that followed as a kind of unificatory fermentation agent, the *Comedy*'s political dimension can account for neither its fame nor its having stood the test of time. In hindsight, the glorification of the empire suffers from the same deficiencies as does the illustration of Paradise. The two apotheoses, and to an even greater degree the intention that binds them together into a veritable garland of hope, leave us sceptical. Can Dante truly have believed it himself? Behind the answerless question lurks, quivering, something we earlier set aside, and to which we must now return.

The least perishable aspect of the *Comedy*—as of the Arthurian cycles—lies in its personification of that which is most human and most universal: love. A man's love for a woman; the poet's love for Beatrice. In speaking her name, known by all those who may have heard even remotely of Dante, one understands how empty, how soulless the *Comedy* is until she is invoked. If there exists a key to the heart of the work, she is that key.

The key cannot be sought anywhere but in the story itself. No need to know what Bice Portinari represented in the life of Dante. Beatrice's true identity, an identity far more certain than any biographical research could possibly establish, is related by the poet, in the poem. This is true of the *Comedy* more than of the *Vita Nova*, which functions as a prelude, and at whose end Dante declares that he no longer wishes to speak of his Beatrice until he is able to invest her with all the dignity she merits. He hopes that enough time remains for him to say of her what has never before been said of any other woman.

That dignity to which none other has ever been elevated resides in the fact that Beatrice literally brings the entire tale alive. She is the incarnation of the strength, the wisdom, and the beauty that, through the agency of Virgil, will enable the poet to accede at last to the supreme truth far from which he has so long wandered. Beatrice is to Dante what Diotime is to Socrates. But she is much more: where Diotime is content to give instruction (not without expressing some doubts about the capacity of the young Socrates to understand her fully), Beatrice acts: she dispatches Virgil to help the fallen poet to his feet; she strengthens the failing will-power of her beloved by the memory of her face and the promise of an encounter, she takes him to task and tears him away from his distractions before guiding him by her own hand into Paradise and making him ready for the sight of God. Contrary to Augustine's *Confessions*, repentance, for Dante, must be sought through woman. The entire *Comedy* can be interpreted as an exercise in loving rehabilitation, the aim of which is to reconquer the lost countenance, and to obtain the forgiveness of her for whose memory the poet has failed in fidelity, when death itself should have made her more precious to him:

> "Never did nature or art present to you beauty so great as the fair numbers in which I was enclosed and are now scattered to dust. And if the highest beauty thus failed you by my death, what mortal thing should then have drawn you to desire for it? Truly at the first arrow of deceitful things you ought to have risen up, following me who was no longer such. Young damsel or other novelty of such brief enjoyment should not have weighted down your wings to await more shots." (*Purgatory*, XXXI, 49–63)

Such is Beatrice's reproach to him who has made his way through the circles of Hell and climbed the ladder of Purgatory before arriving finally at her side. That the poet might once have succumbed to the temptation to seek consolation for the loss of his beloved in the arms of another is understandable enough, but that he would have persisted in such a purposeless endeavor! Not only could no other woman offer him such a perfect body and such lofty release, but most of all her death should have lifted his love for her to heavenly heights where it would reign in majesty, purified of the deceptive dross of the flesh.

Her reproof expresses the full ambiguity of the poet's amorous undertaking. Precisely what salvation does Dante seek in the eyes of his beloved? By transforming Beatrice into the mirror image and the vehicle of Christian love, the poet sends out contradictory signals. We will never know for certain if he is searching for God through her, or if God is not, when all is said and done, his consolation for the terminal destitution that only her glance could remedy. At first glance, no love is courtlier than Dante's. With Beatrice, Dante behaves like the young knight with his lord's lady: the flame he nurtures for the lady of his thoughts brings honor to the husband who possesses her. And, since she is dead, Beatrice belongs indisputably to God. The overall construction of the poem allows not the smallest doubt: divine truth is the ultimate goal, the loftiest of all objectives. But it cannot be reached without the succor of human love. Without Beatrice, there can be no God for Dante. Not only because of her instrumental role as inspiration and guide. Not only because, by virtue of the magic of her carnal attraction on earth, the young woman has touched off in the poet's soul an inexhaustible desire for beauty which ascends, as with Socrates, by degrees until it attains the love of the Beautiful in and of itself, but because it is for her, because he must redeem himself in her gaze, that he has embarked upon his infernal voyage toward the place where she dwells, a place that can be nothing else other than the paradisal ideal of his own gaze.

Paradise does not exist, literally, except in Beatrice's gaze. She so strongly senses it that she admonishes her admirer with tender irony: "Not only in my eyes is paradise" (*Paradise*, XVIII, 21). Yet it is in her eyes and through her eyes that the narrator finds God. Had God not existed, if Beatrice's presence had not brought light to the Empyrean, Dante would not have sought his Eurydice beyond the boundaries of Hell. But Beatrice is not Eurydice. Even if, dazzled and confounded, the poet cannot endure the sunlight of her eyes, he need not—unlike Orpheus—turn away from his beloved.

> "O lady, in whom my hope is strong, and who for my salvation did endure to leave in Hell your footprints, of all those things which I have seen I acknowledge the grace and the virtue to be from your power and your experience. It is you who have drawn me from bondage to liberty by all those paths, by all those means by which you had the power so to do. Preserve in me your great munificence, so that my soul, which you have made whole, may be loosed from the body, pleasing unto you." So did I pray; and

she, so distant as she seemed, smiled and looked on me, then turned again to the eternal fountain. (*Paradise*, XXXI, 79–93)

Here, in the thirty-first canto of Paradise, in a parting scene that throbs with restrained emotion, the poet's wanderings reach their end. The two final cantos are purely descriptive, though the thirty-third canto opens with an oration to the Blessed Virgin. Spoken by Saint Bernard, who has "taken the place" of Beatrice at the pilgrim's side, its function is clearly to generalize the unceasing prayer uttered to his beloved. But if the Virgin is to the human race what Beatrice is to the poet, she loses in intensity what she has gained in breadth. Though he may wish to endow it with universality, his own love, distilled from earthly dust, is what Dante has come to seek out.

Abruptly, this transubstantiation invests the descent into Hell with meaning. By a deft substitution, Dante suggests that in accompanying him in thought on his infernal peregrinations, Beatrice herself has suffered for having left her footprints behind. That which is thus redeemed suddenly becomes much more than the mere fault of the poet: it is all that which, on both sides, became an obstacle to their love. This obstacle need neither be named nor sought in the biography of the protagonists. It is earthly life itself, of which Hell is the representation. To descend into Hell is to confront the hideous realities from which human beings believe they can escape astride vain pleasures. Hence the poet's suggestion, at the very end, that they have followed one another in the descent, though at a distance. Beatrice cannot wield her redemptive powers except in her foreknowledge of the sorrowful, distressing realities of the world. Both must understand the world in which they could not join together, says Dante, and thus agree to enter into it, and to fix their gaze upon it. It is only when they are rid of their worldly vanities that the lovers may truly discover one another. Beatrice admonishes the poet *as a lover* for having taken so long to grasp the fact. Her admonitions seem too severe at first, but they are nothing in comparison to the truth that follows them, when Virgil's earlier promise to his companion consigned to Hell comes to pass:

"When you are before her sweet radiance whose fair eyes see all, from her you shall know of your life's journey." (*Inferno*, X, 130–132)

The glow that, to this day, radiates from the *Comedy* is the warmth of love. Each time she who occupies the thoughts and the gaze of the poet is invoked, a tender light gleams. Each of these few instants (hardly more than twenty, some of them quite brief, others longer) resonates with a singular sense of the genuine—in a poem where beauty is hardly lacking. These auspicious moments are also, for the most part, those in which the poet's lyricism is at its most restrained, most solemn, most poignant. Solemn, too, is the presence of Beatrice, who appears in person only at the end of the *Purgatory*. Dante's immense love poem has lent its object the rarity without which it would be less precious. Though absent for the better part of the time *because* she is absent, Beatrice exercises an irresistible attraction that draws us, as it has drawn the narrator, toward her smile.

If we take Dante's trilogy as a poem of love, God then must be seen as the metaphor for love purified by death, and Christian dogma as spiritual elevation's ideological armature. Once the passion for Beatrice casts off its carnal (and deceptive, says Dante) weight and acquires redemptive value, Christian mediation becomes the only refuge, for one excellent reason: in the sphere of the absolute where the poet has located it, there can be no other legitimacy. The Dantean enterprise is so audacious—it flirts with the blasphemous substitution of Beatrice for the Virgin—that orthodoxy must be more than scrupulously respected. The poet goes a step further: extreme doctrinal rigidity suits the poet's political intentions by making it possible for him to confound the ecclesiastical hierarchy without adverse impact on the idealized expression of his feelings. Paradoxically, it is his impeccable—and undoubtedly genuine—fidelity to the teachings of the Church that gives Dante full freedom of judgement and speech. But the paradox is in our eyes alone, for we confuse the Church with its institutions and with the repression that they have inevitably exercised throughout their long history.

Within the framework of Catholic theology as tempered and reinvigorated by the "Angelic Doctor" (Thomas Aquinas), the *Comedy*, written in the vulgate (as opposed to the Latin of the educated classes), is the poetic expression of freedom of conscience. Its freedom is not tragic; the *Comedy* ends happily; the narrator blazes his own trail to the truth. He succeeds, of course, with the aid of Virgil and, to an even greater degree, thanks to Beatrice, but with no assistance from the priests and institutions that have betrayed their mission. In choosing for himself guides from outside of the Church, the poet demonstrates his independence. And though his pride may seem overweening, he affirms the individuality and the oneness of his path. Truth is one, indivisible—though triple—but man is free to hew to it or to turn away, free to choose among the numerous paths that lead to it, free to go astray in the forest of the world by persisting in his ignorance of the dark, infernal forces that rule over it. Dante himself could not immediately grasp the full extent of the grace descended upon him from Beatrice's eyes. Such is necessity: she has first to die that he might make up for her loss in some other way, that he will attempt to retrieve her beauty in the bodies of others only to understand, through the sense of shame he experiences with these poor replacements, that the physical attraction of the beloved is the starting point of a superior necessity. It is, in fact, the mirror of a loftier, remoter beauty, which can only be gained after a long, hard struggle against oneself—the descent into Hell. It is a descent that the poet denies to persons without character, to "these wretches who never were alive" (*Inferno*, III, 64) for whom he cannot find words harsh enough, and whom he hurls down into the vermin that teem in the antechamber of Hell.

Truth exists and it is Christian: of this there can be no doubt. But how it manifests itself to each of us remains a mystery. Dante relates his own mystery. His mystery has a name, a face that, in dying, invites him to follow it beyond the flesh. It may well be that all beings receive, without necessarily being able to capture or to comprehend it, the hidden call of beauty, that ephemeral spark of eternity amid the falsehood that is the world. The mystery is that of grace, which neither poet nor theologian can elucidate. But the poet, better than the theologian, can capture the instant of illumination. He can rescue it from oblivion and, in so doing, decisively alter the way in which his reader sees the world. Dante pours all his art into the unique and irreplaceable testimony that he lays at the feet of his readers. He tells us that through the beauty of a vanished woman he has learned how to travel the road of life. We should not be surprised that the flesh should efface itself, and that the memory of her face shed beauty upon all that the wears of the world has fatally withered. More than Beatrice, death has set him on beauty's path. Beautiful is the truth; loving the gaze that leads us to it.

For all that, the poet's gaze brings with it the nostalgia of the flesh. Purified though it is, Beatrice's celestial beauty remains too powerfully felt not to elicit the dream of an embrace. Of course, the poet is careful not to give voice to such a dream, but he cannot stop it from hanging there, shimmering, between the lines. As he aspires to become one with the soul of the woman he loves, Dante attempts—an effort as subtle as it is magnificent—to fuse *eros* and *agapé*, Platonic love and Christian love— which we know, contrary to received opinion, to be quite different. The poet's conclusion, in all sincerity, and perhaps in ignorance, is that such a marriage is impossible. Leaving her lover at the threshold of the heavenly throne, Beatrice goes off to meet the Rose of Heaven in all its total remoteness. Neither the Virgin nor God can bridge the chasm of ultimate separation. Only with high tension, behind a façade of serenity, does *agapé* resign itself to parting with *eros*; only with great regret does the poet resolve to leave behind forever the tender ardors of the body, to forgo the salt of life for the definitive illumination of death.

The dialogue between the immanence of all that is perishable and the transcendence of all that is eternal can carry on into infinity. For all its salt, life has no meaning other than in the hereafter whose occasional reflection it reveals—the very reflection that the poet captures in the eye of his beloved, the reflection that transports him into that other world to which the things of this world appear base and worthless. But it is of this muddy world that the poet speaks—despite his knowledge, despite his hopes in the radiance of heaven. Having one's head above the clouds does not keep one's feet warm. No matter how high the spirit may soar, it can never take flight except by setting its feet firmly in the world below that nourishes it and to which it remains deeply attached, like a kite to the hand that has launched it, until death cuts the string. In like manner the transport to paradise does not bring the poet full detachment from the affairs of the world. Dante's hopes for an imperial restoration are not erased by divine expectation; in fact, they are reflected in it.

We must remember that, for Dante, the two worlds are not cut off from one another. On the contrary, the narrator's voyage confirms that they are one: earth, hell, purgatory and heaven are joined in a continuous vision of the universe. It is only that truth does not possess in all its parts the same brilliance, and can shine in full splendor only in proximity to God. Between the darkness of hell and the brightness of paradise, there is no discontinuity. God's will reigns in hell as it does in heaven: it casts down into obscurity those who have scorned light. And as for life, which is neither paradise nor hell, it is that ill-defined zone only half-illuminated by truth, and in whose faint light everything is played out for each one of us. In the half-light the poet learns—and teaches us—to read the signs. But the flickering flame that allows us to read them has been snuffed out by the onrush of ultimate truth. Truth has ceased to be a possibility open to everyone and become a certainty all must accept. Is this a necessary compromise, or profound belief in dogma? I cannot pretend to know. Something in the grandiloquence of the final scene rings false, as if theological truth must be displayed as triumph. But the scene also reminds us of the profound paradox of faith: Christian dogma and free will endlessly trade the same arguments in an unending play of mirrors.

The intent of Dante's story is far from single-minded. In perhaps the most obvious sense—as in Saint Augustine's *Confessions* and the Arthurian legend of the Grail, but on a far grander scale—the *Comedy* accomplishes what philosophy has always dreamed of. Borne on wings of faith, the poem soars far beyond the truth to which philosophy aspires. "The evidence of that not seen" (*Paradise*, XXIV, 22), the magnificent definition of faith that Dante hammers out drawing on Paul (Heb. 11:1), allows him to *state* what philosophers can only *speculate* on. Suddenly it becomes clear how radically the triumph of Christianism, by abolishing doubt, annihilates with the same blow the plurality of meaning. The identity, omnipresent and invisible, that permeates the Christian narrative, from the Gospel to the *Comedy*—justly called divine by the poet's contemporaries—is single-faceted and immutable. But since it is located only in God, only in an afterlife that remains inaccessible to mortals, it cannot inhabit humans except as hope and expectation; or as threat for those who reject it. Free will becomes the freedom to choose between two poles: negative and positive; between acceptance and rejection of the only possible revelation. From this choice, like the sword of Damocles, death hangs suspended. Death, as horrible as it is definitive, is the certain reward of him who is excluded from truth—the death that our Western civilization, particularly now that the path of salvation has been lost to us, seems less able than ever to accept with serenity.

The promise of truth elevated to identitarian necessity repulses death. As he dies, the believer travels toward his own eternity, like Dante toward Paradise; while the unbeliever, the heretic, the apostate, the pagan, perishes irrevocably in his hell. The radical otherness of violent death gathers in all imaginable "others," all that self-certainty has driven away, including the secret portion that certainty itself denies. Dante begins by "abandoning all hope" at the threshold of his painful descent into this, the unavowed part of himself: if the *Inferno* today remains the most troubling panel of his triptych, it is because it embodies another truth to be explored, a truth that is not at all celestial, yet to which the poet lends his entire weight. "Good" truth can only be had at the price of the "bad," as Dante reminds us so ceaselessly. But an exclusively Christian reading of the *Comedy* cannot easily grasp the Socratic imperative to know oneself. The hell—or its opposite—of truth can neither be explored nor understood. As a locus of sin and eternal punishment, hell is transformed into something to be avoided, or expelled from ourselves at all costs. Under the threat of this expulsion, love of truth leads to hatred of the Other, to the abjectness of the death to which that other is explicitly condemned.

Dante speaks, despite himself, of the irreducible distance that separates Platonic erotics from the Christian conception of salvation, where love of one's neighbor has little tolerance for differences. Such love has little or no place in the *Comedy*, which is focused on the personal progress of a narrator torn between a lover's dream and an imperial vision. The attraction of the two opposites seems to nullify the communal space in which love of one's neighbor might flourish. Love of one's neighbor is possible only through the universal extension of the Eucharist that bound the original sect together. This extended space, the achievement of the Roman Empire which "Christian" popes and princes are doing their utmost to destroy, lies in ruins. Faced with the moral and political collapse that threatens the immense whole of Christendom, the believer may well be forced to fall back upon himself for his own salvation. As an incarnation of the necessity of individual inspiration Beatrice, as a perfect looking glass, a person in whom amorous passion and divine expectation meet, is far more vital than the Church.

The figure of Beatrice leads us in another direction, less immediately visible than that of Christian dogma, but probably more powerful and, above all, much more likely to speak to us today. Following in the footsteps of the tales of Tristan and Lancelot, but trading the sword for the quill, the *Comedy* resituates the locus of truth, and does so without openly calling Christian dogma into question. Once collective, this locus has now become individual. With increasing clarity, the quest for truth becomes the quest for oneself. The individual quest had been, to a certain extent, that of Saint Augustine. With the difference that Augustine cannot find himself, as he confesses having long attempted to do, outside the Christian community. He stands in intense need of God's help. The help Dante resorts to is, contrariwise, both earthly and carnal, no matter how sublimated Beatrice is. But the last resort is in fact literature, poetry itself, personified by Virgil and, finally, Dante's poem itself: writing as act.

If the poet possesses the formidable power to body forth the world in his language, it would come as no surprise were he, like Virgil in the *Aeneid*, to contribute, in the relating of his dreams, to the making of history. Virgil, when he crowns Augustus with the numinous wreath of legend, justifies and magnifies the emperor in full knowledge. Dante and the storytellers of the Celtic cycle unconsciously prepare Europe for adventure, and herald the spirit of the modern West. The adventure will be an archaic one, and it will overturn the world. It will turn upon a quest at once utopian and concrete that will inaugurate a new era as it fulfils the ancient myth, now given Christian form, of the promised land: the conquest of America. I cannot help thinking that truth, the Grail, and paradise, the inaccessible object of Christendom's chivalrous, amorous and poetic quest, combine to find their historic fulfilment in the discovery, for Europe, of a new continent—and that the man who incarnates it, like the intrepid knight, gives every appearance of having done so on his own. Individual exploit will become the threshold and the symbol of a new civilization.

Whether Christopher Columbus knew he had discovered a new continent, or whether he did not[117] is of secondary importance. His uncertainty changes not a whit the spirit that guided him. Standing at the point where two historical moments in Christianity intersect, Cristobal Colon is simultaneously the last of the Crusaders and the first of the modern-day adventurers. The Grand Admiral of the Ocean Sea, in his address to his Most Christian sponsors, leaves no doubt that he will be setting sail at the very moment when, in 1492, with the fall of Grenada, the war against the Moors has come to a victorious end and the expulsion of the Jews from Spain has begun. Their Catholic Majesties Isabelle and Ferdinand have dispatched him "to the so-said land of the Indies ... by the way of the West" in his capacity as a "foe of the sect of Mahomet and of all idol worship and heresy."[118]

It is hardly a coincidence that the eviction of the Jews, the first act in a long effort to eradicate all that was not authentically Christian from the Iberian Peninsula, began at the same time as the colonial adventure. In fact, it had immense symbolic significance. If the West expelled the Jews, it could only be to seize definitively from them the status of the chosen people that for centuries Christendom had claimed for itself against them. Not for nothing did Columbus sign his letters *Christo Ferrens*, "he who bears Christ." Just as Robert de Boron's Merlin transferred the blood of Christ from East to West, Columbus carried the Cross farther westward still, toward the new promised land of the far West, whose inhabitants today believe themselves more than ever before to be the elect of the planet: a purely imaginary continuity, of course, but no less effective for being so. Columbus, precisely because this construct of the Western imagination had a greater impact on him than upon most of his contemporaries, took risks, and ventured where more experienced navigators dared not. As Michel Lequenne writes, the discovery of the New World called for an "adventurer of the spirit."[119] The admiral stood apart from his peers precisely in his mysticism and in his prophetic powers. All of which allows me to add, with a smile, that

117. Today, the thesis of ignorance is difficult to credit; Columbus was quite aware of the importance of his discovery.
118. Christophe Colomb, *La découverte de l'Amérique* (Paris: La Découverte, 1991), p. 32.
119. Michel Lequenne, introduction to Christophe Colomb, *La découverte de l'Amérique*, op.cit., p.18.

Columbus, *Christo Ferrens*, is a kind of Perceval who has stepped into history, the conquering spear-point of a genealogy founded by Virgil, sanctified by the Church, and sung by the Celtic cycles.

The man whose discovery was taken from him and who lived out his days in relative obscurity can, for all his ill fortune, boast a name more illustrious and better known than all those who were to follow (including Amerigo Vespucci, whom most people cannot even identify as the man who gave his name to the new world). His renown derives not simply from the magnitude of his accomplishment, nor from the fact of being first (the first known, in any event) to have travelled that route. His reputation as the first discoverer owes just as much to the fact that, for us, he represents the living connection, in a real individual, between the myth and the history that have fashioned the West's imaginary self. He is, in one sense, the tangible confirmation that our civilization has long been following the right path, on the path of the truth promulgated by the Church, and that it alone can cross into that place of sorrow where the sun sets, that is, conquer death's very dominion.

Part Five

SUDDENLY, DOUBT

RABELAIS, CERVANTES, SHAKESPEARE, AND DESCARTES stand as four heroic signposts lining the pathway of truth, each pointing to a break with what had come before. Pantagruel and his companions eat, drink, and carouse their way through life seen as a valley of tears in which no authority can resist their joyous laughter. That anachronistic, ill-armed hero Don Quixote strikes out at all certainties: the idea of reality itself shudders beneath the blows of his crooked lance. Hamlet, in a more lugubrious vein, meditates upon the absence of God: if there is no truth, he cannot act to discharge his duty of revenge. Heroism becomes unthinkable.

In the face of mounting uncertainty, Descartes, that hero of thought, lays hold of doubt, sets it in a narrative and transforms it into his trump card: methodical doubt is the lever by which truth can be pried from nothingness, a truth that is stronger and yet weaker, but distinctly other. A modern truth is struggling to replace the old. But the dawn of this new enlightenment already prefigures its twilight.

13

THE MAGIC LANTERN

R ABELAIS MAY NOT always make us laugh. But even when he is not joking, he is never serious. Seriousness runs off him like water from a duck's back. Monstrous exaggerations, merry pranks, unexpected turn-abouts, racy episodes, crude language, grotesque incongruities, and endless drinking bouts: all are part of his stock in trade. For the erudite, the pedants, the academics, and other masters of the pretentious, his bill of fare is supremely repulsive. From verbal diarrhea to word fights, from farting contests to spoonerisms, from outright inanity to the most prodigious fabrications, the narrator of *Pantagruel*[120] thwarts the boldest attempt at learned interpretation, undermines every "lesson" before it starts. He hews strictly to the facts and faithfully limits himself to what he has seen: "I speak like St. John in the Apocalypse: *Quod vidimis testamur*"[121] (*Pantagruel*, prol., 169). Thus begins an ironical relationship with truth to which he fully intends to testify—an irony that the "wretched devils plagued by pox and gout" will oblige him to temper in subsequent editions. The narrator indeed wishes to tell things as they are, but not at the cost of his own skin: his tale will go only as far as "the teeth of hellfire" (*Pantagruel*, prol., 168). Tragedy be damned!

The spectacle of such an outpouring of joyous nonsense can only cause us to wonder by what enchantment Rabelais, whose work has enjoyed an almost uninterrupted success down to the present day, came to be considered, along with Montaigne, as one of the two "great" French prose writers of the

---

120. Chronologically speaking, *Pantagruel* is the first book written by Rabelais. In all editions of his work including those published during his lifetime, *Gargantua*, though it was written after *Pantagruel*, logically heads up the five books that make up his oeuvre. The *Tiers*, *Quart* and *Cinquisiesme livre*, though written after *Gargantua*, continue the tale of Pantagruel. But *Pantagruel* cannot be seen as a sequel to *Gargantua* even though, from a narrative viewpoint, the son follows the father genealogically.
121. "We relate what we have seen."

sixteenth century, or even as one of the giants of all French literature? For here we are speaking of a literature dominated from the ensuing century on by a ponderous classicism at whose heavy hand it narrowly escaped suffocation. For all its majesty, however, French classicism was unable to devalue the unrestrained writing that gives every appearance of having rejected its splendid equilibrium before the fact. *The Mighty and Inestimable Chronicles of the Huge Giant Gargantua* and *The Heroic Deeds and Words of Good Pantagruel* provided the French reader with thick slabs of bawdiness where a part of the national self-image would certainly feel at home. But self-satisfaction alone can explain neither the long-lasting nor the sweeping nature of their success. No matter how "Gallic" he may be, Rabelais's renown has far outstripped the boundaries of his native land. There is something about him, behind the foolishness, despite the crude mixing of styles, that forces our respect, and makes him an object of admiration. Without that "something" he would simply be gross, incoherent, uninteresting and probably, like so many jesters of lesser calibre, would have fallen into oblivion. Rabelais is the most human, the most vital of humanists; his ferocious humor brims with tenderness. But perhaps it is also because he knows that he finds himself, a child of the age of the printing press and of the great expeditions, at a historical turning point. Today, his *oeuvre* gives every appearance of standing at a crossroads whose importance we can only judge from the comfort of hindsight. Rabelais seems to be telling the Europe of his day of a path quite different from that which the hunger for the far-away and the thirst for conquest were leading it: the tortuous, unpredictable, multi-colored roadway where, so close at hand and yet so often dismissed, the wonderment of life awaits us.

Mining the rich vein of vivid farce that still flourished in his era, Rabelais, a son of good family from Touraine with a solid grounding in Greek and Latin, transforms our silk purses into sows' ears. But for all their laughable guise, our physician of pranks contrives to fill these purses with purest gold.

Master Alcofribas, "abstractor of quint essence," furnishes first-hand instructions for use of his medicine. First, and briefly, in the introduction to the *Pantagruel*, which, though it styles itself as a panacea against sadness, ennui, and pain, is quick to inform that the little gaieties that calm the pangs of gout or of the pox have "greater profit in them than a rabble of critics would have you believe" (*Pantagruel*, prol., 167). Then later, at greater length, in the author's prologue to *Gargantua*, Rabelais invests all his vitality and all his impertinence in making clear his pedagogical intentions. For a full taste of his piquancy, one must read the prologue from beginning to end:

Hail, O most valiant and illustrious drinkers! Your health, my precious pox-ridden comrades! To you alone, I dedicate my writings. Suffer me, therefore, to draw your attention to a dialogue of Plato's called the Banquet.

In this work, Alcibiades, praising his master Socrates (undoubtedly the prince of philosophers), happens, among other things, to liken him to sileni.

Sileni, in the days of yore, were small boxes such as you may see nowadays at your apothecary's. They were named for Silenus, foster father to Bacchus. The outside of these boxes bore gay, fantastically painted figures of harpies, satyrs, bridled geese, hares with gigantic horns, saddled ducks, winged goats in flight, harts in harness and many other droll fancies. They were pleasurably devised to inspire just the sort of laughter Silenus, Bacchus' master, inspired.

But inside these sileni, people kept priceless drugs such as balsam of Mecca, ambergris from the sperm whale, ammonium from the cardamom, musk from the deer and civet from the civet's arsehole—not to mention various sorts of precious stones, used for medical purposes, and other invaluable possessions.

Well, Alcibiades likened Socrates to these boxes, because, judging by his exterior, you would not have given an onionskin for him. He was pill-shaped, ridiculous in carriage, with a nose like a knife, the gaze of a bull and the face of a fool. His ways stamped him a simpleton, his clothes a bumpkin. Poor in fortune, unlucky when it came to women, hopelessly unfit for all office in the republic, forever laughing, forever drinking neck and neck with his friends, forever hiding his divine knowledge under a mask of mockery ...

Yet had you opened this box, you would have found in it all sorts of priceless, celestial drugs: immortal understanding, wondrous virtue, indomitable courage, unparalleled sobriety, unfailing serenity, perfect assurance and a heroic contempt for whatever moves humanity to watch, to bustle, to toil, to sail ships overseas and to engage in warfare.

Alcibiades? Socrates? The sileni? Why all this introductory flourish? Let me explain to you only, O my beloved disciples, and to such other idlers and idiots as read my works. Having noted the flippant titles of certain books of my invention—Gargantua, Pantagruel, Drownbottle, The Dignity of Codpieces and

Trouserflies, Of Peas and Bacon, with Tables and Sauce Material, etc.—you jump to the conclusion that these tomes are filled with mere jests, vulgarities and buffoonery. Alas! You leap at the outward and visible sign; you swallow the title in a spirit of levity and derision without pausing to make further inquiry. How unseemly to consider so frivolously the works of humankind! Is it you who profess that clothes do not make the man nor robes the monk? Do I quote you when I declare that a fellow most monasterially apparelled may turn out to be a downright infidel whereas another draped in a Spanish cloak, may possess every virtue on earth except Castilian pride and daring? Well then, you see why you should look beyond my title, open my book and seriously weigh its subject matter. The spice secreted within the box is more precious, far, than its exterior promised. In other words, the topics treated are not so foolish as the title suggested at first hand.

Again, supposing you find enough tomfoolery to live up to the title, must you tarry there, as Ulysses tarried at the song of the sirens? Certainly not. Instead, you should lend a loftier sense to what you first believed written in the exuberance of humor.

Have you ever uncorked a bottle of wine? God help us, do you remember the look on your face?

Or have you ever seen a dog fall on a marrowbone? (The dog, I might add, is, as Plato says in Book II of the *Republic*, the most philosophical beast in the world.) If you have seen my dog, you may recall how intently he scrutinizes his bone, how solicitously he guards it, how fervently he clutches it, how warily he bites his way into it, how passionately he breaks it, how diligently he sucks it. What forces move him to act so, what hopes foster such zealous pains, what recompense does he aspire to? Nothing but a little marrow. (To be sure, this is no more toothsome than large quantities of any other meat, for—as Galen testifies in Chapter III of his *Concerning the Natural Faculties*, and Chapter XI of *Concerning the Uses of the Various Parts of the Human Body*— marrow is the most perfect food elaborated by nature.)

Modelling yourself upon the dog, you should be wise to scent, to feel, and to prize these fine, full-flavored volumes. You should be fleet in your pursuit of them, resolute in your attack. Then, by diligent reading and prolonged meditation, you should break the bone of my symbols to suck out the marrow of my meaning—for I make use of allegory as freely as Pythagoras did. As you read, you must confidently expect to become valiant and wise. For here you will find a novel savior, a most abstruse doctrine; here you will learn the deepest mysteries, the most agonizing problems of our religion, our body politic, our economic life.

Do you honestly believe that Homer, penning his *Iliad* or *Odyssey*, ever dreamed of the allegorical patchwork subsequently inflicted upon him by Plutarch, by Heraclides Ponticus, by Eustathius, by Cornutus the Stoic, or by Politian, the Italian who filched his criticism from the lot of them?

If you do, you are miles away from my opinion, for I hold that Homer no more dreamed of all this allegorical fustian than Ovid in his Metamorphoses dreamed of the Gospel. Yet whenever he met folk as witless as himself, a certain Friar Jabbernowl, a true glutton for bacon and misinformation, strove to establish the Christianity of Ovid. Fit lids, that audience, for such a pot, say I, quoting the old saw.

If you agree with the Friar, why refuse the same consideration to my own original mirthful chronicles? Yes, even though I, writing them, gave the matter no more thought than you, who were probably also drinking. I may add that in composing this masterpiece I have spent or wasted more leisure than is required for my bodily refection—food and drink to you! Is that not the proper time to commit to the page such sublime themes and such profound wisdom? Homer, the paragon of all philologists, knew it perfectly well and Ennius also, the father of the Latin poets, as Horace testifies, though a certain sorry clown has said that his poems smelled more of wine than of oil.

So, too, spoke a third-rate cynic about my books, but a ripe turd to the fellow! Oh, the sweet fragrance of wine! How much more reconciling, smiling and beguiling wine is than oil! Let the world say I spent more on wine than on oil: I shall glory in it, like Demosthenes when they accused him of the opposite. For my part, I consider it honorable and noble to be reputed a sportsman and a wit, for as such as I am welcome wherever two or three Pantagruelists are gathered together. Did not a certain surly bore denounce Demosthenes because his Orations smelled like a filthy rag in an oilcan? No so, I!

Accordingly, take in perfect part all I write and do; revere the cheese-shaped brain, which feeds you this noble flummery; strive diligently to keep me ever jocund.

And now, my hearties, be gay, and gaily read the rest, with ease of body and in the best of kidney! And you, donkey-pizzles, hark!—may a canker rot you!—remember to drink to me gallantly, and I will with a toast at once![122]

In the prologue to the *Pantagruel*, Master Alcofribas dedicates his merry pranks to those "most illustrious and most valorous champions, gentlemen and all others who delight in honest entertainment and wit" (*Pantagruel*, prol., 167). Here, in the prologue to *Gargantua*, the master addresses himself, quite philosophically, to drunkards and syphilitics. In their total physical disarray, these unfortunates can only rejoice at the idea that the illustrious Socrates was hardly better than they are, and swill down Alcibiades' orations like a fine vintage, thrilled that the vilest container can conceal the most precious content. The same can be said of the book dedicated to them, *Gargantua*: written expressly for them, in their image, malformed on the outside, divine on the inside.

A second Platonic wink follows hot on the heels of the first. Like dogs, elbow-benders are philosophers by nature. Here, the very authority of Socrates is invoked. But a malicious slippage of meaning has taken place. The young thoroughbred dog that Socrates proposes as a model for the guardians of the ideal city is a philosopher in that he is able to distinguish between those persons familiar and unfamiliar to him; such an attitude implies a love of knowledge—*philo-sophia* in the literal sense (*Republic*, 375e–376b). With Rabelais, the Socratic analogy takes a farcical and all the truer turn: what makes the dog the paragon of philosophers is that he holds fast to his bone like a drunkard to his bottle. Both know the true value of the object of their jealous attention. The whiff of marrow with which Rabelais hopes to tempt his readers is given a stature equal to wine, which can be said to represent—along with the contents of the codpiece—the unchanging value of the Pantagruelian pentalogue. Buffoonery is ever ready to reassert itself.

Only alluded to, the true marrow of substance itself is held up to ridicule, compared to the "symbols of Pythagoras" and, in an amalgam of blasphemous irony, compared to the "deepest mysteries and the most agonizing problems" of religion, politics, and the economy. We have been warned: we, like the learned commentators of Homer and Ovid, can hope to gain nothing from unending annotation; the shred of knowledge that we can hope to extract by gnawing on the Gargantuan bone is insignificant, laughable—in other words, inversely proportional to the size of its heroes.

---

122. François Rabelais, *The Five Books of Gargantua and Pantagruel*, trans. Jacques Le Clercq (New York: The Modern Library, c1944), pp. 3–6.

And for the dullest-witted of all, the narrator adds that he wrote his book while drinking and carousing.

In many ways, the prologue to *Gargantua* is a condensation. It quite precisely prefigures the spirit and the letter of the Pantagruelian *magnum opus*. Or to put it in slightly different terms, it establishes *distance*. Taken by itself, the prologue—as we have already seen, though in a less lighthearted mode, in Chrétien de Troyes—is a wink from the narrator to the reader: a way of underlining the writer's presence with a display of detachment, accentuated by laughter. Writing, as jest, puts distance between itself and the world in a century whose hallmark is adventure. Impertinence, the characteristic of the Rabelaisian narrative, has acquired a historical dimension. It bursts forth at an exceptional moment, which compels our full attention.

If we look closely at the differences between Dante's world and that of Rabelais, we can identify some of the points of contrast between the two eras—the low Middle Ages and the Renaissance—that overlap as much as they stand apart. A sharp and radical shift, as everybody knows, took place in Europe between 1450 and 1550. Rabelais was among the eyewitnesses. Born in 1494, two years after Christopher Columbus's first transatlantic crossing, and died in 1553, he was a contemporary of Jacques Cartier (1491–1557), who set out to find the fabulous North-west passage and ended up exploring the St. Lawrence River in 1534, the very year when *Gargantua* was published. Exploration of the New World followed shortly after the rediscovery—artistic and intellectual—of the ancient, a coincidence that was to leave an indelible imprint on the European conception of time and space. Western Europe began to conceive of itself, in both historical and geographical terms, as the pivotal point between Antiquity and the future, between the eastern basin of the Mediterranean and ultra-Atlantic vastness.

It was a sense of self that needed time to take root, and we are courting anachronism if we project upon the "West Indies" all that we know today of the Americas. Early on, from 1507 in fact, the new name and, with it, the idea of a new world, had gained wide currency. In 1520, Magellan passed through the strait that would bear his name: the roundness of the Earth became historical reality, a yawning chasm snapped closed. In one single movement the horizon turned in upon itself and broadened. The reassuring enclosure of terrestrial space whetted the appetite for adventure. Adventure did not need to be imagined; it had henceforth become possible, no longer limited to Dante's fanciful after-life, nor to the Arthurian universe of marvels, but open to the here and now of this world, with all its new promises: land, gold, slaves.

No need to bring down a verdict here on the amply debated question of non-belief in Rabelais's century.[123] It would be singularly ill-advised to describe as generally irreligious the era that witnessed the spread of the Reformation. It is enough to observe that in society's most dynamic strata the spiritual had receded, that it no longer occupied the same mind space as before. The shift was fraught with conflict, and was to cause fractures that troubled the Church. But the Church joined in the movement, throwing itself into the evangelization of the Indians and the "savages," an undertaking that touched off dangerous controversies on the plurality and relativity of beliefs.[124] As greater value was shifted away from the spiritual to the earthly adventure, the intolerance of the religious hierarchy, both Catholic and Protestant, was sharpened. Neither without risk nor good reason did Rabelais wax ironical on the fires of the inquisition.

But we would be wrong to conclude, either from his irony or his flagrant disrespect for ecclesiastical institutions, that he was an unbeliever.[125] It may even be precisely because he was so profoundly devout that the good doctor wielded with such overwhelming joviality a sense of derision, which, the king of France aside, spared nothing and no man. Like the explorers, the sea captains, the merchants, and the missionaries who so richly peopled his century, his hero belongs to the seething, bubbling world in which his narrator is immersed. But his *joie de vivre* is no blind replicate of his contemporaries' ambitions. As Pantagruel loves life, so he loathes everything in human stupidity that needlessly weighs it down, holds it back. Keenly aware of the new possibilities being revealed day by day, Rabelais, a passionate eye-witness to the great explorations that would so powerfully alter the face and mind of Europe and construct the "West," whose self-image we are attempting to bring to book, holds out to us the promise of adventure of another kind altogether.

The exploits of Pantagruel and Gargantua are cast in the shape of a rough spiral that stretches from the Pichrocholine wars—whose cramped and familiar theater, the region of Chinon, the narrator's homeland, provided his protagonists with a preposterous sense of disproportion—then broadens its

123. See Lucien Febvre's classic *Le problème de l'incroyance au 16e siècle: La religion de Rabelais* (Paris: Albin Michel, « L'évolution de l'humanité », 1942, 1968).

124. Tzvetan Todorov, *La conquête de l'Amérique, La question de l'autre* (Paris: Seuil, 1982).

125. It must be born in mind that our subject is not Rabelais the man, who must remain unfathomable, but the oeuvre, the story, and its potential "charge." In any event, this chapter cannot be seen as anything other than our reading.

sweep to the ultramarine expedition in pursuit of drink in some remote island of a fantasy-land Atlantic, by way of the less-distant though equally indefinable land of the Amaurotes (by way of allusion to Thomas More's *Utopia*) whom the Dipsodes, the thirsty folk whom Pantagruel will ultimately vanquish and rule over as king, are attempting to conquer. Rabelais's spiral, after a consultation with the ethylic oracle, will return straight to its point of departure. There can be little doubt that its curious itinerary hews close to the process of composition, a process that at first has no specific objective.[126] The objective, the sacred wine bottle and its sovereign female pontiff Bacbuc, makes its appearance only in the *Tiers Livre*, after Panurge has exhausted, to no avail, all the advice and all the available authorities in an attempt to decide whether or not he should wed. The grotesque disparity between the expedition and what it hopes to achieve—the answer to a problem that one can only solve for oneself—raises to the Pantegruelian power the question that pervades the entire tale, and for which marriage stands as an allegory: the question of knowledge and, more precisely, the question of how to lead one's life—a substantive and distinctly Socratic piece of marrow.

The sudden appearance of the figure of Panurge and his haunting matrimonial obsession is of capital importance. Prior to his entrance, knowledge is approached from a rather classic point of view—even though the concept of scientific experiment has already made an audacious breakthrough in the episode where Grangousier the father praises his prodigious son: "O my splendid little boy ... you are wise beyond your years! Meanwhile, proceed with the scutscouring you told me of ..." Following upon a series of experiments each one more thorough than the preceding, the young Gargantua lays before his father his inescapable conclusion:

> "But to conclude: I affirm and maintain that the paragon of arse-cloth is the neck of a plump, downy goose, provided you hold her head between your legs. Take my word of honor on this score and try it for yourself. You will experience a most marvellously pleasant sensation in the region of the scutnozzle, as much because of the fluffy under plumage as because the bird's warmth, termpering the bumgut and the rest of the intestines, actually reaches your heart and brain." (*Gargantua*, XIII, 46)

---

126. The narrator of the *Tiers livre* is no longer quite the same as that of *Pantagruel*. The tone and the subject of the narration have shifted, adapting themselves to the narrative flow.

And he goes on to invoke Maistre Jehan d'Escosse (the celebrated philosopher Duns Scotus) in support of his theory. Grandgoussier compares his son's down-to-earth common sense with that of the young Alexander when he realized that the skittishness of his horse was due to its fright at the sight of its shadow. So perspicacious, so profound does he find the lad that he is certain that Gargantua "will attain a supreme degree of wisdom" (*Gargantua*, XIC, 47). But, lo and behold, things are not so simple as they seem, and the various pedagogical experiments—not to mention other kinds—which Gargantua performs in Paris provide more than abundant material for ridicule.

The same can be said of Pantagruel. Having shattered his cradle and thus cast off the chains used by adults to fetter childhood, he tours the universities of France. Aside from those of Poitiers and Bourges, from which he contrives to profit, they are remarkable for the gambling that flourishes within their walls, by their ritual bonfires, by their innumerable feasts and orgies—when the stench of the professors does not destroy the pleasures of the palate and the flesh. Pantagruel, "fearful lest he strain his eyes ... took good care not to study too hard." (*Pantagruel*, V, 190), and all the less so since very little studying is needed to obtain a degree.

On his arrival in the capital, Pantagruel discovers the wealth of the library of Saint Victor, whose interminable catalogue (*Cobbler or Pierre Cordonnier, a Doctor of the Sorbonne, against Whatever Consorted with Scoundrels and why Scoundrels are not damned by the Church ... Cacatorium medicorum, Of the Medical Dungers ... The Chimney Sweep of Astrology ... The Fields of Enemas by S.C. or Syphorien Champier, a Doctor of Lyons ... The Poopdrawer of Apothecaries ... The Arsekisser of Surgery ... Justinianus: De cagotis tollendis, Of the Toleration of Bigots, by Justinian*, to give only the slenderest of samplings) provides eloquent proof of the narrator's opinion of such a prestigious accumulation of knowledge. Scholasticism is not the only target of Rabelais's mockery. His irony strips away the varnish of pedantry so fashionable at the time and, along with it, its nasty veneer of ancient culture: at Orleans, close to the gates of Paris, Pantagruel encounters a Limousin who, in an attempt to pass himself off as a Parisian, prattles on in an incomprehensible French larded with stilted Latin, until finally the giant grabs him by the throat, forcing him to cough up his scullery Latin and revert to his natural vernacular.

As if to demonstrate his genuine appreciation for education and the art of fine speaking, the narrator's catalogue is followed by a letter from Gargantua to his son, Pantagruel, a kind of spiritual and intellectual

testament. The letter is truly magnificent: a deeply felt, humanist profession
of faith that is far from parody. It is one of those rare passages in the *oeuvre*
which clearly are not intended to amuse the reader, and which can be taken
literally. No son could hope to receive a finer letter from his father. After
having given thanks to God "for having granted me the joy of beholding in
my old age blossom anew in your youth," Gargantua sets down his
conception of a rounded education at a moment in history when, with the end
of the "dark clouds of ignorance" during which "we suffered the calamitous
consequences of the destruction of good literature by the Goths," new
horizons of knowledge are revealing themselves to humanity:

> "To-day, the old sciences are revived, knowledge is systematized,
> discipline re-established. The learned languages are restored:
> Greek, without which a man would be ashamed to consider
> himself educated; Hebrew, Chaldean and Latin. Printing is now in
> use, an art so accurate and elegant that it betrays the divine
> inspiration of its discovery, which I have lived to witness. Alas!
> Conversely, I was not spared the horror of such diabolic works as
> gunpowder and artillery.
>
> "To-day, the world is full of learned men, brilliant teachers
> and vast libraries: I do not believe that the ages of Plato, Cicero or
> Papinian afforded such facilities for culture. From now on, it is
> unthinkable to come before the public or move in polite circles
> without having worshipped at Minerva's shrine. Why, the robbers,
> hangmen, adventurers and jockeys of today are infinitely better
> educated than the doctors and preachers of my time. More, even
> women and girls aspire to the glory, the heavenly manna of
> learning."

[He goes on to exhort his son to study languages, geography,
history, arithmetic, music, astronomy (and not the divinatory art of
astrology), civil law, philosophy as well as all branches of natural
history.]

> "Then carefully consult the works of Greek, Arabian and
> Latin physicians, without slighting the Jewish doctors, Talmudists
> and Cabbalists. By frequent exercises in dissection, acquire a
> perfect knowledge of that other world, which is man.
>
> "Devote a few hours a day to the study of Holy Writ. Take up
> the New Testament and the Epistlés in Greek; then the Old
> Testament in Hebrew. Strive to make your mind an inexhaustible
> storehouse of knowledge. For you are growing to manhood now:
> soon you will have to give up your studious repose to lead a life of

action. You will have to learn to bear arms, to achieve knighthood, so as to defend my house and help our allies frustrate the attacks of evildoers.

"Further, I wish you to test what profit you have gained from your education. This you can best do by public discussion and debate on all subjects against all comers, and by frequenting learned men both in Paris and elsewhere.

"But remember this. As Solomon says, wisdom entereth not into a malicious soul, and science without conscience spells but destruction of the spirit. Therefore serve, love and fear God, on Him pin all your thoughts and hopesl by faith built of charity, cling to Him so closely that never a sin come between you. Hold the abuses of the world in just suspicion. Set not your heart upon vanity, for this life is a transitory thing, but the Word of God endureth forever. Be serviceable to your neighbor, love him as you do yourself. Honor your teachers. Shun the company of all men you would not wish to resemble; receive not in vain the favors God has bestowed upon you.

"When you realize that you have acquired all the knowledge Paris has to offer, come back so I may see you and give you my blessing before I die." (*Pantagruel*, VIII, 202–206)

Gargantua's program is so obviously immense that no ordinary man could hope to complete it. But it also reflects the deeply humanist desire for a complete and balanced education, in which knowledge of nature need not be sacrificed to book knowledge. Here, sheer size, in my estimation, plays only a secondary role: the tone of the letter causes us to forget the gigantism that the narrator never loses an opportunity to play upon elsewhere in the work. Gargantuan optimism may be excessive only in the confidence that it places in the new amenities available for study. But Gargantua makes gentle fun even of these in the only humorous passage of the letter: even robbers and hangmen are better educated than the erudite of yore. In doing so, he kills two birds with one stone: the first are the old fogies; the second, the excessive expectations that accompany the spread of printing.

In a letter whose dominant tone is tenderness and gravity, the ironic aside in no way diminishes the hopes expressed by its writer. Gargantua is conscious of the great changes that have been set in motion around him in the space of only a few decades. Not only have the works of antiquity become more accessible, but placed now at our disposal are ways and means that the ancients did not possess. His consciousness of novelty, of light shining forth in the darkness in a world drunk on discovery and conquest, contains the seeds of much of the spirit we today call "modern." But it lacks the arrogance of certainty. Gargantua's moderate confidence is accompanied by a sense of disquiet: "Alas! Conversely," alongside all the beneficial inventions loom evil ones, like artillery. Still, his letter breathes a confidence in mankind that would have been unthinkable even one or two generations before. For all the breadth of his curriculum, the concern for balance tempers an appetite for knowledge that might appear to be bulimic.

To know all, to take all into account, to map the world, and to master nature are the founding ambitions of modernity, whose origins we normally assign to humanism. For better or for worse, by placing man and his earthly achievements at the center of its concerns, humanism has put man in control and paved the way for the development of the technoscientific development that is ours today. This simplistic, linear view of evolution that transforms the past into the "preparation" of a "predictable" outcome that history continually "bears out" is itself an outflow of the temporal, spatial, and mental revolution that we have supposedly inherited from the Renaissance. In seizing the entire world, and in reclaiming the inheritance which the dislocation of the Roman Empire and the barbarian invasions had all but consigned to oblivion, Renaissance man shaped before our eyes the world view and the conception of history that are ours today, and that allow us to make an "accurate" reading of the Renaissance itself. For us, it embodies the movement that leads to the free exercise of reason and to human self-determination—to the celebrated "majority" of the Kantian *Aufklärung*. Thus, insidiously, the idea of an ineluctable historical continuity leading toward the advent of liberty takes shape. In its ignorance of itself, the modern vision of history has created a vicious circle, one from which even today it is struggling to escape.

If we understand Gargantua correctly, the desire to understand, which Aristotle had long before ascribed to man as natural, stands at the threshold of a new awakening. But for him, it seems, this appetite suffices in and of itself; it has no end beyond the satisfaction it provides. Lest there be any doubt, the father advises his son to leave behind the peace and quiet of his studies and learn the arts of arms—much more immediately useful subjects—in order to defend hearth and home. Far from seeking some putative mastery of inanimate objects, Gargantuan wisdom is wary of the abuses and the vanities of the world. This transitory life is worth being devoted to friendship, in the respect of God whose "word is eternal." The words Gargantua attributes to Solomon—so often invoked every which way—here assume their full power: "Wisdom entereth not into a malicious soul, and science without conscience spells but destruction of the spirit." Science can indeed be ruinous; it has no connection with wisdom, and no amount of knowledge can make an ill-turned spirit wise. Here, Rabelais is far closer to Plato than he is to us.

For all that, Gargantua's exhortations to accumulate knowledge appear to lead nowhere. Though Pantagruel, like his father and grandfather before him, often displays flashes of both wisdom and moderation, everything seems to happen as though the ship of humanism, or at least its bulkiest cargo, is about to founder in the ocean of human buffoonery. The arrival of Panurge irresistibly pulls the story toward parody, toward the absurd, even toward the fraudulent. Unlike the Socratic Silenius, Panurge, though raggedly clad when Pantagruel encounters him in his path, is "of fine stature and handsome mien" (*Pantagruel*, IX, 207) while also of unusually insubstantial character. Mischievous and fond of the fast life, this ladies' man is quickly revealed to be a rascal, a coward, and a liar. It would hardly be an understatement to say that the ingenious rowdy is singularly lacking in both perspicacity and decisiveness when it comes to his own affairs. He may have Ulysses' cleverness, but he has none of Ulysses' boldness and often displays an alarming credulity. Unable to weigh the advantages and disadvantages of marriage, torn between the fierce necessity of ejaculation and the terror of cuckoldry, he rushes from one bit of advice to another and journeys to the ends of the earth to be told what Pantagruel has been telling him all along.

Yet Pantagruel quickly develops an affection for the newcomer that will never falter. His friendship for Panurge is unconditional; his forbearance cannot be shaken, not even by the youth's spinelessness. It is as though Pantagruel has found, in this heaven-sent friend, a kind of "scale model" double; as though the good giant, the incarnation of fidelity, recognizes a part of himself in this roguish pleasure seeker so full of human imperfections and—because he is so human—so touching. The recognition is immediate, instinctive: Pantagruel takes to him at first glance, even before the vagabond, who first attempts to conceal himself behind a façade of languages as unusual as they are foreign, reveals that he is a native of Touraine—which makes him a native of the same region as both the hero and the narrator. Panurge is nothing quite so much as the *alter ego* of both. Is not the "other world, which is man" that Gargantua refers to in his letter ultimately meant for each and every one of us?

Alcofribas remains torn between these two complementary characters, one of whom, Pantagruel, bodies forth the aspiration for wisdom while the other, Panurge, conveys a sense of folly and disarray. Wisdom (or the desire for it) is contained within a caricaturally grotesque, utopian body: at the inner core of an average physique full of natural elegance lies weakness. Wisdom leads weakness to the far reaches of dithering and vacillation. The progression makes a mockery of the great discoveries. The narrator, as he sails from one island to another, carries out a comic inventory of human institutions and sports with worlds. The other world is by no means what we thought it was.

Signs are visible even before the trans-oceanic expedition begins, at the end of the *Pantagruelion*. In his campaign against the Dipsodes, the giant shelters his army from a sudden downpour by covering it with his tongue. Seizing the occasion, the narrator makes his way along it and enters the giant's mouth, where he comes upon mountains, meadows, forests, and great cities no less fine than Lyon or Poitiers. His first encounter is with a man who is planting cabbage, whom he asks, astonished:

> "What are you doing here, friend?"
> "Planting cabbages!"
> "Why? How?"
> "Faith, sir, we can't all sport ballocks as heavy as mortars and we can't all be rich. I earn my living planting cabbages here and selling them in market in the city yonder."
> "Good Lord, is this a new world?"
> "No, no, there is nothing new about this place. Though they do say there is a world beyond here somewhere—a new world too—with a sun and a moon in it and all sorts of fine jobs for a man. Maybe so, maybe not. At any rate, this is the old world.
> "Really?" I pondered the question for a moment. Then: "This city where you sell your cabbages—what do they call it?"
> "It's called Aspharage; the citizens are good Christians and friendly souls. They will give you a rousing welcome."
> On his recommendation I decided to go. On my way, I came upon a man lying in wait for pigeons.
> "Good morning, friend. Those pigeons you get—where do they come from?"
> "From the other world."
> I concluded that when Pantagruel yawned, the pigeons, believing his throat to be a dovecote, doubtless flew in flocks."
> (*Pantagruel*, XXXII, 306–307)

Not only do the two worlds correspond, they are perfectly inter-changeable. One's new world is the other's old, and each possesses its "other world," the only difference being that the inner world,[127] that world so near that we know nothing of it, is the only one of the two that is aware of the other's existence. To the narrator's great surprise, nothing distinguishes one side of the borderline from the other. Congruent with Pantagruelian anatomy, the borderline shifts and extends indefinitely, precisely because it is imaginary. Above or below, inside or out, each of us has cabbages to plant. Here, novelty is the product of our ignorance, our fears, or our hopes.

The celebrated long stay in the "new world" located behind the teeth of Pantagruel (marvellously analyzed by Auerbach)[128] prefigures the long transatlantic voyage of the merry pranksters toward truth. Truth, as everyone knows, is ever elsewhere, ever distant. Its remoteness is all the more startling in that its subject, the possibility of taking a wife, is a particularly futile one. There is no reason why the theme of marriage cannot lend itself to reflection, but such reflection can take place just as well, if not better, at home than at the antipodes. What we have is an immense parodic voyage that draws on elements of the *Odyssey*, the *Aeneid*, the expeditions of Columbus, and the quest for the Grail. In the course of this voyage, under the most extravagant of external appearances, the travellers at every turn come upon our world, with all its defects, abuses, and absurdities. After having experienced the inevitable storms, overcome the sea monster, massacred the Andouilles (whom a stream of mustard suffices to set back on their feet); after having encountered the fanaticism of the Papimanes, studied the mores and customs of the Gastrolatres, and suffered the extortions of the Chats fourrez (papists, economists, and judges respectively), the Pantagruelian expedition, after countless other episodes, finally arrives in the land of the Lanternois.

As the name implies, it is a land inhabited by lanterns, where our boon companions are given permission by the queen to select the finest to light their way to the subterranean realm of the Holy Bottle. An inscription, less dire than that which graces the portals of Dante's Inferno is emblazoned atop the entry arch:

> Before you pass beneath this noble arch,
> Find a good Lantern to direct your march.

Overcome with trepidation, Panurge swears that he has heard Cerberus growl, and begs the Lantern in terms that hark back ever so slightly to the

---

127. An expression used to designate man's internal anatomy.
128. Erich Auerbach, "Le monde que renferme la bouche de Pantagruel," chap. XI, in *Mimesis, La représentation de la réalité dans la littérature occidentale*, traduit de l'Allemand par Cornélius Haim (Paris: Gallimard, 1968).

Florentine poet: "O wondrous lady, I beg you, with contrite heart, to go back" (CL, XXXVI, 859). But Friar John quickly collars him, proclaiming his readiness, if necessary, to defend him against eighteen devils. And since "fate guides him who consents, and pulls him who resists [DUCUNT VOLENTEM FATA, NOLENTUM TRAHENT]," and that "toward this all things move [PROS TELOS AYTON PANTA KINETAI]," as the inscriptions on the portals of the temple proclaim, our heroes appear before the pontifess Bacbuc, where at last they hear the voice of the oracle of the Bottle. Its message is a single word: TRINCH. "Drink," the priestess wisely interprets, to the immense joy of the supplicants who, in transports of Bacchic enthusiasm, strive to outdo one another in a poetic frenzy, beginning with Panurge, who has suddenly put all doubt behind him and swears in elaborate rhyme how he will soon wed and tend his wife with wild abandon. The entire expedition to the Bacbucian Grail has served but one purpose: to initiate the travellers into their favorite pastime, drinking themselves to a stupor, which they have not for an instant ceased to do before and during the voyage.

Though Panurge learns nothing more from his initiatory journey than what he should have known before he set out, and what Pantagruel has been belaboring him with from the very beginning, the experience will not have been entirely for nought. Deaf to the knowledge of others, man must often go to the most absurd and yet necessary lengths to find himself, to understand the meaning of what he has always done as a matter of course. No matter how ridiculous it is, the illumination that floods over Panurge is real enough: in his joyous drinking bouts with his friends, he has been imbibing all along from the fountain of truth (*en oïno alétheia, in vino veritas,* "in wine truth," reads the inscription on one of the temple doors). There is drinking, and there is drinking with full knowledge and lucidity; the two are not the same. The celebrated rule of the Abbey of Thélème, FAY CE QUE VOUDRAS—"DO AS THOU WILT" (*Gargantua,* VVII 159)—is complicated by the fact that our will is rarely as unambiguous as we imagine it to be. Only after multiple tribulations does Panurge gain access to the poetic inebriation that disentangles him from all his anxieties. The oracle does not at all enjoin him to "get married!" Ultimately, the Holy Bottle's advice seems the most succinct, the most ludicrous, and the most hermetic of all he has extracted from the diverse authorities, learned and not-so-learned, whom he has petitioned before setting out. The adventure may have taught him nothing new, but it has seasoned him, in that he has more than once been forced to overcome the obstacle of his fear. At last he is capable of grasping the full significance of the advice he receives from the Holy Bottle as it bids him drink: to do what he has always done: "Be thou the interpreter of thine own enterprise" (CL, XLV, 883).

Pantagruel says "It is impossible to do better than does this venerable pontifess" (*Ibid*). The gentle giant had long ago understood, and has accompanied his friend as one would a patient whose cure can only come from within himself (psychoanalysis would venture, cum grano salis, that Pantagruel is, with regard to Panurge, in the position of the analyst). In his search for himself, man cannot rely upon any other authority; the journey is his alone and must be quite independent of the teachings of others. Such is Gargantua's humanist program. If the narrator, to convey his message, must employ all the resources of burlesque and buffoonery, it is because the sense of awareness and the sense of identity are not to be taken too seriously. Panurge does not "find" himself in the dramatic sense of the term; he merely experiences a Bacchic moment that reveals the meaning of his own inconsequentiality. "Let flower within you that joyous love of life that is yours," advises the Bottle. Then and there, Panurge experiences the desire to procreate, and alongside that desire, the fear of being cuckolded—which has driven him to embark on his journey—dissipates. Panurge reaps no great self-mastery; in fact, he barely realizes the simple yet hidden truth by virtue of which he will henceforth be able to interpret what is happening to him. That modest truth is the gift of friendship.

As he takes his leave of the travellers, and before setting them on the road that will return them directly to Sables-d'Olonnes, Bacbuc the sorceress prays that they gain more happiness in bestowing and giving than in taking and receiving, then adds:

> "Go, my good friends; may you depart under the protection of that intellectual sphere, whose centre is everywhere, whose circumference is nowhere, and whom we call God. When you return to your world, bear witness to your fellow men that the greatest treasures and the most wonderful things lie hidden deep underground—and not without reason....
>
> "Your philosophers who complain that the ancients have left them nothing to write about or invent, are obviously very much mistaken. The phenomena you see in the sky, the wonders earth, sea and river offer you are not to be compared to what is hidden in the womb of earth.
>
> "For this reason, the subterranean ruler is in almost every language accorded the epithet of rich—Pluto, Dis and countless others. Your philosophers must learn to apply their energies and to

direct their studies toward the search for eternal truth. They must pray for the assistance of the sovereign God, Whom the Egyptians of old used to call, in their language, the Hidden, the Concealed, the Absconce... Whom they used to invoke by that name ... Whom they used to implore to reveal and manifest themselves unto them ...

"When your philosophers have had done with this, God will discover and make Himself known unto them. He will not only teach them to know his creatures, but Himself also. Thus they will be guided by his good Lanterns.

"For all the philosophers and sages of antiquity have deemed two things essential in order to pursue safely and pleasantly the search for wisdom and the road to God: first, God's guidance; then, man's aid." (CL, XLVIII, 888)

Thus ends the tale, on a serenely mystical, pantheistic profession of faith that assigns everything human, including the quest for self, to its proper place. Bacbuc's magnificent definition of God would soon be taken up almost word for word by Pascal to define the universe. In Pascal, the universe remains distinct from God, while the Rabelaisian priestess unites them audaciously in what may seem, in hindsight, a prefiguration of the Spinozan equation between God and the All of the world.

In a century that (re)breathed new life into the human adventure and redefined in its own terms the great ancient epics; in a century in which Christopher Columbus and his emulators more resembled heroes who had stepped straight out of fiction into reality, that brought together the exploits of Ulysses, Roland and Perceval; in a century when, in the name of truth, the discovery of the world and the conquest of the other began, Rabelais suggested with a laugh that, if we gave it even the most cursory thought, we would never seek anything but ourselves—the "other world which is man." The encounter itself is meaningless except in relation to that unmapped intellectual sphere we call God. Like Ulysses, Panurge does little more than return home, but his treasure is pathetic and no one seeks to usurp his place (the woman he will marry has neither name nor face). Like Perceval, he reaches the threshold of truth, but truth has become a mirror in which he can read only that which he is becoming. Rabelais is taken in neither by vast spaces nor by "the inner voyage." In every respect, his pentalogy sets itself up in opposition to the "great stories" we have read thus far; even more patently, to the truth narrative developed as historical myth in the *Aeneid*;

then, as they so affirm, as an absolute in the Gospels and in the Christian literature inspired by them.

Rabelais avoids transposing into the lower realm—that of worldly affairs—the thirst for truth that Christianity holds out for the hereafter. In fact, he proceeds as though he feared the possibility of an eventual slippage of truth from divine to human. To set oneself free from dogma is to emphasize the mystery of creation and of our presence in the world. Far from revoking the mystery, Rabelais accepts it wholly and without reserve—as long as it assumes the Christian form. Far from being a punishment or an obstacle, submission to the divine sphere is the condition of true *joie de vivre*: consciousness of the indescribable immensity surrounding us shrinks apace the poverty and the injustice that afflict the "ego." "I loathe a sad and cheerless spirit that slides above the pleasures of life, and that revels in discontent" (822),[129] Montaigne would say, in the same vein. From the Rabelaisian "ego" to that of Montaigne, however, a certain distension has taken place: "I wish to be master of myself, in every way," (824) writes the author of the *Essais*, who declares himself "hungry to make [himself] known" and to seek himself "down to his entrails" (824).

There is nothing in Alcofribas of the "egotic" importance which, from Saint Augustine to Rousseau, by way of Montaigne, so laboriously attempts to reveal itself in its most intimate "truth"—perhaps even by painting a picture of excessive bleakness. The game of life cares little for the ego's obsessive fears. The Rabelaisian subject is in a constant state of composition, decomposition, and recomposition, according to circumstances; it floats upon the ocean of the world (*Fluctuat nec mergitur* could well be its motto) and takes amusement from the constant flux that surrounds it. Of course, he spends the better part of his time gorging and boozing, but the feasting burdens him not at all. The hugeness of his banquets is joyous, never bulimic. The narrator takes enormous pleasure in jibing at the stomach-worshippers and their potbellied god, "Master Gaster, the master of all truths," who subordinates all human activity to his insatiable appetite.

> He only speaks by signs. But let him make them, and everyone observes them more rapidly than the edicts of prætors or the decrees of kings; he does not admit of the slightest delay or postponement in the execution of his orders....
>
> None but labors to serve him, none but bustles to do him reverence. As a reward, he confers a benefit upon mankind the

129. Montaigne, *Œuvres complètes* (Paris: Gallimard, Bibliothèque de la Pleiade, 1962).

invention of all arts, machines, trades, engines and crafts.... And all for the sake of their guts. (*QL*, LVII, 696)

Revelry has nothing to do with the tyranny of accumulation. Good wine and good food are, for Rabelais, the fuel of friendship, of festivity, of play. For life above all is worth being celebrated, enjoyed; it can only be properly enjoyed at the "mediocre" median position, far from the anguish of ambition and the embarrassments of power, which allows each and every one of us full freedom to invent and to imagine ("Strive then for mediocrity," enjoins the prologue to the *Quart Livre*).

Before leading them into the precincts of the Holy Bottle, Bacbuc invites her visitors to drink at her fountain, then asks them how they find her water. As they wax dithyrambic about its crystalline purity, their hostess derides the insensitivity of their palates and has them served "fine and jolly hams, fine, fat and jolly smoked beef tongues" by way of "rasps" to scrape their gizzards. Once the "cleansing" has been completed, the priestess suggests that they drink again while imagining that they are tasting their favorite wines. The miracle takes place: they are ecstatic, one about his Beaulne, another, his Graves, yet another, his Mirebeaulx, etc. "Drink once, twice, thrice more. Change your imagination, every time you drink. You'll find this water's bouquet and body exactly that of the wine you thought of," says Bacbuc (CL, XLIII). So it is with the fountain of life: its taste varies according to the drinkers' imagination. The Pantagruelian tale, in all its incredible variety, its lunacy, its vitality, in all its unquenchable verbal creativity, is the finest literary illustration of the imaginational openness Rabelais lays before us and without which, like the "shitchewing" monks and other sin-eaters of the same poor cloth (*Gargantua*, XK, 118), we would be reduced to ruminating on the unhappiness of the world. The same is true of speech, which possesses the power both to enliven and to blight the spirit, much as "the impostors who poison the soul" are worse than the plague, which "kills only the body" (*Gargantua*, XLV, 131). Life and its enjoyments are here; they are of this world, close at hand, far more real than all the promises of another world.

Rabelais has enjoyed consistent success in Western literature—probably because he gives us, whether consciously or not, a sense of nostalgia for the freedom of mind and the sad memory of the mad magic of life that the growing rationalism of the succeeding centuries has driven from us. Not that our roguish doctor has no desire for reason. But, for him, reason is suspicious of itself; it can go beyond its self-recognized limits and find other reasons to rejoice, other reasons for being—fragile yet alert—beneath the infinite vault that far exceeds our grasp. Alcofribas leaves in our imagination the faint traces of a comet's passage through a sky that is no more, a sky different from our own, and whose return seems anything but likely.

Four and one-half centuries after its creation, the Rabelaisian epic, that amalgam of ancient wisdom and of the broad popular farce that was still flourishing, can be seen as a locus of intense and exceptional condensation, in which Christian truth assumes a new life, and with it, a more earthly, more affable face, from which all fear is banished. The Reformation did not move Rabelais; he has another, more upbeat version to offer us, incarnated in the Abbey of Thélème, from the Greek *thelemos*: that which flows naturally, and which bubbles up of its own accord. Closed to the Pharisees, to the usurers, to the envious, and to the grumblers, it stands fully open to "all fair companions" (*Gargantua*, LIV). As he strolls leisurely through its pages with its creator, the reader may even surprise himself in dreaming of a quiet, gentle faith in life and friendship in a society freed of all its weighty dogmas, seeking peacefully for a thousand glistening truths; remote from that unique and tyrannical society in whose name the Church assigns true life to the heavenly kingdom, while for the greater glory of Christ, conquerors bloody the new world they believe they have discovered.

With Rabelaisian laughter, the truth that Chrétien de Troyes dusted so lightly with irony, that Dante lent a human form in the face of his beloved, dissolves in joyful noise. Frail and faraway, our literature's happy song seems to come to us from that mournful crossroads where the history of our civilization has taken a wrong turn.

14

A Singular Madness

… but what cause has your worship for going mad?
—Cervantes, *Don Quixote*

A S THE FIGURE who launches the modern novel, he stands out as the most celebrated character in Western literature. But few know his story. Only fragments remain—random episodes, blurred images, fleeting silhouettes. Don Quixote is the madman who does battle with windmills. Depending on your point of view, he is either ridiculous or tragic. Need we really add that this mindless categorization has come to define him? So great is his celebrity that it has extinguished his story. And yet the story, in all its magnificent absurdity, takes liberties with truth unlike any before it. The game it plays is complex; to join the game, we must chart its inner workings with all the diligence we can muster.

Here is a book whose narrator claims to be both a scholar and the translator of a tale originally written by an Arab historian of unimpeachable sincerity. Drawing upon the most reliable sources, he has reconstructed the story of a *hidalgo* on the threshold of his fiftieth year who, mind addled by excess consumption of chivalrous romances, decides to transform himself into a knight-errant and by his heroic feats go on to eternal renown. This he will accomplish for both himself and for the lady of his dreams, Dulcinea of Toboso, to whom, sight unseen, he has devoted himself body and soul.

In a world where chivalry has disappeared, Don Quixote seems fated to be flung from hope into absurdity, from chimera into defeat, and from extravagance into disgrace. His first sally comes to an abrupt end when, having had himself fitted out as a knight by an innkeeper whom he imagines in his ravings to be a squire, our hero tumbles from his horse in a raid on harmless merchants, only to return bruised and battered to his point of departure with the help of a passing peasant returning on donkey-back from the mill. His first attempt at knightly deeds is little more than a prelude to the story of the second sally which, in a dizzying cavalcade of twists and turns, makes up the remainder of the first volume of *The Ingenious Gentleman Don Quixote of La Mancha* (1605). Having evaded the watchful supervision of his friends and family (his governess, his aunt, his niece, his barber, and the curate), who have convened in an effort to shake him out of his madness, our fine flower of knighthood issues forth once more, accompanied this time by the extraordinary Sancho Panza, a neighboring peasant who is convinced that his master's brilliant success will win him, a doughty but insignificant stable hand, the governorship of some distant island. The second sally ends as ingloriously as the first: caught in an impasse, hoodwinked by the conniving curate and barber who have set out to find him, Don Quixote returns to the village "all lean and yellow and stretched out on a truss of hay on an ox-cart" (I, VII).[130] At the end of the first volume, a third sally is mooted, in the course of which—according to local tradition—the knight travels to Saragossa to take part in a famous tournament where he wins a measure of fame. These few details aside, the chronicler can tell us nothing about the end of his life, and finds nothing but sundry sheets of parchment containing two versions of his epitaph.

The second volume, a direct result of the popularity of the first, appeared in 1615, one year after the publication of an apocryphal "second part" by a lesser author (*The Quixote of Avellaneda*) which Cervantes denounced as a fabrication. The sequel, given over entirely to the third sally of the Knight of the Rueful Countenance, plays upon the celebrity won by the story of the character's feats, and sets the scene for an engagement with the mischievousness of certain of his readers. Among them are a duke and a duchess who, in their wealth, rank, and idleness, have little better to do than to stage diversions in which their invited paragon of chivalry is all too ready to play—blindly—his assigned role. After numerous adventures in the course of which Sancho for three days plies the demanding trade of governor, the sally ends with a serious reverse, which will prove irreparable. One of his ironic admirers, a young bachelor in league with the curate, disguised as the knight of the White Moon, challenges the hero to man-to-man combat. Unhorsed at the first exchange, Don Quixote is forced to accede to the conditions he had accepted before the joust: he must return home and forgo

---

130. Miguel de Cervantes, *Don Quixote*, trans. John Ormsby (London, 1919).

all knight-errantry for one year. In his mortification, the hero considers becoming a shepherd, but he rapidly languishes and is soon carried off by death. Before dying, he recovers his full lucidity and with it, his true identity, that of a certain Alonzo Quixano. Then and there he repudiates knight-erranthood and all his exploits with the same fervor with which he once embraced them: "Now I perceive my folly, and the peril into which reading them brought me; now by God's mercy schooled into my right senses, I loathe them" (LXXIV, 500). One can never be too careful: the curate, as the secular arm of truth, commissions a notary to draw up, on the death of the repentant, an attestation of conversion. Forgers and imitators take heed: henceforth, no man will be able to raise him from the dead, nor claim for him new acts of derring-do.

Thus ends the cycle of excess that delivers over "to the detestation of mankind the false and foolish tales of the books of chivalry, which, thanks to that of my true Don Quixote, are even now tottering, and doubtless doomed to fall for ever" (II, LXXIV, 504).

These are the words penned by the cautious historian of the quixotic adventures, Cid Hamet ben-Engeli, which his faithful interpreter (or "second narrator") places at the end of the work, as if to bring it full circle. Don Quixote, that one-time madman, has become *in extremis* a hero of common sense, claims the historian; the inept righter of wrongs—with the involuntary assistance of this apocryphal double—is transformed into a prodigious toppler of ineptitudes.

At first glance, *Don Quixote* has all the appearances of an extraordinary entertainment, of a high-humored battle against literary extravagance. It is quite possible that Cervantes' original intention had been little more than to mock and to divert. But there exist few works in which the author's intentions are of less moment than this one. During his lifetime, the immensity and the longevity of his success trapped him; he was caught with a character that surpassed him, as testified by the need for a second volume. Cervantes' genius was to have created a novel of such truth, such verve, that its characters, whoever they may be, ended up foiling his best efforts to control them. It is all well and good for him to register his repentance, to bury it beneath the ground, but Quixote and his world have long since taken on a life of their own. If Cervantes represents a significant shift in Western fiction, it is because he has demonstrated, perhaps even in spite of himself, that the imagination is as powerful as the real, sometimes more powerful; better yet, the former is part and parcel of the latter, and the borderline between the two registers is often blurred.

Don Quixote's "modernity" cannot be reduced to some kind of putative "realism." No, it derives from the sequence of shocks that the story sets up between what we commonly term "reality" and that other, imaginary reality. Quixote's "madness" is a form of mental discrepancy, the identitarian dichotomy that is indispensable to the incongruous meeting of the two worlds. Fiction takes full advantage of its freedom to lay down a counterpoint—one is even tempted to call it a fugue—between dream and reality, between the hero who "imagines himself" and the world against which the self-image he struggles to construct collides. But what is at issue in this collision, and in the joyous shower of sparks it spews forth, is not the power of imagination, but the very status of reality itself.

Reality can here be taken to mean that part of our universe which we judge the least disputable because, under normal circumstances, it is the least dependent on our will; realism, then, means that we cannot reduce the real to our desires. What could be harder, or more "real," than the reality against which the quixotic ideal unfailingly bangs its head? With every passing moment the world around him and his own entourage remind the unfortunate knight how deceptive the works of his imagination are. Windmills are not giants, wineskins are not bodies, and flocks of sheep are not armies. But against all these discrepancies, Quixote has an irrefutable explanation: he has fallen under the spell of those who wish him ill. They transform giants into windmills and warriors into sheep, all in order to deprive him of the fruit of his daring deeds, to rob him of the glorious fruits of his efforts. But these evil spirits can only fool the simple-minded. He, Quixote, can see beneath appearances as he demonstrates in the famous episode of Mambrino's helmet. Sancho attempts to warn him against any further illusions, but he snaps back:

> "How can I be mistaken in what I say, unbelieving traitor?" returned Don Quixote; "tell me, seest thou not yonder knight coming towards us on a dappled grey steed, who has upon his head a helmet of gold?"
>
> "What I see and make out," answered Sancho, "is only a man on a grey ass like my own, who has something that shines on his head."
>
> "Well, that is the helmet of Mambrino," said Don Quixote; "stand to one side and leave me alone with him; thou shalt see how, without saying a word, to save time, I shall bring this adventure to an issue and possess myself of the helmet I have so longed for...."

The fact of the matter as regards the helmet, steed, and knight that Don Quixote saw, was this. In that neighbourhood there were two villages, one of them so small that it had neither apothecary's shop nor barber, which the other that was close to it had, so the barber of the larger served the smaller, and in it there was a sick man who required to be bled and another man who wanted to be shaved, and on this errand the barber was going, carrying with him a brass basin; but as luck would have it, as he was on the way it began to rain, and not to spoil his hat, which probably was a new one, he put the basin on his head, and being clean it glittered at half a league's distance. He rode upon a grey ass, as Sancho said, and this was what made it seem to Don Quixote to be a dapple-grey steed and a knight and a golden helmet; for everything he saw he made to fall in with his crazy chivalry and ill-errant notions.

[Don Quixote charges and, to his great satisfaction, the barber flees, abandoning both animal and utensil.]

He told Sancho to pick up the helmet, and he taking it in his hands said:

"By God the basin is a good one, and worth a real of eight if it is worth a maravedis," and handed it to his master, who immediately put it on his head, turning it round, now this way, now that, in search of fitment, and not finding it he said, "Clearly the pagan to whose measure this famous head-piece was first forged must have had a very large head; but the worst of it is half of it is wanting."

When Sancho heard him call the basin a headpiece he was unable to restrain his laughter, but remembering his master's wrath he checked himself in the midst of it.

"What art thou laughing at, Sancho?" said Don Quixote.

"I am laughing," said he, "to think of the great head the pagan must have had who owned this helmet, for it looks exactly like a regular barber's basin."

"Dost thou know what I suspect, Sancho?" said Don Quixote; "that this wonderful piece of this enchanted helmet must by some strange accident have come into the hands of some one who was unable to recognise or realise its value, and who, not knowing what he did, and seeing it to be of the purest gold, must have melted down one half for the sake of what it might be worth, and of the other made this which is like a barber's basin as thou sayest; but be it as it may, to me who recognise it, its transformation makes no difference, for I will set it to rights at the first village where there is a blacksmith, and in such style that that helmet the god of smithies forged for the god of battles shall not surpass it or even come up to it; and in the meantime I will wear it as well as I can, for something is better than nothing; all the more as it will be quite enough to protect me from any chance blow of a stone."

"That is," said Sancho, "if it is not shot with a sling as they were in the battle of the two armies, when they signed the cross on your worship's grinders and smashed the flask with that blessed draught that made me vomit my bowels up." (I, XXL, 194–195)

The knight's fertile imagination stands in opposition, as it must, to that of his plodding squire. Sancho's common sense, however, is not always reliable. When it suits him, he can fabulate in his own way. Out of his powers of invention grow hopes and dreams (to be appointed governor), but rarely do they have any effect on what he sees around him. In the scene we are examining, however, his grasp seems firm enough, which the narrator takes pains to confirm in a rather laborious explanation of an altogether improbable apparition: a barber hurrying along with his basin atop his head. Nothing is spared to make the circumstances plausible: local geography, the rain, the new hat, the metallic gleam of the shaving basin (under a rainy sky!), as though the author feared accrediting his hero's capricious imagination. As though reality had to be burdened with a maximum of verisimilitude, lest someone mistake the shaving basin for a head piece. At this point, enchantment all but takes leave of us. Quixote notices it himself, and casts about for a "reasonable," factual explanation for the transformation that has seen a warrior's helmet take on the appearance of a vulgar shaving basin.

The imagination of the Ingenious Gentleman comes in response to the narrator's efforts to justify the scene. The only difference is that Quixote's job is the harder one: he must account for the physical transformation of an object, where the author need only describe the circumstances of that transformation. In his indirect dialogue with the author, the hero suspects that his explanation will simply convince no one, and brings the discussion to an abrupt end by invoking authority: whatever the reasons for the metamorphosis, he, Quixote, knows what is behind it, and feels no obligation to offer a convincing argument. In so doing, he is half admitting that his story is as wobbly as the shaving basin atop his ahead. Sancho is quick to point out the precariousness of the situation, reminding him maliciously that his discovery will not protect him from another thrashing.

Don Quixote leaves little to doubt: the narrator is continually pointing out, reiterating clearly and unequivocally, that for all his knightly daydreaming, Don Quixote is no madman; that he is in fact a man of great sagacity. The passage quoted *in extenso* above goes farther still: at the very heart of his madness, the hero secretly knows what to expect, knows precisely what the score is with reality—a reality he wants nothing to do with; a reality he rejects, one that he will even fight against.

As he encounters some prisoners being led away to the galleys, our valorous knight knows quite well that the men he sees are miscreants thrown into chains by order of the king. He takes them neither for angels, nor for bedevilled brothers in arms. He listens carefully to the catalogue of their offences, but is entirely at odds with their punishment. At his own expense he has them released, only to be partially relieved of his personal effects by a handful of them soon thereafter. Freeing them is a new act of madness but it is "madness" of an entirely different kind, which now involves taking a stand, if not against the established order then at least against one of its dispositions. Flight into the utopia of chivalry is already, in and of itself, one way of rejecting the world. With the episode of the galley slaves, his refusal suddenly takes on new, active, lucid form. To an old man who relates how he has been condemned to the galleys for pimping and sorcery, Quixote answers that, as far as he is concerned, the function of the procurer should be assumed, and not suppressed, by the State. On the second count, the knight declares, "I know well there are no sorceries in the world that can move or compel the will as some simple folk fancy, for our will is free, nor is there herb or charm that can force it" (I, XXII, 206).

The shift is ironic indeed: the victim of sorceries now denies their power. But the contradiction is an apparent one only. Don Quixote proclaims to anyone who cares to listen that no sorcery in the world has power over him. He is proud of his ability to resist it and of his perseverance in hewing to the path of glory from which those evil spirits would like to divert him. The hero is a model of consistency: in doing battle with windmills, he expresses his free will, and affirms his determination. It is not because reality has become a travesty that he intends to resign himself, to succumb to the charm of its disguises. No more is he impressed by pretense than by royal justice. No authority can force his conscience to consider as just what in his eyes is unjust; no man can oblige him to consider as real that which is not, nor to give the lie to what he considers as reality. If we are to admit that our senses can deceive us (as philosophers and men of science do), if we accept the possibility of a disconnection between what is *seen* and what *is*, Quixote's logic is impeccable. But it remains unreasonable. Not only is logical reasoning not synonymous with reason (in the sense of capacity for thought that yields the well-considered experience of life) but the rigor of this very logic itself is a powerful, restrictive implement for any mind that refuses to draw lessons from real-life experience and that relegates itself to the closed circuit of a single way of thinking.

While it can be fruitful or at least benign in its cognitive effects, free will can have troublesome social consequences when it is exercised on the moral level, as the ugly turn of events involving the galley slaves illustrates. Free will obliges man to reflect, but the duty of reflection does not mean that he can be guided only by his conscience, though he might place it under God's protection, in the manner of Don Quixote. Neither God nor conscience can replace the law. By ignoring the indispensable limitation placed upon public life, our hero goes astray. Here law and reality merge in one sole principle, one sole necessity, and one sole "reality." But this reality wounds him in a way that remains unelucidated, mysterious. Quixote cannot accommodate himself to it. And in this sense, he rejects it. But his rejection is not total. No matter how radical he may be on occasion, he holds a grudge only against that part of reality that thwarts the fulfilment of his dream: the dispenser of justice, the righter of wrongs can tolerate no resistance from iniquity, be it on order of the king. Therefore he resists. The combatant cannot accept that an opportunity for victory slip away from him; nor can the lover conceive that there exists any woman more beautiful, more admirable than Dulcinea.

Our *hidalgo* is at his most unbending on the subject of love. The respect he demands from one and all for the lady of his dreams can tolerate not the slightest divergence. In this respect, Quixote is no different from any lover whose critical faculties are blurred by passion at the merest mention of the object of his affection. Perhaps that is why it is startling to see, on the treacherous field of love, precisely where his honor is at its touchiest, the hero display flashes of a disarming lucidity. In Dulcinea, he confesses with a sigh to a boon companion who delights in egging him on, "all the impossible and fanciful attributes of beauty which the poets apply to their ladies are verified" (I, XIII, 127). Quixote knows all too well that his lady love is a fantasy. Yet he keeps her alive, for "to deprive a knight-errant of his lady," he will much later profess to the Duchess, "is to deprive him of the eyes he sees with, of the sun that gives him light, of the food whereby he lives. Many a time before I have said it, and I say it now once more, a knight-errant without a lady is like a tree without leaves, a building without a foundation, or a shadow without a body that causes it." When his interlocutor, whose reading of his earlier adventures is still vivid in her mind, suggests that his Dulcinea is not of this world, that she is in fact a lady created from the whole cloth of his imagination, our hero replies evasively: "God knows whether there be any Dulcinea or not in the world, or whether she is imaginary or not imaginary; these are things the proof of which must not be pushed to extreme lengths" (II, XXXII, 229).

Truth to tell, our Ingenious Gentleman is not really in love. Love is merely an emotion essential to his undertaking. So much the better that he excels in such matters, as he confides to Sancho during the penance he performs in honor of Dulcinea in the Sierra-Morena. After the freeing of the galley slaves, Quixote agrees to accept his squire's advice and seek refuge in the mountains where he may hope for absolution by Saint Hermanadad, on condition that it never be said that he has acted out of cowardice. The bitter solitude of the heights quickly sweeps away his apprehensions and instils in him the desire, he proclaims, to perform "among them an achievement wherewith I shall win eternal name and fame throughout the known world." To calm Sancho's fears at the prospect of yet another hazardous undertaking, the master explains to his intrepid squire that he fully intends to draw inspiration from the ascetic regimen of Amadis de Gaule, pole star and radiant sun of knighthood, to prove his steadfastness and his despair at the hands of the disdainful Lady Oriana. For, he adds, "it is easier for me to imitate him in this than in cleaving giants asunder, cutting off serpents' heads, slaying dragons, routing armies, destroying fleets and breaking enchantments." Though he is tempted to approve of his master's effortless ease, the squire remains sceptical about his motives:

> "It seems to me," said Sancho, "that the knights who behaved in this way had provocation and cause for those follies and penances; but what cause has your worship for going mad? What lady has rejected you, or what evidence have you found to prove that the lady Dulcinea del Toboso has been trifling with Moor or Christian?"
>
> "There is the point," replied Don Quixote, "and that is the beauty of this business of mine; no thanks to a knight-errant for going mad when he has cause; the thing is to turn crazy without any provocation, and let my lady know, if I do this in the dry, what I would do in the moist....
>
> ... and so, friend Sancho, waste no time in advising me against so rare, so happy, and so unheard-of an imitation; mad I am, and mad I must be until thou returnest with the answer to a letter that I mean to send by thee to my lady Dulcinea.... (I, XXV, 234–235)

Here Don Quixote reveals a finely honed sense of his own limitations. The limitations are physical, above all: he can never hope to equal the great knights in combat. They are also amorous: because he has no motive for jealousy, no reason to despair of a lady whom he has never seen, his mad mortification soars to the summits of improbability. In fact, the absence of a veritable passion is what makes it possible, on this specific point, for his excesses to outstrip the unsurpassable prowess of his idol, Amadis de Gaule. Finally, the limitations are structural, governing the framework within which his knightly extravagances unfold. They are, in other words, limitations upon the game he plays, a game whose meaning his acolyte has such difficulty in grasping.

Shortly after his outburst, Quixote suddenly attempts to find out where Sancho has hidden Mambrino's famous helmet, of which so much has been made. The return of his obsession enrages the squire who, tired of his master's delirious ravings about the dented, tarnished shaving basin, expresses the most serious reservations about his mental health, and fears for the promises made to him by the knight. Far from taking offence at his servant's insolence, Quixote fires Sancho's exasperation straight back at him, in amazement at his narrow-mindedness:

> Is it possible that all this time thou hast been going about with me thou hast never found out that all things belonging to knights-errant seem to be illusions and nonsense and ravings, and to go always by contraries? And not because it really is so, but because there is always a swarm of enchanters in attendance upon us that change and alter everything with us, and turn things as they please, and according as they are disposed to aid or destroy us; thus what seems to thee a barber's basin seems to me Mambrino's helmet, and to another it will seem something else; and rare foresight it was in the sage who is on my side to make what is really and truly Mambrino's helmet seem a basin to everybody, for, being held in such estimation as it is all the world would pursue me to rob me of it; but when they see it is only a barber's basin they do not take the trouble to obtain it. (I, XXV, 235–236)

Because there exists a closed field of particular sensitivity to enchantment restricted to knight-errantry, the truth of the events and the objects that exist within it are beyond the capacity of ordinary people to perceive. Quixote knows that he exists on two distinct levels of reality, a duality that the simple Pancho, who has never known but one, that of the hard ground on which he walks, cannot grasp. Because he knows nothing of the cohabitation of the two parallel worlds, the doughty squire passes from one to the other unawares: if his master is mad, then his assurances are nothing but so much hot air (I, XXV, 235). Sancho believed—and still hopes to obtain his island to govern *in quotidian reality*—something that will only come to pass through a subterfuge organized much later by the Duke and Duchess, who will take pleasure in lending the fiction they have so enjoyed reading an ephemeral appearance of reality. Sancho behaves rather like an adult who takes literally the daydream of a child playing at Robin Hood. While aware that he is making it up as he goes, the child, like our knight-errant, is totally immersed in the story he is inventing, but he would have a low opinion of the adult who would treat his adventure as though it were a reality of the same order as, for instance, that which obliges him to go to school on Monday morning. Quixote's behavior is no different than that of the child—the subtlety of his argumentation aside. Though he plays on the plurality of worlds and on the relativity of objects as they relate to each other, he insinuates that a certain reality—his own—has greater weight or at least, greater value, than the other, in the way that Mambrino's helmet is a thousand times more precious than a shaving basin. Not only because it is made of gold but because, above all, there is none other like it.

Quixote yearns to be extraordinary, like his helmet. "I know who I am," he tells the peasant who, after picking him up at the conclusion of his first sally, attempts to return him to the reality of his identity, "and I know that I may be not only those I have named, but all the Twelve Peers of France and even all the Nine Worthies, since my achievements surpass all that they have done all together and each of them on his own account" (I, V, 76). His confidence in his own strength of arm, as we have seen, will not always be quite so unshakable, but the conviction that in one way or another he will surpass his models never abandons him. He imitates them only to rise higher, to win incomparable renown. Singularity is no longer enough for him; it must be visible, it must shine in everyone's eyes, it must cause tongues to wag, it must remain forever etched in memory. Renown and the writing that alone can transmit it have become more important than their object—witness the knight's interest in the unflattering epithet his squire publicly bestows upon him. Sancho informs the handful of unfortunate penitents whom his master has just finished upending that they have just been routed by "the famous Don Quixote of La Mancha, otherwise called the 'Knight of the Rueful Countenance.'" When the Don inquires about the title,

"I will tell you," answered Sancho; "it was because I have been looking at you for some time by the light of the torch held by that unfortunate, and verily your worship has got of late the most ill-favoured countenance I ever saw: it must be either owing to the fatigue of this combat, or else to the want of teeth and grinders." "It is not that," replied Don Quixote, "but because the sage whose duty it will be to write the history of my achievements must have thought it proper that I should take some distinctive name as all knights of yore did ... and so I say that the sage aforesaid must have put it into your mouth and mind just now to call me 'The Knight of the Rueful Countenance,' as I intend to call myself from this day forward; and that the said name may fit me better, I mean, when the opportunity offers, to have a very rueful countenance painted on my shield." "There is no occasion, senor, for wasting time or money on making that countenance," said Sancho; "for all that need be done is for your worship to show your own...." (I, XIX, 177–178)

So mightily does Quixote aspire to the other reality he has discovered in the knightly narratives that he thenceforth assumes the life of a fictional character. There can be no tangible cause for his hangdog look, and Sancho's trivial explanations hardly touch him, since his discovery is the product of a cause that utterly escapes the squire's comprehension. Whatever of significance happens to Don Quixote (from the first volume on) has meaning only in terms of the tale to come, which will enshrine his glory. As knightly narratives are of scant interest to squires, it is hardly surprising that Sancho interprets events mistakenly. Totally mistakenly, in the event, from the fictional viewpoint of the Quixotic hero who, for all his thirst for a surplus of reality, cannot completely overlook the fictitious aspect of his quest; but quite correctly nonetheless, as seen from the down-to-earth outlook of his man-servant who must bear the retainer's burden. So it is that each of the two experiences the same events in two distinct spheres: Quixote from high in the clouds, Sancho from his donkey on the ground.

Neither compartment is entirely airtight. In the image of the lead characters themselves, the two are joined. The dialogue between master and man-servant is almost incessant. Each one, while holding fast to his position, shares a portion of the other's reality. Quixote is not unaware of contingencies, and keeps a perspicacious eye upon them to make sure that they do not endanger his dream. Meanwhile, Sancho unshakeably believes, despite his moments of discouragement, in the governorship that his master's exploits will deliver into his hands. In fact, he throws his full support behind any initiative likely to bring the blessed moment nearer. In so doing, he contrives to espouse his master's literary obsessions. Sancho, thinking back to the Don's explanation concerning the soubriquet of the Rueful Countenance, points out to his noble companion what a waste of time it is to accumulate feats of bravery on the highroads, for "there is no one to see or know of them," and so they "must rest untold forever." How much better it would be to offer his services to an emperor or some great prince, for thus would his valour be rewarded. "And there you will not be at a loss for some one to set down your achievements in writing so as to preserve their memory forever," concludes the clever squire (I, XXI, 197). Quixote is forced to admit that his man-servant has spoken well, but he too has a rejoinder which is hardly less telling: glory must precede the knight's arrival at the prince's court; far from having to ask for permission to serve, the champion may do the prince the signal favor of placing his sword-arm at his disposal.

So it is that the concerns of the two companions join and partake of one another, partially, subtly, without ever entirely abandoning their respective registers. The two voices blend without losing their own particular tonality in a kind of ambiguous intelligence that lends them a punctilious compatibility. The incessant conversation of Sancho and Quixote, where each one pretends to ignore his borrowings from the other and his tacit acceptance of that which he has rejected, makes for one of the richest, most savory dialogues of the deaf in all of Western literature. Their respective deafness is not total though; fragments of truth are always turning up. Truth is volleyed back and forth like a ball; it remains with neither the one nor the other, but in constant motion between the two. The game is played out within strict limits, which are rarely exceeded. With a few exceptions, each holds to his own ground; roles are not interchangeable, but almost always complementary: Sancho is cautious when Quixote is mad, and mad when his master is cautious. The incessant exchange of wisdom and madness, which functions as a passageway linking the two levels of reality where each man's spirit normally resides, ends by weaving between the two companions strong ties of common cause and friendship. The two men fool themselves, and love one another at the same time. This is what makes them so real, and why we become so attached to them.

One of the episodes that throws their ambiguously complementary relationship into sharp relief takes place at the beginning of the third sally (in the second volume). In it, the knight and his valet are making their way toward Toboso in quest of Dulcinea. A fear that cannot speak its name has overcome both men, at the prospect of a final confrontation with the truth:

the knight dreads the collapse of his dream, and the squire the discovery of his deception (contrary to his detailed report to his master, Sancho has never set foot in Toboso, nor ever met the woman whose message of love he claimed to have delivered). Quixote seeks refuge in a grove and sends his man-servant off for news of his lady. Perplexed, Sancho pretends to go off to the village, but no sooner is he out of his master's sight than he dismounts from his donkey and sits down at the foot of a tree to dialogue with himself on the fine mess into which he has plunged himself. Finally, from his feverish thoughts emerges a solution:

> I have seen by a thousand signs that this master of mine is a madman fit to be tied, and for that matter, I too, am not behind him; for I'm a greater fool than he is when I follow him and serve him, if there's any truth in the proverb that says, 'Tell me what company thou keepest, and I'll tell thee what thou art,' or in that other, 'Not with whom thou art bred, but with whom thou art fed.' Well then, if he be mad, as he is, and with a madness that mostly takes one thing for another, and white for black, and black for white, as was seen when he said the windmills were giants, and the monks' mules dromedaries, flocks of sheep armies of enemies, and much more to the same tune, it will not be very hard to make him believe that some country girl, the first I come across here, is the lady Dulcinea; and if he does not believe it, I'll swear it; and if he should swear, I'll swear again; and if he persists I'll persist still more, so as, come what may, to have my quoit always over the peg. Maybe, by holding out in this way, I may put a stop to his sending me on messages of this kind another time; or maybe he will think, as I suspect he will, that one of those wicked enchanters, who he says have a spite against him, has changed her form for the sake of doing him an ill turn and injuring him."

> With this reflection Sancho made his mind easy, counting the business as good as settled, and stayed there till the afternoon so as to make Don Quixote think he had time enough to go to El Toboso and return; and things turned out so luckily for him that as he got up to mount Dapple, he spied, coming from El Toboso towards the spot where he stood, three peasant girls on three colts, or fillies- for the author does not make the point clear, though it is more likely they were she-asses ... [Sancho trots off toward his master to prepare him for the apparition] "Holy God! what art thou saying, Sancho, my friend?" exclaimed Don Quixote. "Take care thou art not deceiving me, or seeking by false joy to cheer my real sadness." "What could I get by deceiving your worship," returned

Sancho, "especially when it will so soon be shown whether I tell the truth or not? Come, senor, push on, and you will see the princess our mistress coming, robed and adorned- in fact, like what she is. [A superlative description of their beauties and adornments follows.]

By this time they had cleared the wood, and saw the three village lasses close at hand. Don Quixote looked all along the road to El Toboso, and as he could see nobody except the three peasant girls, he was completely puzzled, and asked Sancho if it was outside the city he had left them. "How outside the city?" returned Sancho. "Are your worship's eyes in the back of your head, that you can't see that they are these who are coming here, shining like the very sun at noonday?" "I see nothing, Sancho," said Don Quixote, "but three country girls on three jackasses." "Now, may God deliver me from the devil!" said Sancho, "and can it be that your worship takes three hackneys—or whatever they're called—as white as the driven snow, for jackasses? By the Lord, I could tear my beard if that was the case!" "Well, I can only say, Sancho, my friend," said Don Quixote, "that it is as plain they are jackasses—or jennyasses—as that I am Don Quixote, and thou Sancho Panza: at any rate, they seem to me to be so."

"Hush, senor," said Sancho, "don't talk that way, but open your eyes, and come and pay your respects to the lady of your thoughts, who is close upon us now," and with these words he advanced to receive the three village lasses, and dismounting from Dapple, caught hold of one of the asses of the three country girls by the halter, and dropping on both knees on the ground, he said, "Queen and princess and duchess of beauty, may it please your haughtiness and greatness to receive into your favour and good-will your captive knight who stands there turned into marble stone, and quite stupefied and benumbed at finding himself in your magnificent presence. I am Sancho Panza, his squire, and he the vagabond knight Don Quixote of La Mancha, otherwise called 'The Knight of the Rueful Countenance'." Don Quixote had by this time placed himself on his knees beside Sancho, and, with eyes starting out of his head and a puzzled gaze, was regarding her whom Sancho called queen and lady; and as he could see nothing in her except a village lass, and not a very well-favoured one, for she was platter-faced and snub-nosed, he was perplexed and bewildered, and did not venture to open his lips. (II, X, 69–71)

The village lasses rudely send their admirers packing, and an inconsolable Don Quixote concludes that the evil genius dogging his footsteps wishes to deprive him of the happiness he would have experienced had he gazed upon his lady "in her veritable being."

Sancho's trick has accomplished its aim, but not at all in the way its author expected. For once, although he finds himself at the heart of the web of hallucination, Don Quixote does not allow himself to be fooled, and sees things exactly as they are. But he does not, in a matter of such sovereign importance as this, doubt for an instant his man-servant's good faith. It would never have occurred to him that his plucky companion could simultaneously muster such finesse and such cunning. Thus he *logically* comes to the well-known conclusion. The stratagem begins to break down because the Ingenious Gentleman—failing a new, more effective *mise-en-scène* that would be beyond the squire's capacity—can only be deceived by his own imagination. This is, of course, the pretender's ultimate recourse: if the man in love refuses to play the game, he is bound to discover within himself the motives for his disenchantment. It goes to show how deeply the servant has, perhaps unconsciously, penetrated into his master's mindset, even though he persists in not grasping its meaning. But this extraordinary penetration must remain concealed, for if it is not, the relationship of the priceless duo would be irremediably compromised. Until the very end, Quixote will never know.

Sancho and Quixote are held together as a couple by the equivocation that, in each one's mouth, carefully surrounds the question of truth, and that makes it possible for them, for all their incessant bickering, to love one another. The portraits they draw of each other give us a moving testimony to the depth of their friendship:

> "I would have your graces understand [declares Quixote to the duke and duchess] that Sancho Panza is one of the drollest squires that ever served knight-errant; sometimes there is a simplicity about him so acute that it is an amusement to try and make out whether he is simple or sharp; he has mischievous tricks that stamp him rogue, and blundering ways that prove him a booby; he doubts everything and believes everything; when I fancy he is on the point of coming down headlong from sheer stupidity, he comes out with something shrewd that sends him up to the skies. After all, I would not exchange him for another squire, though I were given a city to boot, and therefore I am in doubt whether it will be well to send him to the government your highness has bestowed

upon him; though I perceive in him a certain aptitude for the work
of governing ..." (II, XXXII, 231)

Sancho will go on to demonstrate remarkable sagacity in his brief tenure
as governor. But he finally abandons the position on his own initiative when
faced with the absurd requirements of the trade. We soon find the same
perspicacity at work in his word-portrait of Quixote, in the course of a
confidential conversation with the duchess:

> "And the first thing I have got to say is, that for my own part I hold
> my master Don Quixote to be stark mad, though sometimes he
> says things that, to my mind, and indeed, everybody's that listens
> to him, are so wise, and run in such a straight furrow, that Satan
> himself could not have said them better." [He relates the deception
> of Toboso, upon which the duchess observes that he must be even
> madder than his master if he persists in following him and
> believing his promises. Sancho agrees without difficulty:] "if I
> were wise I should have left my master long ago; but this was my
> fate, this was my bad luck; I can't help it, I must follow him; we're
> from the same village, I've eaten his bread, I'm fond of him, I'
> grateful, he gave me his ass-colts, and above all I'm faithful; so it's
> quite impossible for anything to separate us, except the pickaxe
> and shovel." (II, XXXIII, 235–236)

Faith in his master implies faith in his dream that drives him on,
incomprehensible though it may be. One cannot follow Don Quixote, nor
enter his service, without sharing a bit of his madness. It would be hard not to
be half crazy when anywhere close to him. At Toboso, Sancho does nothing
more than extricate himself from a delicate situation; his duplicity is far from
treachery; it is deeply, secretly faithful. He deceives out of love, out of the
rightful intuition of what keeps his master alive. The game may seem cruel,
but the Knight of the Rueful Countenance will contrive somehow to draw
strength from his bitter disappointment at not having beheld his lady in her
"true" splendor, the moment when the truth could have brought about his
death. Cunning notwithstanding, Sancho behaves more justly than he thinks
in sparing Quixote the encounter, even though it is false, with the object of a
love that, to use his own words, must remain "chimerical."

By the same fatality that binds servant to master, the master himself is
not at liberty to choose his fate. In fact, the master is less master of himself
than his valet (who has been able to abandon his own chimera, the

governorship, of his own accord). As the hero explains to his niece on the eve of the third sally: "It will be labour in vain for you to urge me to resist what heaven wills, fate ordains, reason requires, and, above all, my own inclination favours; for knowing as I do the countless toils that are the accompaniments of knight-errantry, I know, too, the infinite blessings that are attained by it" (II, VI, 48–49).

The blessings of which he speaks are as chimerical as Dulcinea herself. It remains to be seen whether that fact alone makes them ridiculous—which leads us to reflect upon the meaning of the fate that Don Quixote claims he must make his own and which he unyieldingly desires to be assigned him, by the tale in which the narrator sets up a dialogue of almost inexhaustible complexity between necessity and free will, between the real and the imaginary.

Without presuming to exhaust its meaning, let us attempt to get a firmer grasp of the nature of Quixotian heroism in its double relationship with fiction and with reality. Where fiction is concerned, there can be little doubt that the hero's fate, as his nickname implies, is to cut a doleful figure; the laughable figure of a hero more pathetic than he is tragic. How can he be taken seriously if he is the sole author of his mishaps? If we limit ourselves to the fiction alone, the entire work is little more than parody, irony, mockery. Such a position is clearly untenable: Quixote is well aware that he is not wandering through the enchanted forest of Broceliande in the days of King Arthur, but through the Spain of the late sixteenth century, a world that is presented to us as perfectly real, where frequent mention is made of historically verifiable facts.[131] Cervantes' tale owes much of its life to this contrast.

The reality against which fiction collides is that of Spain, which, ruled by their Most Catholic Majesties since the fall of Grenada in 1492, has continued to expel, purify, and submit to the Inquisition everything that might be contaminated in any way, shape or form by either Islam or Judaism. Such are the political priorities of the reason-inspired elite that watches over the affairs of this world. I am not attempting to insinuate that Cervantes condemns his government; he does not. I am merely pointing to the presence of this dimension in his work, which invokes—let us not forget—the authority of an Arab historian. The policy of purification constitutes an objective part of the reality in which the hero finds it entirely reasonable to become a madman. The contrast between the reasoning of the madman and

---

131. With his edict of September 22, 1609, Philippe III forbade the Moriscos from residing in Spanish territory on pain of death (II, LIV).

that of the most logical of men, as we shall see in another context, is far from innocent.

The decision to be mad, in Quixote's case, clearly has nothing to do with actuality. It is simply *that which reason demands*, as he tells his niece. It would not be difficult to catalogue the appeal to reason under the heading of Quixotian extravagance. In fact, we would hardly have another option were Quixote truly and fundamentally mad. But as everyone well knows, he is not. He is "mad" only within the narrow confines of his personal foibles. And these foibles have a reason. But what is that reason? How, in other words, does the fiction manage to extract itself from its everyday surroundings to such a degree that Quixote will eventually desire to penetrate it? The erotic image is anything but fortuitous: Dulcinea, for all the ambiguity of courtly love, stands as the emblematic figure of the fiction which Quixote would *really* love to penetrate and to possess, not so much the lady as his glory. Yet he no more lives in this fiction than he encounters Dulcinea. The *hidalgo's* love for both is necessarily unrequited, and his reputation is anything but glorious. In returning to reality, he abjures his dream. Though he fails to carve out a place for himself in chivalrous fiction, Quixote succeeds in spite of himself in doing so in the burlesque fiction that makes a mockery of the original: his story is printed and widely read, to the great amusement of those into whose hands it falls.

This comic circularity does not, however, exhaust relations with the real, for it never explains exactly why Quixote succumbs to madness and to the charms of narrative fiction, chivalrous or not. He can only be understood in terms of the reality that has been his from the very beginning:

> In a village of La Mancha, the name of which I have no desire to call to mind, there lived not long since one of those gentlemen that keep a lance in the lance-rack, an old buckler, a lean hack, and a greyhound for coursing. An olla of rather more beef than mutton, a salad on most nights, scraps on Saturdays, lentils on Fridays, and a pigeon or so extra on Sundays, made away with three-quarters of his income. The rest of it went in a doublet of fine cloth and velvet breeches and shoes to match for holidays, while on week-days he made a brave figure in his best homespun. He had in his house a housekeeper past forty, a niece under twenty, and a lad for the field and market-place, who used to saddle the hack as well as handle the bill-hook. The age of this gentleman of ours was bordering on fifty; he was of a hardy habit, spare, gaunt-featured, a very early riser and a great sportsman.

> They will have it his surname was Quixada or Quesada (for here there is some difference of opinion among the authors who write on the subject), although from reasonable conjectures it seems plain that he was called Quexana. This, however, is of but little importance to our tale; it will be enough not to stray a hair's breadth from the truth in the telling of it.
>
> You must know, then, that the above-named gentleman whenever he was at leisure (which was mostly all the year round) gave himself up to reading books of chivalry with such ardour and avidity that he almost entirely neglected the pursuit of his field-sports, and even the management of his property. (I, I, 51)

We know nothing more about the character before his reading turns his head. An obscure inhabitant (we are not even certain of his name) of a village that is itself anonymous, defined by his repetitive diet, his accoutrements, and his mediocre entourage made up of a governess, a niece, a boy of all work, a nag, and a hound. His only visible occupation is hunting, which for all intents and purposes is not enough to extract him from his quasi-permanent state of sloth. He is becalmed on a sea of boredom, a man of fifty. He has nothing to look forward to but the endless, monotonous repetition of all that has come before. In a century rich in possibilities for adventure, our *hidalgo* might well have offered his services to the King, taken to sea, marched off to colonize the New World. Despite his apparent good health, perhaps it is too late; the bed of his life has been made, he has been crushed by the weight of inertia. Imagination, compensating for the emptiness of a life by now almost over, revives his slumbering hopes and dreams and lifts him from the confines of daily life— while never carrying him too far afield. The tale of knight-errantry propels him into a real world long separated from him by rural idiocy. The paradox is that *through fiction*, either thanks to or because of it, our valorous Quixano comes into contact *with a far greater reality*.

We cannot simply claim that Quixote is fleeing reality. Instead, he is escaping his minuscule day-to-day world the better to fling himself into the wider world—the altogether relative immensity of the Manchegan plain that still contrives to open new horizons to him. The problem is that the path he has elected to follow belongs to a bygone era, if indeed such an era ever existed. Don Quixote has entered into the wrong world. But he has done so more consciously than less. Surely he suspects that in a century he could not become a part of as a young man, no other form of adventure is possible. Not satisfied with experiencing adventure from his armchair, he seeks it along the farthest limits of the world. This is the world he must enter into, and with which he inevitably will collide, for he is proceeding blindfolded. Quixote does not reject reality out of idealism, but simply because he can do nothing else except to die from boredom in his hole.

Don Quixote is indeed a tragic figure. But his tragedy is that of not being understood by the world through which he makes his way, an incomprehension that he accepts with some dignity, and from which he draws the best of his pride. His tragedy is twofold: first, to have passed himself by; second, to have been forced to relinquish his dream. Only too late does Quixano discover the desire to set himself apart. All that remains is to throw himself into extravagance with total abandon. His only madness lies in his failure to understand that this singular manner of attaining lasting renown is to make him far more illustrious than the absurd nature of his undertaking ever could. But by the same token, only by refusal can he preserve his dignity. Not as a ridiculous hero, but as a hero *of* the ridiculous; the Ingenious Gentleman has come to personify the precariousness of the heroic stance. Perched atop his frail Rocinante, he canters along the edge of the void into which *all* heroes are at constant risk of tumbling. Trapped between the mediocrity of his daily life and the excessiveness of his ambition (to stand out at any cost), the hero must continue to blind his eyes to his true situation.

There is nothing extraordinary here; his is the kind of situation we must all, to a greater or lesser degree, confront: the ridiculous lies in wait for us at the most tragic moments of our lives, at the moment when we are the least apt to realize it. Quixote finds himself exposed to it with particular frequency and intensity due to the permanent state of misalignment in which he exists, but his lot is ours as well. No one makes his or her way through life untouched; no one lives without masking a considerable part of his or her reality, without interpreting reality to his or her advantage. Reality, the hardness of which breaks our dreams, becomes endurable only insofar as it can be strained through the edifying filter of our interpretation. *Don Quixote* is the tragic caricature of this necessity, the same necessity that, for the eponymous hero, has assumed heroic proportions. Quixote is inconsolable at the collapse of his self-image. His lucidity, by reducing that self-image to his mediocre identity, kills him. Life is no longer worth living. This does not make him the first anti-hero of our literature. Indeed, he may well be its last authentic hero: he strives for the impossible, and perishes in the attempt. He lives out his dream, and it is the death of him. Abjuring his "error" cannot save him. Only in death does errancy such as his remain possible.

The character of Quixote may be archaic, but the absurdity of his situation could hardly be more modern. In a world where, as we have seen in Rabelais, earthly adventure claims (or reclaims) all its rights, in a world where the individual feels all but compelled to give meaning to life in the growing solitude of his ego, the imaginary structures that sustain meaning slip imperceptibly from the collective to the individual. The ego must, increasingly, contrive to survive in the illusion of its success—or perish, if not in reality, at least symbolically, or become what we call a "less than nothing"—the void that threatens us all. It comes as no accident that Quixote's attempts to draw attention to himself take place in the fictional universe of chivalry. We know now to what extent this universe has already magnified the personal exploit that, unlike the prowess of the heroes of old, is a sign of truth. The Arthurian knight finds the truth within and beyond himself at the same moment, in the combat against the Other; truth and identity are mortally interconnected. The quest for the Grail unfolds in a social and symbolic framework that makes such fusion possible. This is the outdated structure that Quixote pretends to wish to reinstate, and whose obsolescence condemns him to isolation, to derision, to defeat.

Insofar as, if we are to believe the narrator, "it is, from beginning to end, an attack upon the books of chivalry" (I, prol., 47), Cervantes' novel does not only deliver a devastating verdict against an outdated heroism, it also prefigures, with broad brushstrokes of sarcasm, the condition of the modern ego. To this ego has been assigned a task that is, for all intents and purposes, overwhelming, if indeed its sole responsibility is to give meaning to the real. It is a burden that Quixote, by conforming to the code of knight-errantry, by taking refuge in an outmoded grandeur, refuses to bear. Everything that is familiar to him, his day-to-day universe, is too obviously devoid of meaning; his reading of the marvellous awakens him to his own internal mediocrity, invites him to strike out for that land of impossibility whose meaning has already been given. But those in whose eyes he becomes a public laughingstock (but a published one, let us not forget) are one hundred times more mediocre than he is. They know not what they mock: feet mired in reality into which Quixote regularly tumbles, they mechanically take the world for granted. Their lives make even less sense than that of their laughable hero; the Duke and the Duchess have nothing better to do than to make him the butt of their pathetic distractions. For his part, Cid Hamet the historian "considers the concocters of the joke as crazy as the victims of it" (II, LXX, 479). In their well-anchored reasoning, they draw meagre comfort from the spectacle of Quixotian "madness." But their reasoning is void. The non-sense that they take pleasure in pointing out in others exempts them from the suffering their own truth inflicts. Their reading of *Don Quixote* has the same effect on them as do tales of chivalry upon Quixano : it *distracts* them from their reality. Interpreting the Other's reality (in the event, his madness) means that they need not interpret their own. They have not read Rabelais.

Perhaps now we can understand somewhat better how problematic reality is in *Don Quixote*: the spiritual underpinnings of those who laugh at the Ingenious Gentleman's misadventures may well not be quite as solid as they imagine. Cervantes inserts his story within a story for the best of reasons: the reality in which most of his secondary characters believe themselves so firmly rooted is in fact a part of the fiction. Quixote and Sancho are not the only ones to provide narrative material; the readers themselves, like the Duke and the Duchess, like Samson Carrasco, all contribute actively to its growth. Carrasco, it must be said, brings it also to an end, by toppling the hero bearing the coat of arms of the Knight of the White-Moon. But this champion of common sense does not know what he has gotten into, and Don Quixote's host in Barcelona, the Gentleman Antonio Moréno, loses not an occasion to let him know: "May God forgive you the wrong you have done the whole world in trying to bring the most amusing madman in it back to his senses" (II, LXV, 450). God's name may not be invoked as vainly as it might appear, and Samson surely does not appreciate the implications of his act: if madness no longer looms on the horizon, how is reason to define itself? Samson shares in the "disenchantment with the world" that deprives men of their dreams. But where the champion is convinced that he has acted properly, the gentleman has his doubts: a world without dreams, without madness, with no other madness than that which consists of taking reality for reality, stands in danger of being annoying in the extreme.

I have no intention of suggesting that Cervantes' "modernity" lies in his premonition of boredom; that, beyond the "end of myth" lies a critique of the new world taking shape on both sides of the Atlantic. The same can be said of reality itself: its status, in the story, remains uncertain. The light that brutally illuminates it, like the sun of La Mancha on a white-hot summer midday, leaves so little shadow that it becomes unreal itself—as if the clarity of reason could reign forever, effortlessly. The piercing gaze that the story turns upon its lead characters is not enough to disperse all ambiguity, nor does it even attempt to do so—beginning with the ambiguity of the narrator who, as we have seen, designates himself as "second author" and hides behind an Arab source of which he claims to offer us a simple translation accompanied by the occasional commentary, touching for the most part on its reliability. What could be more reliable? With the exception of a few minor details, the first author, Cid Hamet ben-Engeli, has clearly hewed scrupulously to the historian's obligations. If any possible objection is to be raised as to the sincerity of the tale, he adds,

> it can only be that its author was an Arab, as lying is a very common propensity with those of that nation; though, as they are such enemies of ours, it is conceivable that there were omissions rather than additions made in the course of it. And this is my own opinion; for, where he could and should give freedom to his pen in praise of so worthy a knight, he seems to me deliberately to pass it over in silence; which is ill done and worse contrived, for it is the business and duty of historians to be exact, truthful, and wholly free from passion, and neither interest nor fear, hatred nor love, should make them swerve from the path of truth, whose mother is history, rival of time, storehouse of deeds, witness for the past, example and counsel for the present, and warning for the future. (I, IX, 101)

If we are to take these remarks seriously, the first author, because he is an Arab, would be inclined to minimize Quixote's merits—which supposes that the second author knows the "true" nature of this "so worthy a knight." In which case, the Ingenious Gentleman could only be less mad than he appears to be. But the providential circumstances that deliver the Arabic manuscript into the hands of the Spanish narrator, at the very instant when the sources upon which he has been depending have left the tale hanging in the midst of a ferocious combat—the only true, man-to-man combat which Quixote will have had the opportunity to engage in throughout all his adventures. This unlikely scene, in the tale, of the story of the tale itself, combined with excessive praise for the virtues of historical discipline, all indicates that this "criticism of sources" is in fact part and parcel of the comic apparatus designed to enhance the ridiculous aspect of the entire enterprise: both that of the hero, and of his historians. The obsession with historical accuracy becomes the means that the only true author, Cervantes, employs to muddy the waters and to place himself beyond reach, like truth itself. There is no way of knowing for certain where reality lies nor, in the final analysis, what things it holds dearest.

Clearly, Cervantes makes abundant use of the comic register and does so admirably. But it is much more difficult to ascertain what exactly he is holding up to ridicule: madness or reason, otherness or identity, dream or reality, fable or truth? The further we read, the more difficult it becomes to make up our minds. This all but insoluble difficulty leads me to conclude that Cervantes refuses to reduce life to these alternatives. We cannot entirely overlook his concern for the censors, but that seems to me a secondary consideration in a work respectful of the established order and hardly likely to be considered as a thought crime. If Cervantes is critical of any "order," it is neither specifically political or religious, but rather the general order of things that we take for granted, the certainty of his varied characters that they are in "good order." For Quixote, this means belonging to the order of justice; for his readers, to that of reason. Far more than the censorship of the king or the Church, Cervantes' tale would have had more to fear from the reductive function that, down to the present day, threatens to transform his book into a hymn in praise of oneiric flight, or into its opposite, an apology of realism.

Don Quixote's ambiguity is pedagogical. It causes us to reflect on what Hegel was later to term "the false familiarity of things." Cervantes goes quite far in this direction. To sustain ambiguity to the bitter end, he sacrifices his hero to it. Despite the affection he feels for his creature, almost in spite of himself, he allows him to travel down the road to ruin. Don Quixote does not return any wiser than when he departed, and his last-minute conversion is a pure defeat: it preserves none of the dream that he so unhappily attempted to live. He denies himself with the same strength that he had dreamed himself. His return is no greater cause for reflection than his earlier life, or his departure. Though it is real enough, his wisdom will be of no help to him whatsoever—perhaps because of that particular cleft of the soul through which the honorable gentleman would have vainly attempted to escape from himself, and which the narrator takes great pains not to explain.

In burying Don Quixote, and along with him his cleft soul, Cervantes makes certain that no one will be able to manipulate him. Uncertainty he leaves intact. Just as he leaves intact the paradox of his masterwork. In what we might well term the precursor in book form of modern heroism—assuming it is still possible to speak of heroism—Don Quixote, in grafting the fictional onto the real at that historical point where the old and the new intersect, sets in sharp relief the individual imperative to make one's self singular. But in the same breath he sweeps aside the dream that had been destined to carry the hero's singular madness to its ultimate conclusion. In this disenchanted world can one be a hero, if only in one's own eyes? Can an individual, alone, create meaning?

15

The Ghost of Truth

I F ANY MAN can be said to ruminate on the solitude of meaning, that man is certainly Shakespeare's most celebrated, most commented-upon hero.

Night has fallen. It is cold. A silent form clad in all the majesty of the recently deceased king, a suspicious figure who has usurped his lordly bearing and his noble features, prowls the ramparts of Ellsinore. Officers of the guard attempt in vain to restrain him: "Stay, illusion!" Hamlet, homonymous son of the dead man, has been warned: the ghost will speak to him. It reveals that his father died not of snakebite, but of venom from the viper of fratricide, adultery, and incest that now wears his crown and sleeps with his widow.

The atmosphere in which Hamlet learns that his uncle, King Claudius, his mother's new husband, is in fact his father's killer crackles with dark electricity. The inexorable dynamo of vengeance has begun to turn.

But the telling of the tale unfolds disjointedly. The man who seeks revenge hesitates, procrastinates. And because he cannot bring himself to act, vengeance will never be his. Only death. Death upon death, which will leave the Danish throne unguarded, left at the mercy of the Norwegian enemy against whose intrigues preparations are being made as the play opens. The original victory, that of Hamlet the father over Fortinbras, King of Norway, will have been for naught: the murderous dissolution of the royal family will deposit the crown of Denmark upon the head of Fortinbras the son.

Let us begin again.

The lawful king is dead. From the secret revelation of the initial murder bubbles a thirst for revenge that is slow to assume overt form. Indecision touches off a spate of killing: first Polonius, counsellor to the usurper, hidden behind the curtains in the queen's apartments, whom Hamlet blindly runs through in the hope of striking his uncle; the seemingly suicidal drowning of Ophelia, daughter of Polonius, who has fallen wildly in love with her father's killer; the poisoning of the queen who carelessly drinks from the cup that her husband had prepared for Hamlet in the event the prince survived the rigged duel organized by the king with the connivance of the vengeful wrath of Laertes, son of Polonius and brother of Ophelia; the fatal wound dealt to Laertes by the poisoned blade with which he has just struck down Hamlet and which the two combatants have inadvertently traded in the heat of the action; the death of the king at the hand of his nephew, to whom Laertes reveals before expiring; the conspiracy of regicide; and last but not least, Hamlet himself, from the blow dealt by his adversary before their swords changed hands. Reckonings are postponed, characters hesitate, identities are mistaken, and things go suddenly awry: against all expectations and despite the best of calculations, everything seems to lead to the grotesque dance of death. Inaction far more than action, error far more than shrewdness, is the protagonist's guide.

Stripped of its flesh, reduced to its denouement, the tragedy collapses headlong into a heap of bones. Clumsy composition is not a factor: what we witness is tragedy itself, the raw and primal tragedy of a story with neither beginning nor end, the mirror image of the decapitated and rotten kingdom in which it unfolds. The tragedy is one of indecision, indecision hard to fathom in a hero who lacks neither lucidity nor courage, a man toward whom the reader is inclined to be quite forgiving. Perhaps precisely because in him, lucidity paralyses action and the consummate art of sarcasm does far greater damage than would any sword. For all that, speech, and language triumph over nothing, and perish with him. Whether by tongue or by rapier, Hamlet gives every *appearance* of impotence.

Doubt may excuse his excessive prudence: there is no certainty that the ghost he beholds is an emanation of the devil, nor that it has taken on the beloved face of his father all the better to deceive him. But our hypothesis cannot hold water for long: the hero utilizes the arrival of a group of travelling players to stage a barely concealed representation of the murder of his father, at which King Claudius promptly betrays himself. Doubt is no longer possible, yet still Hamlet refuses to act. He lets the perfect occasion slip by, on the pretext that the fratricide and usurper is at prayer; therefore he does not wish to strike him down while he is in God's good graces, but must wait to find him in a state of sin (as his father had been). Called to his mother's chambers, a mortified Hamlet gives vent to his rage against a suspicious drape in the nebulous hope of slaying the king by mistake: with one fell—and blind—swoop a filial duty will be accomplished, the scandal suppressed, the shame washed away. But the corpse proves to be only that of the wretched Polonius, the pitiable "intelligence" of the state, the ears of the king concealed with the queen's collusion.

Weakness of character? The explanation carries no water. The hero's impotence has other causes, outside himself, which he is strongly aware of yet can only partially grasp. Though sensitive to everything that is going on around him, he does not have—any more than do we, as readers or spectators—the means to understand all that is happening, the circumstances of the initial murder to begin with. What precisely was queen Gertrude's role? How deep was her involvement? Does she even know that a murder has taken place? More than probably she is implicated, but can we be absolutely certain? Whatever the case, the ease with which she moves from one brother to the other, from authentic majesty to tainted royalty, the facility with which she leaves such a great love behind raises far more questions than it answers. Before he encounters the ghost the son expresses his disgust, though he is not yet aware of the murder. The viands of the funeral banquet, says his friend Horatio, were hardly cold when they were served at the nuptial feast. "Frailty, thy name is woman" (I, ii, 122).

Uncertainty swirls not only about the queen's head. It touches too the nature of the relationship between the two brothers, the stature of the killer, and even the innocence of the slain king—all perplexities that do nothing but aggravate the hero's indecision. Not that he can truly doubt the villainy of his uncle, but because the incriminating events belong to a state of pre-existence that the tale deliberately leaves to bathe in a sort of star-lit chiaroscuro.

Ambition, jealousy, and covetousness are the motivations that the spectator spontaneously attributes to Claudius's crime, though the text never directly says as much. But as soon as it becomes clear that the same evidence cannot be applied to the queen's motives, we will never know how she could ever have succumbed to such a wretch's charms. The ghost itself is reduced to lending to his brother an occult seductive power (I, v, 42–47). That which cannot be explained is bodied forth: the queen's behavior remains totally incomprehensible. The psychological enigma that she represents stands in startling contrast to the spirit of revenge that impels Clytemnystra in Aeschylus's *Agamemnon*: the abandoned spouse of the Atrides has simply filled the void left by her husband's absence by taking Aegisthus as a lover; as for the murder, it is made inevitable by the sacrifice of Iphigenia, whom Agamemnon had shamefully handed over in order to win from the gods the fair wind he needed for his expedition, placing the honor of his brother Menelas above his own duty as parent and spouse.

No such causal sequence can be found in *Hamlet*.[132] The fratricide stands outside the tragedy it unleashes; it forms a portion of its premise and as such needs no explanation. Not unlike the ruler's madness in *King Lear*, the first scene does little more than expose an irreversible decision the cause of which is unknown to us, and which can, at best, be attributed to the ageing monarch's senility. In both instances, a kind of initial fatality weighs upon the entire tragedy to follow. But where Lear probably does little more than carry his age, and with it the load of a reign of which we know nothing, upon Hamlet's shoulders suddenly falls the burden of the preceding generation. Dramatically, the human condition is amplified: each one must, in one way or another, come to grips with the visible and invisible, the honorable and the shameful inherited from one's parents, the full extent of which is only revealed with their disappearance.

This, at least, is what happens to Hamlet. The death of his father leaves him all the more alone in that it deprives him at the same time of his mother. Here the Œdipean tragedy seems to play itself out in reverse: instead of granting access to the mother, the suppression of the father estranges her forever from the son's love. If *Hamlet* were nothing but Hamlet's dream— which it may well be—it would be easier to attribute the act of parricide and the incest with which he charges his uncle to the unconscious desire of the dreamer. For the uncle is the double negative of the father, whose unworthiness would allow access to the forbidden road by freeing the son of the feelings of guilt aroused by his incestuous impulses. Even assuming that the meeting with the ghost is purest hallucination (which the hero would have to share with his friend Horatio and two other officers), the Œdipean interpretation cannot satisfactorily account for the whole of the drama. At most, it generates a secondary meaning by shedding light on what the playwright is saying in spite of himself. To do so would be to read, behind the text itself, Shakespeare's subconscious. But such a reading would be forced to pretend to distinguish with a modicum of certainty what, in his work, the playwright has "intended" from what he has not. Not only does the task seem impossible, but to make a distinction actually hinders analysis. Any text worthy of attention warrants reading and reflection, empowers the reader to draw from it all the power and meaning he is capable of, independent of the author's intentions. So, without losing sight of the possibility that he may be an unconscious Œdipus, an Œdipus incapable of

---

132. William Shakespeare. *The Tragedy of Hamlet, Prince of Denmark.*

facing up to truth, Hamlet is, it seems to me, well and truly an orphan, alone against the putrefaction of the world.

The father's absence looms over the hero, and over the entire play. The king is present only as a corpse and, fleetingly, as a ghost. A ghost who, from the immaterial prison that is his, *cannot say everything*. If he could, he confides to Hamlet, he would tell him a tale whose least word would freeze his young blood (I, v, 13–16). It is unclear whether the prohibition concerns the circumstances of his assassination or his condition as a wandering soul. But we understand that something essential and abominable lurks there, something that the living must not know, an "eternal blazon" that ears and blood cannot bear to hear—and about which not another word will be spoken throughout the play. The father possesses a terrible, impenetrable secret, which we can only believe is the secret of death.

The father, or rather, the father's spirit ("I am thy father's spirit," he tells his son) is damned to wander by night, and by day to expiate his father's crimes in fire (I, v, 9–12). His nocturnal soul is half-pagan, lacking even the resources to pay its entry into Hades; his diurnal soul, the half-Christian one, is exposed to the purifying fire of purgatory. Nothing is said of the crimes it must expunge, except that they are *foul crimes*. Perhaps it is merely a stylistic flourish to describe a commonplace state of affairs: all men enter the hereafter with their bulging bags of filth. The deceased King Hamlet, in this regard, is no different from his fellow men, and the insistence with which he dwells on his sins may have no other purpose than to add to the horror of his murder, carried out while he slept, that is to say, in circumstances that prevented him from repenting his sins and commending himself to God. In all other respects, the sinner had proved an excellent king, a faithful and attentive husband, a father worthy of love and respect, whom disappearance has only helped to idealize. The spirit of the father, the ideal father, constitutes that which we could also call the "good part" of the father. In comparison with it, the uncle, who henceforth holds effective paternal power, incarnates the evil part. The son invokes the ideal father, the spiritual father, to rid himself of the real father, all the while showing himself incapable of taking action despite the success of the play-within-a-play that he has employed to unmask him. It is as if the higher authority that he has invoked is no longer sufficient to reverse the order of usurped power.

There is something religious, something metaphysical about the taboo that prevents Hamlet, whether consciously or unconsciously, from taking action. In comparing the two brothers, the nephew describes his uncle as being no more like his father than he, Hamlet, is like Hercules (I, ii,

152–153). The confession is a capital one: the son places the ideal father in a mythical, heroic, and near-divine world to which he himself does not belong. In doing so, Hamlet not only forgoes the hero's role, he also admits that he is of the same foul smelling world as his uncle. Alongside the evil father, he tramples about in the muck of earthly concerns. In the name of what should he kill him whom he so closely resembles? In the name of the higher order given to him alone to hear? The order is an enigmatic one; it comes *in such a questionable shape* (I, iv, 43), and that which it demands remains, yet again, uncertain:

> Let not the royal bed of Denmark be
> A couch for luxury and damned incest.
> But, howsoever thou pursuest this act,
> Taint not thy mind, nor let thy soul contrive
> Against thy mother aught: leave her to heaven
> And to those thorns that in her bosom lodge,
> To prick and sting her.
>
> (I, v, 82–86)

The ghost says no more, satisfied that Hamlet is intent on seeking prompt revenge. But his promise is made under the influence of emotion, at the moment of painful exaltation that tests filial love: "List, list, O, list! If thou didst ever thy dear father love" (I, v, 22–23). No sooner has he returned from his hallucinatory encounter than Hamlet makes known to his friend Horatio (while revealing nothing of what he has heard) that he will almost certainly be forced to play the fool, as though he knows already that the task is beyond him, that he feels himself threatened by a madness so real that he might not have to feign it: "The time is out of joint. O cursed spite. / That ever I was born to set it right!" (I, v, 188–189)

Playing the fool and feigning madness form part of the tactical necessity of preparing revenge in secret. But the secrecy is weak indeed, so much so that the keen eye of the king is quick to see through it despite the efforts of Polonius, who clumsily attempts to forestall the looming crisis by blaming Hamlet's erratic behavior on his unrequited love for his daughter. Polonius is a model advisor, taking upon himself the responsibility for a situation he claims to be able to untangle with the royal couple's approbation, for he can force Ophelia to reject the man she loves. Like any courtier over-eager to serve, Polonius shuts his eyes the better to blind his master's. But Hamlet's excesses foil his own best-laid plans: his eccentricity quickly betrays far more than it conceals. Dissimulation, in fact, is hardly the hallmark of his behavior.

Hamlet's "madness" derives from his having been assigned an impossible task. Its impossibility is profound, arising from the very order of the world, from the insupportable distance that separates him from what we might term the order of the ideal father. In Hamlet's consciousness, this distance is expressed as madness.

It finds its first expression in the way he approaches Ophelia, doublet unbraced, stocking fouled, ungartered. She is the narrator:

> He took me by the wrist and held me hard;
> Then goes he to the length of all his arm;
> And, with his other hand thus o'er his brow,
> He falls to such perusal of my face
> As he would draw it. Long stay'd he so;
> At last, a little shaking of mine arm
> And thrice his head thus waving up and down,
> He raised a sigh so piteous and profound
> As it did seem to shatter all his bulk
> And end his being.
>
> (II, i, 87–96)

Naïve Ophelia has been taken in by her suitor's performance. In this instance, simulation is all the more effective in that it is not total. Poor theatre though it is (the playwright will not represent it on stage), the scene speaks to a necessity deeply experienced by the character: to take his leave of her whom he loves, whom he would have liked to have loved. When, shortly thereafter, we encounter the two in one another's presence, the tone has shifted. On sight of Ophelia, Hamlet holds back the emotion that lends him his beauty and keeps a cool distance. He denies ever having given her what she so tenderly claims he has promised to return, and bewilders her with an unpleasant argument on the incompatibility of honesty and beauty. Then, he says abruptly:

> Get thee to a nunnery: why wouldst thou be a
> breeder of sinners? I am myself indifferent honest;
> but yet I could accuse me of such things that it
> were better my mother had not borne me: I am very
> proud, revengeful, ambitious, with more offences at
> my beck than I have thoughts to put them in,

imagination to give them shape, or time to act them
in. What should such fellows as I do crawling
between earth and heaven? We are arrant knaves,
all; believe none of us. Go thy ways to a nunnery.

. . . .
Or, if thou wilt needs
marry, marry a fool; for wise men know well enough
what monsters you make of them. To a nunnery, go,
and quickly too. Farewell.

(III, i, 122–131, 139–141)

Hamlet cannot conceal his emotions. He turns the accumulated hatred of
the woman who brought him into the world against Ophelia; his mother's
infamy so disgusts him that he cannot bring himself to love again, and it
reveals to him his own monstrousness. The king, who is looking upon the
scene from his hiding place, is not deceived: in the prince there is neither
love nor madness, but a melancholy pregnant with danger. And most of all,
he is a man to be watched.

Hamlet is unaware that the king has overheard him. The monarch had not
waited to surprise them before placing his nephew under surveillance. Prior
even to his encounter with the ghost, the prince had ostensibly taken his
distances from the royal couple and refused to be associated with the new
ruling house. To Claudius, who addresses him as "my son" and who
expresses surprise that clouds of mourning still hang heavy about him,
Hamlet fires back: "Not so, my lord, I am too much in the sun" (I, ii, 67).
Which can be read as: I am too closely watched by his majesty, and by
consonance between *sun* and *son*, more of a son than I would wish. Or, put
more succinctly: you may spare me your royal and paternal solicitude.

Far from tempering his audacity, the revelation of the crime tends to
exacerbate it. Not only is Polonius, the king's eyes and ears, treated to
sarcasm and rebuff, Claudius himself is not spared. As the play within a play
that will betray him begins, the king worries (an opening pantomime reveals
the theme):

KING CLAUDIUS
Have you heard the argument? Is there no offence in 't?

HAMLET
No, no, they do but jest, poison in jest; no offence
i' the world.

KING CLAUDIUS
What do you call the play?

HAMLET
The Mouse-trap. Marry, how? Tropically. This play
is the image of a murder done in Vienna: ... you shall see
anon; 'tis a knavish piece of work: but what o'
that? your majesty and we that have free souls.

Hamlet speaks here with all the self-assuredness of a director, hardly bothering to conceal his intentions: the prey need not worry; the trap into which it is about to stray is not meant for it.

The prince's insolence reaches its climax after the death of Polonius. The king attempts to learn where Hamlet has hidden the corpse:

KING CLAUDIUS
Now, Hamlet, where's Polonius?

HAMLET
At supper.

KING CLAUDIUS
At supper! where?

HAMLET
Not where he eats, but where he is eaten: a certain
convocation of politic worms are e'en at him. Your
worm is your only emperor for diet: we fat all
creatures else to fat us, and we fat ourselves for
maggots: your fat king and your lean beggar is but
variable service, two dishes, but to one table:
that's the end.

KING CLAUDIUS
Alas, alas!

HAMLET
A man may fish with the worm that hath eat of a
king, and eat of the fish that hath fed of that worm.

KING CLAUDIUS
What dost you mean by this?

HAMLET
Nothing but to show you how a king may go a
progress through the guts of a beggar.

(IV, iii, 16–31)

This is the third and last dialogue between the protagonists (whose meetings are as rare as they are brief). In injecting Claudius with the venom of his words—the same poison his uncle poured earlier into his father's ear—Hamlet has already dispatched into the realm of worms the man whom he here refuses to kill by his own hand. He will finally kill him, of course, at the play's very end, but in the heat of action unforeseen. The dagger of words is no substitute for the sword by which Hamlet is loath to carry out a task that he would have preferred to leave to vermin alone. Beyond his bottomless contempt for the royalty of this particular king looms his immense apathy for the affairs of the world. Not only will Hamlet follow the same path as King Claudius—that goes without saying—he has already considered preceding him down that path.

His cynical outlook toward death finds resonance in the famous monologue in the third act: "To be or not to be …" Is it "nobler in the mind to suffer the slings and arrows of outrageous fortune or to take arms against a sea of troubles?" wonders Hamlet. Who would hesitate "to die, to sleep; to sleep, perchance to dream"? "For in that sleep of death what dreams may come"[133] no man can "bear the whips and scores of time, the oppressor's wrong, the proud man's contumely," when we can deliver ourselves by a simple dagger's blow, there remains "But that dread of something after death" (III, i, 57–89).[134] Dread not of death itself—for death would be deliverance!—but of an eventual *something* thereafter, of which we know nothing. This is the cowardice of conscience, which, in Hamlet, reduces all enterprise to nothing. It is the sole failing that prevents him from taking leave of the "sterile promontory" of the world (II, ii, 294).

On the approach of his childhood friends Guildenstern and Rosencrantz, who have been commissioned by the king to watch him and to pry information from him, Hamlet's welcome to them tinges assiduity with irony:

133. [Translator's note: Quotation appears in English in the original text.]
134. [Translator's note: Quotation appears in English in the original text.]

HAMLET

What's the news?

ROSENCRANTZ

None, my lord, but that the world's grown honest.

HAMLET

Then is doomsday near: but your news is not true.
Let me question more in particular: what have you,
my good friends, deserved at the hands of fortune,
that she sends you to prison hither?

GUILDENSTERN

Prison, my lord!

HAMLET

Denmark's a prison.

ROSENCRANTZ

Then is the world one.

HAMLET

A goodly one; in which there are many confines,
wards and dungeons, Denmark being one o' the worst.

ROSENCRANTZ

We think not so, my lord.

HAMLET

Why, then, 'tis none to you; for there is nothing
either good or bad, but thinking makes it so: to me
it is a prison.

ROSENCRANTZ

Why then, your ambition makes it one; 'tis too
narrow for your mind.

HAMLET

O God, I could be bounded in a nut shell and count
myself a king of infinite space, were it not that I
have bad dreams.

(II, ii, 233–252)

If the world were nothing but a prison, the prince could peacefully dream there. But the world intrudes, like a splinter implanted in thought. The infinite space of the mind cannot liberate it from its internal divisions. To kill the king would not drive the world from the sphere of thought. Were he to ascend to the throne over his uncle's dead body, Hamlet would be merely climbing the ladder of nightmare. Of all his subjects the king is the least free to dream, as Claudius's agitation clearly demonstrates. The king is far too close to the world to understand that his nephew's disgust is so deep that it has placed him beyond reach of revenge. Stricken by Hamlet's gaze and obsessed with escaping it, the king ends by plotting his own demise. In imposing his logic, the fixation on power, which is the monarchical expression of *raison d'État*, turns against the man who wields that power. King Claudius may be a villain but he craves life. Craves it so miserably that he has killed in order to enjoy it as he is convinced a true sovereign must. Hamlet loves nothing; he has no position to uphold, no throne to consolidate. His cynicism, in the image of the kingdom of the spirit, knows no limits. It is this very detachment from the things of this world which, as the drama concludes, allows him to attend the duel to which he has invited the king while aware that he is probably walking toward his death—a death that would not weigh more heavily than the fall of a sparrow:

> If it be now,
> 'tis not to come; if it be not to come, it will be
> now; if it be not now, yet it will come: the
> readiness is all: since no man has aught of what he
> leaves, what is't to leave betimes?
>
> (V, ii, 209–213)

Were it not for the maturity of his responses and the philosophical distance they body forth, Hamlet would personify the crisis of adolescence. Perhaps a crisis of that order lies latent in him, never overcome, insurmountable, preventing him, as the royal couple chides him, from bidding his father final farewell. "But, you must know, your father lost a father;" Claudius tells him. "That father lost, lost his" (I, ii, 89–90). If we forget for a moment the active role that the speaker has played in the loss (and whom the hero at that moment totally ignores), his remark is wise indeed. There is a time for mourning. Hamlet, though, has never taken that time. The haste with which the funeral gives way to the wedding has something sacrilegious about it, to which the prince refuses to grant his endorsement. His inability to complete his mourning arises precisely from the fact that, beginning with his mother, *no mourning has ever taken place*. Above and beyond the respect owed to the dignity of the departed, Hamlet is tormented by the scorn of the world—the world of pleasure and power brought together in the new royal couple—for all that is sacred.

Paradoxically, for all his torment, our hero can barely bring himself to believe in the notion of the sacred. Mourning for him assumes a particular intensity, in that its object proves so vacillating. For all his finer qualities, the murdered king has not been able to win his brother's respect, nor hold his wife's love. Behind his worldly and political impotence lurks a weakness, a more fundamental flaw. In the figure of the ideal father, the ideal of the father, and above and beyond it, the principle of truth, God himself, has been struck down. Hamlet encounters only the ghost of truth. Existing in the form of a plaintive shadow, it requires the aid and comfort of the living in order to prevail. Here then is the son's task: to serve this pallid truth, this doubtful ideal while revealing the sordid truth that has dispatched the personification of the ideal into the other world (not unlike in the Christian myth, the son is called upon to die for his father; here he will do so by sacrificing not himself but his progenitor, even though he risks his life in doing so). There is nothing reassuring about the ghost; the hero alone can hear his voice,[135] and if he speaks of the other world, he offers only the palest reflection of transcendence.

Hamlet may well wish to conform to the canon of heroism, but he is caught in a contradiction from which he cannot extricate himself: he must act in the name of a truth in which he no longer believes, to the extent of expecting only nothingness after death. If his expectations are well founded, if life is nothing but a bad dream (of which the ghost's apparition is as much a part as any other untoward event), what remains to avenge? Why relieve the murderer of the burden of his crime? Hamlet's sardonic watching and waiting, his cynical presence, are the only torments the tyrant warrants, the only revenge to fit the crime. Quite precisely because this torment of his has become unbearable, the king unconsciously arranges for his own death—and along with it, the deaths of all, in a final hecatomb worthy of a *grand guignol*. The drops of poison King Claudius has deposited in the ear of his brother, and that Hamlet in turn transmits by his words, end up spreading uncontrollably and killing everyone.

Hamlet, just like all the others, dies stupidly, stung by the venom of power—a power he has never sought. His death is neither glorious, nor spectacular, nor even tragic. The lack of heroism is deliberate: throughout the play Hamlet has refused to play the hero's role and turns his back on revenge, or rather, distils it as a slow-acting poison. He does act, but only in allowing

---

135. In the great confrontation between Hamlet and his mother, the ghost makes a brief appearance and addresses the hero. But the queen neither sees nor hears it, and believes her son to be mad as she sees him "with the incorporal air do hold discourse" (III, iv, 102–139).

events to happen, limiting himself to deflecting blows (particularly in redirecting toward Guildenstern and Rosencrantz the sealed order they bear and by which King Claudius enjoins the king of England to execute Hamlet). His only act, a blind thrust of his sword, an impulsive demonstration of virility and impotence performed for the benefit of his mother, fails: the mediocre Polonius has not deserved as much. To pass himself off as a hero, Hamlet would have had to be convinced that justice and truth were on his side. Not only the justice of men, which reduced to its essentials is nothing but a settling of accounts or reflections of a balance of power, but also that superior, transcendent justice in which, as a legitimation of action, he has ceased to believe. All men have the same worth, and "Man delights not me" (II, ii, 304).

Life itself is not only a game, but a sinister game at that. For example, the actor on occasion plays it so perfectly, incarnating characters that are of little concern to him, that his performance becomes almost revolting:

> Is it not monstrous that this player here,
> But in a fiction, in a dream of passion,
> Could force his soul so to his own conceit
> That from her working all his visage wann'd,
> Tears in his eyes, distraction in's aspect,
> A broken voice, and his whole function suiting
> With forms to his conceit? and all for nothing!
> For Hecuba!
> What's Hecuba to him, or he to Hecuba,
> That he should weep for her? What would he do,
> Had he the motive and the cue for passion
> That I have? He would drown the stage with tears
> And cleave the general ear with horrid speech,
> Make mad the guilty and appal the free,
> Confound the ignorant, and amaze indeed
> The very faculties of eyes and ears. Yet I,
> A dull and muddy-mettled rascal, peak,
> Like John-a-dreams, unpregnant of my cause,
> And can say nothing.
>
> (II, ii, 540–559)

So masterful is the actor's simulation that he moves us where Hamlet remains silent: a virtuoso performance that convinces the prince to use the stage to bring truth to light and unmask the king. Life and the theatre are in constant communication; reality and fiction share the same sphere, fable and truth are one—as Nietzsche would put it. But if there is no difference between the world and its representation, God is then defined as nothing but the fabrication of our thought process, and that process is sufficient to annihilate him. If his existence depends on men alone, he may as well be absent.

Like the ideal father, God himself is the ghost of our imagination. Truth has no substance, and heroism, in circumstances such as these, has no meaning. Ever since the triumph of Christianity, there can be no other hero than truth—one and indivisible. If truth fluctuates according to each individual's lights, then each is nothing but the laughable hero of his own illusion. Such is the derision that Hamlet refuses to carry to its highest degree, and which we could term the heroism of refusal. Hamlet's heroism resides precisely in his discarding of the heroic role the situation demands of him. In fact, it brings about a clean break with the very idea of heroism itself.

His refusal and his clean break are what make him the most "modern" of the heroes we have thus far encountered, if not the most "modern" of those yet to come. In a certain sense, Hamlet has already moved beyond modernity. He could well be considered, using a deliberate anachronism, as the archetype of the "postmodern" hero. The modern hero still has truth on his side, even though he may no longer designate it (not necessarily, at least) by the name of God, whom he no longer hesitates to replace, thus attaining with greatest difficulty what might be considered as the heights of absurdity. Hamlet takes pains, however, to stay far from these heights, as though he already knew that nothing, no one, one's self least of all, could possibly take the place of supreme absence. Knowledge like this makes him a dangerous man, a man to be watched and eliminated: under his caustic gaze all falls apart, beginning with the political and social hierarchy that is the cement of the state.

What is most striking about *Hamlet* today is that its eponymous hero shows hardly a wrinkle. If Hamlet is indeed our contemporary, if we can effortlessly make him one of us now, at the beginning of the twenty-first century, it is because at the dawning of the modern age, well before the beheading of kings in the name of the people, well before the "Rule of Law" and the "death of God," nearly forty years before the publication of the *Discourse on Method*—that modern quest for truth—he already gives voice to the void of meaning which, over the last several decades, has resulted from the disillusions of modernity and of its political and social assumption. Hamlet may well be both pre-classical and postmodern. He is the forerunner of modernity in gestation, and the precocious herald of its defeat as a political idea.

But his powers of anticipation make sense only for us. Hamlet is neither prophetic nor divine. He embodies perhaps the most sinister portion of the sensibility of his age, a kind of Montaignian scepticism carried to its darkest extreme and a fair match for his humor, radical in its opposition to Rabelaisian impertinence. Against these three varieties of scepticism (farcical in Rabelais, measured in Montaigne, radical in Shakespeare), classical thought will attempt with regard to truth a "rectification campaign," which will lead, not without an occasional setback, to the philosophy of the Enlightenment and to the political project of modernity—in whose light Hamlet's dark thoughts seem momentarily "archaic." If, for all that, his thoughts seem up-to-date, it is because they convey, beyond their allotted time, the deep restlessness that excess and finitude, the absence of standards, and the loss of truth have aroused in us ever since mankind began to tell tales.

To Ophelia, as she watches the masque he has devised, Hamlet confides that the actors cannot hold their tongues, that "they'll tell all" (III, ii, 135). Seek no further. The theater is within the theater, as the tale lies within the tale in Cervantes. The circularity is identical, the only difference being that in *Don Quixote* the status of reality remains ambiguous, and the question of truth is suspended. Nothing of the kind in *Hamlet*, however: there is no truth to be sought outside the spectacle that man stages for himself. Could there be any better reason for toying with the king rather than killing him? In holding out to him the mirror of his mortal insignificance, Hamlet gains the only revenge possible in a world closed upon itself, a world from which the only escape is death. If God exists, he is the impenetrable mystery that awaits us in the hereafter, and which Hamlet hopes amounts to nothing. If God exists, he cares nothing for mankind.

If we conclude that *Hamlet* (which was first staged c. 1600) reflects or portends the spirit of an entire age, it must foreshadow, in the form of a narrative transformed into disorder, the death throes of truth as transcendence. It would deal a fatal blow to the idea that a truth awaiting us in a promised afterlife can invest our lives with meaning. Henceforth truth will be earthly, trivial, comical, ugly or beautiful, sad or joyous, depending on the humor of the moment, but always multiple, fleeting, changing, unpredictable, diminished or magnified by death and, in the final analysis, cancelled out by it, as brief and fragile as the love of Romeo and Juliet. Shakespeare (after Rabelais and Montaigne, and at the same time as Cervantes) may well signal the beginning of an era in which the idea of metaphysical truth begins to decline, but there were to be several efforts to reverse the trend of this decline, which to this day has not entirely run its course. The most significant of these efforts, in the generation immediately following Shakespeare's, one upon which all subsequent efforts would come in varying proportions to depend, is that of Descartes.

16

THE HEROISM OF REASON

THAT OUR READING should end with Descartes, that it should be drawn to him, and find in his work a point of conclusion—provisional though it may be—may well raise eyebrows. Yet, as conclusion, it brings us full circle, back to the question that lies at the very heart of our investigation, that of the conflict between narrative and philosophy and the stakes in that conflict: the status of truth and its relationship with death. If narrative, better than philosophical speculation, can grapple with the meaning and the finitude of life, if philosophy, more than it would care to concede, is a narrative in spite of itself, then it may be no accident that we find Descartes reaffirming philosophy in the form of a story. Conceived at a historical moment when the metaphysics of truth had begun to falter, and when experimental science had begun to assert itself, his *Discours de la Méthode pour bien conduire sa raison et chercher la vérité dans les sciences* (1637)[136] stands forth both as an attempt to re-establish an endangered truth and as the narrative of a new and strikingly original adventure of the mind.

If the discoveries of science had become more clearly separated from biblical revelation, and acceptance of Church dogma had grown weaker, then truth stood at grave risk and theology had ceased to be its best guarantor. New, far more solid foundations were needed than those of distant historical accounts whose veracity could always be called into question and which non-Christians had no reason whatsoever to espouse. Descartes's life work would be to dissociate truth from theology while taking the greatest care not to contradict it,[137] thus laying down a metaphysical foundation for science

---

136. René Descartes, *Discourse on Method* (London: J.M. Dent & Sons, 1916).
137. In a letter to Père Mersenne in late November, 1633, the former student of the Jesuit college of La Flèche writes to his former master and friend: "As I would not, for anything in the world, wish that I might utter the slightest word of which the Church might disapprove, I would thus prefer to suppress it [the

without having to plead, cap in hand, for each of its discoveries at the Sorbonne or at the Vatican. If it were only possible to obtain that approbation once and for all, men of science would be able to work and to publish in peace. By no means in irony does Descartes dedicate his *Meditations* "To the Very Sage and Illustrious Dean and Doctors of the Sacred Faculty of Theology of Paris," but in an attempt to convince them of the soundness of his approach, and to win them over to his cause:

> I have always been of the opinion that the two questions respecting God and the Soul were the chief of those that ought to be determined by help of Philosophy rather than of Theology; for although to us, the faithful, it be sufficient to hold as matters of faith, that the human soul does not perish with the body, and that God exists, it yet assuredly seems impossible ever to persuade infidels of the reality of any religion, or almost even any moral virtue, unless, first of all, those two things be proved to them by natural reason. (*M*, 257)[138]

Quite apart from science's troubled relationship with theology, there arise more fundamental problems dealing with the role of knowledge in giving order to the world and in bringing longevity to the social order. The very sage and illustrious doctors of the Faculty of Theology of Paris are by no means unaware of "the disorders that doubt of these truths produces." Without desiring to "commend at greater length the cause of God and of religion to you, who have always proved the strongest support of the Catholic Church" (*M*, 261), Descartes still finds it necessary to prescribe the remedy of philosophy to the truth of metaphysics.

It is indeed a sovereign remedy, a double-acting *pharmakon*, whose inherent dangers Descartes is far too clever to ignore. Theology and the Church can only emerge weakened from their course of medication. Philosophy had repeatedly proven its weakness; far from throwing up an unassailable obstacle in the path of metaphysics, it had carved out a road of doubt—such, at least, had been its practice before being transformed into the handmaiden of theology. The reversal of this situation is not without its risks.

Traité du Monde] rather than to see it crippled." Descartes goes on to add that there already exist so many philosophically disputable opinions that his own are no more certain and "cannot be approved without controversy," he prefers to abstain from publishing them (L, 948). His desire to live and reflect restfully is more powerful than any ambition, he writes in a subsequent letter (L, 951). 'L' here denotes the letters collected in Descartes, *Œuvres et Lettres* (Paris: Gallimard, Bibliothèque de la Pleiade, 1978), and the Arabic numerals to the page numbers of that edition.

138. *M* for *Meditations*, *DM* for *Discourse on Method*.

In the first place, Descartes, dissatisfied with the scholastic training he has received, is keenly aware of the inadequacies of philosophical speculation. The re-foundation on which he embarks must be the object of a flawless process whose strength all can vouch for. The stakes far exceed the fate of theology: nothing less than the very possibility of truth, and thus of the future of science, lies in the balance.

Such is the spirit in which Descartes makes public the story of an intellectual adventure that can be shared by any human being capable of reason: a task to which the narrative form lends itself particularly well. It gives his demonstration the captivating power of a perilous exploration from which the narrator emerges victorious. As witness to his own progress, Descartes at the same time testifies to the truth to which his path has led him. The power of conviction of his testimony depends on three factors: the universality of common sense, the clarity of the process, and the acceptance of doubt.

The first of these three conditions is, at the very beginning of the *Discourse*, the subject of an irony which may be difficult for us to properly appreciate:

> Good sense is, of all things among men, the most equally distributed; for every one thinks himself so abundantly provided with it, that those even who are the most difficult to satisfy in everything else, do not usually desire a larger measure of this quality than they already possess. (*DM*, I, 176)

But by relating it to universal self-satisfaction, Descartes rapidly undercuts his premise. It is as though he were relying more upon self-satisfaction than good sense in an effort to encourage the largest possible number to accept his discourse. Here, irony teases out a difficulty whose comical character masks its cutting edge: the philosopher is by no means certain that things are so nicely shared as he has supposed, to the extent that the punctilious reader might lose patience had his vanity not shield him from an irony that is applicable only to one's neighbor. But if the *Discourse* is addressed only to an elite (to the elite of an elite, the cream of the erudite), it then ignores the down-to-earth mortals who share in common sense. In his self-satisfaction, Descartes adds that, in its self-conceit, every man's pretension to possess good sense speaks a truth the full extent of which not every man can grasp:

> And in this it is not likely that all are mistaken: the conviction is
> rather to be held as testifying that the power of judging aright and
> of distinguishing Truth from Error, which is properly what is
> called Good Sense or Reason, is by nature equal in all men; and
> that the diversity of our opinions, consequently, does not arise
> from some being endowed with a larger share of Reason than
> others, but solely from this, that we conduct our thoughts along
> different ways, and do not fix our attention on the same objects.
> For to be possessed of a vigorous mind is not enough; the prime
> requisite is rightly to apply it. (*DM*, I, 126)

The explanation is not as simple as it appears. We must hear it out while
reminding ourselves of the irony of the beginning. Descartes postulates an
equality that those infatuated with knowledge have the greatest difficulty in
acknowledging. *The power of judging aright* has nothing to do with the
accumulation of knowledge. I am not addressing myself to those who know,
says the narrator, and it matters little if everyone understands, and even less,
as we shall see, that everyone makes precipitously for the narrow path that I
have taken, for there are risks involved in rushing ahead without preparation.
The essential consideration is that this path may be followed by anyone who
is prepared to abandon his prejudices and make the necessary effort to
understand:

> My present design, then, is not to teach the Method which each
> ought to follow for the right conduct of his Reason, but solely to
> describe the way in which I have endeavoured to conduct my own.
> They who set themselves to give precepts must of course regard
> themselves as possessed of greater skill than those to whom they
> prescribe; and if they err in the slightest particular, they subject
> themselves to censure. But as this Tract is put forth merely as a
> history, or, if you will, as a tale, in which, amid some examples
> worthy of imitation, there will be found, perhaps, as many more
> which it were advisable not to follow, I hope it will prove useful to
> some without being hurtful to any, and that my openness will find
> some favour with all. (*DM*, I, 127)

The word 'tale' (a wink in Plato's direction?) indicates that the
autobiographical relationship cannot be absolutely faithful (and we know
that it is not). It is partially fictitious, because it is a reconstruction, a
remodelling to which the act of writing has contributed. Thus the *Discourse*
is itself part of the progression that it relates, so much so that the narrative

becomes one with its object—hence its vigor: Descartes tells a story, his story, which, as he reconstitutes it, takes shape in front of our eyes.

The narrator begins by reconstituting the journey that, beginning with his school years and threading its way through his active life, his travels, and his dealings with his fellows, has led him to rely only upon his own resources. Quite unexpectedly, at the end of his studies, he finds himself "involved in so many doubts and errors" that he benefits only from the discovery of the growing extent of his ignorance (*DM*, I, 128). For all his near-Socratic discovery, he passes a carefully weighed judgement on his experiences as a student. Contrary to the cliché that depicts him as making *tabula rasa* of the little he has learned (the expression does not occur either in the *Meditations* or in the *Discourse*), Descartes takes some pains to "to hold in esteem the studies of the Schools" and congratulates himself on having cultivated the languages necessary to the understanding of the books of the ancients, for "the perusal of all excellent books is, as it were, to interview with the noblest men of past ages" (*DM*, I, 128). A critical evaluation follows, begun in an ironic tone, and then becoming more serious, touching on the diverse disciplines taught at the time.

As a lover of poetry, sensitive to eloquence, the narrator quickly grasps that inspiration cannot be learned, and that rhetoric does not teach one to reason well (as Plato tirelessly repeated). Respectful of theology, aspiring "as much as any man to gain heaven," he understands "that the way is not less open to the most ignorant than to the most learned, and that the revealed truths which lead to heaven are above our comprehension." Jurisprudence, medicine, and the other sciences "secure for their cultivators honours and riches." As for philosophy (and all the sciences that borrow their principles from it), aside from the fact that it "affords the means of discoursing with an appearance of truth on all matters, and commands the admiration of the more simple," he finds nothing in it, for all the excellent minds of ages past, that is not still in dispute—and as a young bachelor, he "did not presume to anticipate that my success would be greater in it than that of others" (*DM*, I, 129–130). One sole discipline, in fact, meets with his approval:

> I was especially delighted with the Mathematics, on account of the certitude and evidence of their reasonings: but I had not as yet a precise knowledge of their true use; and thinking that they but contributed to the advancement of the mechanical arts, I was astonished that foundations, so strong and solid, should have had no loftier superstructure reared on them. (*DM*, I, 130)

With a keen sense of disappointment, but enriched by his studies and determined to cultivate his "most earnest desire to know how to distinguish the true from the false" the narrator makes up his mind to devote the remainder of his youth to travel, to meet men of other positions and ranks; in a word, to continue to seek out science in himself or in "the great book of the world" (*DM*, I, 131). He joins the army. But intercourse with others—other men, other peoples—brings him to the discovery that there exists in the wider world as much diversity and uncertainty as among the philosophers, and that the ideas commonly received in his own land are seen in other countries as exotic, and vice-versa. All that remains for him, from that moment on, is to apply his resolution to make himself an object of study. This he finds the free time to do, in the serene seclusion of a well-heated room in his winter quarters.

One of the first thoughts to occur to the narrator is that "there is seldom so much perfection in works composed of many separate parts, upon which different hands have been employed, as in those completed by a single master" (*DM*, II, 132). Architecture, the disposition of cities, and legislation all provide eloquent proof. But the proof is not entirely convincing, for it is rare that on the public or collective level it is possible to begin all over again; Descartes takes great care to challenge the presumption that states can be reformed:

> Large bodies, if once overthrown are with great difficulty set up again, or even kept erect when once seriously shaken, and the fall of such is always disastrous.... Hence it is that I cannot in any way or degree approve of those restless and busy meddlers who, called neither by birth nor fortune to take part in the management of public affairs, are yet always projecting reforms; and if I thought that this Tract contained aught which might justify the suspicion that I was a victim of such folly, I would by no means permit its publication. I have never contemplated anything higher than the reformation of my own opinions, and basing them on a foundation wholly my own. And although my own satisfaction with my work has led me to present here a draft of it, I do not by any means therefore recommend to every one else to make a similar attempt. Those whom God has endowed with a larger measure of genius will entertain, perhaps, designs still more exalted; but for the many I am much afraid lest even the present undertaking be more than they can safely venture to imitate. The single design to strip one's self of all past beliefs is one that ought not to be taken by every one. The majority of men is composed of two classes, for neither

of which would this be at all a befitting resolution: in the first place, of those who with more than a due confidence in their own powers, are precipitate in their judgments and want the patience requisite for orderly and circumspect thinking; whence it happens, that if men of this class once take the liberty to doubt of their accustomed opinions, and quit the beaten highway, they will never be able to thread the byway that would lead them by a shorter course, and will lose themselves and continue to wander for life; in the second place, of those who, possessed of sufficient sense or modesty to determine that there are others who excel them in the power of discriminating between truth and error, and by whom they may be instructed, ought rather to content themselves with the opinions of such than trust for more correct to their own Reason. For my own part, I should doubtless have belonged to the latter class, had I received instruction from but one master, or had I never known the diversities of opinion that from time immemorial have prevailed among men of the greatest learning. (*DM*, II, 134–136)

If we are to take his reservations literally, the narrator in person should credit the need to seek out his own path to his good fortune at having had many masters, at having been able to compare the most learned opinions. As for the rest, so binding are the restrictions that they appear to cancel out his introductory affirmation of the generality of good sense.

Had we not known him to be careful to avoid seditious utterances, we might conclude that Descartes *truly* wishes to dissuade anyone else from following his example. But the hypothesis is contradicted by the intent of a discourse written, let us not forget, in the vulgate, that is to say, in French, for a wide readership ("width" being an entirely relative notion at the time). Though there can be no doubt that the narrator wishes us to follow him, we cannot rule out that he judges his own method to be inimitable, or at least that he considers any attempt to repeat it as superfluous, even undesirable. It is enough that his method be rigorous, its conclusion irrefutable, for others to be spared the necessity of retracing his steps: each and every one may henceforth venture forth onto the safe path that circumstances have allowed him to open, and, following his example, develop science without concern for its metaphysical underpinning that would be solidly established once and for all. It is a way of reintroducing, implicitly, the argument from authority at precisely the juncture where each person should, through his own personal experience, arrive at his own conclusions. No need to resolve the narrator's contradictions; the deeply conservative aspect of Cartesian innovation stands apparent, and with it, how strongly its author, for all his modesty, sees it as decisive. Hence his extreme care, in *Meditations* and even more so, in *Discourse*, to ground his proof in full.

For all that, his proof is by no means provided for others alone; it also corresponds—perhaps above all—to an internal necessity. One can only take the full measure of the Cartesian adventure by reading it as it sees itself: necessary and authentic. There is no finer way to sink one's teeth into the act of reading than to confront the paradox it raises: few thinkers have entertained fewer doubts about the reality of the world than this explorer of radical doubt. Truth to tell, the paradox is not as great as it seems: it is because Descartes possesses such great inward solidity, whatever its reasons, that he is able to drive his thought to the point of vertigo.

The narrator himself ventures an explanation for his precautions: Part III of the *Discourse* is almost entirely devoted to moral considerations that are not justified at that juncture except by the risks inherent in the expedition he proposes to embark on. Descartes takes certain measures, just as a mountain-climber preparing to descend a sheer cliff attaches a lifeline to his harness: he sets up a practical structure, an apparatus of moral maxims "so that I might not remain irresolute in my actions, while my Reason compelled me to suspend my judgment" (*DM*, III, 140). In sum: to obey the laws and customs of his country and to abide, insofar as received ideas are concerned, by the most moderate; remain firm and resolute in action, hold fast to his chosen course; overcome oneself rather than fortune, change one's desires rather than the order of the world and accustom oneself "to the persuasion that except our own thoughts, there is nothing absolutely in our power" (*DM*, III, 141–143), and concluding:

> Having thus provided myself with these maxims, and having placed them in reserve along with the truths of Faith, which have ever occupied the first place in my belief, I came to the conclusion that I might with freedom set about ridding myself of what remained of my opinions. And, inasmuch as I hoped to be better able successfully to accomplish this work by holding intercourse with mankind, than by remaining longer shut up in the retirement where these thoughts had occurred to me, I betook me again to travelling before the winter was well ended. And, during the nine subsequent years, I did nothing but roam from one place to another, desirous of being a spectator rather than an actor in the plays exhibited on the theatre of the world; and, as I made it my business in each matter to reflect particularly upon what might

> fairly be doubted and prove a source of error, I gradually rooted out from my mind all the errors which had hitherto crept into it. Not that in this I imitated the Sceptics who doubt only that they may doubt, and seek nothing beyond uncertainty itself; for, on the contrary, my design was singly to find ground of assurance, and cast aside the loose earth and sand, that I might reach the rock or the clay. (*DM*, III, 144–145)

To these maxims he adds, *in extremis*, the capital element of faith. It is not, I believe, a simple clause of the kind inserted to placate the ecclesiastical censors. It must be viewed, instead, as a precondition of the Cartesian method. But wait! Suddenly, his audacity is reduced to nothing: if faith is the condition on which adventure may be undertaken, truth is then assured and adventure vanishes. No longer is there any veritable doubt, no longer is there any risk. Let us say, instead, that there is no longer any *a priori* existential risk, in the sense that the narrator nowhere suggests that he has *spontaneously, tragically* come to doubt the existence of faith (as Hamlet doubts the existence of God). His risk is purely intellectual: the risk that metaphysical truth cannot be rigorously demonstrated. For a man who has placed in this demonstration his highest ambitions, failure remains a distinct possibility, and the consequences of failure cannot be foreseen.

Cartesian doubt, while purely cerebral, is far more than empty intellectual posturing; it is radically necessary to the credibility of his enterprise. Precisely because doubt is abroad in the land, feeding off the minds and spirits of his contemporaries, it must be located at ground zero of the Cartesian method. The hypothesis of nothingness must spare nothing to win the loyalty of true sceptics. The refusal to be fooled by appearances constitutes the only true freedom of the spirit. The spirit can only claim its independence by saying "no" to the world. A deceitful God, whatever his power, cannot impose his falsehood upon him who refuses it. Against such a God, against deceit and illusion, doubt remains the only unquestionable strength thought possesses; this is why Descartes begins, must begin, by revoking all items of evidence. All except one, which cannot be destroyed: the very activity by which refusal assumes shape and form. As long as it is radical, refusal becomes the first and only certainty of the thinking being. Descartes transforms absolute doubt into the firm spot on which he can stand to move his thought:

> I thought that a procedure exactly the opposite was called for, and that I ought to reject as absolutely false all opinions in regard to

which I could suppose the least ground for doubt, in order to ascertain whether after that there remained aught in my belief that was wholly indubitable. Accordingly, seeing that our senses sometimes deceive us, I was willing to suppose that there existed nothing really such as they presented to us; and because some men err in reasoning, and fall into paralogisms, even on the simplest matters of Geometry, I, convinced that I was as open to error as any other, rejected as false all the reasonings I had hitherto taken for demonstrations; and finally, when I considered that the very same thoughts (presentations) which we experience when awake may also be experienced when we are asleep, while there is at that time not one of them true, I supposed that all the objects (presentations) that had ever entered into my mind when awake, had in them no more truth than the illusions of my dreams. But immediately upon this I observed that, whilst I thus wished to think that all was false, it was absolutely necessary that I, who thus thought, should be somewhat; and as I observed that this truth, I think, hence I am, was so certain and of such evidence, that no ground of doubt, however extravagant, could be alleged by the Sceptics capable of shaking it, I concluded that I might, without scruple, accept it as the first principle of the Philosophy of which I was in search. (*DM*, IV, 147–148)

The logical chain which from *I doubt* leads to *I am* by way of *I think* is self-evident. Doubt, no matter how radical, cannot erase the thinking subject without cancelling out itself. Note that there is no longer any dispute over the association between the subject (the *I*) and thought; it goes without saying, or so it seems (we could well imagine a more radical position that would eliminate the I altogether and simply certify: there is doubt, there is thought, leading to the conclusion: there is being). Not for an instant does Descartes call into question the thinking I. On the contrary, he insists on its presence even before the process of reasoning has begun: "I am in doubt as to ..." "I thought that," and further along: "I supposed that." Or: "I thus wished to think." It would be difficult to indicate with greater clarity that the thinking subject's resolve precedes the act of doubt that it imagines. The chain, in its entirety, stands thus: *I am resolved to doubt, I doubt, I think, therefore I am*; or, *having resolved to doubt, I may doubt everything except the* I *that has taken this resolution. I* stands poised at the point of departure as it does at the point of arrival. Were Descartes to stop there, his reasoning would lead to a pure tautology. But Descartes goes further, immediately adding:

In the next place, I attentively examined what I was, and as I
observed that I could suppose that I had no body, and that there
was no world nor any place in which I might be; but that I could
not therefore suppose that I was not; and that, on the contrary,
from the very circumstance that I thought to doubt of the truth of
other things, it most clearly and certainly followed that I was;
while, on the other hand, if I had only ceased to think, although all
the other objects which I had ever imagined had been in reality
existent, I would have had no reason to believe that I existed; I
thence concluded that I was a substance whose whole essence or
nature consists only in thinking, and which, that it may exist, has
need of no place, nor is dependent on any material thing; so that
"I," that is to say, the mind by which I am what I am, is wholly
distinct from the body, and is even more easily known that the
latter, and is such, that although the latter were not, it would still
continue to be all that it is. (*DM*, IV, 145–146)

No sooner can the narrator *suppose* (or imagine) that he has no body but
not *suppose* that he could not think (assuming that to *suppose* is in itself an
act of thought), he concludes: first, that his thought (or his thinking
substance) possesses a reality that is more certain than his body; second, that
it is distinct from that body. If the second deduction does not rest upon
anything demonstrable, the first, the establishment of thought as the first
certainty, indissociable from the *I*, constitutes the first *tour de force*, and the
pivot upon which the entire Cartesian discourse turns.

What Descartes, in his search for truth, contrives to establish most
forcefully is not his existence, which has never been in doubt, but the
primacy of thought: *the thinking being in me is that which has the greatest
reality*; if it is not true that I think, then nothing is true. The *cogito* of *I think,
therefore I am*, from simple tautology at the beginning, now takes on another
meaning, acquires a more specific, more troubling sense: for thought,
thought is primary. In other words, the "thinking *I*" precedes all other *I*s, all
other things, the world, and even—whatever the narrator claims—God
himself.

That Descartes deducts with no convincing argument that the soul is a
substance distinct from the body takes nothing away from the impact of the
preceding primacy. Though it may not be possible to conclude that we are
capable of thinking without a body (no more than it can be established that
the body is indissociable from thought), there is no obstacle, as Husserl has

noted, to "think of a conscience without body."[139] By demonstrating that consciousness is the only thing that consciousness cannot obliterate, Descartes implicitly reverses the priority of philosophy: its first subject is no longer the world, but thought. Even if it could be proven that, ontologically, the first precedes the second (supposing of course that the proposition makes sense), thought (or consciousness) comes methodologically first. Subjectivity immediately captures itself as having been experienced, it imposes itself upon us absolutely, while the world and "objective reality" become relative, and have no further existence except in the focused beam of thought. True enough, Descartes himself does not go quite so far; but that, nonetheless, is what his *cogito* implies.

The primacy of thought, at this early stage, does not permit us to be certain whether or not the world exists outside of our thought. Unless that thought itself leads us to the certainty of an outside power without which it could not think. This is the famous proof of the existence of God. Emboldened by the first conclusion (the *cogito*), i.e., that his thought process is capable of formulating a true proposition on condition of being able to conceive of things "very clearly and very distinctly," the narrator returns to the imperfection of his nature:

> In the next place, from reflecting on the circumstance that I doubted, and that consequently my being was not wholly perfect, (for I clearly saw that it was a greater perfection to know than to doubt,) I was led to inquire whence I had learned to think of something more perfect than myself; and I clearly recognised that I must hold this notion from some Nature which in reality was more perfect. (*DM*, IV, 148)

> ... for how could I know that I doubt, desire, or that something is wanting to me, and that I am not wholly perfect, if I possessed no idea of a being more perfect than myself, by comparison of which I knew the deficiencies of my nature? (*M*, III, 294)

The argument gives ample cause for reflection. The idea of perfection, quite obviously, cannot arise out of nothingness. But we also know that nothingness is an outmoded supposition, now that it has been established beyond the slightest doubt that something exists—that is to say, thought. Defective though it may be, thought need not be perfect in order to grasp

---

139. Edmund Husserl, *Idées directrices pour une phénoménologie*, traduit de l'allemand par Paul Ricoeur, (Paris: Gallimard, 1950, collection « Tel », 1985), p. 182.

perfection. Life offers us ample occasions for measuring ourselves against greater perfection (that which is more beautiful, stronger, more adroit, etc.) than ourselves for us to become aware of our deficiencies. The idea of perfection, from earliest childhood, is never anything but the idea of whatever is more perfect than us. As for perfection itself, in absolute terms, if it exists, it is impossible for us to form an adequate image: God, by definition, remains unknowable. Here Descartes confounds two distinct levels: he extrapolates a metaphysical reality from an existential sentiment, that of emptiness, which can be experienced quite well without metaphysics.

His second demonstration thus lacks the power of the first. Here, as Pascal detected, Descartes is indeed "uncertain and ineffective." God's existence is not a matter of proof, but of belief. One must speak either for or against. Descartes does so, but without avowing it. But his failure has the merit of leaving open a question which, in the history of Western thought, remains both crucial and unanswered: *where does the idea of truth come from?* In an intellectual tradition that, from the Greek origins it claims as its own down to the present day, has never ceased to consider truth as its central concern, Descartes's intuition continues to trouble us. If Descartes has failed to ground truth in the bedrock of metaphysics, he has at least demonstrated that this truth cannot be only half accepted. The power of the Cartesian argument is this: if there is no God, then we can be certain of nothing, and no significant truth is possible in any science. In other words, for Descartes, science can neither be possible nor worthy of pursuit except in the unity of truth. But such a position is virtually a nihilistic one, for if Descartes's demonstration should fail to convince, it helps undercut the very principle it seeks to establish.

Kant will see the danger clearly, which is undoubtedly the reason why his struggle against scepticism will take another path. In stark contrast to Descartes, he labors to separate scientific activity from the idea of God. But in separating what Descartes had intended to unify—scientific and metaphysical truth—Kant, whether or not he intended to do so, provided justification for the sciences to pursue their particular truths, or, more precisely, their respective efficacies. It may not have been Kant's desire to extend this freedom to moral considerations, for the validity of which God remains absolutely necessary; scientific praxis, now become technoscience, follows its own movement with no particular consideration for the Sovereign Good whose existence God is understood to guarantee. That which Descartes may well have feared most has come to pass: truth has become diluted, fragmented, and pragmatism has today occupied all spheres of knowledge and morality. But, curiously, the fragmentation wrought by pragmatism has not altered, in its principles, the need for truth that upholds the intellectual universalism of our civilization. Though it has destroyed the pedestal on which truth stands, the West continues to carry its torch (the giantess who raises hers above the port of New York can only be called "Liberty" out of guile, or because of the semantic confusion of her designers, for no liberty can pretend to illuminate the world), without noticing that the torch that should burn with a perpetual flame has been reduced to little more than a stick of wood smouldering in the damp drizzle of nihilism and commercialism.

Concern for truth and conviction of the universality of reason had, in Descartes, at least the merit of being restricted to the rather precise sphere of that which is "geometrically" demonstrable. Descartes takes pains, expressly, in the *Discourse*, to extend the empire of universal reason to the immense domains of values, of manners, of politics, and of morality. If he accepts the laws of his country, it is because they are accepted by those with whom he must live, and not because he judges them as being superior to those of Persia or China (*DM*, III, 141). His wise sense of limitation is precisely what the Enlightenment and, more specifically, Kantian practical reason were later to reject in the name of a new man summoned to bestow upon himself an ahistoric reason. The consequence being that our civilization, while wrongly believing itself rid of its metaphysical heritage, still proposes to impose its morality upon others based on a universality which, in the West, has totally lost its foundations. Of the truth in which we have ceased to believe remains only its negation and its destructive impact. And what remains of Descartes in our collective imagination is nothing more than the sad caricature of a utilitarian rationality whose sources and measure—absent the texts—we can no longer see.

For, in Descartes, the unity of the true has consequences both for the way he views science and the way he leads his life. In enunciating the first of his *Rules for the Direction of the Mind* ("The end of study should be to direct the mind towards the enunciation of sound and correct judgments on all matters that come before it"), he inveighs against the tendancy to cultivate the sciences "each taken separately from all the rest," considering that "the sciences taken all together are identical with human wisdom which always remains one and the same, however applied to different subjects," adding that "there is nothing more prone to turn us aside from the correct way of seeking out truth than this directing of our inquiries, not toward the general end, but towards certain special investigations" (*RDM*, I, 37–38). Such unity, whose contemplation "is the only joy in this life that is complete and untroubled with any pain," encompasses as well the moral, practical sphere: knowledge possesses utility not to facilitate material existence but to "increase the natural light of reason ... in order that his understanding may light his will to its proper choice in all contingencies of life" (*RDM*, I, 38–39).

Descartes's avowed utilitarianism, his supposed ambition to master and possess nature (on the basis of a single phrase almost always separated from an "as" that substantially qualifies its scope),[140] his systematic manner of reasoning step by step from one obvious fact to another, the importance he attaches to experimental verification, the entire machine for thinking in a rational and useful manner, hardly jibes for us, today, with the idea that *the true*—from physics to metaphysics by way of practical experience—is indivisible and dependent upon the existence of God. It cannot be said often enough: what gives Descartes his originality and his power is precisely the tension that joins the comprehensible with the incomprehensible, the human with the divine, in the mighty bow of truth. If the human spirit can pull taut the bow-string and hope to attain the real with its arrow, it is because the truth exists: "The certitude of all other truths is so absolutely dependent on it that without this knowledge it is impossible ever to know anything perfectly" (*M*, V, 315). God, as supreme truth, is simultaneously the condition of science and its end. Whatever its practical utility, man is not the end: "We may say that all created things were made for us in the sense that we may derive some utility from them; but I do not know that we are obliged to believe that man is the end of creation" (*Letters*, to Chanut, June 6, 1647, 1275).[141] We certainly cannot speak of Cartesian utilitarianism in the modern and purely pragmatic sense of the term. For Descartes, wisdom remains science's greatest "utility."

In his quest for truth as supreme happiness, Descartes does not stray far from the two great philosophers of classical Greece. At first glance, his

---

140. By way of demonstrating the progress achieved in his time by physics, Descartes praises its newest notions in these terms: "For by them I perceived it to be possible to arrive at knowledge highly useful in life; and in room of the Speculative Philosophy usually taught in the Schools, to discover a Practical, by means of which, knowing the force and action of fire, water, air, the stars, the heavens, and all the other bodies that surround us, as distinctly as we know the various crafts of our artizans, we might also apply them in the same way to all the uses to which they are adapted, and thus render ourselves the lords and possessors of nature. And this is a result to be desired, not only in order to the invention of an infinity of arts, by which we might be enabled to enjoy without any trouble the fruits of the earth, and all its comforts, but also and especially for the preservation of health, which is without doubt, of all the blessings of this life, the first and fundamental one; for the mind is so intimately dependent upon the condition and relation of the organs of the body, that if any means can ever be found to render men wiser and more ingenious than hitherto, I believe that it is in Medicine they must be sought for" (*DM*, VI, 168–169).

141. René Descartes. *Descartes: Philosophical Letters*, trans. & ed. Anthony Kenny (Oxford: Clarendon, 1970), p. 222.

rationalism and scientific optimism resemble Aristotle's. But he diverges from and criticizes the ancient master on two critical counts: Descartes refuses to argue from ends, nor does he believe that, in interpreting the world, intelligence can be satisfied with the dictates of our senses. The "great book of the world" is not as accessible as we might think; the language of nature, even though intelligible, is not directly readable. A key is needed. In this regard, Descartes is closer to Plato: while not being accessible, God, or our idea of him, impels us toward truth. Toward the truth that, like *Eros*, we lack, yet both the notion of which and the desire for which we have within us. Yet he distances himself from it through his excessive confidence in the capacity of our thought processes to make up for our lack. More than Plato, Descartes is possessed by the rational desire for God.

The desire is eternal; the method exceptional. Orthodox in his metaphysical pursuits, pioneering in his method, Descartes contrives to make science compatible with the truth of Christianity, which he fully intends to reinforce by placing it atop new foundations, on firmer bases of reason. A slippage has taken place, from a revealed truth to a reasoned one, from a specific (for all the pretensions of the *Catholic* Church) truth to a universal truth. The shift is a tiny one, but of immense consequence. The hypothesis of radical doubt that provides Cartesian thought with its point of departure nourishes an unprecedented will to certainty: the truth that would contemplate using this initial obscurity as its point of departure draws from it an extra measure of force and universality capable of arming reason with a far more despotic power than the truth of Scripture ever possessed. For Scripture leaves in a state of relative uncertainty the extent of divine intervention in the affairs of the world, while reason seeks total dominion over them. Not that we can attribute such intentions to Descartes himself. In fact, as we have seen, quite the opposite is true. But the propensity itself may well be located, in spite of him, in the radicalism of his method. At no point does the Bible ever lose its character as a story, while the story of the *Method* abandons itself to its outcome, to such an extent that no one considers the Cartesian *Discourse* as a narrative. There is a loss to be reckoned with here: the adventurer of the mind becomes the geometer of reason; the lover of truth, the priest of absolute rationality. But he has become a priest who, for all his insistence to the contrary, may officiate without God.

Whatever the power of conviction—and it is far from negligible—with which Descartes demonstrates the scientific necessity of God, the path that leads to such a necessity must, for the briefest of moments, pass through the intimate, isolated consciousness of the reasoning *I*. There is a moment within the Cartesian progression during which consciousness (thought) is utterly alone with itself, up to the possibility of raising the hypothesis of the negation of God. Who could doubt that he raises the hypothesis the better to conclude, hurriedly, that such negation is impossible, that it would be a denial of itself, that its autonomy is unthinkable. But the thought itself has been thought by negation! If God were to "return," it would be because *it* has so decided. In this brief moment of self-reflection, the *I* becomes the sovereign witness to its truth before becoming witness to God. This "swollen ego" has already appeared, let us recall, in Saint Augustine, but the Augustinian *I*, entrapped in the scandal of will, is a weak one, whose suffering will only be ended in God. Descartes's thinking *I* uses God, recreates Him far more than it seeks shelter in Him, and bolstered by this support, which one is tempted to claim he owes only to his thought, he moves serenely along the edge of the abyss that his truth draws closed behind him as he goes.

Where Saint Augustine absorbs in faith the inner otherness that torments him, Descartes would seem to overcome uncertainty in science. In reality, for him, science merely prolongs long-standing conviction. Cartesian nothingness is essentially its provisional instrument. In establishing God and reason as equal, he simultaneously places reason on an equal footing with the intimate emotion of truth. I, reason, speak the truth. The *I* is right; it can afford to be—we are constantly saying, without a second thought: "I'm right." Ultimately, reason becomes one with itself. Where the presence of God, of the Incomprehensible, diffused though it may be, leaves the narrative unfinished and the road open to a trace of otherness, reason left to itself tends to occupy the entire field, until it establishes itself within us as an unconscious authority. The man we consider as one of the principal thinkers of modernity, far from establishing what we customarily, and rather unthinkingly, call the "objectivity" of science, has, in spite of himself, laid the groundwork for its subjectivity.

Descartes captures the latent doubt that winds through much of the literature of his day and lays hold of it in the indecisive state in which it lies (as a sense of uncertainty regarding the existence of any truth other than the simple truth of our lives) the better to fashion a tool for philosophical speculation. Where in *Hamlet* (as in Montaigne) doubt has an effect on belief, on values, on the afterlife, for Descartes it affects the reality of the world. *Don Quixote* does not cause us to doubt reality, only the firmness of that which, in our light-headedness, we are wont to call realism; it calls into question our capacity to grasp it and blurs the distinction we believe ourselves capable of establishing between the fictitious and the real. Descartes begins by throwing the fictitious and the real into the same bag, in such a way as to cast doubt on the entire world and upon his own existence. But were this doubt experienced at the level where the philosopher pretends to locate it, that is to say, as an absolute, it could not but annihilate him who has thought it, could simply not even be thought. Hamlet's cry, *to be or not to be*, would remain unutterable. If nothing of the kind has happened, if the hero of thought has survived his radical doubt, it is because there has already been an implicit transfer of the locus and of the function of doubt, which in Descartes is method.

Not once, let us repeat, does Descartes truly doubt either himself or the world. He simply scrutinizes what takes place when the intellect, in him, plays at acting *as though* all were naught but illusion and deception. His simulation is none the less dizzying; it brings into sharp relief the bottomless pit over which the intellect must bend once it reflects upon itself. But at the same time, in risking the rapture of the abyss—for this mental exercise is not without the risk of madness—Descartes shows that thought is, for itself, that which is most indestructible. Thought, now certain of its resilience, can return to the world and reflect on its weakness, on its insufficiency. For the inability of thought to destroy itself does not establish its unbridled power. Far from it. Its self-certainty and persistence can in no way guarantee its reliability, since as both dreams and madness show, no *a priori* consideration can protect it against delirium, and his senses do not provide a sufficient basis for the establishment of his certainties. Descartes, like a practiced judoka, uses this undeniable weakness, and in a more general sense, the absence that lies at the heart of the human condition, to re-establish *a contrario* the idea of truth. For all its ingeniousness, the maneuver is a perfectly circular one. The idea of perfection, troubling though it may be, does not prove the existence of perfection beyond us, it is only a different, sublimated expression of the absence upon which it intends to construct itself. The re-establishment that Descartes has effected does little more than confirm the initial incompleteness; it has merely transposed the state of absence to a higher plane. In spite of himself and more radically than ever before, he has introduced the impossibility of absolute certainty.

In seeking to make methodical doubt the unerring lever of a new truth, Descartes, hero of thinking subjectivity, opens a mortal aperture in the truth he intends to save. For this reason he satisfies and dissatisfies everyone. Those who follow a religious conception invoke or revoke him, and only the free thinkers who strive to bring down transcendent truth once and for all see in him truth revealed. These are vain polemics. First and foremost, they forget that the Cartesian narrative makes ultimate sense only within the narrow limits of geometry, and that its scope is therefore historic rather than scientific.

For having overlooked this limit, the Enlightenment has bequeathed to reason an impossible task, and given Western science limitless ambitions and destructive hopes. Today, as the belief in progress is no longer able to carry all before it, we can discern more clearly the cost of having believed that we could repatriate to this world the promise of salvation and truth that Christianity had reserved for the life that lies beyond death.

AFTERWORD

THE CREAKING TRUTH that the West has discovered, dismantled behind the torn stage settings of metaphysics is not the truth which stood dominant before the rise of the Gospel story. Something of the Christian promise has survived, if only negatively, in the modern, Western manner of understanding life. Life itself is not enough, as it was for the Greeks; it must accomplish here, on earth, the salvation after death proclaimed by the Gospel. Such an accomplishment is clearly impossible; the finite cannot promise the eternal. So great is this infirmity that it seems incurable: life itself has become unequal to the task. The insufficiency of our earthly life, given the limits which have been handed down to us, has become the most vivid relic bequeathed by the Christian sense of expectation that has long since ceased to believe in an afterlife.

Our civilization must therefore succeed in history, in the here-and-now, in making possible exactly what the expectancy of death denies each of us: eternal life. There could be no finer guarantee of such a life-span than growth projected as an infinite process. The modern hero, in the West, is he who by his own actions contributes in one way or another to this limitless expansion. But the depreciation that the world has undergone when confronted by the promise of the hereafter has transformed this world into that which is most precious to us and at the same time most neglected. Acting upon the world, regardless of the cost, surpasses all other pleasure, all other contemplation, and all other existence. The world is not the locus of life but an immense quarry from which we must with all our might extract, as though it were the most precious of all minerals, the sense of our own importance. The need to act and the need to grow have overwhelmed the joy of living.

Whether it be territorial expansion, economic accumulation, cultural hegemony or scientific and technical progress, the sign of our immortality as a civilization resides in the inexorable expansion of its ascendancy over the rest of the world, including "nature." We allow what we term nature to survive only as parkland, set aside for that purpose; we accept other cultures as folkloric enclaves and tourist destinations. Otherness has its place, alongside beauty: in museums and protected sites. Museums, reserves (botanical, wildlife, ethnic) can only have been Western inventions. Only a civilization in anguish at its destructive power and haunted by the fear of its final disappearance could have conceived of setting aside in specially planned areas the wrecks that have escaped the ravages of time past and time future. This precaution we first extended to the ancient civilizations of which we considered ourselves the direct or indirect heirs. The museum confirmed our mastery of the world for in it could be found the remains of its history. But today's museum mania spares nothing—up to and including ecology itself, which, by extending the concept of the museum to the whole world, provides us with a pious echo of the excess of our ambitions. Since everything now is at risk of vanishing under the onrushing sweep of our desire to endure, all is worthy of preservation and protection from the obliterating forces that we have set loose in our limitless exploitation of the world. Our ecological concerns form the ultimate expression of the contradiction between the desire to endure and the preservation of the very space upon which this desire wreaks its devastation, the world. Not for nothing has science fiction envisaged the need to ensure the survival of humankind in intergalactic space, beyond the earthly habitat that it has completely ravished.

The "story" is the classic form taken in almost every culture by the desire for self-perpetuation. To tell our story is not to die. Such desire finds expression in words, in the writing of narrators who know well that they are mortal; it is for this very reason that they tell stories, to provide nurture for the memory of those who will follow in their footsteps. To tell the story, and to die; to die at peace for having lived and transmitted it to the next generation. Today we may well have reached a point at which, if we are not careful, our stories may be unable to convey such a message. Henceforth, no longer able to write down anything lasting, the intent of our stories will be to divert, to induce forgetfulness. For several decades now, some authors have attempted to deal with this insufficiency by multiplying subtle shadings of the insignificant. To say as much as can be said about almost nothing. To write in order to say nothing, for there is nothing to say, nothing lasting that might be worth transmitting, for the story has ceased to be that privileged place where one generation's legacy is passed on to the next. The will to endure has become hardened in perpetual action: transmission takes place more and more through the production of objects or, more precisely, by the accelerated activity that produces them on an increasingly vast scale. Great stories may no longer be possible, for there remains nothing to be transmitted other than incessant economic, scientific, and technical amplification, which has been assigned the task of assuring our salvation, and which our capacity for self-imagination, dominated by the fear of the void, the spectre of sickness, and the rejection of death, has so powerfully fostered.

It may well be that the reification of the world is nothing more than a difficult passage toward something that we cannot yet perceive. We already have an indication of what it might be in the phenomenal growth of the production of symbolic goods spurred on by the rapid development of computer and communication technology. The virtual, ramified world that has created itself across the worldwide web provides the imagination with an unlimited space in which everything seems possible, in which each can tell everyone a story and each can learn from everyone else. In a certain sense, we may be entering more than ever before into the era of the story, at a historical moment where the difference between reality and fiction has become increasingly blurred. But what to relate, and what to learn from this superabundance of dispersed stories? What new tales today weave the web whose short-term destination is not the trash basket? Is not every text launched bravely on the web a bucket of water poured into the sea? What will remain of these billions of daily signs? What memory can we possibly have of that which no longer has the time to be written down? There can be no doubt that, for all the danger of dilution, the web can carry the story as printing once did. But this may only happen if the desire to create meaning by telling a story is not simply swamped in the onrush of the disposable.

For the desire is not dead. In a certain sense it has reasserted itself, now more concerned—but also more engaged—by the decline of metaphysical truth. The next step will be to illustrate how, beginning with the classical age, the modern novel has struggled, at least up until Proust, to keep meaning alive in our lives through the actual exercise of a narrative that is free to lay down its own rules.

The pause in our exploration will only, I hope, be short-lived. I feel myself standing at the threshold of a new journey as though at the edge of an immense, rich landscape, in which I fully intend to lose my way in a subsequent book, should this present volume contrive to stimulate readers' interest. My words should be taken neither as modesty nor as stylistic flourish, but perhaps even as excess confidence, in imagining that this book might have some value as a test, that its reception might be a significant indicator of the importance we attach to our narrative tradition, so strongly do I hope that it will contribute, even in the smallest ways, to reveal to us a reborn desire to draw from that tradition a richness of meaning that I believe to be inexhaustible.

A real apprehension, greater than that of simple failure, troubles me at the conclusion of this first adventure: that the great stories may, for us, be great no longer, and that my efforts to demonstrate their wealth and fertility may seem, in the end, to be obsolete; that the great stories themselves may have become diversions that we encounter only on the screen; that it has become increasingly difficult to transmit the enthusiasm that their *reading* can touch off. If I have pursued the task of reading with doggedness and passion over the course of several years, it is with the conviction that our narrative heritage—so rich in its ignored wealth—is more than worth reading, and re-reading. I said it at the beginning, and I repeat it here, by way of conclusion: this book will have attained its goal if it rekindles the desire, if it provides us with a stimulus to return to the texts themselves once more.